HEMINGWAY

VS.

FITZGERALD

THE RISE AND FALL
OF A LITERARY FRIENDSHIP

SCOTT DONALDSON

JOHN MURRAY
Albemarle Street, London

© Scott Donaldson 1999

First published by The Overlook Press, Peter Mayer Publishers Inc., in the United States of America

First published in Great Britain in 2000
by John Murray (Publishers) Ltd.,
50 Albemarle Street, London W1X 4BD

A catalogue record for this book is available from the British Library

ISBN 0-7195-5483-7

Printed and bound in the United States of America

HEMINGWAY VS. FITZGERALD

TO VIVIE,

WHO KNEW IT COULD BE DONE

CONTENTS

PREFACE

As every writer knows, when you're "living in the book"—as Fitzgerald put it—the characters begin to inhabit your life. They are in your mind as you work, and do not go away when you leave your desk. Often they make a call during the night, leaving behind a reminder of something you overlooked during your conscious hours, or of something—as Frost said of the thrill of discovery in poems—that you did not know you knew. Sometimes they invade your dreams.

During the early morning hours of March 31, 1999, I dreamed about Ernest Hemingway and F. Scott Fitzgerald. Perhaps it was the blue moon outside the window that brought them to life, but there they were, in the ring, boxing. I knew this made no sense. There is no record that Scott and Ernest ever duked it out, and it would have been a terrible mismatch, with the larger and heavier and more experienced Hemingway liable—as Maxwell Perkins used to say about him, as a fighter—to "kill" the slightly built Fitzgerald.

And yet...Scott got into his share of fights when drunk, and was regularly beaten up for his trouble. It was a tangible, physical expression of his compulsion to court humiliation. Ernest loved to fight, and was proud of his prowess. He did not move with the grace of an accomplished boxer, but as Morley Callaghan and others have testified he loved to hit and could hit very hard. In a real fight, he would surely have knocked Fitzgerald out.

In the dream, that did not happen. Traditionally boxers have been taught to go first for the body, and to deliver the crushing blow to the head only after the opponent's hands come down. In the dream bout, Hemingway went for Fitzgerald's upper arms instead. He punched and jabbed at Scott's biceps until they grew numb. So immobilized, Fitzgerald could neither strike back with force nor do much to protect himself. After that, Ernest simply used Scott as a punching bag, hitting him at will with enough force to inflict pain, but not enough to bring the torture to a conclusion. It was terribly cruel.

This was only a dream, and proved nothing about Hemingway or Fitzgerald or the relationship between them. Yet there was a logic to the fight my imagination conjured up. At the beginning, the friendship between Scott and Ernest was extraordinarily close. These days people ask if they were lovers. The only sensible answer is that one cannot know for certain, but that it was extremely unlikely. Both men shared the homophobic sensibilities characteristic of the times and their midwestern upbringings. But to another question—did they love each other?—the answer almost certainly is yes. The letters of the mid-twenties show that Scott and Ernest shared an extraordinary warmth. The feeling lasted much longer for Fitzgerald than for Hemingway. Ernest tried to break things off by way of insult, time and again. Scott took the blows and came back for more.

What the dream suggested was that Hemingway wanted or needed to strike out at his former friend at least as much as Fitzgerald wanted or needed to be hurt.

In David Levine's wonderful drawing, the two writers appear as a song-and-dance team, natty in polka-dot bow ties and shuffling off to Buffalo behind the stage lights. Both of them carry pens. Hemingway smiles toothily at the audience as he embeds his pen in Fitzgerald's heart. Fitzgerald, maintaining the trace of a grin, looks like a startled ghost.

For half a century now, I have been reading and writing about Fitzgerald and Hemingway. For thirty years I have been teaching their fiction. I wrote my 1950 senior honors thesis on Hemingway's short stories, a choice of subject grudgingly allowed by a Yale English department committed to British authors and distrustful of any writer still alive. The family connection to Fitzgerald may go back even farther in time. My mother grew up in the same St. Paul neighborhood Fitzgerald occupied. I like to think that she danced with him and he flirted with her. But she died young, just as he did, so that by the time the question occurred to me, there was no one left to ask.

This is not the first book on the friendship between these two writers, or even the second. In two separate volumes Matthew J. Bruccoli has provided "a documentary reconstruction of their friendship and estrangement." The documents he presented—letters mainly, but also notes and comments from the published writings—constitute an invaluable resource for aftercomers. You cannot, after all, interview the dead. What I have tried to do is to engage those documents, along with many others, in telling the *story* of the Fitzgerald-Hemingway relationship. I've had a still more difficult goal in mind, too: to arrive at an understanding of their failed friendship and what it has to tell us about each of these two great writers and their work.

When Hemingway was writing *A Moveable Feast* in the late 1950s, his wife, Mary, read a few chapters and objected that this was not autobiography at all. Ernest was writing about other people, not himself. "It's biography by *remate*," he explained. *Remate* is a jai alai term meaning a two-wall shot. In *Hemingway vs. Fitzgerald*, also, I've tried to work by reflection and rebound, bouncing the material off others who knew both men well. Maxwell Perkins is the principal example, but he is joined in the pages ahead by Gerald and Sara Murphy, Gertrude Stein, Morley Callaghan, and Edmund Wilson—all of whom become characters in the story.

So do Clarence and Grace Hemingway, and Edward and Mollie Fitzgerald, the parents whose importance in shaping these writers' lives and personalities can hardly be overstated. Ginevra King and Agnes von Kurowsky, the young women who jilted Fitzgerald and Hemingway during their most vulnerable years, play major roles in that process as well. I've taken up the painful issue of alcoholism as a malady afflicting both writers, and considered in some detail Hemingway's unfortunate assault on Fitzgerald's reputation. Finally, and with trepidation, I've drawn on the assistance of psychological interpretation in coming to account with Scott and Ernest.

Who is the better writer? people ask, Which of them do you *like* better, or at all? These are the wrong questions. Fitzgerald was a great writer and so was Hemingway, each in his incomparable way. They may have thought themselves in competition, but the race is over and both tortoise and hare have won. Hemingway was a difficult human being and so was Fitzgerald, again in markedly different ways. I have no wish to judge them—only to tell their story and to arrive at some understanding. If that gets done, it will be enough.

—SCOTT DONALDSON
Scottsdale, Arizona

11

HEMINGWAY VS. FITZGERALD

CHAPTER I

LOVESHOCKS: AT HOME

According to the adage, the best training for a writer is an unhappy childhood. Both Scott Fitzgerald and Ernest Hemingway qualified, but for markedly contrasting reasons. As Tolstoy put it in another famous saying, "[H]appy families are all alike; every unhappy family is unhappy in its own way."

Scott Fitzgerald grew up embarrassed by his mother and alternately proud and ashamed of his father. Edward Fitzgerald came west to strike it rich, and in a way he did, for in St. Paul he met and married Mollie McQuillan, the daughter of an immigrant from Ireland who had amassed a small fortune in the wholesale grocery trade. On his own, Edward did not do well. First, he failed in the wicker furniture manufacturing business that brought him to St. Paul. Then, after a decade in sales with Procter & Gamble in upstate New York, he was fired in 1908, in his mid-fifties. It was too late to start over. The Fitzgeralds returned to St. Paul in mild disgrace. McQuillan money supported them. Edward Fitzgerald was given an office to go to but no further responsibilities.

Contemporary reports agree that Scott Fitzgerald's father was small of frame, good-looking with his Vandyke beard, possessed of perfect manners, and invariably well-dressed: in appearance, every inch the gentleman. But he came from "tired old stock" in Maryland, and lacked the drive to succeed in business. He also drank more than was good for him.

Scott did his best to reason away his father's failures. Edward was "caught" in the panic of 1897, he wrote, then became a victim of the "rush to weed older men out of business." All his life Scott remembered the times he had spent with his father in boyhood. The walk downtown on Sunday morning to get their shoes shined before mass. His father's instinctively correct gesture, at a party where he knew no one, of introducing himself to the oldest woman there. The "Confound it!" oath he would utter in moments of supreme exasperation. Byron's "The Prisoner of Chillon" recited from memory. Civil War tales from his Maryland boyhood (Edward was twelve when the war ended) that Scott inflated into his father's having functioned as "an integral part of the Confederate spy system."

Though he grew up in some of the nation's northernmost cities, Scott was on the side of the Confederacy from the beginning, as on the side of lost causes and underdogs generally. Among his juvenilia are two stories and a 1913 play that spin improbably romantic tales of Southern gallantry. One of the first stories he remembered reading was about a struggle between the large animals and the small animals, whose leader was the fox. The small animals won the first battle, but the sheer size of the elephants and lions and tigers eventually overwhelmed them. Scott identified with the small animals. "I can almost weep now when I think of that poor fox," he wrote at twenty-one. Even as a young boy, he thought, he must have sensed "the wearing-down power of big, respectable people."

As much as any American writer, Scott Fitzgerald was extraordinarily aware of social gradations. In 1928, he recorded his version of St. Paul's social hierarchy. At the top were "two or three nationally known families," followed by third-generation families whose grandparents had brought "a vestige of money or culture" from the East. Next in line were families of the "big self-made merchants" who had arrived in the 1860s and 1870s, ranked in descending order by nationality: American-English-Scotch, German, and Irish. Finally there were well-to-do "new people" whose background was cloudy and "possibly unsound."

Edward Fitzgerald belonged among the new people, but his background set him apart, for he brought with him instead of wealth the prestige of a very old American family. Scott was proud of his father's roots, which connected him to the early days of the republic and such Marylanders as "Caleb Godwin of Hockley-in-ye-Hole, or Philip Key of Tudor Hall, or Pleasance Ridgley." His own name paid homage to this background. He was christened Francis Scott Key Fitzgerald, in recognition of his relation to the composer of the national anthem. The famous Key had been his "great-uncle," Scott wrote in 1935, probably reflecting received legend in the Fitzgerald family. Actually, Francis Scott Key was his second cousin, thrice removed.

A notable fact about Scott and Zelda Fitzgerald, as about Scott's parents, is that they never owned a home, never sank roots. But his father's childhood home was the place he came to love the best. Maryland was "the loveliest of states," he thought. He felt comfortable there; everything was "civilized and gay and rotted and polite." It was where his "great-grandfather's great-grandfather was born," where he went to live in the 1930s, where he chose to be buried.

At the head of his mother's side of the family, Grandfather McQuillan exemplified the self-made merchant class that Scott thought of—with a measure of snobbery—as "straight 1850 potato famine Irish." Actually P.F. McQuillan emigrated in 1843 and took the steamboat upriver from Galena, Illinois, to St. Paul in 1857, where he started his grocery business. He was "in trade," though Scott sought to minimize the condescension inherent in that phrase by making the point that at least his grandfather had pursued a career as a *wholesale* rather than a *retail* merchant. There was some money on his mother's side, some breeding on his father's. The combination left him uncertain about his own status.

He summed up his feelings in a 1933 letter to John O'Hara, another writer with an Irish heritage and a strong sense of social insecurity:

> I am half black Irish and half old American stock with the usual exaggerated ancestral pretensions. The black Irish half of the family had the money and looked down upon the Maryland side of the family who had, and really had, that certain series of reticences and obligations that go under the poor old shattered word "breeding.". . .

As a result, Fitzgerald added, he had developed "a two-cylinder inferiority complex." Even if he were elected king of Scotland, he maintained, he "would still be a parvenu." Unlike his father, he did not know how to act in challenging social situations. His youth had been spent "alternately crawling in front of the kitchen maids and insulting the great."

Edward Fitzgerald was thirty-seven and Mollie McQuillan thirty—ages that placed them on the brink of permanent bachelor and spinsterhood—when they married in February 1890. Their only son Scott was born six years later, on September 24, 1896. He was his mother's third child, but the first to survive. His two older sisters, one and three years old, died only three months before his birth. "I think I started then to be a writer," Fitzgerald observed, by which he meant something about the effect upon him of the way his mother, in the aftermath of her emotional trauma, coddled and cosseted him. It made him different from other youths, more self-absorbed and more emotionally vulnerable.

To Mollie, her good-looking baby boy must have seemed a gift from God, the more so when, three years later, she lost another female infant only an hour after birth. (The Fitzgeralds tried once more, and in July 1901 produced Scott's sister Annabel, his only surviving sibling.) It was no wonder that in the Fitzgerald household every childhood sniffle was a cause for alarm. Nor did Mollie's over-protectiveness disappear over time. In a 1923 article, Fitzgerald criticized just such a mother, whose every moment was tortured by groundless fears that her daughter was on the verge of a breakdown or that her son wasn't getting enough rest. Like the "Mrs. Judkins" of this article, Mollie Fitzgerald's perpetual worry-ing drove her children to distraction.

Mollie also liked to dress up her son and show him off. Master Scott would be summoned to accept the admiration of the visitors, and proceed to astound them with a delivery of Brutus's "Friends, Romans, countrymen" speech. Alternatively he would recite a poem or sing a ballad. "He used to sing for com-pany—God!" a mature Fitzgerald wrote of his boyhood self, stabbing the pen through the page in disgust. Yet there was no doubt that he had a strong theatri-cal bent, both personally and professionally. In his adolescence he wrote plays and acted in them, reserving the best parts for himself. At Princeton he threw himself into the Triangle Club musicals, both as author and sometime chorus girl. One of the great disappointments of his career came in 1923 when his comedy, *The Vegetable,* bombed in Atlantic City. Twelve years later, he wrote his agent Harold Ober that he wanted "to try a second play. It's just possible that I could knock them cold if I let go the vulgar side of my talent."

Fitzgerald might have been inclined to forgive his mother all her solicitude had she been more attractive. But Mollie was, unfortunately, rather dowdy in appearance and lacking in social graces. She did not smile to please others, only when she was amused. She said whatever came into her head. She wore prepos-terous hats. Her shoes did not always match, for she had the eccentric habit of breaking them in one foot at a time. The neighborhood children in St. Paul were rather frightened of her as she strode along, dour expression on her face and umbrella in hand. At home, she ruled the family, and for good reason. "Where would we be," she could point out, "if it weren't for Grandfather McQuillan?"

Which gives rise to another question: where did Scott Fitzgerald's genius come from? Not from a mannerly but unenergetic father, surely, and not from a mother whose tastes in reading ran to the sentimental rubbish of the time. As a boy, Scott dreamed of himself as a foundling, descended from royalty and unaccountably left at the door of unworthy parents. This was juvenile arrogance, and uncharming, but in fact the elder Fitzgeralds had little in common with their talented son. Neither of them approved of his decision to become a writer. They thought of authors as "distinctly peculiar," if not downright disreputable. In a February 1926 letter to his editor Maxwell Perkins, Fitzgerald disparaged his parents for the handicaps they had bequeathed to him. "My father is a moron and my mother is a neurotic, half insane with nervous pathological worry.... If I knew anything I'd be the best writer in America."

One of the unfortunate qualities his mother ingrained in him was an unrealistically elevated social ambition. Scott's first spoken word was "Up," Mollie recorded in his baby book, and that was the direction she hoped he and his sister Annabel might go. Edward Fitzgerald's failure in business and Grandfather McQuillan's Irish Catholic roots worked against the rise, but Mollie saw to it that Scott and Annabel mingled with those at the top of St. Paul's hierarchy. Scott attended St. Paul Academy, the city's leading private school, before being sent east to the Newman school and Princeton. He went to Professor Baker's dancing school with the children of the leading families. His father belonged to the University Club in town and to White Bear Yacht Club in the suburbs, but unlike the boys he went to school with and the girls he flirted with, Scott had to ride the streetcar out to White Bear for summer outings. The family could not afford a second home at the lake. The Fitzgeralds lived, in fact, in a succession of row houses on or near Summit Avenue, St. Paul's most elegant residential boulevard. Every year or two, they moved from one such rental property to another, within walking distance of, yet worlds removed from, the mansions nearby.

Another important legacy from his mother was a sense of himself as superior to others and hence not subject to discipline. Throughout childhood Mollie Fitzgerald forgave her beautiful baby boy all misbehavior. No matter what Scott did, he was just her "bad brownie." So thoroughly did his mother spoil him that, as he later commented, until he was fifteen he "did not know anyone else was alive." His youthful cockiness and propensity for showing off did not sit well with other boys. In his *Ledger,* Scott recorded a series of childhood humiliations. No one came to his birthday party. Boys at a potato roast told him to go away. He was "desperately unpopular" at camp. A letter in the St. Paul Academy school paper recommended that someone "poison Scotty or stop his mouth in some way." At Newman, he got into fights, earned poor marks, and achieved a measure of notoriety as the "freshest boy" on campus.

Girls liked him better, thank heaven. Even in pre-adolescence he understood how to play the game of courtship. Upon meeting an attractive girl, he would flatter her and then—to hold her interest—tell her that he had a particular adjective in mind that exactly suited her. She would have to wait to find out what it was.

In two unusual documents of his youth, Scott made it clear that he considered wooing a highly competitive game. His "Thoughtbook," written when he was fourteen, related the results of his early flirtations, carefully ranking his standing with various girls. "It was impossible to count the number of times" he kissed Kitty Williams during one afternoon of playing "postoffice" in Buffalo, he commented in one entry. When he went home he "had secured the coveted 1st place" and held it until spring, when another boy demoted him. Alida [Bigelow] was thought to be the prettiest girl in Professor Baker's dancing school, another passage stated. Although Scott and Bob Clark went to see her almost every night, "she liked Art [Foley] 1st, Egbert [Driscoll] 2nd, I third & Bob 4th."

Still more revealing was the letter Scott wrote for the benefit of his sister Annabel when *she* was fourteen and he was "19 or so." This extraordinary document, divided into sections like a scholarly treatise, instructed Annabel how to win the admiration of young boys. In the area of conversation, for example, Scott supplied his sister with "leading questions" to use and parallel ones to avoid. She might say, "I hear you've got a 'line,'" for instance, but should not ask about school or college unless the boy brought up the subject. The important thing was to get a boy talking about himself. Once that was done, she'd have him "cinched and harnessed."

In his letter Scott repeatedly counseled his sister to work on her social skills. On the dance floor she should maintain "a graceful and athletic carriage" and "remember to dance hard." Dancing counted as nothing else did, and Annabel should make it a point to *practice. "You can not be lazy."*

Annabel smiled on one side of her face, he told her, and that was all wrong. She should get in front of a mirror and *practice* a good radiant smile, *practice* it on other girls and on the family, *practice* it when she felt bored or unhappy, *practice* it until she was sure of it "as a good weapon in tight places." A laugh wasn't as important, but here too Annabel should *practice* until her artificial laugh was as engaging as her natural one. She should also cultivate a pathetic appealing look, best achieved "by opening the eyes wide and drooping the mouth a little, looking upward (hanging the head a little) directly into the eyes of the man you're talking to." *Practice* this, he counseled.

Next Scott undertook an inventory of his sister's good and bad points, taking up hair, features, complexion, figure, and so on. Where she was deficient, he advised her to make improvements. Exercise would give her healthier skin, and she ought to rub cold cream into her face regularly. She should brush and wet and train her splendid eyebrows "every morning and night," as he'd long ago suggested. To ward off her tendency toward physical clumsiness, he recommended that she imitate the graceful walk of a girl she admired. *Practice* it now, he implored her, for she couldn't practice when boys were around. It would be too late then.

Annabel Fitzgerald never commented on her brother Scott's ten-page letter of advice, but she might well have come to two conclusions about it. First, playing the courtship game sounded like exceedingly hard work. Second, her brother had an obsessive interest in how the game should be played. The truly successful player—the one who would rank "first"—must be capable of putting him- or herself in the place of the competitor of the opposite sex. Here young Scott Fitzgerald had an advantage over other boys, for he could think like a girl. "I'm half feminine," he said, "—at least my mind is."

In advocating a series of techniques for manipulating others, Scott's letter to Annabel betrayed a certain streak of cynicism. Yet that hard-heartedness coexisted with a romantic strain that made him idealize the very girls he courted with such calculation. Reading Fitzgerald's *Tender Is the Night*, the novelist Elizabeth Spencer was arrested by a description of Rosemary Hoyt, early in the novel: "The night had drawn the color from her face—she was pale as pale now, she was a white carnation left after a dance." That passage evoked for her a time when Americans believed in "romance, the high, breathless kind, the kind that went deep." Only Fitzgerald could have written it, she decided. For him, it was not enough to say that Rosemary was "wan or weary" after a long day and night in Paris in the company of Dick Diver. "No, she is flower-like, and she is a white carnation, she is what a gentleman wears on his lapel to a dance."

Four hundred miles east and south of St. Paul, Ernest Hemingway was born in the Chicago suburb of Oak Park on July 21, 1899, nearly three years Fitzgerald's junior.

The two had a number of things in common. Both were middle western middle-class youngsters. Both grew up dreaming of sudden success they read about in the books of Horatio Alger. Like almost all male American writers, both were children of dominant mothers and dominated fathers. But their upbringing—and the shape of the personality that derived from it—could hardly have been more different.

On the surface, the tall and bearded Dr. Clarence Edmonds Hemingway and his tall and amply-figured wife, Grace Hall Hemingway, made an impressive couple. Ernest was the second of the six children they produced over a span of two decades. The children were sturdy and sailed through the dangerous childhood illnesses of the period. Dressed in their Sunday best for services at the First Congregational Church, the Hemingways looked like a model turn-of-the-century family, hale and handsome embodiments of the American dream. These appearances were deceptive.

"Teach us to sit still," T.S. Eliot prayed, but for Dr. Hemingway inner peace was neither a goal nor a possibility. He had tremendous resources of energy, and was forever rushing from one task to another. In addition to his medical practice, Clarence Hemingway performed a considerable amount of charitable work. He also did much of the cooking and household supervision for the family. If he found any of his children idling away an hour, he would scold them off the davenport and into some form of physical activity, preferably outdoors.

Outdoors, Dr. Hemingway was in his element. During their summers at Walloon Lake in northern Michigan, he taught his youngsters to hunt and fish. He also taught them about the natural world. When Ernest and his sister Marcelline were old enough, Dr. Hemingway organized an Agassiz club that he led on weekend trips into the woods. With his incredible eyesight—he could see like an eagle—he showed the youngsters how to look at nature, unveiling birds' nests concealed in the crotch of a tree, wildflowers budding beneath the leaves of springtime.

Clarence Hemingway was a stern disciplinarian who believed in the benefits of physical punishment. The children were spanked hard, and afterwards instructed to kneel and ask forgiveness for their sins. These included disobeying their parents, of course, but also being late for appointments or family gatherings, for their father was passionate about punctuality. Dr. Hemingway held puritanical views about most forms of entertainment, as well. He would have prohibited his children from learning to dance, if his wife had not contravened his commands.

His father was "unsound" on questions of sex, Ernest felt. In "Fathers and Sons" Nick Adams—Hemingway's most autobiographical character—recounted the advice he received from his father. Dr. Adams "had summed up the whole matter by stating that masturbation produced blindness, insanity, and death, while a man who went with prostitutes would contract hideous venereal diseases and that the thing to do was to keep your hands off of people." In Dr. Hemingway's view, the function of literature was to instruct and enlighten. He did not know what to make of *In Our Time*, Ernest's first book of stories. "The brutal you have surely shown the world," he wrote his twenty-six-year-old son. "Look for the joyous, uplifting, and optimistic and spiritual in character."

Opposites attract, Marcelline wrote about her parents. Something of a tomboy in her youth, the strong-willed Grace Hall insisted on riding her brother's bicycle at a time when doing so was thought to be, for girls, both unseemly and risky. Yet for the most part she was an indoor person, since her congenitally weak eyes were sensitive to strong light. Her interests were concentrated in the arts instead of science. She came from a musical family, and had a fine soprano voice. Clarence Hemingway first came to know Grace Hall well when he attended her mother during a fatal illness in the fall of 1895. He asked Grace to marry him then, but she put him off in order to go to New York and work with a famous voice coach. She spent six months at the Art Students League, practicing day and night. Her blossoming talent, Grace later told her children, led to an audition for the Met and a concert at Madison Square Garden.

Back to Oak Park in the spring of 1896, Grace once more postponed Dr. Hemingway's suit, this time to travel to Europe with her father, Ernest Hall. She thought her father "the finest purest noblest man" she had ever known, and Clarence Hemingway could wait. They finally married in October, and immediately moved into her father's home. Determined to keep her independence, Grace began giving voice lessons. According to Marcelline, very much her mother's advocate in her memoir called *At the Hemingways*, the newlywed Grace Hemingway soon was earning as much as $1,000 a month from her pupils, ten times more than her husband was making from his general practice of medicine.

Marcelline arrived in January 1898, about eighteen months before Ernest, and Grace Hall Hemingway did a highly unusual thing with these two first-born children. She twinned them. They were dressed alike, at Oak Park "in gingham dresses and in little fluffy lace tucked dresses with picture hats" and at Walloon Lake in matching overalls. Grace also had their hair cut the same way, often in a style called the Dutch dolly, bangs across the forehead and squared off below the ears. As biographer Kenneth Lynn has pointed out, dressing little boys in girls' clothing was conventional enough at the time. There is a photograph of young Scott Fitzgerald in bloomers, for example, but his hair is cut short so that in spite of his prettiness there is no question of his gender. What was different, in the case of Grace's twinning of Ernest with his sister, was the combination of feminine attire and feminine hair style. As early as two, Ernest rebelled when his mother called him her Dutch dolly. "I not a Dutch dolly," he declared, stamping his foot. "I Pawnee Bill. Bang, I shoot Fweetee [his pet name for his mother]."

Another oddity about Grace Hemingway's twinning experiment was that it lasted so long. Ernest wore dresses until he entered kindergarten, or about twice as long as most boy children of the period. Even then, his mother continued to treat her two oldest offspring as twins. Marcelline was held back so she and Ernest could enter first grade together. Their play knew no distinctions of gender. They had china tea sets just alike, and dolls alike, and when Ernest was given a little air rifle, so was his sister. "Mother was doing her best to make us feel like twins," as Marcelline put it in all innocence.

Marcelline wrote openly about her mother's twinning of herself and Ernest, but avoided discussing two other difficulties: Clarence Hemingway's mental illness and Grace Hemingway's intimate companionship with a longtime pupil. Brother Leicester kept the silence in his book of reminiscence, as did sister Sunny in hers. Even Ernest, who was not averse to exploring taboo psychological terrain, shied away from these family secrets. Certain things were not to be spoken of.

Clarence Hemingway was beset by depression all his life. Michael Reynolds, whose multi-volume biography has emerged as the primary source for information about Ernest Hemingway, has documented Dr. Hemingway's spells of depression through the cache of letters the family left behind. The best cure for his troubles, Clarence obviously believed, was to get away from home. A week's vacation in New Orleans over Thanksgiving 1903 had been his salvation, he wrote Grace. Five years later, he took six weeks off for a postgraduate course in obstetrics in New York City. Oak Park was not aware that the course was only four weeks long, and that Clarence had spent the last two weeks on his own, again in New Orleans. "Try to rest the worry place in your brain," his wife advised him. "Just make a business of eating and sleeping and forgetting."

Whatever their short-term benefit, these rest cures worked no permanent magic. In October 1909, Dr. Hemingway sent his family a letter of instruction about how to proceed in the event of his imminent death. He had secured $50,000 in life insurance policies from eleven different firms, and gave his wife specific instructions about how to collect on them. At stake was the future "of the darling children and your own self—Grace my darling," he wrote, and she must not let her grief prevent her from acting in a sensible businesslike fashion. She should tell each company the same story, for example, and not tell them everything she knew. "[S]hould there be any doubt at all as to the cause of death," he provided her with the names of two doctors who would best represent her interests at a coroner's inquest. Dr. Hemingway did not use the word "suicide," but evidently he did have in mind a particular way to die. "[I]f *Accident* is Blood Poisoning," he told Grace, "you can realize on the Aetna Policy."

Clarence Hemingway survived that crisis, but other dark periods ensued. The trouble intensified in 1919. His son Ernest had come back from the war with a burden of physical and emotional wounds, but Dr. Hemingway's concerns lay closer to home. He and his wife were not getting along.

In May Grace Hemingway contracted to build a cottage of her own a mile away from Windemere, the Hemingway family place at Walloon Lake. She had bought the land with her inheritance, after her father died in 1905, and for many years had planned to have a cottage, only holding off because of the objections of her husband. Now she was going to build her retreat despite those objections. To make his position clear, Dr. Hemingway wrote her contractor in Michigan that he would not be responsible, in any way, for his wife's debts.

In a letter to her husband about this dispute, Grace made the case for her new cottage. Windemere had been "pleasant and adequate" for the first eight or nine years, she acknowledged, but since then had become hateful to her. Summer after summer she suffered there, "shut in by the hills and lake, no view, no where to go, acting the part of the family drudge, standing at sink and cook stove until the agony in my spinal nerves forced me to lie down...the very sight of Windemere brings tears to my eyes and a sob to my throat." A small place of her own, she concluded, would save her nerves and serve as "a demonstration in neatness cleanness simplicity and wholesomeness which is sorely needed right now by my four daughters who have an idea that excitement is the only form of happiness worth while."

That final appeal was well contrived, for as Grace well knew, Dr. Hemingway feared that their daughters were running wild. Still, he would not be moved. The cottage across the lake seemed an indulgence, and it was probably associated in his mind with Ruth Arnold. He could not prevent his wife from spending her small inheritance on a cottage of her own. By summer's end, though, he laid down the law on the subject of Ruth Arnold. She was no longer to live with the Hemingways, or even permitted to visit.

Ruth Arnold took her first voice lesson from Grace Hemingway in 1907, when she was twelve years old—only three years older than Marcelline. She moved into the Hemingways' house in 1908 to continue her studies and function as a part-time baby sitter and cook. Ruth was not particularly talented, and not terribly bright, but she was quiet and attractive and absolutely worshipful toward her teacher. In effect she repudiated her own family—she was the youngest daughter, and outshone by her sisters—and chose Grace as surrogate mother and ideal.

Over the years, Ruth became an integral part of the Hemingway family, and the bond between herself and Grace Hemingway grew closer. Dr. Hemingway spent the sweltering summer of 1919 in Oak Park, unwilling to be a party of any sort to the construction of Grace Cottage, as his wife called it. But Ruth went north with the Hemingway daughters in June, where she eagerly shared Grace's delight as her private retreat went up. "No distance can separate my soul from the one I love so dearly," Ruth wrote Grace after she returned to Oak Park early in August. Dr. Hemingway imposed what distance he could by barring her from the house.

From Walloon Lake, Grace mailed Clarence a letter of protest. If his mental attitude was really not within his control, she pointed out, he could count on her to give him all the help she could. But others needed her as well, including her "blessed children" and "dear faithful Ruth, who has given me her youth and her loyal service for these many years." Her platform was that they were all as dear to her as life herself; she would desert none of them. A closing clause simultaneously assured Dr. Hemingway of her love, and chided him for his suspicions. "[N]o one," Grace wrote, "can ever take my husband's place unless he abdicates it to play at petty jealousy with his wife's loyal girl friend...."

Ruth could hardly be so bold. She continued to see Grace and to correspond with her, but as circumspectly as possible. In the summer of 1920, she wrote Grace about a possible visit to Walloon Lake. Ruth realized she could not come north if Dr. Hemingway were there, yet if he decided to spend all summer at the lake, it was all right with her. She would be brokenhearted not to visit Grace, "but would far rather be, Dearest, than have any talk." If she *could* come up, she would make sure that Grace was not lonesome. Meanwhile, "Dearest when I choose to send a little love gift up, please don't mention it to Dr. It seems so silly to make this request but will explain later."

The affection between Grace Hemingway and Ruth Arnold lasted until Grace died. Ruth moved in with Grace during the 1930s, after Dr. Hemingway's death, and tongues wagged in Oak Park. Grace scolded two of the gossips for repeating "an old malicious story." She and her husband had been "loving and sympathetic" every day of their thirty-two years together, she maintained. As for Ruth, Grace had "known and loved her nearly 30 years, and she has always been loyal and true to the Hemingway family." The children were fond of Ruth too, and "grateful for her many kindnesses." These kindnesses continued. When Grace's health began to fail, in the 1950s, Ruth Arnold was on hand to care for her.

Ernest apparently shared his father's sentiments about this relationship. He forbade his own sons to visit their grandmother Hemingway on the grounds that she was "androgynous." Ernest also believed that his mother had emasculated his father. In December 1928 Clarence Hemingway shot himself behind the right ear with his own father's revolver. The death could not be construed as an accident, to insurance companies or anyone else, but neither was there any public mention of the doctor's "nervous breakdowns." Poor health and financial worries caused Dr. Hemingway to take his life, the family explained. Ernest held his mother responsible. He "hated" her, he insisted, and would not back down from that verb when others protested. The alienation between Ernest and his mother had been brewing for a long time before his father's suicide. It boiled over in the summer of 1920.

Back from the war and limping slightly from his wounds, Ernest Hemingway cut a rather romantic figure. His parents were proud of his wartime service, but the war had been over for nearly two years and it bothered them both that Ernest continued to idle away so much of his time. Ernest could not go to college, he was later to claim, because the money had been spent on Grace Cottage. This statement was misleading—Marcelline was sent to Oberlin, and he could have gone if he wished—and characteristic of his propensity to blame every conceivable misfortune on his mother. The fact was that he wanted to be a writer, and neither college nor full-time employment fitted into his plans.

Ernest and his friend Ted Brumback spent the first part of the summer of 1920 at Walloon Lake, dodging the chores his mother assigned. Dr. Hemingway had come up from Oak Park for a few weeks, and returned to his practice deeply concerned about the moral status of the family. Ursula and Sunny, seventeen and fifteen respectively, defied the strict rules he tried to impose on them, and Ernest was openly insubordinate with Grace. It may be that Ernest, who reached his twenty-first birthday on July 21, was trying to precipitate a break with his parents. Surviving letters demonstrate that he succeeded. "Try not to be a sponger," Dr. Hemingway advised his son the day after his birthday, in a letter that sounds very much as if it were written at the behest of Mrs. Hemingway. "It is altogether too hard on your mother to entertain you and your friends, when she is not having help and you are so hard to please and are so insulting to your dear mother." It would be "best" for Ernest and Ted "to change camps," his father pointed out. "[P]lease pack up and try elsewhere until you are again invited" to Windemere. Clarence Hemingway's mild language—"try," "please"—undercut the authority of his message. Ernest stuck around for a few more days.

Ruth Arnold arrived at Walloon Lake July 25. The following night, the tension between mother and son erupted. Ernest and Ted accompanied Ursula and Sunny and a few of their young friends to a secret late-night cookout and sing-along at Ryan's Point. It was past midnight when the mother of these friends discovered her children missing and, suspecting Ernest, confronted Grace Hemingway, who was startled to find Ursula and Sunny's beds empty. Ruth, who had been let in on the secret, finally told the frantic mothers about the clandestine outing. When the youngsters returned at three A.M. for their dressing down, Ernest was anything but contrite. He "called me every name he could think of," Grace wrote her husband. She didn't think anything particularly "wicked" had happened at Ryan's Point, but could not countenance "the general lawlessness that Ernest instills into all young boys and girls." Without seeking further assistance from the good doctor, she ordered Ernest and Ted off the premises, and presented her son with a letter of condemnation she had been working on for days.

This remarkable document took the form of an extended financial metaphor, comparing a mother's love with a bank account. A very young child drew upon this account every day, Grace began, and continued to make withdrawals as he grew, only occasionally depositing a few pennies. Then the rebellious period of adolescence left the mother-love bank account "perilously low." When a child like Ernest reached manhood, the bank could not continue to pay out. The account needed some deposits in the form of "[f]lowers, fruit, candy, or something pretty to wear, brought home to Mother, with a kiss and a squeeze." But there had been none of these deposits from her son, only supercilious remarks and selfish misbehavior.

> Unless you, my son Ernest, come to yourself, cease your lazy loafing, and pleasure seeking,—borrowing with no thought of returning;—Stop trying to graft a living off anybody and everybody, spending all your earnings lavishly and wastefully on luxuries for yourself. Stop trading on your handsome face, to fool gullible little girls, and neglecting your duties to God and your Savior Jesus Christ, unless, in other words, you come into your manhood,—there is nothing before you but bankruptcy.
> *You have over drawn.*

Grace went on to remind Ernest that the world was crying out for "real men, with brawn and muscle, moral as well as physical—men whose mothers can look up to them, instead of hanging their heads in shame at having borne them." Ernest had been born of a race of gentlemen, men who "were clean mouthed, chivalrous to all women, grateful and generous." Until he was ready to take his place beside them, he need not bother to return.

In the parlance of a later time, this letter might stand as an example of "tough love," designed to shock the recipient into a behavioral change. The love-as-bank-account metaphor certainly fits into that category. But Grace Hemingway was not content to style herself as a cold-blooded banker. No, she would gladly have been Ernest's "best girl" as well, joyfully receiving the sweet and thoughtful presents that he would not supply, the "little love gifts" that she could count on only from Ruth Arnold.

Grace's letter did not work. If anything, it hardened Ernest's heart against her. "Do not come back," she commanded him, "until your tongue has learned not to insult and shame your mother." In that sense, he never did come back. As the eldest son, he felt it his duty to establish a trust fund for his mother's support after the death of his father. But he paid no duty calls to Oak Park, and repeatedly denigrated her in correspondence with his siblings. You know, Ernest told his sister Carol in 1945, he "could never stand to look at [their brother Leicester] on acct. he looked like our mother." Nor could he abide what he thought of as her sanctimonious pronouncements. "Had a lovely letter from our Mother," he added, "in which she was sure God would look after me no matter how little I deserved it."

In the summer of 1920 at Walloon Lake, the year he passed his twenty-first birthday, Ernest cut the cord.

CHAPTER 2

LOVESHOCKS: JILTINGS

Being jilted is a rite of passage that few people, in a dating culture, are lucky enough to avoid. There is something terribly banal about rejection by a loved one, particularly by a first love. We are inclined to smile about the indignity of it, as we might smile at *Reader's Digest* accounts of "Life's Most Embarrassing Moments." But the smile only emerges retrospectively, or when it is someone else who has been jilted. At the time, rejections hurt, for they strike directly at one's sense of self-worth.

One indication of the emotional cost of a jilting is that the word itself has almost vanished. College students talk of being "dumped," and social scientists reject even that term, with its visually comic overtones. "I haven't heard anyone use *jilted* in twenty years," one of them said recently. "Nowadays we talk about 'failed relationships' instead." This psychobabbling phrase nicely skirts the issue, for if it is the *relationships* that fail and not the people in them, there need be no question of assigning blame, or of acknowledging one's own shortcomings and another's fickleness and cruelty. Alternatively, one can say that "things didn't work out," as if euphemism could make the pain go away.

Fitzgerald and Hemingway suffered through their jiltings at about the same age, when they were nineteen to twenty years old. But the circumstances were very different, as were their attempts to deal with the aftershocks.

According to his *Ledger*, Scott Fitzgerald first heard "the name Ginevra

King" when he was fourteen, and heard it again eighteen months later, in January 1913. It would be another two years before he met her, but during the interim the name resonated in his mind with the unmistakable ring of American aristocracy. "Ginevra" with its Italianate flavor promised a measure of sophistication, and she was indeed the king's daughter as in the fairy tale, only to be won by the worthiest of suitors.

Ginevra came from Lake Forest, Chicago's most socially prominent suburb. As a matter of course the family belonged to the exclusive Onwentsia Club. Her father, Charles King, pursued a successful career as a banker and—like Tom Buchanan in *The Great Gatsby*—was rich enough to keep a string of polo ponies. Ginevra did not need this most fortunate of backgrounds to get herself talked about. As a young girl, she earned her own reputation as a beautiful and brilliant competitor in the battle of the sexes.

Scott's former flame Marie Hersey invited Ginevra, her classmate at exclusive Westover school, to visit St. Paul during the 1914-1915 Christmas holidays. She wanted to see what would happen when Scott and Ginevra met. That meeting took place January 4, 1915, during a dinner dance at the Town and Country Club. Reluctant to abandon Chicago during the holiday's social season, Ginevra, sixteen, had just arrived in town. Scott, eighteen, was supposed to leave for Princeton that day, but postponed his train trip in order to attend the party. The evening must have gone much as Fitzgerald described it in *This Side of Paradise*, the highly autobiographical 1920 novel that established his reputation as an expert on and spokesman for the Jazz Age generation. In that book, as in much of his fiction, Fitzgerald displayed an uncanny knack for double vision. On the one hand, he was very much involved emotionally in the story. On the other hand, he stood back, observed, and made notes like an anthropologist immersing himself in another culture.

In his novel, Fitzgerald made his protagonist a few inches taller than himself, but otherwise the descriptions of Amory Blaine (Scott) and Isabelle Borge (Ginevra) were true to life. "Amory was now eighteeen years old, just under six feet tall and exceptionally, but not conventionally, handsome." He had "rather a young face" with "penetrating green eyes, fringed with long dark eyelashes." Although he lacked "that intense animal magnetism that so often accompanies beauty in men or women," people never forgot his face.

The lack of physical magnetism troubled Fitzgerald. In the notebooks he assembled during the 1930s, he calculated his personal assets. "I didn't have the two top things— great animal magnetism or money. I had the two second things, tho', good looks and intelligence. So I always got the top girl." This was whistling in the wind, for Fitzgerald had discovered by then that he would come in second (or lower) when matched against someone with great animal magnetism like, say, Ernest Hemingway, or against a "top girl" who had *both* the magnetism and the money, like Ginevra King.

"Flirt smiled from her large black-brown eyes and shone through her intense physical magnetism." So Fitzgerald introduced Ginevra's fictional counterpart Isabelle. And as he recounted their meeting, Amory's rumored inconstancy in love rather appealed to Isabelle. The fact that "every girl there seemed to have had an affair with him at some time or other" made him a more worthy adversary in the game they would be playing. She had an almost unlimited capacity for such affairs, herself.

Amory and Isabelle confronted each other as competing performers in a contest they both enjoyed. Amory gained an early advantage with two conversational gambits. They were to be dinner partners, he announced. "We're all coached for each other." The remark made Isabelle gasp. She had the temperament of an actress, and felt "as if a good speech had been taken from the star and given to a minor character." Amory followed with the line about the adjective that just fit Isabelle but that he didn't know her well enough yet to reveal.

"Will you tell me — afterward?" she half whispered.

He nodded.

"We'll sit out."

Isabelle nodded.

Isabelle regained some momentum with a compliment. "Did anyone ever tell you you have keen eyes?" she inquired, and it seemed to him that her foot just touched his under the table. During the dancing, she reigned. Boys cut in on her every few feet. She gazed up at them with that pathetic "poor little me" look Scott had instructed his sister to gain command of, and sent each one away with a squeeze of the hand intended to convey how much she had enjoyed dancing with him. Yet by eleven o'clock Amory and Isabelle had escaped the dance floor to "sit out" alone in the den upstairs. She told him about the twenty-year-old college boys who were supposedly courting her. He affected an air of blasé sophistication. Wearing masks, they both understood, was part of the game.

It grew late, and Amory turned out the electric light above their heads. He was mad for her, he said, and was going back to college for six months. Couldn't he have "just one thing to remember her by"?

"Close the door," he barely heard her murmur. The music from outside sounded wonderful, Isabelle thought, as she revelled in anticipation of the romantic scene to come. She envisioned "an unending succession of scenes like this: under moonlight and pale starlight, and in the backs of warm limousines and in low, cozy roadsters stopped under sheltering trees—only the boy might change, and this one was *so* nice." But others burst in on them, and the moment was lost. "Damn!" Isabelle muttered to herself as she went to bed later that night. Amory had such a good-looking mouth.

In fact, Scott was the more smitten of the two. "Ginevra - Triangle year," he headed the *Ledger* diary entries for the year he was eighteen. With the exception of his grades, Fitzgerald's sophomore year at Princeton was a series of successes. In February 1915, he was elected secretary of the Triangle Club. (He wrote lyrics for the Triangle musical comedies in both 1914 and 1915.) This meant he would almost certainly rise to vice president and then president of the club, if he could stay eligible. In March, he turned down three other bids to join University Cottage Club, exactly the club he had been angling for.

Things were also going well with Ginevra, that year. A month after their first meeting in St. Paul, he traveled from Princeton to see her at Westover, but such meetings were necessarily rare. Westover kept a short leash on the fashionable girls it was in the business of preparing to lead fashionable lives. To solidify his position, Scott wooed Ginevra through the mails, writing long letters almost daily. Usually designed to entertain, the letters were accompanied by drawings and bits of doggerel and dialogue. Occasionally, though, he chastised her for encouraging other suitors. There were probably more of these than he imagined. At the time, Ginevra later admitted, she "was definitely out for quantity not quality in beaux." Scott was "top man" for the moment, but she still coveted attention from others and was not about to change her ways. She had never asked to be placed on a pedestal, she reminded him. Besides, it was her cohort of admirers that attracted him in the first place.

In June 1915 he took Ginevra to see *Nobody Home* on Broadway, and danced with her afterward at the Ritz hotel's Midnight Frolic. He saw her again in Chicago, on his way back to St. Paul for the summer. Observing Ginevra in her own milieu, Scott began to understand the handicaps he faced in courting her. The notation in his *Ledger* for that visit reads: "Stopping off in Chicago. Midge Muir. House Party. Jimmy Johnston. Deering: I'm going to take Ginevra home in my electric." Midge Muir effectively vanished, and there exists no account of the house party. More would be heard of Jimmy Johnston, the Harrison Johnston who was to become United States amateur golf champion. It was Deering's offhand remark/boast that troubled Scott, who had himself no automobile either gas- or electric-powered to take home the young lady he liked to think of as his girl. The distance between Ginevra's overprivileged surroundings and his own was driven home further when Courtney Letts told him that Deering, the boy with the electric, was "as poor as a church mouse."

Scott spent much of the summer in Montana, on the ranch of Sap Donahoe, his classmate and friend both at Newman school and Princeton. "No news from Ginevra," he somewhat ominously observed in his *Ledger* for August 1915. Back in college, he launched into a junior year "of terrible disappointments & the end of all college dreams. Everything bad in it was my own fault." First off, he flunked a makeup exam in mathematics, and became ineligible for his Triangle Club office. "There were to be no badges of pride, no medals, after all," he realized. His career as a leader of men was over. Throughout the fall, he continued to neglect his studies. In December, he and the dean reached an agreement that it would be better for him to leave and try again the following year. "Went home early sick," he laconically noted in his *Ledger*, without mentioning his academic difficulties.

During those despairing months, Fitzgerald "lived on the letters" he was writing to Ginevra. They had dinner together in Waterbury, Connecticut, one evening in October 1915, and he did not see her again until the following summer. Meanwhile, Ginevra was "fired" from Westover for flirting with a boy from the window of her room after the senior dance. The next morning headmistress Mary Hillard (who was, incidentally, the aunt of the poet Archibald MacLeish) summoned Ginevra to her office, delivered the standard cautionary tale about "foxes in the henhouse," and dismissed her from school. Perhaps it was on the ride back to Chicago that she encountered Jimmy Johnston. Scott's *Ledger* for April includes "Ginevra & Jimmy on the train." That cryptic comment may prefigure Dick Diver's jealousy in *Tender Is the Night* when he hears about Rosemary Hoyt's intimacy with a traveling companion on a train trip. Almost everything about Ginevra King found its way into his stories and novels, eventually.

In August 1916, Ginevra invited Scott for a second visit on her home grounds, and this time it was even more forcibly brought home to him that in courting this golden girl, he was reaching beyond his grasp. The shorthand of his *Ledger* recreated the experience: "Lake Forest. Peg Carry. Petting Party. Ginevra. Party. The bad day at the McCormicks. The dinner at Pegs. Dissapointment. Mary Buford Pierce. Little Marjorie King & her smile.

Beautiful Billy Mitchell. Peg Cary stands straight. 'Poor boys shouldn't think of marrying rich girls.'"

Nothing has come to light about the bad day at the McCormicks or Mary Buford Pierce. Everything else in the cryptic catalogue signifies. Margaret (Peg) Cary was a close friend of Ginevra's. With Courtney Letts and Edith Cummings, they made up the "Big Four" debutantes of the time, girls so legendary for their beauty that they were known by that designation for the rest of their lives. In the late 1970s, I met a fellow from Lake Forest at the Yale Club bar in New York City, and asked him if possibly he had heard of "the Big Four," who would have been at least a decade his senior. He had indeed— everyone in Lake Forest had—and he could tell me about their subsequent marriages and divorces as well.

The generic "Petting Party" Fitzgerald made famous in *This Side of Paradise*, revealing to a shocked older generation "how casually their daughters were accustomed to be kissed." The Popular Daughter of the day (P.D.) was a good deal more liberal with her favors than the "belle" who preceded her, he explained. "The 'belle' was surrounded by a dozen men in the intermissions between dances. Try to find the P.D. between dances, just *try* to find her." Like as not she would be inside someone's limousine, with the boy of the moment. Amory Blaine "found it rather fascinating to feel that any popular girl he met before eight he might quite possibly kiss before twelve."

"Little Marjorie King," Ginevra's younger sister, suggested that it might have been their father Charles King who made the devastating remark that "[p]oor boys shouldn't think of marrying rich girls." Certainly those were the sentiments of his generation and class on the subject. By most standards of measurement, of course, Scott Fitzgerald was not a poor boy. But in the scale of Lake Forest, which Scott thought of as "the most glamorous place in the world," he was poor all right. Especially so in comparison to "Beautiful Billy Mitchell," who like Charles King was rich enough to maintain polo ponies and who was to marry the beautiful Ginevra King two years later.

Scott's courtship of Ginevra did not end after his visit to Lake Forest, but it might as well have. There remained the fiasco of the Princeton-Yale game in October 1916. Ginevra and Peg Cary came to Princeton for the game and the associated parties. When Scott and Peg's date delivered them to the train station in New York, the girls said their good-byes, and then rendezvoused with two Yale boys—oh, the disloyalty—who were secreted behind the pillars. "Final break with Ginevra," Scott noted in January 1917, but she did not disappear from his

Ledger, not quite. In June 1917: "Ginevra engaged?" and "Girl at show resembled G.K." In September 1917: "Minnekahda [Minikahda] Club. 'Oh Ginevra.'" Finally in July 1918, the month Scott met Zelda Sayre: "Ginevra married." September 1918: "Fell in love [with Zelda] on the 7th."

Zelda delayed committing herself to Scott until he could demonstrate sufficient capacity to support her. When she broke off their engagement on those grounds, he wrote in a *Crack-Up* essay of 1936, it seemed to be "one of those tragic loves doomed for lack of money." In the end he won Zelda back by publishing a novel and selling a story to Hollywood. But, he pointed out, "since then I have never been able to stop wondering where my friends' money came from, nor to stop thinking that at some time a sort of *droit de seigneur* might have been exercised to give one of them my girl." The images of both Zelda and Ginevra must have conflated in his mind as he wrote those words, though the courtships hardly resembled each other. Zelda came from an old Southern family, but she was by no means rich. And she always took Scott seriously as a suitor, even when she was putting him off. Ginevra, apparently, never did.

"He was mighty young when we knew each other," Ginevra said of Scott in a 1974 interview, adding that she hadn't "singled him out as anything special." He was one of several boys she was carrying on romances with, and in retrospect, by no means the most memorable of the group. She couldn't even remember kissing Scott, Ginevra said. She threw away the hundreds of letters he sent her, and when he had *her* letters typed up and bound into a booklet, she disposed of those as well. She did write him a farewell letter before her marriage in 1918. It was one of quite a few she had to write, for she "was engaged to two other people" at the time. Multiple engagements were easy enough to manage during the war, she explained, "because you'd never get caught. It was just covering yourself in case of a loss." For Ginevra, Scott was an engaging competitor in the courtship game, nothing more. She was not to blame if he converted the game into a passionate quest for an unattainable ideal.

Looking back on their relationship, Ginevra wouldn't have changed a thing. At no time did Scott measure up to her idea of someone she could marry, for he came from a different social universe. Just how different is emphasized in a Chicago newspaper article about her that Fitzgerald pasted in his scrapbook. This society page feature amounts to a puff piece about Ginevra (then Mrs. William H. Mitchell III), whose portrait had recently been completed "by the great painter Sorine." The Ginevra of this account, identified as one of "These Charming People," had a "truly natural beauty" unenhanced by rouge or mascara. She was vibrant and energetic, and when she laughed, which was often, her enormous deep brown eyes sparkled. But Mrs. Mitchell was still more to be admired for her way of life "which combine[d] a tremendously gay amusing time with a thoughtful organized existence." She was "a grand and courageous horsewoman" who followed the seasons to Aiken and Palm Beach and Santa Barbara—resorts where the wealthy took the sun and rode horses. Back in Lake Forest, she ran her own house "to the queen's taste" and supported every worthy charity, in particular St. Luke's Hospital in Chicago.

That kind of life, Scott knew, was beyond his means, and so he invested it with glamour. When he heard about Ginevra's divorce in 1936, he sent her a copy of *The Beautiful and Damned* and asked her on the flyleaf to identify which character had been modelled after her. "They were all such bitches," she said, that she didn't feel like guessing. Yet on a trip to Santa Barbara in 1937, she summoned him from Hollywood for a luncheon meeting. Scott was nervous as a schoolboy about the prospect. "She was the first girl I ever loved," he wrote his daughter Scottie, "and I have faithfully avoided seeing her up to this moment to keep the illusion perfect, because she ended up by throwing me over with the most supreme boredom and indifference." Maybe he shouldn't go, he halfheartedly proposed to Scottie. Of course he did.

At the beginning, Scott and Ginevra got along extremely well during their lunch in Santa Barbara. Then, characteristically, he botched the reunion by falling off the wagon and out of favor. Despite a number of phone calls in the next few days, Ginevra refused another meeting. She was still "a charming woman," he reported to Scottie. "I'm sorry I didn't see more of her." In going out of his life yet again, Ginevra gave him one more failure to cherish, one more humiliation to remember and hang on to, like the list of "Snubs" he carefully preserved in his notebooks, lest they go away.

The only mementos Ginevra had of Scott when the revival of Fitzgerald's literary reputation was getting underway were his Triangle Club pin ("if that's of use to anyone") and a couple of snapshots. She sent those to biographer Arthur Mizener in 1947. She was not, herself, a fan of Scott's writing. "It was quite a while" after their youthful romance, as she put it, "before he developed into what people consider a good writer."

How did Fitzgerald react to his rejection by Ginevra King? According to Ginevra, he sent her a brief "insulting" note when she announced her wedding plans. Beyond that report and the brief notes in his *Ledger*, there is surprisingly little documentation. He did not retire from the social whirl, exactly. The names of a number of girls appear in the *Ledger* entries after the January 1917 "Final break with Ginevra," leading up to that of Zelda Sayre. Still, there can be no doubt that he fell in love with Zelda on the rebound. The hurt of losing Ginevra did not disappear. He wrote about the pain of that loss again and again.

"Mostly, we authors must repeat ourselves," Fitzgerald commented in a 1933 essay. "We have two or three great and moving experiences in our lives... Then we learn our trade, well or less well, and we tell our two or three stories — each time in a new disguise — maybe ten times, maybe a hundred, as long as people will listen." One of those stories for Fitzgerald, the one most often repeated, is that of the poor boy hopelessly in love with the rich girl. It is the story of Amory Blaine and Rosalind Connage in *This Side of Paradise*, of Dexter Green and Judy Jones in "Winter Dreams," of Jay Gatsby and Daisy Fay Buchanan in *The Great Gatsby*. "The whole idea of Gatsby," he said, "is the unfairness of a poor young man not being able to marry a girl with money. This theme comes up again and again because I lived it."

Writing about that emotional trauma did not make it go away. You'll lose it if you talk about it, Hemingway's Jake Barnes maintains, but that depends on *how* you talk about it. In the case of Fitzgerald, even though each of his stories ends in disillusionment for the spurned suitors, he could not bring himself to condemn the characters who elicited the disillusionment. Rosalind is culpably selfish in turning down Amory, Judy lures and drops suitors with a callous recklessness, Daisy will not abandon a hollow but financially secure marriage even for love. Yet as he depicts them, his golden girls remain largely untarnished. Intellectually Fitzgerald understood that "nine girls out of ten marry for money." Emotionally he refused to hate them for doing so, if they were as beautiful and unwinnable as Ginevra King of Lake Forest.

What went wrong with Ernest Hemingway and Agnes von Kurowsky had nothing to do with social position, but still there was a barrier between them — a barrier of age.

Much has been made of the wound Hemingway suffered at Fossalta di Piave shortly before midnight on July 8, 1918. He arrived in Italy five weeks earlier, to serve as an ambulance driver for the Red Cross. The ambulance service was not thought of as particularly dangerous. Ernest, in fact, was the first

American to be injured in Italy (one other had been killed). On the night he was wounded, he volunteered to pass out chocolate and cigarettes to the troops at the front. He was only eighteen, just a year out of Oak Park High School, and like many another immature lad in battle thought of himself as exempt from the laws of mortality. That illusion exploded with the mortar shell that the Austrians' Minenwerfer launched across the river.

Hundreds of shrapnel fragments ripped into Hemingway's legs. He thought he was dying. He could not move, he fought for breath, he felt his soul flutter out of his body like a handkerchief in the wind. When the initial shock abated, he managed to stagger a hundred and fifty yards to the first aid dugout, and to carry a wounded soldier on his back. En route he was struck by two machine-gun bullets in his right leg. The Italians awarded him a medal for gallantry under fire.

Hemingway did not soon outlive that night at Fossalta. In dreams and nightmares, in fiction and in fact, he returned to the scene time and again. One of his characters makes the pilgrimage in order to defecate on the exact spot of the wounding. For years to come, Ernest could not sleep without a light burning in the room.

Psychologically oriented critics have seized on the wounding in Italy as a key to interpreting Hemingway's life and work. As a result, they maintained, he was repeatedly compelled to prove his courage and face down his fears, in the process reliving—and once more miraculously surviving—the terrible trauma. Hemingway lived long enough to read such speculations and dismiss them as in his view absolute nonsense, but they take on a certain credibility when considered in the context of his life and writing. Wounds leave scars, and not all of them heal completely. That much at least was true not only of his physical wounding in World War I, but of the emotional injury inflicted by Agnes von Kurowsky.

Here is the way it was. The badly wounded Ernest was brought to the handsome five-story house on the Via Manzoni in Milan then serving as a makeshift hospital for the American Red Cross. From the roof, you could see the massive Duomo, the Galleria with its shops and restaurants, and the famous opera house La Scala. Hemingway was one of the first patients to arrive. Even lying flat on his back, he projected a winning animal vitality. He was terrified that the doctors might amputate his leg, yet refused to feel sorry for himself. Red Cross officers came to call and went away full of admiration for his high spirits and good humor. Among them was Captain Jim Gamble, a wealthy thirty-six-year-old who took a particular interest in Ernest, and not only because he was in charge of the volunteers for the "rolling canteens" to serve the front-line troops. Then as always, Hemingway easily commanded male friendship.

Women were new to him, however. Physically, he was shedding his adolescent awkwardness and becoming for the first time highly attractive to the opposite sex. Unlike Fitzgerald, he had little experience in courtship. There were no serious girlfriends in high school. Whenever possible, his mother arranged for Ernest to accompany his sister Marcelline to social gatherings. He may, like his autobiographical character Nick Adams, have copulated in the woods with a native American girl, but perhaps not. Visiting an Italian house of prostitution with other young Red Cross volunteers, Ernest turned red with embarrassment when one of the whores accosted him.

The nurses in Milan soon made a favorite of Hemingway. They smiled at his boyish exuberance, and conspired in silence when he drank from the bottle of cognac secreted in his quarters. He was also admired as a patient who had been wounded at the front. The nurses "liked to exhibit him...as their prize specimen of a wounded hero," as fellow patient Henry Villard—who was recovering from jaundice and malaria—remarked with a degree of asperity. He and Ernest, among others, were rivals for the affection of Agnes von Kurowsky.

Agnes was tall and attractive, with chestnut-brown hair. Cheerful and lively, she was like Ernest full of energy and had a considerable appetite for adventure. At twenty-six she was seven and a half years his senior, and independent for her age, having worked in the Washington, D.C., public library before going to nursing school at Bellevue in New York City. Eager to see the world, she joined the Red Cross nursing service early in 1918. Italy was her first overseas post. She arrived in Milan only a few days before Hemingway. An angel had come to him, he wrote home, "in the form of a beautiful night nurse named Agnes," who gave him a hot bath and sent him off to the first good night's sleep he'd had in months.

Agnes was not without experience in affairs of the heart. When she came to Italy, she was officially engaged to the doctor she'd left behind in New York. She did not let that deter her from seeking out new places and making new friends. As she later admitted, she was "pretty fickle" at the time.

Agnes did not mind night duty, and as Ernest's night nurse cared for him during the difficult early weeks when he was operated on twice and his leg immobilized in a cast. By the middle of August, he was wildly in love with her, and she was receptive enough to come to his room in the early hours of the morning for intimate conversation. As their romance developed Agnes and Ernest held hands more or less openly and wrote daily notes to each other during the hours when they were apart. Matters had gone far by the time the crisp fall weather came to north Italy. Then circumstances conspired to keep them apart, perhaps abetted by the powers-that-be in the Red Cross.

On September 24, Ernest and another patient set out for a week's holiday at Stresa, on Lake Maggiore. On October 15, Agnes was transferred to Florence to care for a victim of "the Spanish fever." In late October Ernest went to the Monte Grappa front, contracted jaundice, and returned to the hospital in Milan in the comforting custody of Jim Gamble. Sometime early in November Gamble offered Hemingway a year's stay in Italy, all expenses paid, as his secretary and companion. On Armistice Day, November 11, Agnes came back to Milan. Nine days later she and another nurse were assigned to Treviso where the flu was raging among American troops. Ernest visited her there December 9. During the Christmas holiday, Ernest stayed with Jim Gamble at his villa in Taormina, Sicily. He and Agnes met one final time before he sailed from Genoa to New York on the S.S. *Giuseppe Verdi* on January 6, 1919. It was understood between them that they were to be married when she came back to the United States. Soon thereafter she was posted to Torre di Mosta, where she met and fell in love with an Italian officer named Domenico Caracciolo. On March 7 she mailed Ernest the letter breaking off their relationship.

In later years Agnes invariably contended that she and Ernest had not been lovers. This assertion is largely borne out in the diary she kept from June 12 to October 20, 1918, which was edited and published by Villard and James Nagel in 1989. (This diary provided the basis for *In Love and War*, a disastrously bad motion picture starring Sandra Bullock and Chris O'Donnell.) The sometimes passionate letters she wrote to Ernest in the fall of 1918 appear to tell a different story, however. He saved those letters, while Agnes burned his at the insistence of Caracciolo: just like Scott and Ginevra.

While she was in Florence and Treviso, Hemingway wrote her almost every day, and she replied nearly as often. She yearned for them to be together, she wrote from Florence, so that she could nestle in the hollow space he made for her face and then go to sleep with his arm around her. Then she added a promise: "I love you more and more and know what I'm going to bring you when I come home."

To avert suspicion about their relationship—Red Cross nurses were not supposed to have love affairs with their patients—she posted some of her letters to the Anglo-American Officers Club in Milan instead of the hospital. "This is our war sacrifice, bambino mio, to keep our secrets to ourselves." Right now, she pointed out, the "older world" wouldn't understand, and "would make very harsh criticisms." After the war, they could tell everyone.

The difference in their ages runs like an unacknowledged undercurrent through her correspondence. Ernest is her *bambino mio*, her *dear boy*. He is "Kid" to her "Mrs. Kid." Agnes dispenses advice and praise as to a younger person sorely in need of flattery and approval. She admires the beautifully tailored British uniform he's acquired in Milan. She is proud of him when he promises to cut back on his drinking. An ironic motif concerns her fear that Ernest might abandon her as she had abandoned her doctor fiancé in New York. "I never pined for anybody before in my life," she wrote him from Treviso. "I never imagined anyone else could be so dear and necessary to me...Don't let me gain you only to lose you. I love you, Ernie."

During the mid-November week when both were in Milan, the two lovers solidified their marriage plans. On November 23, Ernest wrote his sister Marcelline that he'd always wondered what it would be like to "meet the girl you will really love always and now I know." Ag loved him too, and so he knew for sure who he was going to marry. In retrospect, Agnes said that she'd only consented to their engagement to keep Ernest away from Jim Gamble, who seemed to be sexually interested in him. Ernest, she thought, would never be "anything but a bum...if he started traveling around with someone else paying the expenses." She and Ernest became engaged soon after Gamble proposed the yearlong holiday to Hemingway. When the captain suggested a journey to Madeira as an added inducement, Agnes warned Ernest against going. If he did go, she was afraid he'd never "be somebody worth while. Those places do get in one's blood, & remove all the pep & 'go' and I'd hate like everything to see you minus ambition." Sometimes, she went on, she wished that they might be able to marry in Italy, but that was a foolish idea. Ernest did not go to Madeira, and soon after his December 9 reunion with Agnes in Treviso, he agreed to return to the States at the first opportunity. In order, as Ernest saw it, to start earning for their marriage. Also in order, as Agnes viewed it, to avoid becoming a bum and a sponger, if not worse. "When I was with Jessup [another nurse]," she wrote him, "I wanted to do all sorts of wild things—anything but go home—and when you [were] with Captain Gamble you felt the same way. But I think maybe we have both changed our minds—and the old États-Unis are going to look très, très bien to our world-weary eyes."

In the light of this triangular complication, it is extremely significant that Ernest never told Agnes—or anyone else—about his trip to see Gamble in

Taormina over Christmas. He even constructed a tall tale to account for his activities in Sicily. At the first place he stopped overnight, he wrote his friend Eric Dorman-Smith, the hostess hid his clothes and kept him to herself for a week. His only complaint was that he'd seen very little of the country. Agnes's letters from Treviso said nothing about his upcoming trip to Sicily. Instead she lamented that she could not get away from her duties, so they would not be together for their "first Christmas." Just make believe "you're getting a gift from me (as you will someday)," she wrote. "And let me tell you I love you." In closing, she raised once more the possibility that their love might not last. "I miss you more and more, and it makes me shiver to think of your going home without me. What if our hearts should change?"

In the context of her loving letters, it seems likely that in encouraging Ernest to reject Gamble's offer of an expenses-paid year in Europe and return to the United States, Agnes hoped *both* to save him from his own worst instincts *and* to save him for herself. But she may also have begun to have second thoughts about the age gap between them. At their last meeting before he sailed home, she and Ernest quarreled about when she would be following. To calm him down, Agnes agreed to come as soon as possible, but she was not really ready to give up her stay in Europe. The issue lay between them across the ocean.

The letters from Agnes to Ernest over the next two months were obviously calculated to prepare him for the end and must have been exquisitely painful to read.

"Well, good night, dear Kid," she signed off one of her first missives to Oak Park. "A riverderla, carissimo tenente, suo cattiva ragazza, Agnes." She was, cheerfully enough, "his naughty girl," but this hardly conveyed a passionate commitment to their love. After she was transferred from Treviso to run the small Red Cross field hospital in Torre di Mosta, Agnes scaled back her letters from twice a week to once every two weeks, and with each one sounded less and less like Ernest's future wife.

Ernest, meanwhile, continued to save money toward their marriage. He must have sensed the increasing chill in Agnes's correspondence, but he was not prepared to admit it to himself—or to the close friends he'd told about their marriage plans. One of these was Bill Smith, in a December 13 letter from Milan. "Bill this is some girl and I thank God I got crucked so I met her," Hemingway wrote. He couldn't understand what she saw in him "but by some very lucky astigmatism she loves me...So I'm going to hit the States and start working for the Firm. Ag says we can have a wonderful time being poor together." All he had to do now was "hit the minimum living wage for two and lay up enough for six weeks or so up North and call on you for service as best man." He only had fifty more years to live, and felt that every moment he spent away from "that Kid" was wasted.

Agnes to Ernest, February 3-5, 1919:

Agnes's enthusiasm is not so apparent. "My future is a puzzle to me, and I'm sure I don't know how to solve it. Whether to go home, or apply for more foreign service is the question just now." (*Hadn't they settled that question?*) "Of course, you understand this is all merely for the near future, as you will help me plan the next period, I guess" (*she guessed!*)...*"*I'm getting fonder, every day, of furrin' parts" (*she'd answered the question already?*) "Goodnight old dear, Your weary but cheerful Aggie." (*Why didn't she sign off "I love you" anymore?*)

Agnes to Ernest, February 15, 1919:

The unreliable Italian mail system had broken down, and she had not seen a letter from him for a while. It was "hard work writing letters when you have none to answer," she complained. (*Hard work? Writing to him?*) She'd had guests for dinner at Torre di Mosta, including the "tenente medico [who was] the funniest and brightest one yet." (*Was this a rival?*) "I have a choice of staying a year in Rome, but I'm thinking of going to the Balkans so I'm rather undecided as yet...work is going to be very dull at home after this life." (*So she had made up her mind to stay overseas another year: wasn't this the same girl who'd sent him home to wait for her?*)

Agnes to Ernest, March 1, 1919:

Now there were too many letters from him. "I got a whole bushel of letters from you today, in fact haven't been able to read them all yet." (*She hadn't read them?*) "I can't begin to keep up with you, leading the busy life I do." (*Her career came first, did it?*) Aside from work, she was having the time of her life and never lacked for excitement. (*With whom?*) She had a star shell pistol and lots of cartridges to fire off on dark nights. (*Alone?*) She had learned to smoke and to play "a fascinating gambling game" called 7 1/2. (*Who taught her?*) She had to admit she was far from the perfect being he thought her. "I'm feeling very cattiva tonight, so goodnight, Kid, and don't do anything rash, but have a good time. Afft. Aggie." (*She wasn't his "cattiva ragazza" now, merely feeling naughty 5,000 miles away, and even the disappointing "Affectionately" came in abbreviated form.*)

Ernest to Jim Gamble, March 3, 1919:

Ernest could hardly have failed to detect the warning signals Agnes was flashing across the seas. He decided to make contact with the benefactor she'd been protecting him from. Perhaps that bridge had not burned down. His long letter to Gamble didn't get around to mentioning Agnes until the sixth paragraph. "The Girl doesn't know when she will be coming home," Ernest admitted, but he'd been saving money against the day. He had "$172 and a fifty buck Liberty Bond in the Bank already...Maybe she won't like me now I've reformed, but then I'm not very seriously reformed."

News of Agnes shared time in this letter with reports of Bill Horne and Howie Jenkins and others who had been in the ambulance service with Hemingway and Captain Gamble. The principal theme, however, had to do with Ernest's deeply felt regret that he was stuck in Oak Park instead of liberated in Sicily with Jim, his old "Chief." "Every minute of every day," Ernest wrote, he kicked himself for not being there. In memory he called back the sight "of old Taormina by moonlight and you and me, a little illuminated some times, but always just pleasantly so, strolling through that great old place and the moon path on the sea and Aetna fuming back of the villa." The thought of what he might have had made him "so damn sick" that he poured himself a glass, and thinking of the two of them sitting in front of the fire after dinner, offered Jim a transatlantic toast: "I drink to you Chief. I drink to you."

"You know I wish I were with you," he closed the letter.

Agnes to Ernest, March 7, 1919:

This was the letter he had been afraid of. Significantly, Agnes addressed him as "Ernie, dear boy." Even before Ernest left Italy, she wrote, she'd been trying to convince herself that theirs was "a real love-affair." She'd only given in *(consented to the engagement?)* to keep him "from doing something desperate" *(accepting Gamble's invitation?)*. Now, two months later, she was still "very fond" of him, but "more as a brother than a sweetheart."

And not only a brother but a younger brother, for the real thrust of her argument was that Ernest was too young for her. Agnes realized that she had made him care for her, and was sorry about that from the bottom of her heart. "But I am now & always will be too old, and that's the truth, & I can't get away from the fact that you're just a boy—a Kid." *(She was no longer "Mrs. Kid," however.)* She expected to be proud of him some day, but it was "wrong to hurry a career." It made no practical sense for a twenty-seven-year-old woman with a profession to marry a nineteen-year-old youth with no occupation or college education or immediate prospects. She'd tried to tell him that when they quarreled at their last meeting, but he'd acted "like a spoiled child" and so she stopped.

The closing paragraph unveiled the rival (Domenico Caracciolo) her previous letters had hinted at. "Then—& believe me when I say this is sudden for me, too—I expect to be married soon. And I hope & pray that after you have thought things out, you'll be able to forgive me & start a wonderful career, & show what a man you really are." (*Or at least, what a man he could become.*)

"Ever admiringly & fondly, Your friend—Aggie," she signed off.

Hemingway went through a number of reactions to his jilting. He sank into a morass of sorrow, he converted the hurt to anger, he affected a stance of philosophical wisdom, he determined to prove the jilter wrong (*Won't she be sorry, though?*), and he tried to exorcise the experience by writing about it.

When Agnes's break-up letter arrived, Ernest zombied around the house in Oak Park in an attitude of leaden despair. Within days, however, he managed to write Bill Horne a curiously two-toned letter about the rejection, appealing for sympathy on the one hand and on the other adopting a pose as expert on affairs of the heart. "She doesn't love me, Bill," he commences. "She takes it all back. A 'mistake.' One of those little mistakes, you know. Oh, Bill, I can't kid about it, and I can't be bitter because I'm just smashed by it... All I wanted was Ag. And happiness and now the bottom has dropped out of the whole world."

Then he put aside his sorrow, amazingly, to make a sweeping generalization. As if to repudiate Agnes's reason for rejecting him—his relative immaturity (which he does not reveal to Horne)—Ernest donned the mantle of experience. The split would never have happened, he asserted, if he'd stayed with Agnes in Italy. "You, meaning the world in general, teach a girl—no, I won't put it that way—that is you make love to a girl and then you go away. She needs someone to make love to her. If the right person turns up, you're out of luck. That's the way it goes." Hemingway could rarely resist playing the expert, and in doing so for Horne's benefit, sought to regain a measure of his damaged authority. If only he, the teenaged tutor, had not taught the older Agnes the joys of lovemaking, she would not have succumbed to another. It was his fault. He was too skillful an instructor.

Still, he longed to do something to ventilate his frustration and anger. He claimed, in his only fictional rendering of the jilting, that in retaliation he contracted a dose of gonorrhea from a girl who worked in a Chicago department store. He told a friend that he burned out Agnes's memory "with a course of booze and other women." Perhaps these tales were true, perhaps not. What is certain is that he became angrier and angrier the more he thought about how she had cheated him out of a wonderful year in Italy. As he wrote Jim Gamble, her letter came as "a devil of a jolt because I'd given up everything for her, most especially Taormina."

In mid-June he had a chance to take a measure of revenge. Agnes's romance with Caracciolo had ended short of the altar, when his family took the view that she was "an American adventuress." According to Hemingway, Caracciolo was the heir to a dukedom, but this may have been exaggeration. Elsewhere he promoted his rival from Tenente (first lieutenant) to Major, and reassigned him to the crack Arditi. No ordinary man could have taken Agnes away, no matter how starved for love Ernest had left her. Anyway, as he wrote Howie Jenkins, there was nothing he could do for poor Agnes now. "I loved her once and then she gypped me." The news of Agnes's misfortune did not entirely assuage his anger. When he heard that Agnes was coming back to the States, Ernest expressed his devout wish that she might trip on the gangplank and knock out her front teeth.

The charge that he was a boy, a kid, a spoiled child still rankled. He set out to demonstrate that she was wrong about that, but the demonstration took time. Two years after the jilting, in the summer of 1921, he married Hadley Richardson, a woman who at almost eight years his senior was a few months *older* than Agnes. (Jim Gamble complicated that courtship as well, by inviting Ernest to join him overseas, this time in Rome.) Eighteen months later, in November 1922, he wrote Agnes about how far he had progressed. He was traveling around Europe, as she had longed to do, as a roving foreign correspondent for the *Toronto Star Weekly*. He was headquartered in Paris, a city that she loved. He was married to Hadley, who was a fine musician and shared his love of the outdoors. His first book—*Three Stories and Ten Poems*—was to be published soon. Did she begin to realize what she'd missed?

This letter does not survive, but much of it can be reconstructed from Agnes's reply. It may be that he made a proposal of some sort about a meeting between them. At the Lausanne conference in the same month he wrote her, he told the famous journalist Lincoln Steffens that he was prepared to leave Hadley if Agnes would come back. If so, her response of December 22 was not encouraging. She filled him in on her activities during the intervening years. Like him, she had wanted to break "somebody or something" when she was jilted by her Italian fiancé. She was delighted to hear about his book. "How proud I will be, some day in the not-very-distant future to say 'Oh yes, Ernest Hemingway—Used to know him quite well during the war.'"

But Agnes went on to insist that events had proven her right in ending their "comradeship." She reiterated the point about the difference in their ages, softening the blow this time by stressing her antiquity instead of his youth. "May I hope for an occasional line from you?" she inquired, but there was no coquetry, no hint of resuming their romance. It was just that she and Ernest had been "good friends" once, and "[f]riends are such great things to have." Then she offered him a firm handclasp, and closed with "best wishes to you & Hadley...Your old buddy Von (oh excuse me, it's Ag)."

Ernest must have concluded that no matter what he achieved, he could not change Agnes's mind. She thought him too young for her when he was nineteen, and she still thought so four years later, never mind that he had married and moved to Paris and launched a promising career. Six months later, he spelled out his lingering resentment in "A Very Short Story."

This story is manifestly autobiographical. Wounded soldier and nurse fall in love, he returns to the States, she proves faithless and writes him a goodbye letter. In its earliest draft, "A Very Short Story" remains sympathetic to the nurse as someone who succumbs to loneliness and muddy weather and the wiles of an Italian lover. But in its final draft, written after Ernest received Agnes's December 1922 letter, the tone becomes heavily sardonic at her expense. The story strains our credulity. "Ag" (excuse me, "Luz," as Hemingway altered the name to avoid a possible libel suit) is too cruel, too unfeeling, too selfish, while the wounded patient-narrator (who is given no name at all) is too good, too noble, too unfairly wronged to be convincing.

The most interesting thing about the story, from a psychological standpoint, is that it drastically distorts the contents of the "Ernie, dear boy" letter. Luz, in the story, wrote the narrator that she regarded theirs as "only a boy and girl affair," and, again, as "only a boy and girl love." Agnes wrote Ernest that their romance was doomed because it was a boy and *woman* affair. This issue Hemingway concealed, in print and out. Looked at dispassionately and from a distance, Agnes von Kurowsky's 1919 letter breaking off her relationship with Ernest bears a strong family resemblance to Grace Hemingway's 1920 letter scolding her son about his overdrawn mother-love bank account. In their different ways, both women were telling him to grow up.

—✳—

In a 1988 article on "Love Survival: How to Mend a Broken Heart," psychologist Stephen Gullo and journalist Connie Church contend that the emotional effect of losing a lover through rejection parallels that of losing a loved one to death. In each case, the one left behind is liable to suffer through the same stages of shock, anger, grief, blame, and denial before reaching acceptance.

A common if misguided reaction to jiltings, according to the authors, is that of *revenge loving*, or the reckless pursuit of replacements for the departed lover. Copulating with shop girls in taxicabs, as Hemingway claimed he did, would certainly qualify. On a more long-term basis, so would the engagements and marriages that both Fitzgerald and Hemingway embarked upon in less than two years' time. Interestingly, both men married women who resembled those who had turned them down. Zelda Sayre was petite like Ginevra, and like her somewhat younger than Scott Fitzgerald and much sought after by other men. Like Agnes, Hadley Richardson was tall, responsible, and substantially older than Ernest Hemingway. But there was one crucial difference. The women who married the two young writers chose to believe in them, and their future.

Another device for surviving rejection was to loose one's fury on the faithless jilter—not getting mad, getting even. In effect, this is what Hemingway did in his attack on Agnes in "A Very Short Story." It took him four years to get his frustration down on paper, but he only needed to do it once. (Some have suggested that Agnes also served as a model for Catherine Barkley in *A Farewell to Arms*, a nurse who falls head over heels in love with Frederic Henry and dies in the attempt to bear his child. But the real nurse and the fictional one share almost no qualities whatever, and of course Catherine does not jilt Frederic.)

In Fitzgerald's case, by way of contrast, the rejection by Ginevra—and later, the same rejection or very nearly so by Zelda—provided him with a basic donnée of his fiction. He took the hurt, hugged it to his bosom, and would not let it expire.

Fitzgerald fell prey to the worst possible reaction cited in the "Love Survival" piece: *idealizing* the girl who turned him down, and *obsessively thinking* about her. As a sovereign remedy to such self-demeaning behavior, Gullo and Church recommend that spurned suitors get in the habit of writing things down. Keep a diary in which you can vigorously express your feelings (including anger), and you'll feel better. Or make lists of the worst qualities of the jilter, and you'll feel *much* better. Or if you're capable and so inclined, write out your story, making the one who abandoned you the villain of the piece, and maybe the hurt will go away.

Hemingway, as it happened, found it easier to write about his physical wound in World War I than about his emotional one, and the process of writing about what happened at Fossalta may have helped cure him of his trauma. Twenty years later, he behaved with conspicuous courage during the Spanish Civil War. Twenty-six years later, during the hell of the Hürtgen forest, he struck General Buck Lanham as the bravest man he ever met.

Unlike the Austrians, Agnes von Kurowsky administered a hurt that time could not heal. Hemingway wrote a story about it, not one of his best, but did not get rid of it that way. Instead, he internalized the lesson that Agnes—and his mother—had taught him: that those who love can be betrayed. After that knowledge, he made sure he did not put himself at emotional risk. Hemingway had many friends, and broke off most of those friendships, sometimes viciously. He was married four times, and at the end of the first three of them he was responsible for the divorce, with a new wife waiting in the wings while the final scenes with the old one were being played out. He also behaved abominably to his fourth and last wife; only the extraordinary staying power of Mary Hemingway kept that union from dissolving as well.

The jilting by Agnes von Kurowsky, and his mother's censure, may have been the most important of the several serious wounds that fate was to deal Ernest Hemingway. In his young manhood, they drove him toward achievement as he sought to belie the charge of immaturity. And throughout his life, they compelled him to sever ties before friend or lover could strike a blow to the heart. Even mortar shells, he had discovered, were less painful.

CHAPTER 3

A FRIENDSHIP ABROAD

One friend in a lifetime is much; two are many; three are
hardly possible. Friendship needs a certain parallelism of life,
a community of thought, a rivalry of aim.

—HENRY ADAMS, *The Education of Henry Adams*

After a good day's work at his craft in Paris, Ernest Hemingway joined a couple
of "completely worthless" characters for a drink in the evening dank of the bar
Dingo. His companions, warming up for the revelries of the night, were Lady
Duff Twysden, with whom he was half in love, and Pat Guthrie, the Scotsman
she was supposed to marry. These two were to appear, without much disguise, in
The Sun Also Rises, but this was late April 1925 and the trip to the Pamplona fiesta ruined by sexual jealousy over Duff's amours—the crucial event that informed
that novel—still lay months ahead.

After a while Hemingway would walk the half-dozen blocks home to
his wife Hadley and son Bumby in their modest apartment above the sawmill
on rue Notre-Dame-des-Champs, but for the present he was having a fine time
absorbing the latest Montparnasse gossip with his clever and entertainingly self-
deprecatory if worthless friends when in walked two men who'd first got to know
each other at Princeton.

One of these, the one Hemingway took a liking to, was a tall and pleasant
fellow named Dunc Chaplin who had been "a famous pitcher" in college and
who seemed "extraordinarily nice, unworried, relaxed and friendly." The other,
who came right over to introduce himself and Chaplin, was Scott Fitzgerald. In
contrast to Chaplin, he was rather effeminate, a man "who looked like a boy with
a face between handsome and pretty." His most striking feature was his long-

lipped mouth that "on a girl would have been the mouth of a beauty." The mouth worried Hemingway, and he was put off too by Fitzgerald's excessive flattery and invasive interrogation. Had Hemingway slept with his wife before they were married? Fitzgerald asked him. "I don't know," Hemingway replied. "I don't remember."

But the most memorable event of that first meeting, as it is described in *A Moveable Feast* (1964), was that as they drank the champagne Fitzgerald had ordered all of the delicate coloring left his face and it turned into "a true death's head" before Hemingway's eyes. No need to worry, Chaplin assured Hemingway as he ushered the comatose Fitzgerald into a taxicab: "That's the way it takes him."

At this stage in the memoir that Hemingway wrote beginning in 1957, thirty-two years after he and Fitzgerald met and seventeen years after Fitzgerald's death, Chaplin disappears. He has done his job as a foil, a likable fellow against whom Fitzgerald's shortcomings are measured, and is no longer needed. For the rest of the three devastating chapters of *A Moveable Feast* devoted to Fitzgerald, Chaplin is replaced by another character whose behavior stands in implicit juxtaposition to that of poor Scott: a hungry, hard-working, happily married young writer totally dedicated to his profession who can hold his liquor and will not allow himself to waste time or money.

This character, of course, was Hemingway himself.

There was another good reason for Chaplin to vanish from Hemingway's account of his first meeting with Fitzgerald. Chaplin was not there, not at the Dingo, not in Paris, not in Europe. Hemingway invented him, in all his authoritative specificity, to lend an air of authenticity to his story. (In another version of that first meeting, cut from *A Moveable Feast* and closed to scholars for twenty-five years after Hemingway's death, he wrote that Fitzgerald was accompanied by a friend at the Dingo, but the friend is neither named nor characterized.)

This does not mean that we should distrust everything Hemingway tells us about his friendship with Fitzgerald. As he warns us in the preface to *A Moveable Feast*, "this book may be regarded as fiction. But there is also the chance," he adds immediately, "that such a book of fiction may throw some light on what has been written as fact." Here Hemingway implies that his rendition reveals *more* of the truth than any straightforward reportorial version. And in a sense he is right: readers of *A Moveable Feast* can learn a great deal about Fitzgerald and, especially, about Hemingway in spite of—or because of—the fictional liberties the author takes with the facts. As all writers know, there are truths that go beyond mere facts.

At the same time, however, it should be recognized that Hemingway's memoir of the years in Paris is far more reliable about his feelings toward Fitzgerald in the late 1950s than in the mid-1920s. The prevailing public view of the Fitzgerald-Hemingway friendship has been shaped by *A Moveable Feast*, a book in which, for whatever reasons but surely including rivalrous instincts aroused in Hemingway by the Fitzgerald revival of the 1950s, the dice are loaded against "poor Scott." For a less biased grasp on the way it must have been when they met and became friends in 1925 and 1926, it is necessary to consult actual documents of the time—letters between the two men and what they had to say of each other to third parties.

When they met Fitzgerald was much the better-known and more-established figure. He was the author of three novels—his masterly *The Great Gatsby* had just been published—and of two volumes of stories, several of which had initially appeared in the high-paying *Saturday Evening Post*. In these stories, collected in *Flappers and Philosophers* (1920) and *Tales of the Jazz Age* (1922), and in his first novel, *This Side of Paradise* (1920), which recounted the adventures romantic and otherwise of a young Princetonian, Fitzgerald's characters drank and smoked and necked in open and reckless defiance of the older generation. So did Scott and Zelda Fitzgerald themselves, as if determined to become public avatars of the flappers and sheiks in his fiction. Living in or around New York, they dwindled into celebrities as the newspapers eagerly recorded their nocturnal exploits—most notably a midnight dip in the fountain outside the Plaza Hotel. They came to Europe in the spring of 1924 in order to escape the frantic partying, but geography could not alter Fitzgerald's public image. For the rest of his life—and beyond—he fought vainly to shake off his reputation as a rather lightweight chronicler of the Jazz Age.

Hemingway, on the other hand, had been based in Paris since the end of 1921. He began as a feature writer for the *Toronto Star Weekly*, with all of Europe as his beat, and returned briefly to Canada for the birth of his son in October 1923. He gave up journalism at the beginning of 1924, in order to devote himself entirely to fiction. Hemingway had published nothing of book length at the time he and Fitzgerald met, only a handful of stories and poems in the little magazines and two slim volumes printed in France in limited editions: *Three Stories and Ten Poems* (1923) and *in our time* (1924), a collection of brief sketches later resurrected as interchapters for *In Our Time*, his first book of stories. He knew about Fitzgerald's work. Hadley had been reading *This Side of Paradise* during their courtship; the book had "the vital throb of youth," she thought. And he had seen Fitzgerald's fiction in the *Saturday Evening Post*.

Five years earlier, Ernest had sent some of his own unpolished stories to the *Saturday Evening Post*, which sent them right back. But those days were over, and now Hemingway was aiming for a higher target. In that sense, he could and did feel superior to Fitzgerald. There was something virtuous about seeking artistic accomplishment, never mind the financial rewards. Few of his close connections among in the avant-garde literary community in Paris were inclined to pay deference to the commercial success and celebrity of F. Scott Fitzgerald.

Edmund Wilson first brought Hemingway's prose to Fitzgerald's attention. A class ahead of Fitzgerald at Princeton, the intellectually precocious Wilson was rapidly establishing himself as one of the nation's leading critics. He showed Scott his copies of *Three Stories and Ten Poems* and *in our time* early in 1924, and reviewed them favorably in the *Dial* for October 1924. In that same month, Fitzgerald wrote his legendary editor Maxwell Perkins from St. Raphaël, where he was applying the final touches to *The Great Gatsby*. The novel would be on the boat within a week, Fitzgerald promised. But the real business of the letter was to tell Perkins about (misspellings included) "a young man named Ernest Hemmingway, who lives in Paris (an American) writes for the transatlantic Review & has a brilliant future." He didn't have *in our time*, Hemingway's collection of incisive vignettes, in front of him, Fitzgerald acknowledged, but he could vouch for them as "remarkable" and counseled Perkins to look Hemingway up right away. "He's the real thing."

That was high praise, and in no way influenced by friendship. It would be another six months before Fitzgerald and Hemingway actually met. As his letter to Perkins suggests, Fitzgerald was acting as a kind of unofficial talent scout for Scribner's. He liked the role of recommending writers, and had already been instrumental in delivering several of them to his publisher, including Ring Lardner, Thomas Boyd, Woodward (Peggy) Boyd, and John Biggs—all, unlike Hemingway, good friends of his. Lardner and Tom Boyd had been successes, Biggs and Woodward Boyd not. Hemingway would break the tie one way or the other. In a December 1924 letter to Perkins, he asked for news of all five of them, and also encouraged his editor to sign up Gertrude Stein and—in translation— Raymond Radiguet's *Le bal du Comte d'Orgel*.

Back in New York, Perkins took immediate action in response to Fitzgerald's tip. He went to considerable trouble to get hold of a copy of *in our time*, recognized the "economy, strength and vitality" of its sketches, and late in

February 1925 wrote Hemingway in Paris asking to see any future manuscripts. This overture from Scribner's came too late, for Hemingway was spending the winter months at Schruns, in the Austrian Vorarlberg, and did not get Perkins's letter until he returned to Paris in April. By that time, he had signed a contract with Horace Liveright, at Boni & Liveright, for *In Our Time,* uppercase, his first full-scale book of short stories, which appeared in October 1925.

Presumably Fitzgerald learned this news at the Dingo bar meeting in late April. On May 1, after chiding Perkins for losing a crop of promising young English writers to Knopf and other firms, talent scout Fitzgerald reported that "Liverite has got Hemingway!" but at once proposed an alternative: "How about Radiguet?" Three weeks later Fitzgerald was ready to concentrate his efforts on Hemingway alone. Their friendship had progressed during the interim. "Hemminway is a fine, charming fellow," Fitzgerald wrote Perkins about May 22, "and he appreciated your letter and the tone of it enormously. If Liveright doesn't please him he'll come to you, and he has a future. He's 27." In fact Hemingway was 25 at the time. Either Fitzgerald, 28 himself, got it wrong, or Hemingway wanted him to think he was older.

Despite his relative youth Hemingway had lived a far more adventurous life than Fitzgerald. In contrast to Hemingway's service with the American Red Cross in Italy, where he was seriously wounded, and decorated by the Italian army, Fitzgerald served stateside. As a newspaperman Ernest interviewed many of the great figures of the time, including Lloyd George, Clemenceau, and Mussolini. During his years overseas he had also become friendly with such distinguished modernist writers as Gertrude Stein, Ford Madox Ford, and Ezra Pound. Over six feet tall, a sturdy 190 pounds, and darkly handsome, he formed a striking contrast to the slightly built, blond Fitzgerald, who stood five feet eight inches and weighed about 140 pounds. And there was an unmistakable charisma about Hemingway. In those days, as Hadley recalled, men loved him, women loved him, children loved him, even dogs loved him—but men most of all, for Hemingway had a remarkable gift for inspiring (and later breaking off) male friendships. Fitzgerald, by way of contrast, was particularly inept at developing relationships with male companions. His tendency was to make heroes out of them, often to the discomfort of both parties.

There was every good reason for Fitzgerald to make a hero out of Hemingway. He envied Hemingway his wartime experience, and admired his learned capacity to face down fear. "As to Ernest as a boy—reckless, adventurous, etc.," he wrote in his notebooks. "Yet it is undeniable that the dark was peopled for him. His bravery and acquired characteristics." Hemingway was given to exaggerating the extent of his military background. He had fought with the crack Italian Arditi, he maintained, although in truth he had been wounded after only a few weeks at the front as a Red Cross ambulance driver. Similarly he pretended to an unwarranted expertise in his athletic endeavors, although he was only a run-of-the-mill football lineman in high school and a somewhat clumsy if quite powerful boxer.

Fitzgerald was never able to shake off what he called his "two juvenile regrets": not playing football at Princeton and not getting overseas during the war. He used to conjure up dreams of glory to ward off insomnia. "Once upon a time they needed a quarterback at Princeton...I weigh only one hundred and thirty-five, so they save me until the third quarter...." Or: "The headquarters staff and the regimental battalion commanders...have been killed with one shell. The command devolved upon Captain Fitzgerald. With superb presence..." It seemed to him that Hemingway had achieved what he could only dream about, and that in consequence he would forever be disadvantaged as a writer. Hemingway was inclined to agree. "[T]he reason you are so sore you missed the war," he wrote Fitzgerald in December 1925, "is because war is the best subject of all. It groups the maximum of material and speeds up the action and brings out all sorts of stuff that normally you would have to wait a lifetime to get." Fitzgerald soon came to admire Hemingway for his discipline and dedication to his craft as well, and adopted him as his "artistic conscience." According to Arnold Gingrich, the *Esquire* editor who persuaded both men to write for his magazine during the 1930s, Fitzgerald "was so 'gone' on Ernest," from the beginning, that "the degree of his admiration was, as among grown men, almost embarrassing."

THE CITY OF LIGHT

Nothing better illustrates the difference between Fitzgerald and Hemingway, and their varying circumstances, than the way they lived in and reacted to Paris. Newlyweds Ernest and Hadley Hemingway sailed from New York to Le Havre in mid-December 1921, and spent most of the succeeding five years in two rented apartments on the Left Bank: during 1922 and 1923 at 74, rue du Cardinal Lemoine in a working-class neighborhood near the place de la Contrescarpe, and from 1924 through 1926 at 113, rue Notre-Dame-des-Champs in avant-garde Montparnasse.

The move from the somewhat gritty Cardinal Lemoine neighborhood, where there was a *bal musette*, or kind of dance hall, downstairs from their apartment, to the artistically advanced and sexually charged milieu of Montparnasse did not signal a change in Ernest and Hadley's financial position. (Hemingway was never so poor as readers of *A Moveable Feast*—a book in which he celebrates the benefits of hunger to a working artist—might assume. Although he and Hadley had to be careful about expenditures, the favorable exchange rates and her small trust fund provided enough to make ends meet.) But the area around the intersection of the boulevards Montparnasse and Raspail, where the cafés Dôme and Select and Rotonde catered to Paris's aspiring young writers and painters and those tourists and expatriates who hoped to be confused with them, did represent a distinct deviation in lifestyle.

Shortly after arriving in Paris Hemingway visited his scorn on the Americans who idled away their time in the cafés of Montparnasse. The "scum of Greenwich Village," he wrote, had been skimmed off and ladled onto the area around the Rotonde. They were "nearly all loafers" pretending to be artists. Instead of actually working, they boasted about what they intended to do and denigrated the accomplishment of others who received any recognition. In early drafts of the beginning of *The Sun Also Rises*, written after the Hemingways had moved to Montparnasse, Jake Barnes as narrator describes the area with similar distaste. The "Quarter state of mind" was principally one of contempt, he maintained. "Everybody...loathes almost everybody else and the quarter itself." Certainly this was true of Jake Barnes himself. He cast a jaundiced eye at the area's drunks and homosexuals, "frail young men" who "take flight like the birds" to visit the Basque Coast, and then "return again even more like the birds." Yet Barnes, like his creator, was drawn to this despised setting because it was where he could find Lady Brett Ashley and enter the world of sexual intrigue depicted in the opening chapters of *The Sun Also Rises*.

The Paris Hemingway recalls with affection in his writing, the Paris where he and Hadley were "very poor and very happy," the Paris that was "the town best organized for a writer to write in that there is," was not Montparnasse but the working-class Paris he first lived in when he came overseas.

As Hemingway's character, the failed writer Harry, is dying in "The Snows of Kilimanjaro" (1936), he thinks of all the places he's never written about and considers trying to capture them by dictation. But, he decides,

[y]ou could not dictate the Place Contrescarpe where the flower sellers dyed their flowers in the street...and the old men and the women, always drunk on wine and bad marc; and the children with their noses running in the cold; the smell of dirty sweat and poverty and drunkenness at the Café des Amateurs and the whores at the Bal Musette they lived above.

The details add up to an ugly cityscape, yet in that quarter "he had written the start of all he was to do" and so for Harry as for Hemingway there "never was another part of Paris that he loved like that, the sprawling trees, the old white plastered houses painted brown below, the long green of the autobus in the round square, the purple flower dye upon the paving, the sudden drop down the hill of the rue Cardinal Lemoine to the River, and the other way the narrow crowded world of the rue Mouffetard." It's a love song, that description, conveying Hemingway's sense of a paradise lost with the end of his Paris apprenticeship as a writer and the end of his first marriage.

Whether living in a working-class neighborhood he later romanticized or in the Montparnasse that simultaneously attracted and repelled him, Hemingway made every effort to integrate himself into the community. Most of his and Hadley's closest companions were Americans or British living in France — writers and newspapermen — but they also learned demotic French and made friends among the Parisians they encountered during their daily rounds. It was different with Fitzgerald.

Scott and Zelda Fitzgerald first came to Europe on a short tour in 1921 and then returned in 1924 to stay for more than two years. The 1921 visit was something of a disaster. Fitzgerald's reaction to Europeans generally and to the Italians and the French in particular smacked of ugly Americanism. England had its attractions; there was a memorable luncheon with Winston Churchill's mother, the famous Jennie Jerome, and a visit to Oxford, which Fitzgerald declared "the most beautiful spot on the earth." Across the channel, however, lay France, which proved to be "a bore and a disappointment" to begin with and then worse. The country made him sick, Fitzgerald wrote Edmund Wilson, along with "[i]ts silly pose as the thing the world has to save. I think it's a shame that England and America didn't let Germany conquer France." Moreover, he thought French culture was on the skids, for culture "follows money" and hence would gravitate to a new capital in New York.

All of his observations, he confessed to Wilson, might be "philistine," but his old Princeton friend did not let him off so easily. Fitzgerald was so "saturated" with American customs and mores, he wrote back, with "hotels, plumbing, drugstores, aesthetic ideals and vast commercial prosperity," that he couldn't appreciate the superiority of French institutions. He hadn't allowed France time enough to sink in. "The lower animals die when transplanted," Wilson sarcastically reminded him.

Three years later, the Fitzgeralds decided to give the Continent another chance, this time for a more extended stay. Tiring of habitual weekend partying on Long Island, Fitzgerald decided to come to France to finish *The Great Gatsby*. As he later put it, "[w]e were going to the Old World to find a new rhythm for our lives, with a true conviction that we had left our old selves behind forever." Fitzgerald managed to complete his great novel within a few months time in France, but he was always a foreigner abroad, never lighting for long in one place, never allowing himself to absorb foreign customs or styles of life. In effect, he and Zelda remained tourists throughout their two and a half years abroad—"rich tourists," as biographer André Le Vot noted, "who spoke the language badly and dealt mostly with paid employees." Hemingway stated the case more damningly in *A Moveable Feast*. At the time, he wrote, "Scott hated the French, and since almost the only French he met with regularly were waiters whom he did not understand, taxi-drivers, garage employees and landlords, he had many opportunities to insult and abuse them."

The Fitzgeralds sailed for France early in May 1924, and after little more than a week in Paris (where for the first time they met Gerald and Sara Murphy, the elegant expatriates whose lives were to intersect so closely with theirs and the Hemingways'), traveled south to the Riviera, initially putting up at Grimm's Park Hotel in Hyères and then taking an elegant villa at Valescure, near St. Raphaël. There Scott finished his novel, and Zelda had an affair with a handsome French aviator named Édouard Jozan. In a satirical piece written for the *Saturday Evening Post* that summer, Fitzgerald skewered the pretensions of American travellers abroad—and to some extent of Zelda and himself.

> "The trouble with most Americans in France," [a young American man remarks], "is that they won't lead a real French life. They hang around the big hotels and exchange opinions fresh from the States."
> "I know," [a young American woman agrees]. "That's exactly what it said in the New York Times this morning."

With his novel safely on its way to Scribner's, Scott and Zelda again pulled up stakes to spend a dismal winter at a series of hotels in Italy. They were still there on *Gatsby*'s publication day, April 10, 1925. Two weeks later they sailed from

Naples to Marseille on the S.S. *President Garfield*, their Renault on board. They planned to drive the rest of the way to Paris, but the car broke down and they left it in Lyon to complete the journey by train. By May 1, Fitzgerald had met Hemingway and leased an expensive but gloomy furnished apartment at 14 rue de Tilsitt near the Arc de Triomphe for the eight months from May 12 to January 12.

As Fitzgerald recalled five years later, Paris was a tonic to his spirits after the unhappy months in Rome and Capri. *Gatsby* was not the financial success he had hoped it would be; he predicted first-year sales of 80,000 copies, and the book sold fewer than 20,000. But some of the reviews were excellent, especially that of Gilbert Seldes in the August issue of the *Dial*. In his novel, Seldes wrote, Fitzgerald has "gone soaring in a beautiful flight," leaving behind him all the writers "of his own generation and most of his elders." Even the qualified approval he got from respected mentors like Wilson and H.L. Mencken was encouraging. With some justification Fitzgerald could regard himself "the biggest man in my profession...everybody admired me and I was proud I'd done such a good thing." In Paris, he easily found convivial companions to help him turn the warm months of 1925 into a summer of "1000 parties and no work." But there were close friendships formed too, with Gerald and Sara Murphy and above all with Hemingway, "an equal and my kind of an idealist." While Zelda stayed home ill, Scott visited the Murphys for cocktails in the garden of their house at St. Cloud, and "got drunk with [Hemingway] on the Left Bank in careless cafés." Booth Tarkington, the famous author of *Penrod*, *Seventeen*, and *The Magnificent Ambersons*, met the two young writers one afternoon. Tarkington thought Hemingway looked like "a Kansas University football beef," while Fitzgerald was "a little tight." They were having a good time together, Tarkington could see. He gathered they'd been up all night.

Hemingway recorded no mutual intoxications in *A Moveable Feast*. There Fitzgerald is repeatedly inebriated, while Hemingway remains sober enough to take charge of the situation. This is especially apparent during their trip to Lyon to recover Fitzgerald's Renault, a journey undertaken soon after their first meeting. In Hemingway's account of that journey, written in the late 1950s and published in *A Moveable Feast*, Fitzgerald emerges as a childish hypochondriac, a foolish spendthrift, an emasculated husband, and a morally flawed artist compromising his talent by writing formula fiction for the slick magazines. He only agreed to accompany Fitzgerald, Hemingway asserted, because he hoped to learn something about writing from a successful older professional. Except for an extensive plot summary of the novels of Michael Arlen, Fitzgerald offered no such instruction. But by his behavior he did teach Hemingway an important lesson about what a writer should *not* do: squander his ability and feel sorry for himself. After a day on the road with Fitzgerald, Hemingway maintained, he "felt the death loneliness that comes at the end of every day that is wasted in your life."

At this point, the caution flag must go up, for there is persuasive evidence that at the time, *both* Hemingway and Fitzgerald enjoyed the trip to Lyon. Writing to Ezra Pound, Hemingway emphasized the amount of wine they'd consumed: "Didn't miss one vintage from Montrachet to Chambertin. Elaborate trip." And in a June 9 letter to Max Perkins, he reported that he and Scott "had a great trip together driving his car up from Lyon through the Cote D'Or." The top of the Renault had been damaged in some way, and Zelda had ordered it cut off entirely. In *A Moveable Feast*, when it begins to rain hard as they are driving to Paris, this foolish decision serves as but one example of Fitzgerald's general incompetence. In correspondence between the two men, however, the car's condition became a kind of running gag. In April 1931, for example, Hemingway wrote Fitzgerald that he "look[ed] forward like hell" to seeing him in Europe in the fall. "We might take one of those topless motor trips," he added. As for Fitzgerald's reaction to the journey, in a letter to Gertrude Stein he reported that "Hemingway and I went to Lyons...to get my car and had a slick drive through Burgundy. He's a peach of a fellow and absolutely first-rate."

According to *A Moveable Feast*, Hemingway was prepared to forgive Fitzgerald all the weaknesses of the Lyon trip once he'd read *The Great Gatsby*. At the time, Hemingway said, he did not think of Fitzgerald as a serious writer, but from the "shy and happy" way Fitzgerald talked about his new novel, he felt sure it would be worth reading. And so it proved to be. After reading *The Great Gatsby*, Hemingway wrote in his memoir, he "enlisted" as Fitzgerald's friend and helpmeet. "When I had finished the book I knew that no matter what Scott did, nor how he behaved, I must know it was like a sickness and be of any help I could to him and try to be a good friend." The effect of this passage is to portray Hemingway as Fitzgerald's benefactor, when in fact it was very much the other way around. One thing Hemingway did do for Fitzgerald, however, was to take him to see Gertrude Stein.

From the start, Hemingway had a knack of ingratiating himself with famous authors and making them his advocates. He arrived in Paris with glowing letters of introduction from Sherwood Anderson, whom he had befriended in Chicago. The twenty-two-year-old Hemingway had "extraordinary talent," Anderson wrote. He and Hadley were "delightful people to know." There were four letters. The first two paved the way to friendships with the engaging and well-connected Lewis Galantiere and with Sylvia Beach, who ran the bookstore–lending library called Shakespeare and Company. The walls of the store were covered with photographs of writers, many of whom Beach knew. An admirer and sponsor of James Joyce, she took to young Hemingway at once. No one he ever knew, he was later to say, had ever been nicer to him.

The other two letters were to Ezra Pound and Gertrude Stein, writers with international reputations. When Ernest and Hadley went to tea at Pound's, the poet held forth while Hemingway sat silent, taking it all in. Soon thereafter, he composed a satirical sketch pillorying Pound's pretentiousness and wild-haired Bohemian appearance. Fortunately, Galantiere talked him out of publishing the piece; Pound and Hemingway subsequently formed a close bond. They boxed and played tennis together, and Pound applied his sharp editorial eye to Hemingway's prose. The work came back to him blue-penciled, and stripped of adjectives. Writing for a newspaper, Hemingway found, was not the same as writing for a poet. His best critic, though, proved to be Gertrude Stein. "Ezra was right half the time," Hemingway told poet John Peale Bishop. "Gertrude was always right."

In March 1922, the Hemingways paid their first call on Stein at 27, rue de Fleurus—a comfortable apartment whose walls were filled with paintings by Picasso and other modern masters. The Buddha-like Gertrude discussed writing with Ernest, while her tiny companion Alice B. Toklas took Hadley aside to chat about domestic matters. Hemingway listened to Stein's pronouncements with passionate intensity. "She has a wonderful head," he wrote Edmund Wilson in November 1923. He found her method invaluable for analyzing anything and for making notes on a person or a place. As for Stein, she liked Hemingway immediately. "He is a delightful fellow," she reported to Anderson. Toklas, who was given to jealousy, thought that Ernest, with his dark luminous eyes and flashing smile, was entirely too attentive to Gertrude. Nonetheless a close bond was formed. Stein and Toklas became godparents to the Hemingways' son. Gertrude read Ernest's early writing, and told him that it contained too much description, and not particularly good description. "Begin over again and concentrate," she advised. She also urged him to quit his newspaper job. If you keep on with journalism, she warned, "you will never see things, you will only see words and that will not do...."

Hemingway profited from her advice, and did what he could by way of recompense. Early in 1924, Pound persuaded Ford Madox Ford to take Hemingway on as sub-editor of the *Transatlantic Review*. Thereafter Hemingway saw to it that substantial sections of Stein's unpublished work, *The Making of Americans*, were printed in the journal, beginning in April 1924. In due course their relationship would turn sour, but as of 1925 Hemingway and Stein were still on good terms. He brought a number of American writers to her salon, and in doing so confirmed his standing in the Parisian literary community. He brought John Dos Passos to call, he brought Archibald and Ada MacLeish, he brought Donald Ogden Stewart and Nathan Asch, he brought Ernest Walsh and Evan Shipman, and in mid-May 1925 he brought Scott and Zelda Fitzgerald.

"Dear Friends," Hemingway wrote Stein and Toklas prior to that meeting, "Fitzgerald was around yesterday afternoon with his wife and she's worth seeing so I'll bring them around Friday afternoon unless you warn me not to." The visit went well, and Fitzgerald left a copy of *Gatsby* with Stein. On May 22, she wrote him from their summer place at Belley: "Here we are and we have read your book and it is a good book." She liked the melody of his dedication, "Once Again to Zelda." She liked it that he wrote "naturally in sentences and one can read all of them." She liked his creation on the page of a contemporary world much as Thackeray had done "in Pendennis and Vanity Fair and this isn't a bad compliment." Fitzgerald must have been delighted with such praise, though less so with Stein's comparison of *Gatsby* with *This Side of Paradise*, a novel published five years earlier that he was half inclined to repudiate. As compared with *Paradise*, Stein asserted, *Gatsby* was "as good a book and different and older and that is what one does, one does not get better but different and older and that is always a pleasure." In closing, Stein asked the Fitzgeralds to call when she returned in the fall. She sent the letter via Hemingway, having misplaced the Fitzgeralds' address.

Ignoring the comment about not getting better since *Paradise*, Fitzgerald replied to Stein with a show of deference. He could only hope to live up to her approbation. He was basically a "second rate person compared to first rate people." He was content to let her, and the one or two people like her who were acutely sensitive, "think or fail to think for me and my kind artistically."

If he could write a book as fine as *Gatsby*, Hemingway felt, Fitzgerald could do something even finer. And settled into his rue de Tilsitt apartment, Fitzgerald was eager to get on with his writing. Most of the previous winter he had done little besides reading and revising the edited manuscript and galleys of *Gatsby*. Now he had a new novel in mind, a book about American expatriates in France that would not emerge as *Tender Is the Night* for another nine years. During the interim Fitzgerald wrote some of his finest short stories, including "The Rich Boy" (1926) and "Babylon Revisited" (1931). But the long gap between novels damaged his reputatation and caused him tremendous personal distress. As Hemingway came to regard the situation, Fitzgerald had two tremendous handicaps to overcome as a working writer: his drinking and his wife.

Two Weaknesses

A friend should bear his friend's infirmities,
But Brutus makes mine greater than they are....

All his faults observed,
Set in a notebook, learn'd, and conn'd by rote.
—Cassius, in SHAKESPEARE's *Julius Caesar*

A man's friendships are, like his will, invalidated
by marriage—but they are also no less invalidated
by the marriage of his friends.
—SAMUEL BUTLER

One of the more cryptic observations in Fitzgerald's notebooks reads: "An inferiority complex comes simply from not feeling you're doing the best you can— Ernest's 'drink' was simply a form of this." It is impossible to date this comment precisely, or to be sure of its meaning. But it seems likely that the inferiority complex in question was that of Fitzgerald himself rather than of the aggressively confident Hemingway, and that "Ernest's 'drink'" referred to a warning from Hemingway that liquor was preventing Fitzgerald from doing his best work. Certainly Hemingway felt that Fitzgerald's weakness for drink was debilitating.

From the beginning Hemingway made fun, in print, of Fitzgerald's trouble with alcohol. In *The Torrents of Spring* (written in November 1925), Hemingway intruded to remark that "[i]t was at this point in the story, reader, that Mr. F. Scott Fitzgerald came to our home one afternoon, and after remaining for quite a while suddenly sat down in the fireplace and would not (or was it could not, reader?) get up and let the fire burn something else so as to keep the room warm." This incident had no bearing on the rest of the story, Hemingway acknowledged, but just the same, he chummily went on, things like this did happen, and "think what they mean to chaps like you and me in the literary game." Before dropping the subject, he observed: "Need I add, reader, that I have the utmost respect for Mr. Fitzgerald, and let anyone else attack him and I would be the first to spring to his defense!"

Hemingway fashioned another version of this same incident twenty-eight years later. In a letter to Charles Poore, he reported that he had sent his Pulitzer Prize check (for *The Old Man and the Sea*) to his son Bumby, now in service as "Capt. John H. Hemingway O-1798575 who helped me write The Sun Also Rises, A Farewell to Arms and rendered a signal service to literature by pulling Mr. Scott Fitzgerald out of the fireplace where he had gone to sleep when we lived at 115 Rue Notre Dame des Champs." Both in this letter and in *The Torrents of Spring*, Hemingway underscored Fitzgerald's immature behavior by referring to him as "Mr."

During their Paris years Hemingway may well have decided that his friend was fair game because of his celebrity. The "Who's Who in Paris" column of the *Chicago Tribune*'s Paris edition for December 7, 1925, featured a handsome photograph of Fitzgerald, accompanied by a story based on Ellin Mackay's observation that "the trouble with our elders is that they have swallowed too much of F. Scott Fitzgerald" and particularly his stories about debutantes like herself. Fitzgerald, the *Tribune* reported, was "popularly credited with the discovery of the flapper" and with exploiting "the gin and jazz crazed milieu of modern New York." This kind of publicity demeaned Fitzgerald in the eyes of his fellow authors. He was as ambitious as the next man, Dos Passos remarked, but he did not covet the Fitzgeralds' kind of Sunday supplement celebrity: that "set his teeth on edge."

In a satirical piece Hemingway raised an eyebrow at Fitzgerald's dilatory work habits, and by implication the drinking that led to them. His comic article, entitled "My Own Life," appeared in the then-new *New Yorker* for February 12, 1927. Therein Hemingway focused on a number of people he'd supposedly broken off relations with (uncannily, in many cases he subsequently *did* end these relationships), including "Gertrude Stein, My Wife, Benchley, F. Scott Fitzgerald, Donald Ogden Stewart" and promising "Next Week How I Broke with Dos Passos, Coolidge, Lincoln, Mencken and Shakespeare." The section on Fitzgerald, cut out of the typescript before publication, read as follows:

HOW I BROKE WITH F. SCOTT FITZGERALD

I tried hard to break with Fitzgerald but the maid said that both Mr. and Mrs. Fitzgerald were sleeping and could not possibly be wakened. I went out and broke with the cabman instead.

In these accounts and in direct correspondence between the two men, Fitzgerald's drinking was invariably treated as a joke, but the humor carried an undercurrent of disapproval. Work and the bottle both figure in the course of a friendly letter to Fitzgerald of May 1926, for example. Hemingway asked how Fitzgerald was feeling and if he were "really working on his novel" and followed that question with another: "Is it true that you have become blind through alcoholic poisoning and had to have your pancreas removed?" To soften that brutal inquiry, Hemingway allowed in closing that he was "thinking of going out in a few minutes, and getting very cock eyed drunk."

Perhaps Hemingway's most interesting document on Fitzgerald's drinking during the 1920s is a handwritten sketch drafted for possible use in *A Moveable Feast*. In this sketch, Hemingway answers his son Bumby's questions about Fitzgerald "[a]fter [he] had taken to turning up drunk quite frequently."

"Monsieur Fitzgerald is sick Papa?"

"He is sick because he drinks too much and he cannot work."

"Does he not respect his metier?"

"Madame his wife does not respect it or she is envious of it."

"He should scold her."

"It is not so simple."

Fitzgerald, temporarily on the wagon, comes to visit Hemingway later that day, and Bumby drinks a *ballon* (half a glass) of beer as an example to show Fitzgerald how a man should control his drinking. After Fitzgerald leaves, "full of mineral water and the resolve to write well and truly," Bumby once more interrogates his father.

Was Fitzgerald "demolished mentally by the war?" he inquires. No, that was not his problem. "Poor Monsieur Fitzgerald," the boy goes on. "He was very nice today to remain sober....Will everything be all right with him Papa?" Hemingway could not reassure his son on that score. "I hope so," he answers. "But he has very grave problems. It seems to me that he has almost insurmountable problems as a writer."

As this excised passage demonstrates, Hemingway believed that Fitzgerald's drinking could largely be attributed to his wife Zelda. And in two of the three chapters on Fitzgerald actually printed in *A Moveable Feast*—"Hawks Do Not Share" and "A Matter of Measurements"—she is portrayed as the single most "insurmountable problem" confronting him. In the first of these, the scene is a luncheon at the Fitzgeralds' ornately but badly furnished apartment, during which Hemingway conceives a strong dislike for Zelda. Everything is contrived to put her in the worst possible light. Hungover from the previous night's party, she does not look her best. Her eyes are tired, her face is drawn, and her "beautiful dark blonde hair" has been ruined by a bad permanent.

Despite her hangover, Zelda accuses Scott of having been a "kill-joy" or a "spoilsport," and she smiles happily with her hawk's eyes as she watches him drink the wine at lunch that would make it impossible for him to work later that day. According to Hemingway, Fitzgerald was trying to stop drinking and to concentrate on his writing, while Zelda—who was "jealous of his work"—encouraged him to indulge himself. In describing his initial reaction to Zelda, however, Hemingway probably misrepresented the facts. By way of contrary evidence there is his letter to Stein and Toklas about Zelda's being "worth seeing," as well as a second version of the luncheon meeting written for *A Moveable Feast* but not published. In this account, Zelda is neither hungover nor jealous of her husband's work. Moreover, although her face was drawn and "the only thing[s] beautiful about her" were the tawny smoothness of her skin, the lovely color of her hair (albeit ruined by the unsuccessful permanent wave), and her wonderful light and long legs, and although she was "very spoiled" and said things that made little sense and he did not like her, that night Hemingway "had an erotic enough dream about her." He told her about it the next time they met, and she was pleased. "That," Hemingway wrote, "was the first and last time" he and Zelda had anything in common.

SPECIAL DELIVERY TO SCRIBNER'S

> Now I know that there is nothing you can do about any
> writer ever. The seeds of their destruction are in them
> from the start, and the thing to do about writers is get
> along with them if you see them, and try not to see them.
> —ERNEST HEMINGWAY, "The Art of the Short Story"

However Ernest Hemingway and Zelda Fitzgerald may have felt about each other at first blush, there can be no doubt that after Scott and Ernest's initial meetings—at the Dingo, at the rue de Tilsitt apartment, at Stein's salon, on the trip to Lyon—F. Scott Fitzgerald became Hemingway's enthusiastic advocate and supporter. Something of the shape and color of their friendship, as it developed during 1925 and 1926, is communicated in their occasional letters. From the beginning Hemingway adopted a tone of light sarcasm at Fitzgerald's expense, a tone meant to suggest his superior wisdom and maturity. Fitzgerald attempted a complementary sort of masculine raillery in response, but that sort of rhetoric did not come naturally to him. Almost always in correspondence, Fitzgerald sounds as if he were on the defensive.

The first surviving letter between them was written July 1, 1925 from Hemingway in Pamplona, where he had gone for the fiesta and bullfights, to Fitzgerald in Paris. In a set piece, Hemingway conjured up two hypothetical heavens. Fitzgerald's idea of heaven, he speculated, would be "[a] beautiful vacuum filled with wealthy monogamists, all powerful and members of the best families all drinking themselves to death." In contrast, Hemingway went on, *his* heaven would include two barrera seats in the bull ring, a trout stream, and two houses, one for his wife and children and the other for his nine beautiful mistresses. Without exactly saying so, this comparison disparaged Fitzgerald's excessive devotion to his wife, his admiration for the rich, and his fondness for the bottle, while drawing attention to Hemingway's aggressively masculine pursuits.

Where Hemingway made light of his friend, the first extant letter of Fitzgerald to Hemingway—written November 30, 1925 after passing out at the Hemingways' flat—struck a characteristic note of apology. Fitzgerald was "quite ashamed" of his drunken behavior, and did his best to pass it off with a joke: "the deplorable man who entered your apartment Sat. morning *was not* me but a man named Johnston who has often been mistaken for me." At the same time, however, Fitzgerald also found it necessary to issue a disclaimer. Perhaps as a consequence of the expansiveness brought on by alcohol, Fitzgerald had inflated the price his stories could command. "For some reason I told you a silly lie—or rather an exaggeration...*The Saturday Evening Post* raised me to $2750 [per story] and not $3000, which is a jump of $750.00 in one month." Either of these figures must have sounded astronomical to Hemingway, who at the time had earned very little for his fiction. Moreover, he did not think it seemly to discuss financial matters so openly. The situation had come up before, at the rue de Tilsitt luncheon when Fitzgerald insisted on showing Hemingway the ledger in which he recorded the dates of publication of his stories and novels along with the amount of money they had brought in. His fiscal triumphs soon became a source of satirical commentary between them.

In his letters, Hemingway acted the role of moral and social counselor to a companion who, while older and more successful, could still use considerable straightening out. This, despite the fact that throughout 1925 and 1926 the established professional Fitzgerald threw himself into a campaign to promote and advance Hemingway's career. The primary goal was to deliver Hemingway to editor Maxwell Perkins at the house of Scribner. This took some doing, since Hemingway had a three-book contract with Boni & Liveright. Yet by early 1926, by virtue of considerable calculation on Hemingway's part combined with Fitzgerald's artful cooperation, the shift of publishers was successfully completed.

Even before Boni & Liveright brought out *In Our Time*, Hemingway was contemplating leaving them. In August 1925, the Paris-based author Jane Heap wrote him that if he wasn't happy with Liveright, she knew a publisher's representative who wanted to see him. (This may have been William Aspenwall Bradley, of Knopf). Hemingway replied that Boni & Liveright had an option on his next three books, but with a loophole: "said option to lapse if they refuse any one book." Although he couldn't "talk business now" he was certainly interested in meeting her friend, for "you can't ever tell what might happen." In fact he was not enthusiastic about his agreement with Liveright. He'd gotten a mere $200 advance for *In Our Time*, and the in-house support for his book was not strong. They made him omit "Up in Michigan" entirely, and altered "Mr. and Mrs. Elliot." Besides, Liveright was the publisher of Sherwood Anderson, who had befriended and encouraged him, and that circumstance might encourage the critics to draw invidious comparisons between them. He wanted to be his own man, not Anderson's or Stein's disciple.

The overture from Jane Heap was but one among several that came Hemingway's way during the summer and fall of 1925. Fitzgerald was aiming him toward Scribner's, and could do so with no pangs of conscience, inasmuch as Boni & Liveright had openly importuned *him* to abandon Scribner's and publish his next book with them. Scribner's sounded good to Hemingway, who was impressed by the supportive letters of Max Perkins. Perkins enthusiastically praised his work, which was more than Horace Liveright had done. Perkins also went out of his way to do the young author a favor. Originally, Perkins had asked him for a copy of the hard-to-obtain *in our time*, but Hemingway said he was sorry, he didn't have a single copy of his own. Thereupon Perkins searched for and secured one, and sent it to the author, accompanied by a request that must have pleased him. If Hemingway should happen to come across *another* copy, Perkins wrote, he'd be delighted if he would sign it and send it to him.

In literary circles, the word was getting around about Hemingway. Well-known novelist Louis Bromfield was singing his praises. So were his friends John Dos Passos and Donald Ogden Stewart. Hemingway's attractiveness as a literary property rose abruptly during the months after the 1925 fiesta of San Fermin at Pamplona. In a nine-week spurt, he completed the first draft of a novel called *Fiesta* (later, *The Sun Also Rises*) based in good part on the people and events of the Pamplona trip. Short stories were one thing, but publishers might make a great deal of money on a successful novel, and now he had a novel to promise them.

In Our Time, Hemingway's book of stories, appeared on 5 October 1925. "Isn't Ernest Hemingway's book fine?" Fitzgerald wrote Perkins immediately. Fitzgerald also turned out a highly laudatory review of *In Our Time*, which did not appear (in the *Bookman*) until May 1926. Meanwhile, the initial notices were extremely strong for a first book of stories. Reviewers admired Hemingway's spare and powerful style. "His language is fibrous and athletic, colloquial and fresh, hard and clean," commented the *New York Times Book Review*; "his very prose seems to have an organic being of its own." Hemingway was more than an accomplished stylist, according to *Time*. "Make no mistake," the newsmagazine announced, "Ernest Hemingway is somebody; a new, honest, un-'literary' transcriber of life—a writer."

Despite such laudatory reviews, Boni & Liveright did little to promote Hemingway's book. The first printing was only 1,335 copies, and the advertising consisted of a single pre-publication announcement in *Publishers Weekly* and two ads in the *New York Times Book Review*. All of the advertisements, like the book jacket itself, relied on blurbs from better-known writers. The jacket featured quotes from anthologist Edward J. O'Brien and critic Gilbert Seldes, as well as writers Anderson, Dos Passos, Stewart, Waldo Frank, and Ford Madox Ford. In the ads, Sinclair Lewis was added to the gallery of endorsers, but the greatest emphasis was placed on Sherwood Anderson, who had recommended Hemingway to Liveright in the first place. "Mr. Hemingway is young, strong, full of laughter and he can write," the *New York Times Book Review* ad of October 11, 1925 quoted Anderson. "The pen feels good in his hand." That was the last effort Boni & Liveright made for Hemingway's book. It was not even mentioned in the firm's two major *New York Times Book Review* ads for the Christmas season.

Understandably enough, Hemingway objected to Boni & Liveright's small first printing and lack of advertising backup. "Evidently they made up their minds in advance that it was not worth while trying to sell a book of short stories whether anyone wanted to buy it or not," he wrote Harold Loeb, the model for Robert Cohn in *The Sun Also Rises* and the author of a novel, *Doodab*, that was published by Boni & Liveright in the same season as *In Our Time*. He thought the massing of blurbs on the jacket put the reader off. And he was undoubtedly annoyed by the clear association of his work with Anderson, a connection that the reviewers spelled out. "Sherwood Anderson is there leading the chorus [of blurb-contributors], and Mr. Hemingway's work is most like his," the *New York Post* observed. Still worse, the *New York Sun* commented that Hemingway's writing did not yet have "the big movement, the rich content of such a book as [Anderson's] *Dark Laughter*." This comparison was particularly galling, since Hemingway believed that Anderson had entirely lost his touch in *Dark Laughter*.

With the first draft of *The Sun Also Rises* completed and his name reverberating around the halls of publishing offices in New York, by November 1925 Hemingway was in a strong bargaining position. He determined then to break his contract with Liveright and switch to Scribner's—or possibly to some other bidder for his services. The way he severed himself from Liveright was to write a lightweight satire, *The Torrents of Spring*, that was clearly a parody of Sherwood Anderson, his former benefactor and Boni & Liveright's best-selling author. He dashed off this 28,000-word book in ten days. It was "[p]robably unprintable, but funny as hell," he wrote Ezra Pound on November 30. "Wrote it to destroy Sherwood and various others."

A week later, he put *The Torrents of Spring* in the mail to Horace Liveright, along with a letter that simultaneously insisted on the merits of his ten-day wonder and talked tough about the conditions he was prepared to demand should Liveright accept it. This was *not* the long novel Liveright was anticipating, Hemingway announced: he'd be rewriting that book, now called *The Sun Also Rises*, over the winter. But the short satirical book he was submitting belonged to the literary tradition established by Fielding's *Joseph Andrews*: Scott Fitzgerald was "very excited about it," and Louis Bromfield thought it was one of the funniest books he had ever read. Still, Hemingway cautioned, "If you take it you've got to push it." Liveright had made a hash of *In Our Time*, but "this book you can sell and it must be given a fair play." Furthermore, he wanted an advance of $500 as a guarantee that *Torrents* would get a fair share of advertising support.

Both author and editor understood (though Hemingway did not articulate this possibility in his letter) that if the firm turned his satire down, that would sever their three-book contract. Hemingway wanted to make it difficult if not impossible for his publishers to accept the book. "The only reason" they might reject *Torrents*, he acknowledged, "would be for fear of offending Sherwood."

But, he pointed out, it would be in Boni & Liveright's interest to differentiate between him and Anderson, "and you might as well have us both under the same roof and get it coming and going"—that is, Hemingway as the comer and Anderson on his way out.

This was not the letter of a man unsure of his ground. Hemingway praised his own work, chided his publisher for past mistreatment, demanded conditions, and in closing asked for an immediate decision. He and Hadley and Bumby were spending another winter at Schruns in Austria; Liveright should cable him there "at once" about his decision, he instructed. If Liveright didn't want to publish it, Hemingway admitted, he had "a number of propositions" to consider. But, he wrote in closing, "I want you to publish it...because it is a hell of a fine book and it can make us both a lot of money." In this letter, Hemingway was having it both ways. Probably he realized that *Torrents* was, for Boni & Liveright anyway, "unprintable." But if they did decide to publish it anyway, he wanted it done on his terms.

To what extent Fitzgerald became involved in Hemingway's contract-breaking scheme is uncertain. Fitzgerald did send Horace Liveright a letter endorsing the merits of *The Torrents of Spring.* "[I]t seems about the best comic book ever written by an American," he said. This was an exaggeration, for as a humorist Hemingway was not in the same league with Donald Ogden Stewart and Robert Benchley. *The Torrents of Spring* is full of attempts at verbal slapstick, only some of which come off. Despite Fitzgerald's overstated enthusiasm for *Torrents*, however, there is no reason to suppose that he was complicit in any sort of subterfuge. In his letter of endorsement, in fact, Fitzgerald admitted straightforwardly that he hoped Liveright would turn the book down, for he was "something of a ballyhoo man for Scribners" and would like to see Hemingway "rounded up in the same coop" with him. That kind of honest talk gave Liveright fair warning about what might happen if he rejected *Torrents*.

Liveright was over a barrel, and did not respond with his decision on the manuscript for three weeks. In the interim, Hemingway in Schruns wrote Fitzgerald in Paris twice, with no mention whatever of Liveright or Scribner's or *Torrents*, except to confess that he had exacerbated a sore throat by reading the entirety of the book aloud to the Murphys. In the second missive, probably written the day before Christmas, Hemingway commented amiably enough that he'd gotten a letter from Fitzgerald and it was good to know that "somebody spells worse than I do." Hemingway was right about that. He was not a good speller, but Fitzgerald was an extremely poor one. He spelled by ear alone, and never developed an eye for the way the word should look on the page. He was especially weak on proper names, and was capable of spelling Ezra Pound's surname as "Pount." So it was natural enough that Fitzgerald persistently misspelled Hemingway's last name, usually as "Hemminway." Writing Archibald MacLeish in December 1925, Hemingway observed that Fitzgerald had invented that spelling and he didn't know why Fitzgerald used two m's unless it was because there were two t's in Scott. Over a period of time, the mistake about his name became a source of exasperation. As Hemingway wrote Malcolm Cowley in 1951, "two mm's mean bastard; Hemenway means Silk Company, and such a long name as Hemingway was really asking too damn much of Scott." In other correspondence at about the same time, Hemingway began to style Fitzgerald as "FitzGerald."

By way of keeping the pot on the boil, Fitzgerald wrote Perkins late in December that he hoped "Liveright would lose faith in Ernest." Horace Liveright didn't do that, exactly. On December 30 he cabled Hemingway in Schruns: REJECT-ING TORRENTS OF SPRING. PATIENTLY AWAITING MANUSCRIPT SUN ALSO RISES. WRITING FULLY. In the promised letter Liveright spelled out his reasons for turning down *Torrents*. "Apart from the fact that it is a bitter, and I might say vicious caricature of Sherwood Anderson, it is entirely cerebral." Who on earth did Hemingway expect to buy the book? Then, without mentioning the conditions of the three-book contract, Liveright reiterated his eagerness to see Hemingway's novel.

Hemingway did not wait for Horace Liveright's letter to cross the Atlantic before taking the next step in his campaign to switch publishers. On December 31-January 1, he wrote Fitzgerald a long letter that in effect commissioned him to serve as his lieutenant in making the change. "I have known all along that they could not and would not be able to publish [*Torrents*] as it makes a bum out of their present ace and best seller Anderson," he confessed. "I did not, however, have that it mind when I wrote it," he added somewhat disingenuously. That sentence makes it seem highly probable that if Hemingway did in fact write *Torrents* for the specific purpose of breaking his contract, he did so without consulting Fitzgerald. The rest of the letter backs up that interpretation, for in it Hemingway describes as if for the first time the provisions of his contract with Liveright. *In Our Time* was the first book, and Liveright had options to publish the next two. But if they did not exercise this option within sixty days of receiving the manuscript of the second book (in this case, *The Torrents of Spring*), their option rights to the third book (*The Sun Also Rises*) would lapse. "So I'm loose," Hemingway asserted. "No matter what Horace may think up in his letter to say."

Hemingway's well-calculated letter to Fitzgerald reiterated his promise to allow Maxwell Perkins first crack at his work once he was released from

Liveright. But now there was competition on the field. He'd been approached by William Aspenwell Bradley from Knopf. And Louis Bromfield, interceding directly with his publisher Alfred Harcourt, had elicited a promise of an advance once Hemingway was free. For Harcourt as for everyone else, Hemingway's novel-in-progress was the prize, with the satirical *Torrents* the second and lesser part of the bargain. As Harcourt wrote Bromfield for relay to Hemingway, "Hemingway is his own man and talking off his own bat. I should say, Yea Brother, and we shall try to do the young man as much credit as he'll do us, and that's considerable. I'd like to see his Anderson piece. It's a chance for good fun, if not for too much money for either of us. Hemingway's first novel might rock the country." In passing on this quotation to Fitzgerald, Hemingway was obviously applying pressure. He wasn't going to "Double Cross" Fitzgerald and Perkins, he maintained. Still, other publishers were interested.

After presenting this situation, Hemingway laid out a scenario involving Fitzgerald as a principal player. "It's up to you how I proceed next," Hemingway claimed. Then he advanced his plan. He was going to wire Liveright to send the manuscript of *Torrents* to Don Stewart at the Yale Club in New York, and then wire Don to deliver the manuscript to Perkins. As for Fitzgerald, "[y]ou can write Max telling him how Liveright turned it down and why and your own opinion of it. I am re-writing The Sun Also Rises and it is damned good. It will be ready in 2-3 months for late fall or later if they wish." To make sure that Fitzgerald did write Perkins, Hemingway stressed that he was jeopardizing his chances with Harcourt by going to Scribner's first. He was only doing so because of the impression he'd formed of Perkins from their correspondence and what Fitzgerald had told him. Besides, he'd like to be lined up with Fitzgerald there.

Time was of the essence, and so Hemingway directed Fitzgerald, "an important cog in the show," to mark his letter for either the *Majestic* or the *Paris*, mail boats scheduled to leave January 5. That way it would get to New York fastest. And oh yes, he wanted an advance of $500 for *Torrents*. In effect Hemingway was relying on Fitzgerald to make his case and negotiate his terms at Scribner's, a role Fitzgerald was eager to play. In closing his letter, Hemingway added the afterthought that perhaps he should go to New York in person to settle things. The trouble was that his passport had run out and the new one he'd applied for would not arrive for a few weeks. Early in February Hemingway did travel to New York to cement the deal with Scribner's. By that time Fitzgerald had done a considerable amount of maneuvering behind the scenes.

As a first step, he cabled Perkins on January 8: YOU CAN GET HEMINGWAYS

FINISHED NOVEL PROVIDE YOU PUBLISH UNPROMISING SATIRE. HARCOURT HAS MADE DEFINITE OFFER. WIRE IMMEDIATELY WITHOUT QUALIFICATIONS. To Perkins, if not to Liveright, Fitzgerald delivered his true opinion of the commercial potential of *Torrents*. Throughout the negotiations of the succeeding six weeks, Fitzgerald played the dual role of adviser-confidant to publisher Perkins and agent-advocate to author Hemingway. Sensing the urgency of the competing "offer" from Harcourt (whose letter to Bromfield was not, in fact, a contractual commitment), Perkins cabled back immediately, PUBLISH NOVEL AT FIFTEEN PERCENT AND ADVANCE IF DESIRED. ALSO SATIRE UNLESS OBJECTIONABLE OTHER THAN FINANCIALLY. On the strength of the critical success of *In Our Time* and Fitzgerald's recommendation, Perkins was willing to commit Scribner's to publish both *The Torrents of Spring* and *The Sun Also Rises*, sight unseen. And he was willing to do so even though he anticipated taking a loss on *Torrents*. But Perkins was worried that his "qualification," the "unless objectionable" phrase, might be "fatal," and on January 11 sent another, more positive cable to back up the first one: CONFIDENCE ABSOLUTE. KEEN TO PUBLISH HIM. His sole reservation, he explained to Fitzgerald in a following letter, was that Hemingway's satirical book might overstep legal boundaries. "I did my best with that cable," Perkins delicately explained, "but there was a fear that this satire—although in the hands of such a writer it could hardly be rightly so upon any theory—might be suppressible." Then he made a sales pitch for Fitzgerald to relay to his friend. He had no criticism of Harcourt, "an admirable publisher." But Scribner's would be better for Hemingway, for they were "absolutely loyal to [the] authors" they believed in, and would support them "in the face of losses for a long time." Hemingway might need that kind of a publisher, for it did not seem likely to Perkins that "he could come into a large public" right away.

Meanwhile, Fitzgerald had heard directly from Horace Liveright, who had not forgotten Fitzgerald's hint about switching Hemingway to Scribner's. Enclosing a copy of the letter about rejecting *Torrents* he'd sent Hemingway, Liveright maintained that he himself liked the satire better than any of his partners, who concurred that it was "just bad." But the point of his letter was that Fitzgerald should not "get so hilariously enthusiastic" about this rejection as to believe that Boni & Liveright were "in any way giving up Hemingway." They had a contract, Liveright was confident that Hemingway had "a big future," and he "absolutely" planned to go through with that contract. He even proposed Doran as an alternative publisher for *Torrents*, one that, presumably, would not try to lure Hemingway away from Boni & Liveright. Fitzgerald might want to give the book to Scribner's, Liveright wrote, but he thought Doran could do more with it. On a friendly concluding note, Liveright mentioned that he'd been "swept off his feet" by *The Great Gatsby*, commented that the firm had just completed its best publishing season, and announced that his partner, T.R. (Tom) Smith, was on his way to Paris where he hoped to see Fitzgerald.

Undeterred by Liveright's letter, Fitzgerald continued to act as unofficial representative of Scribner's in France. Writing to Perkins soon after his January 8 cable, he elaborated on the prospects for *Torrents*. "I loved it, but believe it wouldn't be popular...probable sale 1000 copies." But Hemingway was "*dead set*" on having the satire published in advance of his novel. Ernest thought that Liveright's refusal set him free, but Scott wasn't so sure about that. Harcourt and Knopf were interested, but if Hemingway was legally free, Fitzgerald was "almost sure" he could deliver the satire and novel to Scribner's to be contracted for "*tout ensemble*." In this letter Fitzgerald stressed the importance of his dual function as friend to Hemingway and unofficial overseas representative of Scribner's. He and Hemingway were "very thick," Fitzgerald wrote, but everything he told Perkins about him was to stay confidential. After supplying Hemingway's address in Schruns, Fitzgerald added a cautionary note for his editor: "Don't even tell him I've discussed his Liveright and Harcourt relations with you." In his next letter to Perkins, Fitzgerald emphasized the competitive situation. Without mentioning his letter from Horace Liveright, Fitzgerald told Perkins he was sure Liveright would fight "like the devil" to keep Hemingway, "because he's crazy to get Ernest's almost completed novel *The Sun Also Rises*." Harcourt and Knopf were after him too, and Hemingway was coming to New York to straighten everything out. Perkins could see Hemingway then and was sure to like him. He was "one of the nicest fellows" Fitzgerald had ever known. But Hemingway was also "very excitable" and Fitzgerald couldn't guarantee what he would decide. At the moment he was "favorably disposed" toward Scribner's and inclined to sign with them, provided he wasn't bitched by some terrible contract with Liveright. To hear Hemingway talk, Fitzgerald added, "you'd think Liveright had broken up his home and robbed him of millions," but that was only because he didn't understand publishing.

In fact Hemingway understood the legal side of the business very well, judging from the January 19 letter to Horace Liveright in which he reviewed the terms of the contract and declared himself free to give his future books to whichever publisher offered him the best terms. They had a three-book contract, Hemingway began. *In Our Time* was the first book. *The Torrents of Spring* was in Paris Fitzgerald had been telling Hemingway that he ought to sell his stories to periodicals that, unlike the little magazines, would pay a decent price for them. *Scribner's* magazine was one such market, and luckily it was affiliated with his publisher. To make his point, Fitzgerald took it upon himself to write Perkins on December 1, 1925 asking if Robert Bridges, the editor of the magazine, would like to see Hemingway's "new short pieces." On the strength of an encouraging reply, Fitzgerald submitted Hemingway's "Fifty Grand" for consideration. During the next six weeks, while Ernest was making up his mind about publishers, Fitzgerald repeatedly importuned Perkins about the matter.

Hemingway was anxious "to get a foothold in your magazine," Fitzgerald wrote in one mid-January letter. In the next, he asserted that Ernest was favorably disposed toward Perkins because of the good letters he'd written Ernest and because of "the magazine...if Bridges likes his work and if you'll take *Torrents* he's yours absolutely." Perkins, who was by this time sold on Hemingway, felt the pressure. On February 3, he wrote Fitzgerald enclosing a copy of his letter to Hemingway accepting "Fifty Grand" for $250, with conditions. The story was "magnificent," but it ran longer than *Scribner's* arbitrary 8,000-word limit. Could Hemingway cut it by 1,500 words, so that it would fit?

Perkins concluded his letter to Hemingway, dated February 1, with a curiously offhand remark. *He'd read in the papers,* Perkins said, that Hemingway was working on a novel, and a lot of people, himself included, would be eager to see it. This was a disingenuous observation, considering that Perkins and Fitzgerald had been in correspondence about the possibility of securing Hemingway's novel for some time. Obviously, Perkins did not wish Hemingway to know of this behind-the-scenes work. The point is clearly made in the letter Perkins sent Fitzgerald. It was unfortunate that they had to ask Hemingway to make cuts in the very first story they had seen, Perkins wrote. The stipulated revision might put him off, might compromise Scribner's chances of signing up *The Sun Also Rises*. "Thanks ever so much for sending the Hemingway" story, he told Fitzgerald. "If only we could get the novel!"

A week later, Scribner's did get the novel, leaving the issue of what to do with "Fifty Grand" up in the air. In the light of Hemingway's convoluted dealings with Liveright and Scribner's, there is a certain ironic appropriateness that this particular story should have been involved. "Fifty Grand" is a boxing story dealing with a double cross, or really a double double cross, in which competing fighters bet against themselves and then try to throw the fight by fouling each his second completed book. The contract held that if Liveright did not decide to publish his second book within sixty days of receipt of the manuscript, the firm's option on that book—and on the third—would lapse. The contract also said that one of the three books submitted was to be a full-length novel, but it did not specify that the second book had to be the novel. It could just as easily be a book of short stories or a humorous book. Then Hemingway asserted that he had submitted *Torrents* to Liveright "in good faith," a curious phrase inasmuch as no one, including Liveright, had challenged him on that point. Publishers, he knew, were not in business for their health, but Liveright could hardly expect to reject his books "as they appear while sitting back and waiting to cash in on the appearance of a best seller: surely not all this for $200" [the *In Our Time* advance]. He would come to see Liveright when he got to New York, but the contract was broken, and that was that.

Hemingway crossed on the *Mauretania,* which docked in New York February 9. The next day he fulfilled his promise to Liveright, stopping by his office to officially sever connections. The day after that, he went to see Perkins and signed a contract advancing $1,500 for both *Torrents* and *Sun* against a royalty of 15 percent. "I am extremely grateful to you for intervening about Hemingway," Perkins wrote Fitzgerald March 4. "He is a most interesting chap about his bull fights and boxing." That letter crossed one from Fitzgerald, in which he warned Perkins that Hemingway was "temperamental in business" as a result of his dealings with "bogus publishers" overseas. Be sure to "*get a signed contract*" for *The Sun Also Rises*, Fitzgerald advised, somewhat after the fact. His comments were confidential, he added. "Please destroy this letter."

"FIFTY GRAND" AND MONEY

We secure our friends not by accepting favors but by doing them
—THUCYDIDE:

Scribner's held an advantage over the other firms wooing Hemingway. The: published not only books, but also *Scribner's* magazine, a monthly aimed at middlebrow, middle-class audience. When purchasing stories, the magazin was naturally biased in favor of submissions from Scribner's authors. Bac other. Its 10,000 words make it one of Hemingway's longest stories, longer than everything except "The Short Happy Life of Francis Macomber" and "The Undefeated" among the forty-nine in the 1938 *Short Stories of Ernest Hemingway*. In this instance, Fitzgerald and Hemingway knew something about its length that Perkins did not: that before submitting the story to *Scribner's* magazine, Scott persuaded Hemingway to make some important excisions at the beginning.

The best-known of these, because Hemingway later commented on it with resentment, involved the anecdote that originally led off "Fifty Grand":

"Say, Jack," I said. "How did you happen to beat Leonard?"
"Well," Jack says. "Benny's a pretty smart boxer. All the time he's in there he's thinking and all the time he's thinking I'm hitting him."

Hemingway cut this "lovely revelation of the metaphysics of boxing" when Fitzgerald—who according to Hemingway had heard the story about Jack Britton and Benny Leonard only once before—told him it was an "old chestnut." His "humility" was in ascendance at the time, Ernest explained in "The Art of the Short Story" (1959), and he made the mistake of trusting Scott's judgment. "They will all con you, gentlemen," Hemingway went on in the wise-guy tone of that essay. "But sometimes it is no[t] intentional. Sometimes they simply do not know. This is the saddest state of writers and the one you will most frequently encounter." As it stands, this passage characterizes Fitzgerald as well-intentioned but both ignorant and incompetent. What Hemingway does not reveal—what he never publicly revealed—was that he cut considerably more than that opening dialogue as a consequence of Fitzgerald's suggestions.

Two documents in the Hemingway collection at the John F. Kennedy Library in Boston testify to this fact. One is Hemingway's handwritten comment on a type-script of "Fifty Grand" that reads, "1st 3 pages of story mutilated by Scott Fitzgerald with his [undecipherable]." The other, a brief and apparently incomplete critique of the story in Fitzgerald's handwriting, turned up stuffed inside a late 1925 letter from Sylvia Beach to Hemingway. Fitzgerald's note suggests that Hemingway should lop off the first six (presumably handwritten) pages of his story. "Perhaps its conciseness makes it dull," Fitzgerald commented, "...the very impossibility of fixing attention for amount of time; the very leaving in only high spots may be why it seemed a slow starter." Following Fitzgerald's suggestion, Hemingway deleted about two and a half typewritten pages, or approximately 500 words, most of them devoted to establishing the prizefight ambience of the story through conversations in the gym and in a bar near Madison Square Garden. Half a dozen characters were introduced in this aborted beginning, along with a suggestion appropriate in a story about fixed bouts and double crosses—that heavyweight champion Gentleman Jim Corbett was a good enough "actor" to throw fights. With this background deleted, "Fifty Grand" begins with plot: a reference to the forthcoming fight between champion Brennan and challenger Walcott.

"My loyal and devoted friend Fitzgerald, who was truly more interested in my own career at this point than in his own, sent me to Scribner's with the story," Hemingway wrote in "The Art of the Short Story." This was accurate enough about Fitzgerald's commitment to Hemingway's cause, but pointedly omitted mention of his editorial doctoring. In his 1959 version of what happened, Hemingway ignores Fitzgerald's involvement and presents himself as his own best editor. "I explained without heat nor hope, seeing the built-in stupidity of the editor of the magazine [Bridges] and his intransigence, that I had already cut the story myself." He had cut it "for keeps" when he wrote it, Hemingway asserted, "and afterwards at Scott's request" had even cut out the Benny Leonard–Jack Britton anecdote.

A good place to "amputate" stories was at the beginning, Hemingway also commented in this essay, without admitting that this had already been done. In any case, he knew how difficult it would be to make further excisions, and when Scribner's asked for them, he refused to try. Perkins did not let the matter drop there. Undoubtedly influenced to some degree by Fitzgerald's prodding, he took over as agent for Hemingway's "most excellent" fight story, and shipped it off with his recommendation to other major magazines. It was the first thing Hemingway mentioned to Perkins when he got back to Schruns from his trip to the States and heard that *Collier's* had turned down "Fifty Grand." He was sorry about that, but not surprised, for the story was "quite hard in texture" and not what they wanted at all. It would have "meant very much to me in various ways" for the story to appear in *Scribner's*. Now he supposed the story would come back from the *Saturday Evening Post* and *Liberty*—where Perkins planned to send it next—and so it did.

Troubled by these repeated rejections, Hemingway decided to allow an outsider to try reducing "Fifty Grand" to *Scribner's* magazine length. The writer Manuel Komroff was given the assignment of cutting 1,500 words, but couldn't do it. He managed to reduce the story by only 200 words before returning the manuscript to Hemingway. Further cuts would only harm the story, he believed.

When these initial efforts failed, Perkins enlisted the Paul Reynolds literary agency, and their "man [Harold] Ober, whom Scott knows about," in the attempt to sell "Fifty Grand."

The story was rejected half a dozen times before finally appearing, without any further cuts, in the *Atlantic Monthly* for July 1927. In the interim Hemingway sent Perkins several stories much shorter than "Fifty Grand." He was trying to write "the shortest ones first," he sarcastically reported on April 1, 1926. Hemingway was somewhat mollified when *Scribner's* accepted "The Killers" in September 1926, but the experience with his prizefight story continued to rankle. He'd like to see "Fifty Grand" published "sometime before boxing is abolished," he wrote Perkins. He hoped it would fetch a good price in order to "try and get back some of the postage."

With Hemingway safely delivered to Scribner's, Fitzgerald continued his efforts to promote his friend's career. The review/article of *In Our Time* he had written in the fall of 1925, called "How to Waste Material: A Note on My Generation," finally emerged in the *Bookman*'s May 1926 issue. Fitzgerald submitted the piece first to H.L. Mencken at *American Mercury*, but as he expected—"since it was a blurb for Hemmingway whom you don't like"—Mencken turned it down. Actually, the review was a two-part effort, part two in praise of Hemingway, and part one consisting of a diatribe against various contemporary writers who "botched their books" by trying too hard for prototypically "American" subject matter. Such writers, he declared, were "insensitive, suspicious of glamour, preoccupied exclusively with the external, the contemptible, the 'national' and the drab." Among those he had in mind were novelists who struggled to write "significantly" about city tenement dwellers, small town businessmen, and—especially—farmers. Warming up for his essay, he savaged this last category of book, and his friend Tom Boyd, in a letter of mid-1925 to Maxwell Perkins. A few years before, Fitzgerald urged Perkins to publish Boyd, a newspaperman he met during his 1921-1922 stay in St. Paul, and as a result Scribner's brought out Boyd's World War I novel *Through the Wheat* in 1923. Fitzgerald liked that book, but he did not feel the same about Boyd's second novel, *Samuel Drummond* (1925), a hackneyed tale—as he put it to Perkins—of the "Simple Inarticulate Farmer and his Hired Man Christy." Hemingway encouraged Fitzgerald in these denigrating opinions about his former protégé. "Did you ever read [Norwegian novelist Knut Hamsun's] The Growth of the Soil?" he asked Fitzgerald in December 1925. "And then for Christ sake to read Thom Boyd."

Having disposed of much of the competition, including by implication Sherwood Anderson and Sinclair Lewis, Fitzgerald went on to celebrate the virtues of Hemingway's *In Our Time* and especially "Big Two-Hearted River," which he ranked among the best contemporary short stories. It was the account of a boy on a fishing trip, nothing more, Fitzgerald commented, but he had "read it with the most breathless unwilling interest [he had] experienced since Conrad first bent [his] reluctant eyes upon the sea." In addition, stories like "The End of Something" and "The Three-Day Blow" represented something unself-consciously fresh and arresting in American fiction. There was no exposition at all. Instead, "a picture—sharp, nostalgic, tense—develops before your eyes. When the picture is complete a light seems to snap out, the story is over." Many readers may have grown weary of repeated admonitions to watch this new writer or that, Fitzgerald concluded. This time it was different; he felt "a renewal of excitement at these stories wherein Ernest Hemingway turns a corner into the street."

Fitzgerald manifestly hoped his review would give Hemingway's reputation a boost. "See my article on Hemingway," he advised Perkins in May 1926—"it's pretty good." Then again in June: "Do you think the *Bookman* article did him any good?" Hemingway himself adopted a superior view of the entire endeavor. He was glad that Fitzgerald realized all criticism was "horse shit without horse shit's pleasant smell nor use as fertilizer," he observed in a letter of late April. Hadn't seen the *Bookman*, Hemingway added. "Nevertheless I thank you for services rendered." When Fitzgerald objected to the sardonic tone of that remark, Hemingway smoothed away the issue. "Sorry my letter was snooty," he wrote in late May. "You were saying how little you valued critical articles unless they were favorable for practical purposes...That's what all the services rendered was about."

Hemingway's cavalier attitude did not deter Fitzgerald from his campaign of support. He even attempted to enlist others in the cause. Soon after the appearance of the *Bookman* piece, he encountered novelist Glenway Wescott on a Riviera beach. Drawing Wescott away from a circle of companions, Fitzgerald grasped his elbow and implored him to help launch Hemingway. Why didn't *Wescott* write a laudatory essay on Hemingway's stories? The urgency in Fitzgerald's tone betrayed something beyond mere affection, Wescott thought. Fitzgerald seemed convinced that Hemingway was "inimitably, essentially superior" to both of them, that neither Wescott's 1925 novel *The Apple of the Eye* (which had enjoyed a measure of success) nor *The Great Gatsby* could compare to the superior work Hemingway was doing. It simply didn't occur to him that any "unfriendliness or pettiness" on Wescott's part might inhibit his enthusiasm "about the art of a new colleague or rival." Such extreme devotion to another's cause might seem admirable, but Wescott thought it was bad for Fitzgerald, representing "a morbid belittlement and abandonment of himself." Scott seemed to feel that he could be excused for wasting his energy in hack-writing. Ernest would write the masterpieces.

In addition to professional help on several fronts, Fitzgerald also gave Hemingway money. Having given up feature writing for the *Toronto Star Weekly*, Ernest was almost totally dependent for living expenses on Hadley's trust fund—and occasional loans from others. As artist Kitty Cannell said of Hemingway during those years, he developed "a Tom Sawyerish way of getting money from people and then saying they had embarrassed him by forcing it on him." Cannell, who lived with Harold Loeb for a time in Paris, may have been biased against Hemingway by his unflattering portrayal of her as Frances Clyne in *The Sun Also Rises*. But Fitzgerald certainly did extend him a helping hand, more than once. He loaned Hemingway $400 in the fall of 1925. In April 1926, he sent him $100 in a letter that announced, among other things, that Hollywood had purchased the rights to *Gatsby* for $15,000. The Hollywood windfall should tide him over until Christmas, Fitzgerald remarked, and Hemingway—who was getting along on a small fraction of that amount—seized on his somewhat insensitive comment as a source of satire. "I felt very touched by [Scott's] precarious financial situation," he wrote Max Perkins. *"Don't Worry About Money,"* he sarcastically responded to Fitzgerald himself. He'd instructed Scribner's to send Fitzgerald all future royalties, and called in his attorney to make Scott his heir. Elsewhere in that same letter, however, Hemingway alluded to his own impecunious condition. Getting the manuscript of *The Sun Also Rises* typed up had cost him 1,085 francs, he reported. And he "could use the 250" dollars he could have gotten for cutting "Fifty Grand" (still unsold) for *Scribner's* magazine.

Fitzgerald soon found another way to ease Hemingway's financial difficulties. The Hemingways had arranged to go to Spain early in May, but had to change plans when Bumby came down with whooping cough. Ernest traveled to Spain alone. Hadley and Bumby proceeded to Juan-les-Pins on the Riviera, where the Fitzgeralds were ensconced for the season. Scott and Zelda had rented one house, the Villa Paquita, and then abandoned it to move into a larger and more comfortable Villa St. Louis. So they offered the Villa Paquita to the Hemingways, rent-free, until their lease ran out on June 10. Hadley and Bumby arrived there on May 19, where she and Bumby were more or less quarantined to protect against spread of his disease. It was not a happy time for her. Her letters to Ernest in Spain make it clear that money difficulties were much on their minds and that she felt terribly lonely without him. Between the lines they also reveal her distress at the weakening bonds of their marriage.

She was not being extravagant in going to the Riviera, Hadley wrote Ernest on May 18. Apparently he had some misgivings about the Villa Paquita arrangement, for in her letter of May 24 she insisted that they were "*not* in the hands of Scott & Zelda" but merely using their empty villa at no cost. She was even denying herself the consolations of drink, though in the solitude with no one but an ailing two-year-old to talk to it wasn't much fun. "I'm living here the cheapest possible and *not* being a bad," she movingly assured him. "I've got a headache & a heartache and I work for the common good and am sorrier than I can say I haven't been able to expend myself more on you and not so much on the Smaller Shad." As an inducement for Ernest to leave Madrid and come to the Riviera, she proposed inviting another companion: "Wouldn't it make a great difference to you if Pfeiffer or some other friend turned up to mill around with?"

For some time Hadley had been aware that "Pfeiffer"—Pauline Pfeiffer— was trying to steal her husband. Pauline and her sister Jinny had met the Hemingways in March 1925. The well-dressed Pfeiffer girls were daughters of a landowning squire in Arkansas, and favorite nieces of a bachelor uncle who owned a controlling interest in Richard Hudnut perfumes and who promised to settle substantial funds upon them. Small, dark, and quick of wit, Pauline was working in Paris as an editor for *Vogue*. She thought Ernest rather boorish at first, but was soon overcome with admiration. To see more of him, she attached herself to the family. As Hemingway later generalized the situation,

> an unmarried young woman becomes the temporary best friend of another young woman who is married, goes to live with the husband and wife and then unknowingly, innocently and unrelentingly sets out to marry the husband...The husband has two attractive girls around when he has finished work. One is new and strange and if he has bad luck he gets to love them both.

In the fall of 1925, Pauline accompanied the three Hemingways to Austria for the skiing. She and Hadley gossiped and laughed together, and Pauline also lavished attention on young Bumby. But she was back in Paris when Ernest came through town en route to New York and a contract with Scribner's. In her letters to Hadley, she was disarmingly candid about her feelings. "I'm overjoyed that Ernest will soon be here," she wrote Hadley on January 17. "I'm going to cling to him like a millstone and old moss and winter ivy." And after she and Ernest had spent five days together—Hadley remained in the Vorarlberg, since the Hemingways had sublet their Paris flat for the winter—Pauline reported that she'd seen as much of Ernest as was humanly possible, that he had been "a delight," that she had a new trust fund, and that she was planning to make Bumby one of her heirs. How could Hadley protest? The income from her own trust fund had been severely reduced through mismanagement.

Proposing that Pauline join them in Juan-les-Pins may have been Hadley's way of forcing a confrontation, or of forcing Ernest to come to his senses. In any event, Pauline Pfeiffer had come to the Riviera by the time of Ernest's arrival on the afternoon of May 28. There to greet him when he stepped off the train at Antibes were Pauline, Hadley, and Gerald and Sara Murphy. Later that evening the Murphys gave a caviar-and-champagne party to welcome Ernest to their territory.

A "Golden Couple": Gerald and Sara Murphy

> They were both rich; he was handsome, she was beautiful; they had three golden children. They loved each other, they enjoyed their own company, and they had the gift of making life enchantingly pleasurable for those who were fortunate enough to be their friends.
> —Donald Ogden Stewart

The actress Marian Seldes called them "the golden couple." Don Stewart thought of them as a prince and princess in a fairy tale. "There was a shine to life wherever they were," said Archibald MacLeish. Fitzgerald tried to capture their charm in *Tender Is the Night*. That novel begins with a graceful man in a jockey cap and red-striped tights gravely raking the sand on "the bright tan prayer rug" of the beach at Antibes. Nearby a young woman with a "hard and lovely and pitiful" face is making a list under her beach umbrella. She has pulled her bathing suit off her shoulders to sun her back, and wears a string of pearls around her neck. Fitzgerald gave these characters different names in the drafts of *Tender Is the Night* before calling them, finally, Dick and Nicole Diver. By whatever name, they were mod-elled on the Murphys, the elegant and cultured expatriates whose lives were to intersect so vividly with Scott and Zelda's, Ernest and Hadley and Pauline's.

Fitzgerald wrote of Dick Diver that he bestowed "carnivals of affection" on others, and so it seemed with Gerald Murphy. He knew how to draw people out, how to make them feel important and appreciated. Eight years older than Fitzgerald and eleven years Hemingway's senior, Gerald had grown up in Boston and New York, where his father ran the Mark Cross leather goods company. He went to Hotchkiss and then Yale, where he managed gentleman C's in his cours-es but achieved great success outside the classroom. His talents were concen-trated in the fine arts, and the arts of social intercourse. He managed the Glee Club and served on the Prom Committee. He was elected to Skull and Bones. He was one of eighteen undergraduates chosen as charter members of the Elizabethan Club. In the class history his classmates voted him Best Dressed, Greatest Social Light, and Most Thorough Gent. Tall, slender, and well turned out, Gerald was the kind of boy who seemed more appealing to the mothers of the girls he escorted to dances than to the girls themselves. But Sara Wiborg liked Gerald's gallantry, and his style.

Sara was born in November 1883, more than four years earlier than her husband-to-be. Her father, Frank Wiborg, was a hard-driving Cincinnati indus-trialist who made a fortune as a manufacturer of lithographic inks. The family had social ambitions. The three Wiborg daughters attended private schools in Cincinnati and New York, and were often taken to Europe. They were presented at court. Kaiser Wilhelm invited them for hot chocolate and cakes. All three daughters sang well—they performed as a trio, upon demand—and were thought to be beauties. Sara's blondness and somewhat elfin looks set her apart.

Sara and Gerald married against the advice of both sets of parents. One problem was the difference in incomes. At Mark Cross Gerald was earning $3,000, which would barely cover Sara's clothing allowance. Then too, neither of them paid much obeisance to the Protestant ethic. They were determined to do things their "*own* way." No one was particularly surprised when the two of them decided, in 1921, to abandon commerce and live full-time in Europe, where they could cultivate thair artistic interests. Initially Gerald planned to pursue landscape architecture, but he was soon caught up in the artistic ferment of Paris. Walking in the city one afternoon in October 1921, he happened to glance in the window of an avant-garde gallery and was immediately enraptured. If that was painting, he told Sara, it was what he wanted to do. So he turned his considerable talents to the task. Eventually he was to produce a number of outsized canvases that simultaneously distorted and reflected the reality around him. In December 1925 two of these paintings, *Watch* and *Razor*, were exhibited in Paris alongside the work of his friends Pablo Picasso and Fernand Léger. Picasso admired Murphy's paintings; they were simple, direct, manifestly American. Léger went further. Gerald Murphy was "the only *American* painter in Paris," he proclaimed.

Given thair interests, resources, and amiability, it was only natural that the Murphys gathered around them some of the most accomplished artists and writers of the time. Among the Europeans, Jean Cocteau and Igor Stravinsky in addition to Picasso and Léger. Among the Americans, composer Cole Porter (a friend from Gerald's Yale days), humorists Robert Benchley and Donald Ogden Stewart and the acid-tongued Dorothy Parker, playwright Philip Barry, poet Archibald MacLeish, and novelists John Dos Passos and F. Scott Fitzgerald and Ernest Hemingway. All of these and more found their way to the Murphys' summer head-quarters at their fourteen-room Villa America in Antibes. The Murphys had more or less discovered the potential of the French Riviera as a summer instead of win-ter resort, and took pleasure in inviting others to share its attractions with them.

The Fitzgeralds came to know Gerald's sister Esther back in Great Neck, so the Murphys were among the first people they looked up when they got to Paris in the spring of 1924. From the first the two couples felt a kind of electrical attrac-tion. "Currents race between us regardless," Gerald was later to write. "Scott will uncover for me values in Sara, just as Sara has known them in Zelda through her affection for Scott." But the Fitzgeralds seemed to go out of their way to short-cir-cuit the connection. As compared with Gerald and Sara, who were somewhat older and more settled, both Scott and Zelda behaved like rebellious children.

The Murphys encouraged the Fitzgeralds to go south for the summer of 1924, and were pleased when the Fitzgeralds found a place in Valescure, only a short drive from Antibes. While Scott worked hard on the novel that was to become his masterpiece, Zelda sunned on the beach and flirted with the French aviators stationed nearby. One such flirtation turned into something more serious by midsummer. When Gerald and Sara came to visit the Fitzgeralds, they could not help observing that Zelda and the golden-haired pilot Édouard Jozan were infatuated with each other. "[E]verybody knew it but Scott," Sara said. When Scott finally brought the affair to a halt, Zelda became dangerously reckless. On a drive along the Côte d'Azur, she demanded a cigarette from Scott just as he was negotiating a dangerous curve. She dived at night into the Mediterranean from the thirty-five-foot rocks at the tip of Cap d'Antibes, and dared a terrified Scott into following her. She took an overdose of sleeping pills, and Sara and Gerald took turns walking her up and down all night to keep her awake.

Scott's behavior, less suicidal, was embarrassing in its childishness. The Fitzgeralds "weren't really party people," Gerald said. "It was just that every night they wanted things to happen," whether there was a party or not. Back in Paris in the spring of 1925, they came roaring out to the Murphys' house in St. Cloud late one night and honked the horn. Gerald and Sara didn't let them in. Scott, especially, acted outrageously to attract attention. In a taxi with Sara and Zelda, he stuffed filthy one hundred franc notes into his mouth and started chewing. Sara, who was obsessively devoted to cleanliness and afraid of germs, was horrified. After drinks and dinner with the Murphys and Philip and Ellen Barry, Scott sank to his knees and sobbed to Gerald, "Don't go! Don't leave me here!" Gerald was not amused. "This is not Princeton," he told Scott, "and I'm not your roommate." But the Murphys did not exile Scott and Zelda permanently, as they might have done. In effect, they played indulgent parents to the Fitzgeralds' troubled and misbehaving adolescents.

Why did Fitzgerald behave so badly around the Murphys? Liquor was almost always involved, but there was more to it than drunken theatrics. To begin with, Scott had a severe crush on both Sara and Gerald. As privileged members of an Eastern establishment, they had the kind of assurance he could only yearn for. Sara spoke in a voice "full of money," like Daisy Buchanan's in *Gatsby*, and with a disarming frankness born of absolute confidence. Scott was "sentimentally disturbed by her," Gerald believed, and like a young child was given to demanding, "Sara, look at me." In every social situation, Gerald instinctively understood how to act, how to put others at ease. The word for it was "charm," and at his best Scott could rival Gerald in his capacity to charm other people, mainly women. But he did not like himself when he was expending so much energy simply to please others. Often he would destroy the illusion with an insulting act or remark—and next day, on awaking, try desperately to right the wrong.

If he regarded Gerald Murphy with a measure of hero worship, Fitzgerald also felt compelled to make his hero pay for it. Scott could hardly help resenting Gerald's impeccable manners and air of confidence. There may also have been a certain visceral animosity at work, deriving from Gerald's somewhat effeminate manner and dress. "Are you what they call a fop?" Fitzgerald demanded of the beautifully attired Murphy. No, Gerald replied, refusing to rise to the bait, "dandy" was more like it. He cared about clothes, but was not a slave to fashion.

The Murphys met Hemingway in the fall of 1925, and were immediately captivated by him. Sara "loved very male animals," and with his rugged physicality and intense manner Ernest certainly qualified. His was "an enveloping personality," Gerald observed. Ernest talked so rapidly and passionately that Gerald found himself agreeing with everything he said. Before long the Murphys became enthusiastic admirers of Hemingway's writing. Gerald was impressed by Ernest's devotion to his art, and his determination to strip away ornament and use simple and natural language. It was the same kind of thing Gerald was after in his painting.

In March 1926 the Murphys and John Dos Passos joined the Hemingways in Austria for the skiing. A beginner, Gerald spent two days practicing, then climbed up the mountain in order to ski down. It was an exciting descent, the second half of it through a forest. Dos came down on his back side, tearing a sizable hole in his pants. Ernest, an accomplished skier, waited patiently as Gerald negotiated around the trees, falling a couple of times. Was he frightened? Ernest wanted to know when they got to the bottom. Gerald admitted he had been. Good, Ernest said. He knew what courage was: it was "grace under pressure." Gerald felt elated, as if he'd passed a difficult test. Together they made plans for the summer. The Hemingways must come to the Riviera. The Fitzgeralds would be there, and the MacLeishes, and the Barrys. All were on hand for the party at the Juan-les-Pins casino the night of May 28.

When the Murphys gave a party, they wanted everything to be perfect. To celebrate Ernest Hemingway's arrival, they ordered the best champagne as always and arranged for caviar to be flown in from the Caspian Sea. Gerald, the master of the revels, wandered among his guests, introducing some, starting a conversation with others, making everyone feel clever and bright. Sara was lovely in a long flowing dress, looking as Scott Fitzgerald said more like a "Viking madonna" than one of the short-skirted bobbed-hair flappers in his stories. All eyes were on the handsome Hemingway, tanned from his month at the bullfights in Spain. Hadley hung on every word her husband uttered, while his lover Pauline smiled and nodded at his other elbow. Sara too was drawn by Ernest's magnetism. It was too much for Fitzgerald, who had been drinking in advance of the party. The Murphys were *his* friends, and he had virtually launched Hemingway single-handed. Why was everyone else making such a fuss about Ernest?

While Zelda pointedly ignored him, Scott embarked on a campaign of misbehavior. He stared rudely at a young girl sitting with an older man at a nearby table. He sailed ashtrays from the casino terrace. He draped a throw rug over his shoulders and crawled among the guests, sorrowfully wailing "Sara's being mean to me." He seemed determined to make a fool of himself and ruin the evening, nor would he stop when Gerald remonstrated with him. The very idea of a champagne-and-caviar party was ridiculous, Scott told his host. It got so ugly that Gerald left his own party in disgust.

Either that same evening or on another occasion when the Murphys, Fitzgeralds, Hemingways, and MacLeishes were all assembled, Scott launched into a series of highly personal interrogations of Sara and Gerald. By way of protest Sara wrote him an exasperated letter, demanding that he cease and desist his practice of "analysis & sub-analysis, and criticism." Perhaps he was asking invasive questions for the novel he was working on, but he was old enough to know that you "*Can't have Theories about friends.*" She and Gerald could not be bothered with such "sophomoric situations." They were really very simple people, she insisted. And they were "*literally & actually* fond" of both Scott and Zelda, with no dark subtexts involved.

Fond though they may have been, the Murphys did not regard Fitzgerald in the same hallowed light with which they gazed on Hemingway. Ernest seemed the more dedicated and serious artist, one who was trying for a revolutionary new prose style. Fitzgerald they could not help thinking of as rather frivolous by comparison. Just look at he way he behaved! They were never to know of the invaluable operation that Fitzgerald, as sober and seasoned professional, was about to perform on Hemingway's first novel.

MAKING THE *SUN* RISE

> Nowadays when almost everyone is a genius, at least
> for awhile, the temptation for the bogus to profit is no
> greater than the temptation for the good man to relax....
> This should frighten all of us into a lust for anything
> honest that people have to say about our work.
>
> —F. SCOTT FITZGERALD to ERNEST HEMINGWAY,
> critique of *The Sun Also Rises*, May-June 1926

Nothing Fitzgerald did for Hemingway during their 1925-1926 period of closest friendship was as important as his editing job on *The Sun Also Rises*. In *A Moveable Feast*, Hemingway gives the impression that Fitzgerald had no influence whatsoever on that novel. "That fall of 1925 he was upset because I would not show him the manuscript of the first draft of *The Sun Also Rises*. I explained to him that it would mean nothing until I had gone over it and rewritten it and that I did not want to discuss it or show it to anyone first... Scott did not see it until after the completed rewritten and cut manuscript had been sent to Scribner's at the end of April. I remembered joking with him about it and him being worried and anxious to help as always once a thing was done. But I did not want his help while I was rewriting." This passage is accurate but culpably incomplete. As with many of Hemingway's stories, full understanding of what happened is dependent on The Thing Left Out. "Big Two-Hearted River" only makes entire sense, for instance, if we know or intuit that Nick's nerves have been frazzled in the war. In this case, however, Hemingway was less interested in communicating the truth indirectly than in cannily concealing it. The crucial information omitted in *A Moveable Feast* is that once Fitzgerald did see the manuscript of the novel, he made suggestions that led to its radical improvement.

Hemingway did rewrite *The Sun Also Rises* over the fall and winter of 1925-1926 without showing his work-in-progress to Fitzgerald. They had already discussed the novel by that time, however. "What happened to me is supposed to be funny," Jake Barnes comments in a manuscript reference to his war injury. "Scott Fitzgerald told me once it couldn't be treated except as a humorous subject." Moreover, in a draft foreword to the novel, Hemingway issued a slur against Fitzgerald. The passage recounts the anecdote about Gertrude Stein and the garage owner who told her about "the lost generation," those who had fought in the war. Then it proceeds to differentiate Hemingway's serious attitude toward that generation from that of Fitzgerald in his stories about young people defying the mores of their parents. "This is not a question of what kind of mothers will flappers make or where is bobbed hair leading us," Hemingway wrote. This was probably a slighting reference to Fitzgerald's syndicated articles on such subjects.

In fact, Hemingway was eager to have Fitzgerald's reaction before making final revisions to *The Sun Also Rises*. Around April 20, 1926 he wrote Fitzgerald that the novel was "all done" and ready to ship to Scribner's. He was considering dedicating it

TO MY SON
John Hadley Nicanor
This collection of Instructive Anecdotes

"I'm hoping to hell you'll like it," Ernest went on. "You'll see it in August. [At that time, the Hemingways planned to spend most of the spring and summer in Spain and to join the Fitzgeralds, Murphys, et al. on the Riviera in August. With the advent of Bumby's whooping cough and his and Hadley's stay at Juan-les-Pins, the timetable for seeing Fitzgerald was moved up to late May-early June.] I think may be it is pretty interesting. Later—you wont like it." Clearly, Hemingway hoped that his work would please Fitzgerald, and clearly he felt some uncertainty about that. Subsequently in the same letter, Hemingway repeated that he would have a carbon of *Sun* at Antibes "and w'd welcome your advising me or anything about it. Nobody's read any amount of it yet." The letter closed with a set-piece designed to kid Fitzgerald about both *Gatsby* and the novel he had begun about matricide, a first inchoate draft of what was to become *Tender Is the Night* eight years later.

> The hero, like Gatsby, is a Lake Superior Salmon Fisherman. (There are no salmon in Lake Superior). The action all takes place in Newport, R.I. and the heroine is a girl named Sophie Irene Loeb who kills her mother. The scene in which Sophie gives birth to twins in the death house at Sing Sing where she is waiting to be electrocuted for the murder of the father and sister of her, as then, unborn children I got from Dreiser but practically everything else in the book is either my own or yours. I know you'll be glad to see it. The Sun Also Rises comes from Sophie's statement as she is strapped into the chair as the current mounts.

In reply Fitzgerald took exception to Hemingway's remark about Lake Superior salmon. In *The Great Gatsby* he had described young James Gatz as "a clam-digger and a salmon-fisher" on the shores of Lake Superior. Hemingway, who was an expert fisherman, corrected him on that point, but Fitzgerald argued that the *Encyclopaedia Britannica* did in fact refer to salmon—or at least "salmon trout"—in the lake. Hemingway wouldn't buy that argument. "There are a hell of a lot more salmon in Encyclopaedia Brit. than in Lake Superior," he wrote Fitzgerald about May 20. By then, Hadley and Bumby were in Juan-les-Pins with the Fitzgeralds, where Hemingway would be joining them. He would bring along a carbon of *The Sun Also Rises*, and "you can read it" there, he told Fitzgerald. Fitzgerald had recommended that he drop the part of the dedication about "instructive anecdotes." The book was "obviously *not* a collection of instructive anecdotes," Hemingway agreed, "and...such a hell of a sad story...and the only instruction is how people go to hell." It was not a book for a child to read, but he still intended to dedicate it to Bumby "for reasons that will be obvious when you read the book and also for another reason." The only "obvious" reason that comes to mind is that Bumby—John Hadley *Nicanor* Hemingway—was named, in part, after a bullfighter. The "other reason" undoubtedly had to do with Ernest's desire to make amends for his impending separation and divorce from Bumby's mother.

When he mailed this letter to Fitzgerald, Hemingway still had not heard what Max Perkins thought of his manuscript. By May 28, that word had come through, and it was favorable. Perkins praised the vitality of Hemingway's book. "No one could conceive of a book with more life in it," he commented. The scenes read like actual experience, and covered "an extraordinary range of experience and emotion; all brought together in the most skillful manner...to form a complete design." He could not express his admiration too strongly, Perkins concluded. In fact Perkins did have serious objections. At the in-house editorial conference, he pushed for the book on the grounds that Scribner's would suffer if the word got around among younger writers that they had rejected *The Sun Also Rises*. But "[w]e took it with misgivings," he noted for the record, and he communicated those misgivings to Fitzgerald in a letter of May 29. This letter did not reach Juan-les-Pins until after Hemingway arrived there from Madrid, and after Fitzgerald had read the script of *The Sun Also Rises* and suggested substantial changes at the beginning of the novel.

Hemingway was pleased that Perkins liked his manuscript, but wanted Fitzgerald's opinion as well. So, the morning after Fitzgerald wrecked the Murphys' party, Hemingway delivered the carbon copy of *Sun* to the Villa St. Louis, where the Fitzgeralds were domiciled, and awaited his friend's verdict. Fitzgerald read the script at once—as Hemingway's sponsor with Scribner's he had a considerable investment in the novel's success—and was appalled at the beginning. As it stood, the first chapter of *Sun* presented biographical data about Lady Brett Ashley and Mike Campbell in a chatty, almost flippant manner.

> This is a novel about a lady. Her name is Lady Ashley and when the story begins she is living in Paris and it is Spring. That should be a good setting for a romantic but highly moral story. As everyone knows, Spring in Paris is a very happy and romantic time. Autumn in Paris, although very beautiful, might give a note of sadness or melancholy that we shall try to keep out of this story.

So read the first paragraph, followed by background on Brett's two previous marriages, her beauty and her sitting as a subject for portrait painters, her alliance with Mike, his bankruptcy, and their drinking habits.

In the second chapter of the novel as then conceived, Jake Barnes abruptly and self-consciously intervened to introduce himself as narrator:

> So my name is Jacob Barnes and I am writing this story, not as I believe is usual in these cases, from a desire for confession, because being a Roman Catholic I am spared that Protestant urge to literary production, nor to set things all out the way they happened for the good of some future generation, nor any other of the usual highly moral urges, but because I believe it is a good story.

Jake then went on to describe his job with the Continental Press Association and his cynical opinions about Montparnasse and its inhabitants. The latter subject led him to mention Robert Cohn, "one of the non-Nordic heroes of this book" who had spent two years in the Quarter. Next came an extended anecdote about Cohn's friend Braddocks (Ford Madox Ford) supposedly "cutting" Hilaire Belloc and boasting about it, though in fact the man he snubbed was not Belloc at all. (Eventually, this story was resurrected for *A Moveable Feast*.) The chapter ended with Jake's confession that he never felt the same about Braddocks after this incident, and that he would avoid putting him into the story entirely "except that he was a great friend of Robert Cohn, and Cohn is the hero." After that false lead, the manuscript launched into the passage about Cohn as middleweight boxing champion of Princeton that actually starts the published novel.

Fitzgerald moved cautiously in expressing his objections to this beginning. He was seeing Hemingway daily, and before committing anything to writing warned him that he had certain comments to make. Then he wrote a ten-page handwritten letter that spelled out his complaints. This letter alternates sections of severe and quite possibly hurtful criticism with apologies and reassurances designed to soften the blows. Fitzgerald wanted Hemingway to revise his manuscript, but he did not want to lose his friendship into the bargain.

He began with a rationale for his criticism. Good writers, particularly, owed it to themselves to listen to honest suggestions about their work. In constructing his own novels, Fitzgerald added, he had received and acted on excellent advice from a number of people, including Edmund Wilson, Max Perkins, and his old friend Katherine Tighe, who had probably never even read a novel before making important suggestions about *This Side of Paradise*. Fitzgerald as veteran professional was offering the benefit of his experience to Hemingway as neophyte novelist. *I've listened to others with profit; now you should listen to me.*

With that preliminary out of the way, Fitzgerald got to the point. "Anyhow I think parts of *Sun Also* are careless + ineffectual." To some extent the difficulty was the same one he had isolated in "Fifty Grand": a "tendency to envelope or...to *embalm* in mere wordiness an anecdote or joke." To ameliorate the point, Fitzgerald called attention to a somewhat similar fault of his own—his desire to preserve passages of "fine writing." *Don't feel bad: I make mistakes too.*

The first chapter of the *Sun* manuscript gave an impression of "condescending *casualness*," Fitzgerald observed. "I think there are about 24 sneers, superiorities, and nose-thumbings-at-nothing that mar the whole narrative...." Through the snide commentary of Jake Barnes, Hemingway was writing in much the same wise guy voice that characterized his feature articles for the *Toronto Star Weekly* and *The Torrents of Spring*. "The most obvious mark of the wise guy," as Delmore Schwartz observed in his essay on Hemingway, "is his sense of humor which expresses his scorn and his sense of independence; he exercises it as one of the best ways of controlling a situation and of demonstrating his superiority to all situations." The tone was all wrong, and did not match that of the more maturely ironic Jake who told the rest of the story as narrator. In particular, Fitzgerald detected snobbishness in the account of Brett's past and the effect of the war on her lovers and husbands. He also disliked the background material on her and on Mike. "That biography from you," he chided Hemingway, "who always believed in the superiority (the preferability) of the *imagined* to the *seen not to say to the merely recounted*." In other words, Hemingway had been content to tell without showing, and it didn't matter at all that what he told— about Brett's history—was factually drawn from the experience of her model, Lady Duff Twysden.

In his critique, Fitzgerald commingled sharp rebukes with occasional praise. The passage beginning "So my name is Jacob Barnes" was maladroit; the material about Montparnasse and "the Quarter" was in all the guidebooks; the anecdote about Braddocks was "flat as hell"—the whole beginning was undermined by Hemingway's "elephantine facetiousness." On the other hand, "remember that this is a new departure for you, and I think your stuff is great." And on the other hand also, "I've decided not to pick at anything else [after the first few chapters], because I wasn't at all inspired to pick when reading it. I was much too excited. Besides this is probably a heavy dose. The novel's damn good." *Take these pills—I know they are hard to swallow but they're good for you, and here's some syrup to wash them down with.*

Fitzgerald made his most telling point near the end of his letter. "Apropos of your foreward about the Latin quarter—suppose you had begun your stories with phrases like: 'Spain is a peculiar place—ect' or 'Michigan is interesting to two classes—the fisherman + the drummer.'" In reviewing *In Our Time*, Fitzgerald had marveled at the total absence of exposition. But in writing his novel, Hemingway was guilty of letting merely expository prose take the place of dramatized action. This was true of the introduction of Robert Cohn as well, Fitzgerald thought. In his judgment, the book didn't get going until the start of Chapter III (in the published novel), when Jake picks up Georgette, takes her to the *bal musette*, and Brett appears. But Fitzgerald did not suggest wholesale amputation of the beginning. The section he discussed most thoroughly, up to and including the two brief chapters on Cohn, ran to some 7,500 words, he estimated. He recommended that Hemingway cut them back to about 5,000 words, doing so not "by mere pareing" but by eliminating "the worst of the *scenes*."

Fitzgerald either walked this letter from the Villa St. Louis to the Villa Paquita he was paying for, or Hemingway came to call for it. Reading it over must have been painful, but Hemingway was too much the craftsman to dismiss Fitzgerald's suggestions out of pique. Instead, he took them to heart, talked them over with Fitzgerald, and decided on a drastic remedy. He would not change the beginning chapters, as had been advised, but he would go one step further. Rather than paring them down *or* removing the worst scenes in those chapters—the Braddocks episode, for example—he decided to cut them entirely.

This decision he communicated to Max Perkins in a letter of June 5, accompanied by assurances that Fitzgerald 1) approved of the novel as a whole, and 2) concurred with him about lopping off the beginning. Fitzgerald's opinion, he understood, would count heavily with Perkins. "I was very glad to get your letter and hear that you liked The Sun a.r.," Hemingway began. "*Scott claims to too*" (my italics throughout). Then, after some directions about where to send mail, he revealed his plan. "I believe that, in the proofs, I will start the book at what is now page 16 in the Mss. ["Robert Cohn was once middleweight boxing champion of Princeton"]. There is nothing in those first sixteen pages [about 3,500 words] that does not come out, or is explained, or re-stated in the rest of the book—or is unnecessary to state. I think it will move much faster from the start that way. *Scott agrees with me*. He suggested various things in it to cut out—in those first chapters—which I have never liked—but I think it is better to just lop that off *and he agrees*. He will probably write you what he thinks about it—the book in general. He said he was very excited about it."

That's Ernest on the right (!) with taller "twinned" sister Marcelline, June 1901. Mother Grace captioned it "two summer girls with their peonies." (*Photo courtesy the Hemingway Collection at the John F. Kennedy Library*)

The Hemingways in idealized family portrait, 1903: Ursula, Ernest, and Marcelline with their parents. (*Photo courtesy the Hemingway Collection at the John F. Kennedy Library*)

Up in Michigan with fishing rod, July 1904. (*Photo courtesy the Hemingway Collection at the John F. Kennedy Library*)

Hadley and Ernest Hemingway on their wedding day, September 3, 1921. (*Photo courtesy the Hemingway Collection at the John F. Kennedy Library*)

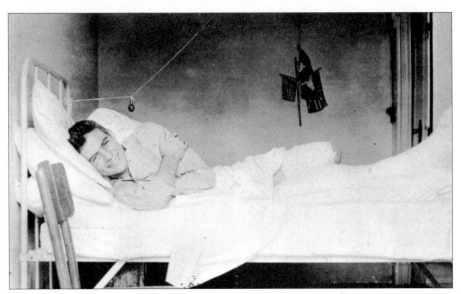

Ernest Hemingway in the Red Cross hospital, Milan, Italy, late summer 1918. (*Photo courtesy the Hemingway Collection at the John F. Kennedy Library*)

Agnes von Kurowsky in her nurse's uniform, Milan, summer 1918. (*Photo courtesy the Hemingway Collection at the John F. Kennedy Library*)

Ernest Hemingway, fall 1918. (*Photo courtesy the Hemingway Collection at the John F. Kennedy Library*)

The injury-prone Hemingway with the scar left when the skylight in his Paris apartment crashed down on him, March 1928. (*Photo courtesy the Hemingway Collection at the John F. Kennedy Library*)

October 1931. Ernest inscribed this photograph "To Scott from his old bedfellow Richard Hallibarton." Hallibarton was a Princetonian who wrote books about his romantic travel adventures. He was widely thought to be gay. (*Photo courtesy the Hemingway Collection at the John F. Kennedy Library*)

Hemingway in beret (with unidentified companion) at the front. Spanish Civil War, 1937. (*Photo courtesy the Hemingway Collection at the John F. Kennedy Library*)

Hemingway in Africa with kudu and oryx horns, winter 1934. (*Photo courtesy the Hemingway Collection at the John F. Kennedy Library*)

The day's drinking has commenced—Ernest with Lauren Bacall in Spain, summer 1959. (*Photo courtesy the Hemingway Collection at the John F. Kennedy Library*)

The magisterial Gertrude Stein—she served as mentor to Hemingway, admired Fitzgerald, and compared their differing "flames." (*Photo courtesy of Corbis/ Bettmann*)

Critic Edmund Wilson, stern and demanding: Fitzgerald's "intellectual conscience" and an early discoverer of Hemingway. (*Photo courtesy of Corbis/Bettmann*)

Maxwell Perkins, an editor who cared about his authors and a go-between throughout the friendship of Scott and Ernest. (*Private Collection*)

Novelist Morley Callaghan—he knocked Hemingway down when Fitzgerald let the round go long, summer of 1929. (*Photo courtesy of Archive Photos*)

In this letter to Perkins, Hemingway acknowledges Fitzgerald's assistance while downplaying its importance. He presents himself as having initiated the revision: it is *"Scott agrees with me"* throughout, not *"I agree with Scott."* Then he invokes Fitzgerald's authority once more before closing. Perkins had objected to the mention of "Henry James's bicycle" in the novel, a reference to a childhood accident that supposedly left James impotent. There were other things in the manuscript Perkins was wary about, but he did not want to bombard Hemingway with them in his initial letter praising the novel. The reference to James's supposed incapacity was too much, however. Though deceased, Henry James had been one of Scribner's most distinguished authors, and there were still people at the publishing firm who knew and admired him. It would be best to eliminate the passage, Perkins wrote Hemingway. Characteristically, Hemingway disagreed. James was "as dead as he will ever be," he pointed out, and had left no descendants to be hurt. No insult was intended. Bill Gorton mentioned him as he would any other historical figure. Besides, *"Scott said he saw nothing off-color about it."*

During the next few months, Fitzgerald acted as referee while Perkins and Hemingway sparred over other changes. In his long letter to Fitzgerald of May 29, Perkins paid tribute to Hemingway's skill but confided his reservations both about the subject matter —Jake Barnes's emasculating injury and Brett Ashley's promiscuity—and about the use of "many words seldom if ever used before in print." "When you think of Hemingway's book you recall scenes as if they were memories...and you recall people as hard & actual as real ones... the mss. wriggles with vitality. The art is marvelously concealed, & yet the whole is composed to the last word. — Yet the book is not an unmixed pleasure because it is almost unpublishable." Perkins regarded the "principle" characters with a jaundiced eye. They are "such people as I suppose you know in Paris," he rather sniffily wrote. "They belong to 'a lost generation.' Several including the girl are what are now called 'disintegrated personalities,' I suppose." Moreover, the romantic situation between the leading characters was complicated by the shocking fact "that he (who tells the tale) has been so wounded that he can not sexually play the part of a man!" Yet he found the book "never erotic,...in a true sense...always clean & healthy." The language posed a serious problem, though. The passage about Henry James simply had to come out. Then there were those dirty words.

In answering Perkins, Fitzgerald acknowledged that he too had certain qualifications about *The Sun Also Rises*. In particular, he thought Hemingway had bitten off more than he could chew in "the mutilated man." And the lady he didn't like, perhaps because he "didn't like the original." Still, he acted as Hemingway's advocate when it came to possible further revision. "Do ask him for the absolute minimum of necessary changes, Max," he counseled their editor. "[H]e's so discouraged about the previous reception of his work by publishers and magazine editors" from whom he'd received a lot of words but "scarcely a single dollar." Some weeks later, Fitzgerald came to Hemingway's defense again. The only censorable passage he found in Ernest's book was the conversation about the bulls' balls. He didn't think "the James thing" objectionable but then it seemed to him that James had been dead for fifty years. (Actually, only a decade had passed since James's death in 1916.)

Perkins thanked Fitzgerald for his opinion, which he valued because he thought of him as "rather strict in that regard." Meanwhile, however, he was waging a campaign to persuade Hemingway to make alterations. By and large, Perkins was a hands-off editor, where Fitzgerald and Hemingway were concerned. When Perkins heard about cutting the first 3,500 words, for example, he wrote Hemingway that he rather liked the original beginning himself, for it delivered the kind of information many readers expected of the conventional novel, but he did not insist on the point: "...[Y]ou write like yourself only, and I shall not attempt criticism. I couldn't with confidence." On the other hand, Perkins *was* vigilant about preserving a measure of propriety in his authors' work, and about avoiding legal difficulties. In order to win Hemingway over, he warned him about "the danger of trouble from referring to real people in a way to reflect upon them, and the danger of suppression." Libel was a possibility, and so was outright censorship. It would be a shame, Perkins pointed out, if so fine a book "should be disregarded because of the howls of a lot of cheap, prurient, moronic yappers." On these grounds Hemingway capitulated. Henry James became Henry, Hilaire Belloc was eliminated, novelist Joseph Hergesheimer's name was changed to Hoffenheimer, and Roger Prescott—too close to the original Glenway Wescott—was altered to Robert Prentiss. In addition, the bulls were unfitted "for a reproductive function" and the dirty word that rhymed with "Irony and Pity" was deleted.

With that issue resolved, Hemingway wrote Fitzgerald around September 7, 1926, offhandedly thanking him for his "sterling attitude on the censorship question. All France is proud of you." Then he signed off on the novel with an implicit recognition of Fitzgerald's editorial advice. "I cut The Sun to start with Cohn—cut all that first part. Made a number of minor cuts and did quite a lot of re-writing and tightening up. Cut and in the proof it read like a good book. Christ knows I want to write them a hell of a lot better but it seemed to move along and to be pretty sound and solid. I hope to hell you'll like it," he concluded, "and I think maybe you will,"

Even after *The Sun Also Rises* was published, Perkins proposed that Hemingway write a foreword summarizing some of what had been omitted in the sixteen pages he and Fitzgerald had decided to cut. He realized that this material had not been written in the same "method" as the rest of the novel. In a brief prologue, he thought, Hemingway "could tell some of the things about Brett which were in the first galleys and did not altogether come out in the narrative." What troubled him, and other readers, was that her scandalous behavior was not adequately prepared for, whereas the discarded beginning created a certain sympathy for her through an account of her troubled past. Hemingway said no. The "Brett biography" contained "some very good dope" on her, but any introduction would break the unity of the book. Besides, Brett was a real person, her story was a real story, and since he'd "protected" James and Belloc and Hergesheimer he might as well protect her too by leaving out the details of her background.

Late in December, Fitzgerald wrote Hemingway how pleased he was with the good press *The Sun Also Rises* was getting. "By the way," he added, "I liked it in print even better than in manuscript." In a note written during the 1930s, Fitzgerald genially poked fun at both his first novel and Hemingway's:

> *This Side of Paradise*: A Romance and a Reading List.
> *The Sun Also Rises*: A Romance and a Guide Book.

But he never sought credit for the excision that markedly improved *Sun*. In a July 1936 letter to John O'Hara, he went so far as to invent a yarn that effectively minimized his role. "[T]he only effect I ever had on Ernest was to get him in a receptive mood and say let's cut everything that goes before this. Then the pieces got mislaid and he could never find the part that I said to cut out. And so he published it without that and later we agreed it was a very wise cut. This is not literally true and I don't want it established as part of the Ernest legend," he concluded, "but it's just about as far as one writer can go in helping another." Fitzgerald had gone a long way to help Hemingway at the beginning of his career. He was willing to go even further, once Ernest's star had risen, to avoid alienating him.

— ✳ —

The End of Something

> God, how much I've learned in these two and a half years in
> Europe. It seems like a decade and I feel pretty old but I wouldn't
> have missed it, even its most unpleasant and painful aspects.
> —F. Scott Fitzgerald to Maxwell Perkins,
> c. August 10, 1926

Scott Fitzgerald and Ernest Hemingway did not have many opportunities to see each other during 1926. Except for his brief trip to New York, the long sojourn to Spain, and two quick visits to the Riviera, Hemingway was in Paris throughout the year. The Fitzgeralds, on the other hand, spent very little time there after the lease on their apartment ran out in December 1925. It was just as well, Ernest wrote, for he believed that Scott would "be a damned sight better off on the Riviera...Paris is poisonous for you." From May to mid-December 1926, Juan-les-Pins was the Fitzgeralds' home base, with a side trip to Paris in June for Zelda to undergo an appendectomy (or, so maintained her writer-friend Sara Mayfield from Montgomery, an abortion). During that visit, the Hemingways were in Spain, but Fitzgerald did run into Michael Arlen. Fitzgerald characteristically celebrated Hemingway's virtues with the British writer. When Arlen declined to share his enthusiasm, the inebriated Fitzgerald accused him of being finished as a writer and jealous of "a coming first-rater." Back on the Riviera, he again sprang to Hemingway's defense when Zelda described *The Sun Also Rises* as full of "bullfighting, bullslinging, and bullshit." She could say anything she pleased, Scott told her, "but lay off Ernest."

Throughout 1926 Fitzgerald was struggling with his novel-in-progress, which by midsummer he was calling *The World's Fair*. In May he reported to Harold Ober that the book was "about one-fourth done" and predicted that it would be finished by the end of the year. That report, like many others he was to make during succeeding years about the progress of *Tender Is the Night*, turned out to be wildly over-optimistic. He completed only four chapters—of a projected twelve—before he sailed back to the States in December. Not much else was getting written, either. He published no stories at all between June 1926 and May 1927. There were a number of reasons for Fitzgerald's lack of productivity during this period. His drinking led the list, but at least part of the dry spell derived from Scott's wholehearted involvement with Ernest's career. Fitzgerald invested much of the psychic energy that might otherwise have gone into his own work in assuring the success of his friend. He was a fan, a devotee, and in the manner of enthusiasts everywhere felt a thrill of exultation when his man Hemingway came through.

The letter of early September 1926 in which Hemingway said he'd cut the novel "to start with Cohn" was full of news. Among other things, it referred to an overture from Fitzgerald's agent Harold Ober, then of the Paul Reynolds agency. The possibility of Ernest's being represented by Scott's agents, now that they had the same book publisher, appealed to Fitzgerald. When Perkins shuttled "Fifty Grand" to Ober in mid-1926, it was apparently done with Fitzgerald's blessing. "Hope you have good luck with Hemmingways work," he wrote Ober in July. " I think he's got a great future." Ober agreed. Though they hadn't been able to place "Fifty Grand," he thought it was "an extremely good and realistic story...I wish we could see something else of his. He certainly has a lot of ability." Ober encouraged Fitzgerald to act as go-between in sounding out Hemingway. "Is he abroad now and do you see him once in a while?" Fitzgerald, at Juan-les-Pins, forwarded Ober's letter to Hemingway in Paris, along with the information that he was "working like hell" and expected to sail for New York from Genoa December 10.

Hemingway did not sign with Ober, perhaps because he finally sold a story on his own to *Scribner's* magazine. The way for a fiction writer to make money, Fitzgerald had told him, was to sell his stuff to high-paying magazines. After the fiasco over "Fifty Grand," Hemingway had his doubts about that, and these were exacerbated when *Scribner's* rejected his grisly "An Alpine Idyll." Hemingway tried again with "The Killers," without much hope. He only sent it, he told Fitzgerald, "to see what the alibi would be" when it was turned down. So he was happily surprised to receive a wire from Perkins in late August accepting "The Killers" for $200. *Scribner's* was a far cry from the *Saturday Evening Post*, where Fitzgerald was commanding $3,000 per story, but it was a start. "Ernest of little faith," his mentor Fitzgerald wrote him, "I hope the sale of 'The Killers' will teach you to send every story either to Scribners or an agent."

As his career swung upward, Hemingway's private life descended into chaos. He and Hadley separated when they came back to Paris in midsummer. Ernest was in love with Pauline, and intended to marry her. The Murphys supported him in this decision. From the first they had been drawn to Pauline, who in her stylishness was much more their sort than the comparatively dowdy Hadley. Hadley was kind and generous and loyal, but in the eyes of Sara and Gerald not the right wife for Ernest. When Ernest's resolve threatened to weaken in the fall of 1926, they advised him to hold firm for divorce. They loved him and had faith in him, Sara wrote. "Bless you & don't ever budge." Gerald put the case more strongly. "Your heart will never be at peace to live, work and enjoy," he told Ernest, "unless you clean up and cut through."

To test the seriousness of the lovers' commitment to each other, Hadley imposed—and Ernest and Pauline accepted—the unusual stipulation that they were to remain apart for one hundred days. At the end of that time, if they still wanted her to, she would divorce Ernest. As a consequence, Pauline returned to the States for the fall months while Ernest remained alone in Paris, racked with guilt. "Our life is all gone to hell which seems to be the one thing you can count on a good life to do," he wrote Fitzgerald. "Needless to say Hadley has been grand and everything has been completely my fault in every way. That's the truth, not a polite gesture." The good news was that he was thinking of bicycling down to Marseille in October and living there for a month or so. That way, he could ride over to Juan-les-Pins and see Fitzgerald.

Were he and Hadley "permanently busted up?" Fitzgerald wrote back. "Anyhow I'm sorry everything's in such a mess and I do want to see you if you come to Marseille in October." In this letter, probably written in mid-September, Fitzgerald began with a rather labored scatalogical parody of the interchapters to *In Our Time*, in an obvious attempt to respond in kind to the satirical forays in Hemingway's correspondence:

> We were in a back-house in Juan-les-Pins. Bill had lost control of his sphincter muscles. There were wet MaFins in the rack beside the door. There were wet Eclaireurs de Nice in the rack over his head. When the King of Bulgaria came in, Bill was just firing a burst that struck the old limeshit twenty feet down with a splat-tap. All the rest came just like that. The King of Bulgaria began to whirl round and round.
>
> "The great thing in these affairs—" he said.
>
> Soon he was whirling faster and faster. Then he was dead.

This passage, written in an irreverent, foul-of-mouth tone that was uncongenial to Fitzgerald, was obviously intended to amuse Hemingway. Before ending the letter, Fitzgerald offered another example of his desire to serve. "Remember," he wrote, "if I can give you any financial help let me know."

With no ready source of income on hand, Hemingway's monetary outlook was dim. He could hardly count on Hadley's trust fund any more. And in his letter to Hadley of November 18, 1926, he promised her all the royalties from *The*

Sun Also Rises. "I would never have written any of them In Our Time, Torrents or The Sun if I had not married you and had your loyal and self-sacrificing and always stimulating and loving—and actual cash support." But she wasn't to worry about his suffering from lack of funds. "I know that I can borrow from Scott, Archie [MacLeish], or the Murphies—all of whom are wealthy people— or that I could accept money from Pauline." The Murphys had already been generous to him. When Ernest and Hadley separated in August, they gave up their apartment on Notre-Dame-des-Champs, and Gerald Murphy turned over his studio with its thirty-foot-high whitewashed walls as a rent-free location where Hemingway could live and work. Fitzgerald apparently did not lend Hemingway money at this time—he did so both before and after the marital crisis—but it was a subject both men touched on in their correspondence.

On the bright side, *The Sun Also Rises* was eliciting extremely favorable reviews. Conrad Aiken in the *New York Herald-Tribune* found Hemingway's dialogue "brilliant," better than anyone else was doing. "Every sentence that he writes is fresh and alive," Burton Rascoe commented in the *New York Sun*. Hemingway's "lean, hard" prose put more conventional English to shame, the *New York Times* observed. A number of reviews detected the influence of other authors on Hemingway. The *Times* saw signs of Ring Lardner and Ford Madox Ford in his work. Aiken thought Hemingway had learned from Sherwood Anderson, F. Scott Fizgerald's *Gatsby*, and Gertrude Stein. Both *Time* magazine and Rascoe commented that Brett Ashley seemed to be modeled on Michael Arlen's Iris March, in *The Green Hat*.

These reviews, and the sales of his novel, were much on Hemingway's mind when he wrote Fitzgerald at Thanksgiving. Career prospects were brightening. *The Sun Also Rises* had gone into a second printing, but what did that "mean in numbers?" he inquired of his more experienced friend. Two publishers had made offers for the British rights. *College Humor* had written asking for essays or stories, short and long. As for the reviews, Hemingway observed in his customary mocking fashion, "the boys seem divided as to who or whom I copied the most from you or Michael Arlen." It seemed "a little premature" to be grateful to Arlen. But he was certainly grateful to Fitzgerald, and was asking Scribner's to insert a subtitle in everything after the eighth printing, reading:

THE SUN ALSO RISES (LIKE YOUR COCK IF YOU HAVE ONE)
A greater Gatsby
(Written with the friendship of F. Scott Fitzgerald
(Prophet of THE JAZZ AGE)

He'd tried to get down to the Riviera to see Fitzgerald before he sailed home, Hemingway wrote. The bad weather made biking impossible, and he couldn't afford the train fare, so he'd been looking for a ride from someone with a car and that hadn't worked out. "God I wish I could see you. You are the only guy in or out of Europe I can say as much for (or against) but I certainly would like to see you." He was beginning to feel less depressed about the divorce. "Have refrained from any half turnings on of the gas or slitting of the wrists with sterilized safety razor blades." But he was strapped for funds, having turned over "all existing finances" to Hadley. "Have been eating one meal a day and if I get tired enough sleeping—working like hell lately—find starting life poorer than any time since I was 14 with an earning capacity of what stories I sell to Scribners very interesting." The only thing he'd ever been decent about was money, and he was "very splendid and punctilious about that."

Fitzgerald was sensitive to the appeal implicit in those remarks. A few days before he left Juan-les-Pins for Genoa, he wrote Hemingway with the hope that everything was going better for him.

> If there is anything you need done here as in America—anything about your work, or money, or human help under any head— remember you can always call on
>
> > Your devoted friend
> > Scott

On board the *Conte Biancamano*, Fitzgerald lamented the unhappy news about Ernest and Hadley's divorce. "I'm sorry for you and for Hadley and for Bumby and I hope some way you'll all be content and things will not seem so hard." He was sorry, too, that Hemingway had not come to Marseille for a reunion. Now he was returning to the States with his novel still unfinished and "with less health and not much more money" than when he came in the spring of 1924.

But his European sojourn had one major consolation, for if Fitzgerald had not come across the ocean they might never have met. "I can't tell you how much your friendship has meant to me during this year and a half," he told Hemingway. "[I]t is the brightest thing in our trip to Europe for me." What's more, "I will try to look out for your interests with Scribners in America, but I gather that the need of that is past now and that soon you'll be financially more than on your feet." Fitzgerald was right about that. Soon Hemingway's star would shine more brightly than his own in the literary firmament. Fitzgerald continued to serve as Hemingway's benefactor in a number of ways during the years ahead, but after December 1926 their friendship was never the same again. One problem was the debt that was owed: Hemingway could ill abide being beholden to anyone. Then, too, they saw each other only rarely. Usually an ocean intervened, and so did the demon of rivalry.

— ✳ —

THE CASE OF HAROLD STEARNS

You've got to be careful who you do favors for —
—F. SCOTT FITZGERALD to ERNEST HEMINGWAY,
December 28, 1928

Both Scott and Ernest could have learned something from the example of Fitzgerald's unwarranted generosity to Harold Stearns. Born in 1891, Stearns was a journalist who published several books during his twenties and thirties. The best known of these was *Civilization in the United States* (1922), an ambitiously titled collection of essays Stearns edited, covering such wide-ranging topics as religion, education, politics, and the arts. For the most part, the contributors to this volume found American institutions badly in need of reform. Stearns felt the same way, so there was a certain logic in his expatriation to France. Once there, however, his career drifted away in a haze of alcoholism. He became a fixture at the cafés of Montparnasse, where he cadged loans from the unwary.

Stearns's name first crops up in Hemingway's *Selected Letters* in a May 1924 communication to Gertrude Stein. Stearns was acting as Paris agent for Horace Liveright, and in that capacity had let Hemingway know that Liveright was turning down Stein's *The Making of Americans*. At that time Hemingway was Stein's admiring friend and pupil, and in his letter he commiserated with her. It was "a rotten shame," but there were other publishers, he would "keep on plugging" for her, and sooner or later she was sure to find one. As for Stearns, his employment by Liveright was of brief duration. In January 1925, Hemingway wrote Stein, Stearns was rumored to be incarcerated for debt in Houston, Texas. He was back in Paris by the fall, frequenting his old haunts and circulating hardluck stories to likely lenders.

Fitzgerald, a soft touch, met Stearns there and undertook to help him out.

Stearns's story that season was that Sinclair Lewis was conducting a vendetta against him, and as a consequence he could not get his articles and essays published in the United States. Fitzgerald was inclined to believe this yarn, though he did take the step of asking Alexander Woollcott, back in New York, to check it out. Stearns had come to him with the claim "that he could *get no answer of any kind*" from the pieces he sent "the [New York] *World* or *The New Yorker*, stuff that was to some extent solicited." Stearns was so "down and out," Fitzgerald reported, that he'd had to pawn his typewriter in Deauville. It was "terribly sad to see a man of his age and intelligence going to pieces" because of "a sort of universal blackball." Could Woollcott check around the *World* office to see if there was any material written by Stearns "lying unused and unpaid for"?

Whatever the reply, Fitzgerald was not deterred from giving Stearns $50. "How did your plan of having Harold Stearns make good in two weeks—after all these years—turn out?" Hemingway, who was anything but gullible about such matters, asked Fitzgerald on December 15, 1925. Hemingway next sent Fitzgerald $400 to repay a loan. "You can keep it yourself or give it to Harold Stearns," he added. Then he warned Fitzgerald about the hopelessness of this lost cause. "I'm sorry as hell for H[arold] S[tearns]," he wrote, "but there's nothing anybody can do for him...except give him money and you've done that and naturally can't asume the continuance of it as an obligation." Panhandling was "no damned fun," he added. "A gent who's drinking himself to death ought not to be constantly having to raise the funds to do it with." Stearns had a good head once, but it was "completely coated with fuzz" now. Personally Hemingway liked Stearns, but he was beyond help. Fitzgerald had done his part for the poor old bastard. "Just don't give him any more dough."

Stearns's impecuniousness and debilitated physical condition figured in two May 1926 letters from Hemingway to Fitzgerald. "I have just given 200,000 francs to save the franc," he announced in one of them. "Harold Stearns is giving the same amount." Then from Madrid Hemingway wrote that the bullfights had been called off because the bulls were too small and sick. "[I]t was a collection of animals Harold Stearns could have killed while drunk with a jack knife." Most notably, Hemingway wrote Stearns into *The Sun Also Rises*. In the original beginning of the novel, he appears under his own name as a habitué of "the Quarter." That was one of the things Fitzgerald thought should be cut, and it was. Thinly disguised as Harvey Stone, however, Stearns does figure in the early Paris scenes of the published novel.

Jake Barnes first encounters Stone sitting outside, alone, at the Café Select in Montparnasse. As usual, Stone has been drinking. "He had a pile of saucers in front of him, and he needed a shave." Stone allows that he hasn't had anything to eat for five days, and Jake—who had lost two hundred francs to him at poker dice three days before—nonetheless responds to this implicit appeal for funds. He gives a hundred francs to Stone, who predictably uses the money for drink and not for food. "When I get like this I don't care whether I eat or not," Stone explains. He's "like a cat" at such times, Stone says, he just wants to be alone. When Robert Cohn comes to their table, Stone openly insults him. "Hello, Robert," he says. "I was just telling Jake here that you're a moron." Cohn responds with a threat—"Some day somebody will push your face in"—but Stone insists that it wouldn't matter to him if somebody did. This scene immediately precedes the series of insults visited upon Cohn by his abandoned lady-love, Frances Clyne, a spectacle to which Jake is an unwilling witness. "Why did [Cohn] sit there?" Jake thinks. "Why did he keep on taking it like that?" To avoid the embarrassment of seeing Cohn savaged, Jake excuses himself. He has to go see Harvey Stone, he says.

At this point, Harvey Stone vanishes from the book, except as a topic of conversation between Jake and Bill Gorton during their hilarious evening together. Bill has been going on wonderfully about the decorative appeal of stuffed dogs ("Certainly brighten up your flat") when he shifts gears. Bill is like the bartender at the Crillon, he maintains: "Never been daunted. Never been daunted in pub-lic...If I begin to feel daunted I'll go off by myself. I'm like a cat that way."

"When did you see Harvey Stone?" Jake wants to know, and sure enough, Bill has just had a drink with Harvey at the Crillon. "Harvey was just a little daunt-ed. Hadn't eaten for three days. Doesn't eat any more. Just goes off like a cat."

Mindful of the caution issued by Hemingway and illustrated in *The Sun Also Rises*, Fitzgerald did nothing more for Harold Stearns until the fall of 1928. The Fitzgeralds spent five months in Paris that year, and shortly before returning to the United States Scott encountered Stearns. "[F]eeling drunk and Christlike," Fitzgerald made a proposal. If Stearns would write an article on "Why I go on being poor in Paris" in the shape of an informal letter addressed to him, he would try to sell it. Stearns turned out the piece, and Fitzgerald sent it to Maxwell Perkins, who bought it for $100. Fitzgerald assumed that Stearns would be delighted. As he wrote Perkins, the "poor bastard" hasn't seen "that much money since I gave him $50 in '25." That should have been a happy ending, but no. According to Fitzgerald's account in a December 28 letter to Hemingway, Stearns wrote him objecting that $100 "isn't very much (as a matter of fact, it isn't much of a letter either) and exhibits such general dissatisfaction that I think he thinks I held out on him...within a year you'll probably hear a story that what started him on his downward path was my conscienceless theft of his royalties."

This incident should have taught Fitzgerald a valuable lesson. Yet when he wrote Ernest that "[y]ou've got to be careful who you do favors for," Scott apparently was thinking only of Stearns and not going beyond the particulars of his case. Specifically, he does not seem to have grasped that those we do the most for rarely exhibit appropriate gratitude, and that often, as in the case of Hemingway himself, they come to resent our ministrations on their behalf. Hemingway, for his part, might have gathered that Fitzgerald's magnanimity toward Stearns was not entirely disinterested, that "Christlike" acts derived at least in part from a compulsion to orchestrate other people's lives. That may have been what Hemingway had in mind when he wrote Arthur Mizener in 1950 that his benefactor Fitzgerald was "generous without being kind."

CHAPTER 4

OCEANS APART

Friendship is like money, easier made than kept.
—SAMUEL BUTLER

The Fitzgeralds had been back in the States only a short time when United Artists hired Scott to write an original flapper screenplay. The script Scott produced, called *Lipstick*, was never filmed, but the month that he and Zelda spent in Hollywood had lasting repercussions. Scott became infatuated with the young actress Lois Moran, who was then not quite eighteen to his thirty. Zelda was naturally distressed, especially after her husband explained that he admired Lois because *she* had done something with her talent through hard work and discipline. In reaction, Zelda burned some of her clothes in a hotel bathtub and threw the platinum wristwatch Scott had given her in 1920 out the window of the train carrying them back east. Once they had settled into Ellerslie, the mansion they had rented on the Delaware River outside Wilmington, she began taking ballet lessons three times a week.

Scott and Ernest had been out of touch during his Hollywood trip, which was as Fitzgerald expressed it the "Goddamndest experience" he'd had for seven years. On his return, however, he resumed his campaign to advance Hemingway's career. During a lunch in Baltimore, he attempted to repair the rift between Hemingway and the influential H.L. Mencken. As editor of the *American Mercury*, Mencken had dismissed the sketches of *in our time* as "[t]he sort of brave, bold stuff that all atheistic young newspaper reporters write." In retaliation, Hemingway dedicated *The Torrents of Spring* jointly to "H.L. MENCKEN AND S. STANWOOD MENCKEN IN ADMIRATION," knowing full well that S. Stanwood Menken (as his name was spelled) was precisely the kind of self-righteous reformer H.L. Mencken detested. He also gave his character Bill Gorton a sarcastic line about Mencken in *The Sun Also Rises*. So there were bad feelings between the two, at least on Hemingway's part. Fitzgerald's job was to persuade Mencken, who was "just starting reading" *Sun*, that his friend Hemingway was a great writer, and to convince Hemingway that Mencken was "thoroughly interested and utterly incapable of malice." As a first practical step in that direction, he got Mencken to say he would pay $250 for anything of Hemingway's he could use in his magazine. "So there's another market" (in addition to *Scribner's*), Scott wrote Ernest in March 1927.

"Isn't it fine about Mencken," Hemingway responded. Fitzgerald's efforts were of limited financial usefulness, as it turned out, for he never published any of his work in the *American Mercury*. Fitzgerald's next agenting overture was only slightly more beneficial. On March 27 he cabled Hemingway that "VANITY FAIR OFFERS TWO HUNDRED DEFINITELY FOR ARTICLE WHY SPANIARDS ARE SWELL OR THAT IDEA." Hemingway replied that as a matter of principle he made it a rule not to write anything to order, but in this case Fitzgerald had cooked up a subject he could write about without "jacking off." In fact, he'd written something the day before, and planned to fix it up and send it along. This piece did not run in *Vanity Fair*, but may have seen the light of day as "The Real Spaniard," in the October 1927 issue of a little-known magazine called *Boulevardier*.

Hemingway's March 31 letter discussing the Spanish article idea was one of the longest and warmest he ever sent to Fitzgerald. While Scott was in Hollywood, Ernest asked Max Perkins for news of him in three separate communications. Obviously, he missed Scott, and after a long silence between them had a great deal of information to pass along.

In the area of literary gossip, Hemingway reported that Harold Loeb (the model for Robert Cohn in *The Sun Also Rises*) was threatening to shoot him, but had not shown up to do so when Ernest sent word about the times he would be sitting unarmed in front of Lipp's brasserie. Then there was a terrible dinner at writer Louis Bromfield's, where "they had a lot of vin ordinaire and cats kept jumping on the table and running off with what little fish there was and then shitting on the floor." On the personal front, most of the news was good. He'd seen Bumby in Switzerland, and it was amicably agreed upon that he could see him regularly. Hadley was happy and "very much in love." Pauline had finally returned from America, and since Ernest had been in love with *her* for a long time it certainly was "fine to see something of her."

In addition, Hemingway emphasized his penury, as usual. The *Atlantic* had taken "Fifty Grand," but had been "too gentlemanly to mention money." He himself had been broke for a couple of months, but happily at the moment that "coincide[d] with Lent." He had been living in Gerald Murphy's studio for months, which was "a hell of a lot better than under, say, the bridges."

At both the beginning and end of his letter, Hemingway emphasized how much the friendship with Fitzgerald meant to him. "And you are my devoted friend too," Ernest began, taking a cue from the phrase Scott used in signing off his letter about Mencken. No one worked harder or did more for him, and "oh shit I'd get maudlin about how damned swell you are. My god how I'd like to see you." At the end Hemingway came back to the same theme. The Murphys had been wonderful to him during the trials of the divorce, and so had the MacLeishes. "If you don't mind, though," he told Fitzgerald, "you are the best damn friend I have. And not just—oh hell—I can't write this but I feel very strongly on the subject."

Fitzgerald sent Hemingway $100 by return mail. The *Atlantic* would pay about $200 for "Fifty Grand," he figured. (Actually, it was $250.) Besides, Scribner's ought to advance him whatever he needed for *Men Without Women*, the book of short stories scheduled for fall publication. As with *The Sun Also Rises*, Perkins called on Fitzgerald for advice in connection with this book. The problem had to do with "Up in Michigan," Hemingway's hard-edged story of seduction that had been cut from *In Our Time* by Boni and Liveright. Ernest wanted to include it in *Men Without Women*, but Perkins had reservations. What did Scott think?

"One line *at least* is pornographic," Fitzgerald advised Perkins, adding that he did not want his name used in any discussion of the matter with Hemingway. He did not see how the story could be amended. What good was a seduction story with the seduction left out? He suggested that Perkins explain to Hemingway that while such an incident might be overlooked in a book, "a story centering around it *points* it." It did not seem to him possible—at the moment, in the United States—that "Up in Michigan" with its physiological details could be published. If that were the case, twenty publishers would be "scrambling for James Joyce tomorrow."

Before the October 14 publication of *Men Without Women*, Max Perkins went down to Ellerslie for a weekend with the Fitzgeralds. The grand old house was solid and high and yellow, with columns front and back, second-story verandas, and a lawn running down to the Delaware. But the atmosphere of the mansion had not as Perkins hoped succeeded in transforming the Fitzgeralds' style of life to one of patrician gentility, with Zelda "a stately lady of the manor" and the drinking confined to "port by candle light, accompanied by walnuts." Instead, Scott was something of a nervous wreck. He needed a month of hard exercise and nothing else, Max thought. He also needed to cut down on smoking and drinking.

Men Without Women, containing half a dozen of Hemingway's finest stories, came out in October. The volume elicited a letter from MacLeish praising its radical reduction of rhetoric: "Ten things 'said' for every word written. Full of sound like a coiled shell. Overtones like the bells at Chartres. All that stuff you can't describe but only do—& only you can do it." Fitzgerald, too, weighed in with favorable commentary. Without mentioning his correspondence with Perkins on the subject, he told Ernest how glad he was that he had left out "Up in Michigan." It belonged to "an earlier and almost exhausted vein," Scott thought. Zelda's favorite story was "Hills Like White Elephants," his own—leaving aside "The Killers"—was "Now I Lay Me." He was also enchanted by the opening words of "In Another Country": "In the fall the war was always there but we did not go to it any more." Fitzgerald sent Mencken a copy of the book, asking him to "please read" it. Hemingway was "really a great writer, since Anderson's collapse the best we have I think."

The reviews were less than Ernest might have hoped for. He was particularly upset by Virginia Woolf's "An Essay in Criticism" and F.P.A.'s (Franklin P. Adams's) parody in his newspaper column. Even Perkins found Woolf's review/essay in the *New York Herald-Tribune* "enraging," because 1) it came out a week in advance of the publication date, and 2) Woolf spent so much of her time "talking about the function of criticism instead of functioning as a critic." Hemingway would have preferred that she not function as a critic at all, for Woolf had little good to say about *The Sun Also Rises* and even less about *Men Without Women*. "Common objects like beer bottles and journalists figure largely in the foreground" of Hemingway's novel, she drily observed. As for his stories, she was surprised that work "so competent, so efficient, and so bare of superfluity" did not make "a deeper dent." The stories were too neatly tied together, too dependent on dialogue, "a little dry and sterile." Furious, Hemingway wrote Perkins that Woolf belonged to "a group of Bloomsbury people" who lived "for their Literary Reputations" and figured the best way to preserve them was to "slur off or impute [impugn] the honesty of anyone coming up."

"Thousands will send you this clipping," Fitzgerald observed as he mailed Hemingway a copy of Adams's parody, based on the tough talk of the hit men in "The Killers." The piece was well meant, he assured Ernest, who could not have disagreed more. He was especially annoyed about a comment by Adams about his "swashbuckling affectations of style," and in a foul mood about the reviews generally. Burton Rascoe in the *Bookman* had reviewed the book without bothering to read it, he maintained. The reviewer in the *New York Times* "missed that lovely little wanton Lady Ashley." Then there was the Woolf. He could count on getting at least *two* thousand copies of "any review saying the stuff is a pile of shit," he chided Fitzgerald. It was enough to make him want to quit publishing fiction "for the next 10 or 15 years."

Another book figured largely in the 1927 correspondence between Fitzgerald and Hemingway. This was Scott's phantom novel, which after one of the longest and most tortuous periods of procrastination in literary history was to emerge in 1934 as *Tender Is the Night*. Yet by early 1927, Fitzgerald was promising imminent delivery of his manuscript to his editor Perkins, his agent Ober, his friend Hemingway, and probably himself. "Book nearly done," he assured Ernest in March. Early in June, Scribner's sent him an advance "without a quiver" for the novel he was "now finishing." In September, Fitzgerald sent Perkins word that he was "hoping...to finish the novel by the middle of November." Perkins loyally supported Fitzgerald despite the repeated delays. Hemingway took a more cynical stance. In a September 15 letter to Perkins complaining about the meretriciousness of literary prizes generally, he proposed that they cook up a new one. "Couldn't we all chip in and get up say The New World Symphony Prize for 1927-8-9 and give it to, Scott's new novel as an incentive that he finish it?" Writing Fitzgerald the same day, Hemingway noted that he was about to produce "a swell novel" himself and added this caveat: "Will not talk about it on acct. the greater ease of talking about it than writing it and consequent danger of doing same."

In this letter Hemingway apologized for not thanking Fitzgerald for his $100 loan in April, and promised to pay it back as soon as *Men Without Women* came out. For the previous five months, he had been living like "the tightest man in the world," subsisting solely on Scott's $100 and $750 from Perkins, while turning down a $1,000 advance from Hearst magazines on a contract for ten stories—$1,000 apiece for the first five and $1,250 each for the second five.

In acknowledging repayment of the loan, Scott wrote that he hoped Ernest—now married to Pauline—was "comfortably off in [his] own ascetic way" and could not resist telling him that the *Saturday Evening Post* had upped his price to "32,000 bits per felony," or $4,000 per story. (This was incorrect: the *Post* was then paying him $3,500 for stories.) He was "almost through" with his novel, but had to do three stories for the *Post* to get his head above water. Hemingway had

113

been wise not to tie himself to *Hearst's* (for one-fourth of Scott's story price), for they had a reputation of feeding on their contracted writers like vultures.

Ernest found Scott's reports on his huge payments as the *Saturday Evening Post*'s "pet exhibit" somewhat annoying. A fragmentary note among Hemingway's papers describes how pleased he was, as a young writer, to receive letters from readers. "Scott Fitzgerald told me," the piece goes on, that "his price for stories was increased according to the number of letters a story brought in to the magazine that published it. Every five thousand letters it brought in they raised him a thousand dollars. He had three uniformed negroes who answered letters day and night and a white overseer picked out a few of the better letters and read them to Scott as he worked."

Fitzgerald was either insensitive to the effect such reports had on Hemingway, or, more likely, unable to refrain from what sounded very much like bragging. Charlie Wales in Fitzgerald's "Babylon Revisited" (1931) commits a similar kind of faux pas about money. But there was more than financial information in Scott's letter to Ernest of early December 1927. He also included, for example, a bawdy passage addressing the rumors that were beginning to circulate about Hemingway's rugged masculinity.

> Please write me at length about your adventures—I hear you were seen running through Portugal in used B.V.D.s, chewing ground glass and collecting material for a story about Boule players; that you were publicity man for Lindbergh; that you have finished a novel a hundred thousand words long consisting entirely of the word "balls" used in new groupings; that you have been naturalized a Spaniard, dress always in a wine-skin with a "zipper" vent and are engaged in bootlegging Spanish Fly between San Sebastian and Biarritz where your agents sprinkle it on the floor of the Casino. I hope I have been misinformed but, alas! it all has too true a ring...

Hemingway used the same tone in his mid-December reply, supplying a sharper edge to the comic effect by references to drugs, sex, and their children, and by sidelong digs at Fitzgerald's monetary extravagance. "Always glad to hear from a brother pederast," he began, introducing a new motif. He had "quit the writing game and gone into the pimping game" as more profitable. "Are you keeping little Scotty off the hop any better?" Ernest inquired. He understood that Scott had to keep up appearances, but nobody could convince him that heroin "really does a child of that age any good." On the bright side, word had reached him about how Scotty "jammed H.L. Mencken with her own little needle the last time he visited at the Mansions." For his part, Bumby had started making up stories. *Hearst's* "offered him 182,000 bits for a serial about Lesbians who were wounded in the war and it was so hard to have children that they all took to drink and running all over Europe and Asia, just a wanton crew of wastrels."

As for himself, he had given up the Spanish Fly game. There was no money in it. But hadn't he got Lindbergh "a nice lot of publicity?" Would Fitzgerald like him to do the same for Scottie or Zelda? Scott was right about the Spanish wine-skin outfit he was wearing, but "it had nothing so unhemanish as a zipper." He had to deny himself little comforts like that, as well as "toilet paper, semi-colons, and soles to my shoes." If he used any of those, people would "shout that old Hem is just a fairy after all"—again, a theme Fitzgerald had not touched upon.

A missive from Gstaad at Christmastime closed out the 1927 correspondence. Often subject to hypochondria, Hemingway could not have been feeling worse during the holidays in Switzerland. The weather was not cooperating, for it persistently refused to snow. But Ernest probably couldn't have skied anyway, beset as he was by temporary blindness (Bumby had inadvertently stuck a finger in his eye), piles, the flu, and a toothache. "Merry Christmas to all and to all a Happy New Year like this one wasn't," he commented sourly. But there was a friendly touch for Fitzgerald. "Wish the hell I could see you. Nobody to talk about writing or the literary situation with. Why the hell don't you write yr. novel?" He and Pauline would be coming to the States in March or April, Ernest added. That was precisely when Scott and Zelda were planning to go to Europe.

Hemingway suffered a further physical misfortune early in March when—at two in the morning—he sleepily pulled the wrong cord in the bathroom of his apartment and brought a decrepit skylight crashing down on his head. The blow poleaxed him, and left a deep gash on his forehead above his right eye. Ernest was losing a great deal of blood, and after trying to stanch the bleeding with toilet paper, Pauline telephoned Archie MacLeish for help. MacLeish rushed the giddy Hemingway to the hospital where nine stitches were needed to close the wound, leaving a scar that was noticeable for the rest of his life.

In a curious example of legend-building, journeyman writer Jed Kiley claimed that Hemingway's injury was no accident but instead an attempt at literary assassination by Fitzgerald! This story was circulated in the London *Times Literary Supplement* (*TLS*) of July 9, 1964, accompanied by some extremely unlikely dialogue. According to Kiley, he had this conversation with Fitzgerald.

"[Hemingway] is a great writer. If I didn't think so, I wouldn't have tried to kill him that time."

"Kill him?" [Kiley] said.

"Sure," Scott said. "I was the champ, and when I read his stuff I knew he had something. So I dropped a heavy glass skylight on his head at a drinking party. But you can't kill the guy. He's not human."

Upon reading this balderdash, MacLeish wrote the *TLS* an account of what actually happened, adding that Fitzgerald would have been incapable of talking in such clichés and more importantly, that he had always been Hemingway's generous supporter. Archie neglected to add in rebuttal that Scott was on the other side of the Atlantic when the skylight came down on Ernest's head.

The episode was symptomatic of two uncommon things about Ernest Hemingway: his susceptibility to physical injuries and his knack for getting himself talked about. Not yet thirty, Hemingway had become a famous person, and the wire services spread the news about his accident. From his base at Rapallo Ezra Pound sent Ernest a humorous question: "Haow the hellsufferin tomcats did you git drunk enough to fall upwards through the blithering skylight!!!!!!!" Writers everywhere were noticing his work, and starting to copy his trademark style. As Fitzgerald observed in reviewing the contents of Princeton's *Nassau Literary Magazine*, the March 1928 issue set a record among American magazines of the year by containing not a single imitation of Ernest Hemingway. "Gosh," Scott wrote Max Perkins, "hasn't [Ernest] gone over big?"

The reversal of roles between Fitzgerald and Hemingway was well underway by this time. Now it was Perkins and Hemingway in back-channel correspondence about Fitzgerald's troubles, and what might be done to right them. In a March 17, 1928, letter to Perkins, Ernest went out of his way to differentiate himself from Scott's procrastination. Progress on his own novel—which was to appear as *A Farewell to Arms* the following year—had been delayed, Hemingway admitted. But he had been laid up by his various ills. "[Y]ou see my whole life and head and everything had a hell of a time for a while and you come back slowly (and you must never let anyone know even that you were away or let the pack know you were wounded)," a parenthetical comment underlining his highly competitive nature. He was, he assured Max, working "*all* the time." It was nothing at all like Fitzgerald's situation. "[F]or his own good" Scott ought to have had his novel out a year or two years ago. He didn't want Max to think he was falling into that pattern of promising and not delivering, or of "alibi-ing" to himself.

Perkins had a chance to observe Fitzgerald in the flesh on April 6, when he and Scott had a long talk on the roof of the Plaza Hotel overlooking Central Park. Scott "has made no progress with his novel for a long time," Max reported, because of "always having to stop to write stories." Worse yet, he was obviously depressed. His nervous attacks—Fitzgerald called them the "Stoppies"—had ended, but the drinking had not. The night before Perkins saw him, in fact, Scott had been partying with Ring Lardner. All of this news Max passed on to Ernest, but neither of them knew about the degrading incident Scott memorialized in his *Ledger* as "Black Eyes in the Jungle." The Jungle was the Jungle Club, a speakeasy in New York. The black eyes were administered by a speakeasy bouncer when an obviously intoxicated Fitzgerald refused to leave without another drink. There would be other incidents like that in the months to follow.

When Perkins's letter about Scott reached Hemingway, he and Pauline were in Key West, checking out the environs as a possible future home site. It was a satisfyingly unliterary place. Nobody believed Ernest when he said he was a writer and "[t]hey haven't even heard of Scott." So Ernest wrote Max on April 21, the same date the Fitzgeralds sailed for Europe, interposing an ocean between them yet again. He offered to cable Scott's ship with a message of support and reassurance. As he saw it, Hemingway told Perkins, Scott was stalled by unrealistically high expectations. After Gilbert Seldes and others said such fine things about *The Great Gatsby*, Fitzgerald figured his next book had to be "a GREAT novel." This scared him, and so he built up "all sorts of defences like the need for making money with stories etc. all to avoid facing the thing through." Scott was really as prolific as a guinea hen but had "been bamboozled by the critics" into thinking he laid eggs like the ostrich or the elephant. Ernest's own novel was proceeding apace, and during the afternoons he was having a fine time "catching tarpon, barracuda, jack, red snappers, etc." in the waters of the Gulf Stream.

Perkins's next letter to Hemingway sounded more optimistic about Fitzgerald, who had called him in good spirits the day before he sailed. Without responding to Ernest's theory about critical overpraise, Max proposed that Scott's worst problems resulted from mismanaging money. "It is true," he wrote, "that Zelda, while very good for him in some ways, is incredibly extravagant." They ran their house in Delaware carelessly, and the servants were robbing them. If only they didn't throw money away, Scott could easily be in a position of independence.

In Paris, the Fitzgeralds settled into a Paris apartment on the rue Vaugirard for six months. Zelda became increasingly abosrbed in the ballet, taking lessons from the distinguished Madame Lubov Egorova, formerly of the Diaghilev troupe. Scott hoped that fresh European surroundings could spur him on to artistic achievement, as they had in the case of *Gatsby*. He wrote Perkins around July 21 that the novel "goes fine" and that those he'd read portions of it to "have been quite excited." He was encouraged when James Joyce announced at a dinner party that he expected to finish *his* novel "in three or four years more at the *latest*." And Joyce worked "11 hrs a day to [Scott's] intermittent 8." His own novel, Fitzgerald promised, would be finished "*sure* in September." Perkins passed on the good news to Hemingway.

It was not true. The change in location did no good. Fitzgerald was not working eight hours a day, or anything like it. And his marriage was coming apart. "You were constantly drunk," Zelda later wrote in accusation. "You didn't work and you were dragged home at night by taxi-drivers when you came home at all. You said it was my fault for dancing all day. What was I to do?" Scott's recollection was that in her passion for the ballet Zelda had retreated into herself just as he had four years earlier, when he was writing *The Great Gatsby* and "living in the book." She was indifferent to him and to Scottie, and paid no attention to the bad apartment or the bad servants. She refused to accompany him to Montmartre nightclubs, and—infuriatingly—did not even seem to mind when he brought home intoxicated undergraduates for meals. He began to go to the Closerie des Lilas alone, where he could recall the happy times he'd had there with Ernest and Hadley, Dorothy Parker and Robert Benchley. He also went to jail twice during that Parisian summer of "[d]rinking and general unpleasantness." Worst of all, "[t]he novel was like a dream, daily farther and farther away."

At midsummer Fitzgerald essayed another of his wisecracking letters to Hemingway. This time, he said, word had reached him that "Precious Papa, Bullfighter, Gourmand" had been seen bicycling through Kansas, "chewing & spitting a mixture of goat's meat & chicory which the natives collect & sell for artery-softener and market-glut." Rumor had it that Ernest was to "fight Jim Tully [a hobo writer] in Washdog Wisconsin on Decoration Day in a chastity belt with [his] hair cut a la garconne." As a fallen-away Catholic Fitzgerald scoffed at Hemingway's conversion that enabled him to marry Pauline Pfeiffer in the church: "Well, old Mackerel Snatcher, wolf a Wafer & a Beaker of blood for me." But he still had Hemingway's career in mind, imploring him to send a story to George Horace Lorimer, editor of the *Saturday Evening Post*, and acknowledging that he had read "Mencken's public apology"—a reference, apparently, to Mencken's largely favorable notice of *Men Without Women* in the *American Mercury*. In closing, Scott urged Ernest to "[p]lease come back" to Paris while he was still there.

Hemingway did not get around to answering this letter until early October. He had been busy finishing the first draft of *A Farewell to Arms* — "God I worked hard on that book" — and took the news of Fitzgerald's working eight hours a day with a healthy dose of salt. "Well Fitz you certainly are a worker. I have never been able to write longer than two hours myself...any longer than that and the stuff begins to become tripe but here is old Fitz whom I once knew working eight hours every day." What was his secret? Ernest wondered. He looked forward "with some eagerness to seeing the product."

Hemingway had also become a father for the second time, this time to a baby boy named Patrick who was built like a brick shithouse, laughed all the time, and slept through the night. He was thinking of hiring out his services as a progenitor of perfect children. Taking up the issue of his new-found faith, Ernest commented that as a prospective father "Mr. Hemingway has enjoyed success under all religions. Even with no religion at all Mr. Hemingway has not been found wanting." Where would Scott be located the end of October? "How's to get stewed together Fitz? How about a little mixed vomiting or should it be a 'stag' party."

Meanwhile Perkins and Hemingway had been continuing their periodic discussion of Fitzgerald. He'd heard a number of rumors about Scott, and wished "to Heaven he'd turn up," Max wrote Ernest September 17. Ernest replied with word that his old newspaper friend Guy Hickok had seen Fitzgerald in Paris "very white and equally sober." Ernest was "awfully anxious to see him," too, though not at all sure that Scott would be better off in the States than overseas. He'd written *Gatsby* in Europe, after all, and drank no more there than anywhere else. On October 2, Perkins announced that Fitzgerald had sailed for the States three days before. Max would let Ernest know "how Scott seems" as soon as he could. "Perhaps the news will be really good."

Perkins was still worried about the Fitzgeralds' extravagance, however, and for a solution he looked to Zelda. "[She] is so able and intelligent," he wrote Hemingway, "and isn't she also quite a strong person? that I'm surprised she doesn't face the situation better, and show some sense about spending money." Ernest was anything but surprised. Instead of regarding her as a possible good influence, he wrote Max on October 11, he held Zelda responsible for "90% of all the trouble" Scott had. Almost every bloody fool thing he had done was "directly or indirectly Zelda inspired." He thought Scott might have become "the best writer we've ever had or likely to have if he hadn't been married to some one that would make him waste *Everything*." Instead of writing the novels he had in him, Scott was pooping away his talent on *Saturday Evening Post* stories.

Ernest didn't blame Lorimer, he blamed Zelda, though he wouldn't for a moment want Scott to believe he thought so.

The following month, Hemingway and Fitzgerald finally saw each other again, after a two-year absence.

— ✳ —

"UNE SOIRÉE CHEZ MONSIEUR FITZ..."

...was the title Hemingway assigned to the tale of his November 17-18 weekend visit to "Ellerslie Mansion on the Delaware River—the ride from the...game— the French chauffeur and the rest of it." In an undated note among his papers, Ernest listed this Fitzgerald encounter as one among half a dozen "Stories to Write." While he was working on *A Moveable Feast* in the late 1950s, he managed to get the beginnings of the story down on paper.

This particular Fitzgerald-Hemingway reunion commenced on the morning of the Princeton-Yale game. Ernest and Pauline came to the campus from New York, accompanied by Henry (Mike) Strater, an artist who had been a friend of Fitzgerald's as a Princeton undergraduate and who later, in Paris, painted two excellent portraits of Hemingway. Scott and Zelda were already at Princeton, staying at the Cottage Club. The five of them were to go to the game at Palmer stadium, and then travel to Ellerslie for the evening festivities.

First, though, Scott and Ernest staged a morning mini-celebration of their own. By the time they arrived at the Godolphins'—Isabel, a childhood friend of Ernest's from Oak Park, had married Princeton professor Francis Godolphin—both were "a bit tight and very cheerful." The two companions struck Francis as "very harmonious, enjoying each other and having a hell of a fine time." Then they left for Cottage Club and the game, which Princeton won, 12-2. The result contributed to Fitzgerald's high spirits, but he maintained a reasonable level of sobriety during the game. The trouble, according to Hemingway's four-page typescript, began on the post-game train ride from Princeton Junction to Philadelphia.

Wandering the aisles of the train, Scott began asking indiscreet questions of absolute strangers. Several women were annoyed by him, but Ernest and Mike spoke to their escorts in order to "quiet any rising feeling" and maneuver Fitzgerald out of trouble. Spying a lone traveler reading a medical book, Scott took the book from him in courtly fashion, returned it with a low bow, and announced loudly, "Ernest, I have found a clap doctor!" When the insult was greeted by silence, Fitzgerald repeated it. "You are a clap doctor, aren't you?" he asked the man. And again, "A clap doctor. Physician, heal thyself." The poor medical student wanted no trouble, and so the Fitzgerald-Hemingway-Strater party got to Philadelphia "with no one having hit Scott."

There to meet them at the station was Philippe, a Parisian taxi driver and former boxer Scott had brought back with him from Paris as combination chauffeur, butler, and drinking companion. Philippe drove them the rest of the way in the Fitzgeralds' Buick. It was "a nightmare ride," for the Buick kept overheating and Scott would not let Philippe stop for oil or water. American cars didn't need oil, he insisted, only worthless French cars did. There was no arguing with him on this point, Philippe told Ernest, and Zelda was even more adamant. As they neared Ellersie, Scott and Zelda quarreled about where to turn off the main road. Zelda thought the turnoff was much further on and Scott insisted they had already passed it. Philippe eventually found the right road when both Fitzgeralds were napping, and the Buick limped home safely. The next morning when he drove Scottie to church, Philippe confided to Hemingway, he would take the car to a garage for service.

Hemingway's written recollection breaks off here, but from conversation and letters it is possible to summon up much of what happened next. Scott was obviously trying to impress Ernest with his surroundings and style of life. Ellerslie itself, with its rolling lawns and big trees, contributed to the effect. So did the six bottles of fine Burgundy Fitzgerald uncorked at dinner. But the false front fell away with the liquor and Fitzgerald's penchant for humiliation. If what Hemingway told A.E. Hotchner was accurate—and many things he told Hotchner were not—Scott began insulting the attractive black maid who was serving dinner. "Aren't you the best piece of tail I ever had?" he repeatedly asked her. "Tell Mr. Hemingway."

A minor crisis developed the next morning. Playing lord of the manor, Scott showed up in blazer and white flannels and demanded that the guests play croquet on his handsome lawns. Ernest, who took no interest in "forced games" and remembered Scott's missing the train from Paris to Lyon, became extremely anxious about getting to the station to catch the one Sunday train to Chicago. He need not have worried so much, judging from the bread-and-butter note he sent Scott the next day. "We had a wonderful time—you were both grand—I am sorry I made shall I say a nuisance of myself about getting to the train on time—We were there far too early." Ernest's letter went on to refer to some unexplained trouble with the police at the station, but that too, apparently, was not of much moment. "It was great to have you both here," Scott wrote back, "even when I was intermittently unconscious." Mike Strater refused to participate in such polite smoothing away of the weekend's rough spots. Three days later, he was only beginning to recover from the hangover. "A bullfight is sedative in comparison," he wrote Ernest. "...And [Scott] is such a nice guy when sober." The worst of it, Mike privately thought, came from the combustible chemistry between Scott and Ernest. "Those two...brought out the worst in each other."

Three weeks later, Ernest was riding another train with his son Bumby, en route from New York to Key West, when a telegram reached him with the news that his father had died. Caught short of cash in the emergency, Hemingway wired Perkins and as a backup telephoned Fitzgerald, who immediately responded by telegraphing $100 to the North Philadelphia station. Ernest left Bumby in the care of a Pullman porter for the rest of the trip to Key West and took the overnight special to Chicago.

"You were damned good and also bloody effective to get me that money," Ernest wrote Scott from Oak Park a few days later. The death, as he must have feared, was a suicide. "My Father shot himself as I suppose you may have read in the papers." The blow hit him hard, the more so because—as he wrote Perkins a week later—"my father is the one I cared about." His mother had thought him irresponsible, and Ernest was out to prove her wrong. He "handle[d] things" at the funeral, he told Max, and realized further that he had to buckle down and finish his book so that he could help out the family (the two youngest children were still in high school). There wasn't much money. His father had cashed in his insurance and invested the funds in Florida real estate, just as the land boom turned to bust.

As good as his word, Hemingway plunged ahead with *A Farewell to Arms* when he got down to Key West. The novel was finished by late January, but Hemingway told Perkins he couldn't have the book unless he came down to get it and went fishing with Ernest and his friend, the artist Waldo Peirce. Why don't you come along? Max proposed to Scott. Perkins was not at all persuaded by the Hemingway-Peirce theory that the sharks were more afraid of him than he was of them, and would feel safer with Scott on board. It was the first of several invitations for Fitzgerald to join Hemingway in male camaraderie and the pursuit of large creatures of the deep. Scott accepted none of them. He was no more an outdoorsman than Ernest was a croquet player.

CHAPTER 5

1929: BREAKING THE BONDS

> It is well, when judging a friend, to remember that he is
> judging you with the same godlike and superior impartiality.
> —ARNOLD BENNETT

During much of 1929—a year in which the Jazz Age and the stock market and a good many other things came crashing to earth—the Hemingways and Fitzgeralds were living in Paris, in the same neighborhood. They saw little of each other, for that was the way Ernest wanted it.

With *A Farewell to Arms* delivered to Perkins for serialization in *Scribner's* magazine and fall book publication, Hemingway sailed for France on April 5. "If you see Scott in Paris write me soon how he is," Max wired Ernest at the boat. As a friend Perkins worried about Fitzgerald's deteriorating condition, and as a publisher he had an understandable interest in the novel Scott had been promising since 1925.

Scott was already in Europe when Ernest embarked from New York. He and Zelda had crossed on the *Conte Biancamano* in March, landing in Genoa and working their way across the Riviera before going to Paris. As in 1924, the Fitzgeralds hoped that a change in scenery might alter the disturbing rhythm of their stateside lives. At Ellerslie Zelda became increasingly obsessive about the ballet, forever practicing before a mirror to "The March of the Toy Soldiers." She thought Philippe rude and insubordinate, and further trouble developed when Mademoiselle Delplangue—Scottie's nanny—fell for Philippe and became "hysterical" about it. When he wasn't drinking, Scott wandered around the property or worked on his Basil Duke Lee stories—anything to avoid the novel. One difficulty, as Perkins intuited, was that he had chosen the almost forbidden subject of matricide as the basis of his plot. *The Boy Who Killed His Mother* was the working title, with the protagonist a Hollywood cameraman bearing the unlikely name of Francis Melarkey.

In November 1928 Fitzgerald sent Perkins the first two chapters of this false start, which was after five more years to segue into something very different. "My God it's good to see those chapters lying in an envelope!" he said. They ran to 18,000 words, and constituted the first quarter of the book. He planned to send Max the rest of the novel in three additional two-chapter segments. Chapters 3 and 4 should be on their way in December.

The deadline came and went, and early in March Fitzgerald apologized to Perkins for "sneaking away like a thief without leaving the chapters." They could be straightened out with a week's work, he estimated, and he could complete them on the boat. Instead he wrote a story called "The Rough Crossing," in which the husband-and-wife principals—who resemble himself and Zelda— become involved in shipboard parties that lead to drunkenness and adultery.

Hearing that Fitzgerald was coming to Paris gave Hemingway "the horrors," he wrote Perkins. On no account was Max to give Scott his address. He and Pauline had found a quiet and comfortable apartment on the rue de Férou, and were afraid that Scott would misbehave and get them ejected. According to Ernest, Scott had already got him kicked out of one apartment the "[l]ast time he was in Paris": a reference, apparently, to the flat he and Hadley occupied on the rue Notre-Dame-des-Champs in 1926. Then too, he and Zelda were given to turning up intoxicated and banging on the door in the wee hours. "I am very fond of Scott," Ernest assured Perkins, but he was prepared to beat him up—"as a matter of fact I'm afraid I'd kill him"—before he'd let him get them "ousted" from their apartment. It had nothing to do with friendship, for that implied "obligations on both sides." The "both sides" phrase connoted a view of friendship as a competitive, if not adversarial relationship.

Despite Ernest's vigorous warnings, the Fitzgeralds and Hemingways did get together in Paris that spring. They could hardly have helped running into each other. The Fitzgeralds rented an apartment on the rue Palatine, only a block around the corner from the rue de Férou, and Scottie was taken to mass at St. Sulpice, the Hemingways' parish church. There was even a dinner at the Hemingways' apartment, where, Scott observed, the atmosphere was tainted by a "[c]ertain coldness." In a list of snubs, he recorded two from 1929: "Ernest apartment" and "Ernest taking me to that bum restaurant.

Change of station implied." The strain was evident in the artificial hilarity of a dinner invitation Scott sent Ernest in May: "Will you take salt with us on Sunday or Monday night? Would make great personal whoopee on receipt of favorable response."

Scott summarized that unhappy time in a personal history written after Zelda's mental collapse. They had been living in Delaware in a state of unhappiness and at a prohibitively expensive rate, he wrote, but upon leaving for Paris

> ...somehow I felt happier. Another spring—I would see Ernest whom I had launched, Gerald & Sara who through my agency had been able to try the movies [Fitzgerald introduced the Murphys to the director King Vidor]. At least life would [be] less drab; there would be parties with people who offered something, conversations with people with something to say....
>
> It worked out beautifully didn't it. Gerald and Sara didn't see us. Ernest and I met but it was a more irritable Ernest, apprehensively telling me his whereabouts lest I come in on them tight and endanger his lease. The discovery that half a dozen people were familiars there didn't help my self esteem.

A Farewell to Criticism

"I'm delighted about Ernest's novel," Fitzgerald wrote Perkins early in April, adding wryly that he himself would be "trying as usual to finish mine."

It was not until late May that Fitzgerald saw the typescript of *A Farewell to Arms*. The novel was then running as a six-part serial in *Scribner's* magazine, but changes could still be made before actual publication of the book. It is unclear whether Hemingway asked for editorial comments, or whether Fitzgerald volunteered them. Unlike the situation three years earlier, when he cut the beginning of *The Sun Also Rises* at Scott's behest, Ernest was neither pleased with the criticism his friend provided on *Farewell*, nor inclined to accept his judgments. He had progressed in his craft, after all, while Fitzgerald's creative engine had stalled. He no longer required Scott to find him a publisher or to intervene on his behalf with Max Perkins. For the most part, he was right to ignore Fitzgerald's suggestions.

If anything, Fitzgerald was even more severe in his comments about *Farewell* than he had been in discussing *Sun*. He attempted to soften the blows in two ways. First, in recommending alterations, he pointed to Hemingway's own previous work as the standard of excellence. Ernest wasn't really listening to his heroine Catherine Barkley in the same way he had to the women characters in "Cat in the Rain" or "Hills Like White Elephants," Scott argued. Nor did some of the scenes in Milan come up to the quality of the fishing trip in *The Sun Also Rises*, where introduction of the seemingly extraneous Englishman Wilson-Harris contributed "to the tautness of waiting for Brett." Second, Fitzgerald balanced his faultfinding with praise, especially near the end of his comments, finishing with the exclamatory "A beautiful book it is!"—an observation that elicited a hand-written "Kiss my ass" in the margin from Hemingway.

Fitzgerald suggested extensive cuts for *Farewell*, just as he had in connection with *Sun*. (He made no comments whatever about the first third of the book: Hemingway may have told him to ignore the beginning chapters.) Fitzgerald rec-ommended excisions, particularly, in the scenes that took place during the peri-od of Frederic Henry's recovery from his war wounds in Milan, and in scenes where he and Catherine conducted their most intimate conversations.

One of the Milan scenes Fitzgerald objected to involved Frederic's after-noon conversation with the two American singers trying to break into Italian opera and with the war hero Ettore Moretti. The passage was slow, Scott thought, and included too many characters and too much talk. "*Please* cut!" he pleaded with Hemingway. At the very least, he should reduce the "rather gassy" half-dozen pages to a brief and self-sufficient vignette.

There was "absolutely no psychological justification" for introducing those singers, Scott asserted. There was, however, a strong *structural* justification for bringing Simmons, one of those singers, onstage, inasmuch as it was to be Simmons that Frederic went to see—and to borrow civilian clothes from—when he made his escape to neutral Switzerland. Similarly, the apparently irrelevant Moretti plays an important *thematic* role in illustrating the consequences of the war. Nothing good could come of it. The only ones who stood to profit were boring and conceited killers who like Moretti bragged endlessly about their battlefield exploits. Ernest had summed up his own views on the subject in an October 1918 letter to his family from the hospital in Milan. "There are no heroes in this war... All the heroes are dead."

In proposing this excision, Fitzgerald was considering the scene in isola-tion instead of as part of the overall fabric of the novel. In his concentration on the trees, he did not see the forest. The same was true of the other seemingly unnecessary scene Scott recommended cutting: the day at San Siro (Chapter 20) that is ruined for Catherine and Frederic by the discovery that the horse races were fixed. "This is definitely *dull*," Scott wrote. If it were up to him, he'd cut it in half and move it to the beginning of the next chapter. Again, considered by itself the racetrack scene is not particularly effective. But when tied into *Farewell*'s pervasive theme of a corrupt world that confounds and defeats the individual, the fixed races convey an important message.

Significantly, the one cut Hemingway actually made among the half dozen proposed by Fitzgerald worked to maintain the novel's suspense. The passage consists of an extended rumination by Frederic in Chapter 40, the penultimate chapter, on the comparative risks of sacred and profane love. The contrast between these two kinds of love constitutes a major theme of the novel, first developed in the opening chapters, and so it made sense to deal with it again toward the end. But with a nudge from Fitzgerald, Hemingway decided against including this passage. It was too long, and it gave away what was going to happen at the end of the book. Here is the excised section, in part:

...They say the only way you can keep a thing is to lose it and this may be true but I do not admire it. The only thing I know is that if you love anything enough they take it away from you. This may all be done in infinite wisdom but whoever does it is not my friend. I am afraid of God at night but I would have admired him more if he would have stopped the war or never let it start... And if it is the Lord that giveth and the Lord that taketh away I do not admire him for taking Catherine away...

I see the wisdom of the priest at our mess who has always loved God and so is happy and I am sure that nothing will ever take God away from him. But how much is wisdom and how much is luck to be born that way? And what if you are not built that way? What if the things you love are perishable?...

The unfortunate disclosure here is that Catherine is about to die.

Among the characters in *A Farewell to Arms*, it was Catherine that Fitzgerald came down hardest on. He particularly disliked the scene in Chapter 21—Hemingway, in reading over this commentary, could hardly have avoided noticing that Fitzgerald was advocating overhaul of *three consecutive chapters* in a novel he had already written and revised to his own satisfaction—where Catherine hesitantly reveals and apologizes for her pregnancy. Many critics have found Hemingway's heroine impossibly noble and self-sacrificing in her desire to please her lover at whatever cost. Fitzgerald, as the first of these critics, counseled extensive deletions as a remedy.

"This could stand a good cutting," he observed about Chapter 21. "Sometimes these conversations with her take on a naive quality that wouldn't please you in anyone else's work. Have you read Noel Coward?" (Fitzgerald's endorsement of the urbane British playwright Coward, whose characters speak a witty café society dialogue, must have bothered Hemingway.) Then Scott went on versus Catherine. "Remember the brave illegitimate mother is an OLD SITUATION & has been exploited by all sorts of people you won't lower yourself to read." Under the circumstances, Ernest should make sure that "every line rings *new*." Scott was not through with his critique. "Catherine is too glib...In cutting their conversations cut some of her speeches rather than his." The trouble was that Ernest, in recalling his own wartime wounding and love affair, was still seeing the nurse through idealizing "nineteen yr. old eyes" while looking back on himself in a more sophisticated way. The contrast jarred: "either the [narrator] is a simple fellow or she's Eleanora Duse disguised as a Red Cross nurse."

Once again, Fitzgerald underestimated the secondary importance of one of Hemingway's scenes, this time for its revelation of character. In reluctantly confessing her condition and offering to take care of all arrangements on her own, Catherine is indeed almost incredibly accommodating—or would seem so were it not for her fragile emotional state, having lost another "boy" she loved to the war. But the scene is crucial in uncovering Frederic's lingering self-absorption and his unwillingness, at this stage, to commit himself fully to Catherine. Upon hearing her news, he says nothing to comfort or reassure her, and more or less forces her to continue talking: ergo, the relative silence that Fitzgerald would have remedied. And when she finally asks him if he feels trapped, Frederic responds with the callous comment that "You always feel trapped biologically"—as if he had impregnated any number of women and invariably felt "trapped" afterwards.

In his critique, Fitzgerald twice objected that the war kept receding from the foreground of the novel. The book became dull during the episodes in Milan, he thought, "because the war goes further & further out of sight every minute." The ending troubled him for the same reason. "Seems to me a last echo of the war very faint when Catherine is dying and he's drinking beer in the Cafe." When Ernest turned his attention directly to the war, as during the retreat from

Caporetto, the result was "marvellous." The scene of Frederic's arrest by the self-righteous battle police, and his dive into the Tagliamento to escape, was "the best in recent fiction," Scott thought. But he did not like the actual ending as it then stood—a roundup of what happened to various characters in the years since Catherine died, culminating in a valedictory paragraph:

> I could tell you what I have done since March, nineteen hundred and eighteen, when I walked that night in the rain back to the hotel where Catherine and I had lived and went upstairs to our room and undressed and slept finally, because I was so tired—to wake in the morning with the sun shining in the window; then suddenly to realize what had happened. I could tell you what has happened since then, but that is the end of the story.

Fitzgerald suggested instead that Hemingway finish with Frederic's eloquent soliloquy the night after he and Catherine are reunited in Stresa. The passage celebrates their love, which now had become strong enough to survive any shocks short of death. "Often a man wishes to be alone and a girl wishes to be alone too and if they love each other they are jealous of that in each other, but I can truly say we never felt that. We could feel alone when we were together, alone against the others." Then too, they loved each other at night just as they did during the day. "[T]he things of the night"—Frederic knew—"cannot be explained in the day, because they do not then exist, and the night can be a dreadful time for lonely people once their loneliness has started. But with Catherine there was almost no difference in the night except that it was an even better time." There follow the five sentences that Fitzgerald suggested might serve to conclude *A Farewell to Arms*: "If people bring so much courage to this world the world has to kill them to break them, so of course it kills them. The world breaks every one and afterward many are strong at the broken places. But those that will not break it kills. It kills the very good and the very gentle and the very brave impartially. If you are none of these you can be sure it will kill you too but there will be no special hurry." Upon reading this soliloquy for the first time, Fitzgerald wrote in the margin of the typescript, "This is one of the most beautiful pages in all English literature." In his letter to Hemingway, he called it "one of the best pages you've ever written."

Hemingway had a famously difficult time deciding how to end his novel. Depending on how you count them up, he tried somewhere between thirty-two and forty-one variant endings, including the one Fitzgerald proposed. What he finally settled upon was, of course, wonderful.

Early in his critique, after accusing Ernest of committing an uninteresting "sort of literary exercise" in the dialogue where Catherine discloses her fear of the rain, Scott added a parenthetical apology. "(Our poor old friendship probably won't survive this but there you are—better me than some nobody in the Literary Review that doesn't care about you and your future.)" Fitzgerald wanted to take the sting out of his comments: he was only doing this because he cared, because of their friendship. From Hemingway's point of view, however, that only made the criticism more painful. With a journeyman reviewer, he could work off his anger with a scornful wave of the hand—or at most with a satirical swipe of the pen, as he had the previous month in his "Valentine" poem for Lee Wilson Dodd, who had the effrontery to accuse him, in *Men Without Women*, of concentrating solely on "the short and simple annals of the hard-boiled."

Fitzgerald's comments could not be so easily disposed of. He was an established and talented writer. He had been Hemingway's sponsor, and was to remain his friend, at least in the near term. And besides, Ernest had not entirely ignored the proposed changes. He cut the long passage of Frederic's musings, he considered Scott's idea for the ending, and he first x'ed out the scene with the opera singers and Moretti before restoring it to the text. So Ernest let the wound to his ego fester for a time before unleashing his powers of invention to discredit Scott's critical overtures.

Fitzgerald reintroduced the topic of revisions to *Farewell* in a June 1, 1934, letter responding to Hemingway's harsh words about *Tender Is the Night*. "[T]he old charming frankness" of Ernest's remarks cleared the air between them, Scott said, and he went on to discuss various literary problems, including how to end a novel. "I remember that your first draft [of *Farewell*]—or at least the first one I saw—gave a sort of old-fashioned Alger book summary of the future lives of the characters: 'The priest became a priest under Fascism,' etc., and you may remember my suggestion to take a burst of eloquence from anywhere in the book that you could find it and tag off with that; you were against this idea beause you felt that the true line of a work of fiction was to take a reader up to a high emotional pitch but then let him down or ease him off. You gave no aesthetic reason for this —nevertheless, you convinced me." As a consequence, he made a "direct steal" from Hemingway and ended *Tender* with Dick Diver drifting off into obscurity.

This letter is noteworthy for its generosity of spirit and manifest unwillingness to offend. Fitzgerald tactfully forgets to remember, for instance, that he had proposed a specific passage for ending *Farewell* ["If people bring so much courage to this world..."], instead leaving such a choice to Hemingway's considered judgment. Even more tactfully he inverts the teacher-pupil status of their relationship. Now it is Scott who expresses his debt to Ernest for showing him how to end his novel, much as Ernest might have (if he could have) thanked Scott for fixing the beginning of *Sun*. Fitzgerald's letter also makes it clear that he and Hemingway talked about these issues in Paris, in June 1929.

One might think that Ernest's bruised ego could have healed in the interim between 1929 and 1934, or that Scott's ameliorative tone might have done the job. One would be wrong. Hemingway did not reply to Fitzgerald's June 1 letter, and instead began a campaign to discredit everything Scott had to say about *A Farewell to Arms*. "[Y]ou may remember," Scott had written, but Ernest chose to misremember the revisions Fitzgerald proposed through a pattern of exaggerations, lies, and outright inventions—the weapons that writers of fiction keep ready at hand to guard their territory.

The first salvo came in a December 1934 letter to Maxwell Perkins. "I will show you some time [Scott's] suggestions to me on how to improve the typescript of A Farewell to Arms which included writing in a flash where the hero reads about the victory of the U.S. Marines." *Invention.* "He also made many other suggestions none of which I used." *Falsehood.* "Some were funny, some were sad, all were well meant." *Patronizing slur.*

Forward to 1942, when Hemingway wrote his lawyer Maurice Speiser granting permission to Edmund Wilson to quote from any of the Fitzgerald's "non-libellous letters" about him in *The Crack-Up,* the 1945 collection of Fitzgerald essays, letters, and notes along with letters and appreciative essays and poems from others. Wilson had sent along a number of letters which referred to Hemingway, including the July 1936 one to John O'Hara where Fitzgerald carefully downplayed his contribution to *The Sun Also Rises* before going on to discuss the ending of *A Farewell to Arms*. Ernest was in doubt about how to end the book, Scott wrote, "and marketed around to half a dozen people for their advice." Fitzgerald "worked like hell" on the assignment, but only evolved a philosophy "utterly contrary" to Hemingway's. Later Ernest convinced him that he was right and so he ended *Tender Is the Night* "on a fade away instead of a staccato."

He had *not* "marketed around" to half a dozen people, Hemingway told Speiser. He had simply shown Fitzgerald the manuscript at his request, and subsequently been appalled by the "idiotic idea" for an ending he proposed: "Lieut. Henry to be sitting in a Cafe and pick up a paper and read that the U.S. Marines had just taken Belleau Wood!" *Invention, elaborated upon.* He "was obliged to reject this suggestion in forceful terms," Ernest wrote, "and Scott was upset about it for a long time." *Probable falsehood.*

Hemingway went on to disparage what he considered to be Fitzgerald's lack of artistic integrity, citing as evidence a conversation between the two writers during 1929, when they were at odds about *Farewell.* "He told me how he wrote a story to please himself and then changed it to sell it to the Saturday Evening Post. I told him if he kept that up he would make himself impotent as a writer and would finally kill himself." Hemingway instructed his lawyer to send his letter along to Wilson, and in a postscript asserted his fondness for Fitzgerald and his inside knowledge of the "real causes of his crack-up, which cannot yet be published."

As time wore on and the posthumous Fitzgerald revival got underway, Hemingway's comments on the critique of *Farewell* became progressively more demeaning. Forward to January 1951, Hemingway to Arthur Mizener following publication of his biography of Fitzgerald. "I have a letter in which [Scott] told me how to make A Farewell to Arms a successful book which included some fifty suggestions" *exaggeration* "including eliminating the officer shooting the sergeant" *invention* "and bringing in, actually and honest to God, the U.S. Marines (Lt. Henry reads of their success at Belleau Woods while in the Cafe when Catherine is dying) at the end." *Invention, further elaborated upon.* "It is one of the worst damned documents I have ever read and I would give it to no one." *A good thing, for it would contradict what he was saying.*

Forward to January 1953, Hemingway to Charles Poore, who was in the process of editing *The Hemingway Reader* for Scribner's. He did the final rewrite of *Farewell* in Paris, Hemingway wrote Poore, and he could be sure of that because he had Fitzgerald's long letter as evidence. "[H]e said I must *not* under any circumstances let Lt. Henry shoot the sergeant" *invention, reiterated* "and suggesting that after Catherine dies Frederic Henry should go to the cafe and pick up a paper and read that the Marines were holding at Chateau Thierry." *Invention, altered with respect to two details.* "This, Scott said, would make the American public understand the book better. He also did not like the scene in the old Hotel Cavour in Milano" *falsehood* "and wanted changes to be made in many other places 'to make it more acceptable.'" *False quotation.* "Not one suggestion made sense or was useful." *Falsehood.* "He never saw the [manuscript] until it was completed as published." *Partial truth.* "...I had learned not to show them to him a long time before." *Declaration of independence, after the fact.*

In his criticism of *A Farewell to Arms*, Fitzgerald warned Hemingway that the rough barracks language of the novel might well lead to censorship. "I think if you use the word cocksuckers here [during the retreat, in two places] the book will be suppressed & confiscated within two days of publication." This was a problem Perkins immediately anticipated upon reading the manuscript in Key West, early in February. "BOOK VERY FINE BUT DIFFICULT IN SPOTS" he wired New York. Later, in a letter to Charles Scribner (who held strict views about what should or should not be printed), he expanded on the point. "It is Hemingway's principle both in life and literature never to flinch from facts, and it is in that sense only, that the book is difficult. It isn't at all erotic, although love is represented as having a very large physical element." Perkins was playing the role of middleman here, trying to reassure his boss (Scribner) that the novel was publishable and to keep Hemingway from erupting in anger when he heard about the emendations that, Max knew, would have to be made.

The plot of the novel itself, involving a somewhat idealized love affair out of wedlock, was "salacious" enough to get *A Farewell to Arms* banned in Boston. More accurately, the second installment of the six-part serial version of the novel in *Scribner's* magazine was banned there by police chief Michael H. Crowley on June 20, 1929. The ruling banned distribution of the magazine by Boston bookstores and newsstands for the run of the serial over the next four months. It did not hurt overall circulation figures of the magazine, and undoubtedly stimulated sales of the book when it was published on September 27.

Still, the Boston censorship gave Perkins a certain amount of ammunition as he and Hemingway went to battle on the question of obscene language. The serial had substituted blank spaces for these words—separate instances of "fuck," "shit," and "balls" as well as "cocksuckers"—on the grounds that *Scribner's* magazine was widely read by young people, girls as well as boys. But Hemingway wanted the words restored for the novel: he was merely re-creating the way soldiers talked. Fitzgerald, who would never himself have written such language for publication, nonetheless secured and delivered to Hemingway a copy of Erich Maria Remarque's *All Quiet on the Western Front*, a war novel then enjoying a phenomenal success in Germany and England, with an American edition about to emerge. Armed with the evidence, Ernest wrote Max that all of his offending words—or all but one, anyway—appeared in *All Quiet*. Remarque's soldiers talked dirty, just as he wanted his to. He hated "to kill the value of [his novel] by emasculating it."

But Hemingway offered Perkins a way out of his dilemma. "If [any given word] *cannot* be printed without the book being suppressed all right." After the Boston ban, Max was able to argue that suppression was a very real possibility.

As Ernest wrote Scott, restoring him to the status of literary confidant and adviser, "Max sounded scared. If they get scared now and lay off the book I'll be out of luck." He wished he'd asked for an advance, because "it is more difficult to lay off a book if they have money tied up in it already." Perkins reassured Hemingway about an advance. He could have $5,000 or more, if he wanted it. At the same time, though, the Scribner's editor presented the company-man argument that an advance could be "very discouraging to an author (take Scott for example)" whose book sold well but who had no royalty coming because of a large advance. He did not add that most writers (including Scott for example) would be more than willing to deal with so rewarding a form of discouragement.

When he heard about the banning of *Scribner's* magazine, Fitzgerald wrote Perkins that *Hemingway* "sounded worried, but I don't see why. To hell with the toughs of Boston." By the end of July, however, Ernest capitulated to Perkins's warnings about suppression. "I understand," he wrote Perkins, "...about the words you cannot print—if you cannot print them—and I never expected you could print the one word (C—-S) that you cannot and that lets me out." Fitzgerald did not get the message that the battle was lost. In an August 23 letter to Hemingway, he took credit for sending Perkins "one of those don't-lose-your-head notes." He'd always believed, Scott added, that if the dispute about dirty words came to a crisis stage Max would "threaten to resign and force [Scribner's] hand."

At their summertime base in Cannes, the Fitzgeralds spent a miserable few months. Zelda went into Nice daily to work on her dancing, while Scott partied with whatever companions he could find. "It's been gay here," Scott wrote Ernest, "but we are, thank God, desperately unpopular and not invited anywhere." According to Zelda, he managed to alienate most of his old friends on the Riviera. "You disgraced yourself at the Barrys' party, on the yacht at Monte Carlo, at the Casino with Gerald and Dotty [Parker]," she wrote. Scott admitted as much, privately, in his *Ledger*: "Being drunk and snubbed."

On the bright side, his unpopularity released time for work, and Fitzgerald did turn an important corner during the months on the Riviera, giving up the matricide theme for his novel and turning instead to the story of a movie director and his wife (Lew and Nicole Kelly) who encounter a stunning young actress named Rosemary on a shipboard crossing to Europe. Fitzgerald was only beginning to reshape the material that would form *Tender Is the Night*. As usual, he exaggerated his progress. "I've been working like hell, better than for four years," he told Hemingway. He was confident that he could finish his novel "before the all-American [football] teams" were picked.

"I can't tell you how glad I am you are getting the book done," Ernest wrote back. He had his doubts, though, for Scott might not be finishing the novel at all "but only putting [him] on the list of friends to receive the more glowing reports." Then Hemingway revealed directly to Fitzgerald what he had been telling Perkins for some time: that Scott had been "constipated" by the reviews of *Gatsby* and especially by Gilbert Seldes's praise. That made him self-consciously decide he had to write a masterpiece, instead of "going on the system that if this one when it's done isn't a Masterpiece maybe the next one will be." He knew there were "other complications," Ernest said, without mentioning Zelda or alcohol. Still, what Scott ought to do was to save "the juice" he wasted on *Saturday Evening Post* stories and use it for his novel.

Actually, Hemingway himself wasn't being particularly productive either. By September it had been a year since he finished the first draft of *A Farewell to Arms*, and not much had been written since. As tended to happen when he was not working, he was beset with physical ailments real and imaginary. Hemingway was in a sour mood waiting for his book to come out, feeling lousy and worried about its reception from the critics and the public and the censors. With his uncanny knack for bad timing, Fitzgerald chose that particular time to place the already fraying ties of their friendship under tremendous pressure.

The troubles began with Scott's unwanted criticism of *Farewell* and his sloppy timekeeping in Ernest's sparring match with Morley Callaghan. During the summer on the Riviera, Fitzgerald managed to complicate his friend's living arrangements in Paris through the Vallombrosa affair. Back in Paris during the fall, he embarked on a series of worrisome interventions in connection with Hemingway's novel. In December, the soirée at Gertrude Stein's brought the issue of rivalry between them into the open.

Most of these vexations derived from Scott's eagerness to be involved in Ernest's life and career. When the two men first met, those involvements worked to Hemingway's benefit. By 1929 they no longer did. To Ernest, Scott's intrusions into his affairs looked like nothing so much as meddling.

To begin with, Fitzgerald could not keep his mouth shut. Ernest and Pauline then planned to maintain a base in Paris—a decision that was countermanded by their return to Key West in January 1930—and with that in mind paid $3,000 to sublet the rue de Férou apartment. After the two men renewed contact in May, Ernest told Scott in considerable heat about the day he was working at home when a group of prospective renters arrived to look it over. He did not want to lose the apartment, and he did not like being interrupted at work.

The Hemingways leased the flat through the good offices of Ruth Goldbeck Vallombrosa, an attractive member of the international set. Ruth happened to be on the Riviera that summer, where Fitzgerald happened to run into her and could not resist telling her about Hemingway's anger. As Scott construed the conversation in his letter to Ernest, it is clear that he viewed himself as having done his friend yet another service.

> Now—Ruth Goldbeck Vallombrosa [actually, Scott spelled it Voallammbbrrosssa, probably for comic effect] not only had no intention of throwing you out in any case, but has even promised *on her own initiative* to speak to whoever it is (she knows her) has the place. She is a fine woman, I think; one of the most attractive in evidence at this moment, and not deserving of that nervous bitterness.

Hemingway replied that although Fitzgerald obviously remembered his "nervous bitterness"—his blowing up about people coming in to look at the apartment—he seemed to have "damned well" forgotten that Ernest came around to see him about it the next day and to explain that under no circumstances did he want Ruth Goldbeck Vallombrosa [Ernest spelled it Vallambrosa] to know how angry he had been. "*She* did not know I was sore and the only way she would ever find out would be through you. You said you understood perfectly and for me not to worry you would never mention it to her."

Fitzgerald tried to calm the waters. "[I]ncidentally," he wrote back, "I thought you wanted a word said to Ruth G. if it came about naturally—I merely remarked that you'd be disappointed if you lost your apartment—never a word that you'd been exasperated." Hemingway could hardly have been reassured on that point, however, for Fitzgerald went on in a highly explicit manner to describe his pattern of behavior when drinking. He tended to dissolve in tears about 11 p.m., and to tell anyone who would listen that he hadn't a friend in the world. Not many would listen for long, Scott admitted, for he would go on and on. He'd never been able to hold his tongue: "when drunk I make them all pay and pay and pay."

In the same confessional spirit, Fitzgerald discussed the long dry period on his novel. He thought Ernest's analysis about overpraise having dammed the flow was "too kind in that it leaves out the dissipation." What really worried him was the remarkable output of 1919-1924: three novels including *Gatsby*, about fifty stories, a play, and numerous articles. That spurt, he feared, "might have taken all [he] had to say too early," especially considering that he and Zelda were then "living at top speed in the gayest worlds [they] could find." He closed with a self-deprecatory bulletin on the financial front. "[T]he *Post* now pays the old whore $4000 a screw. But now it's because she's mastered the 40 positions—in her youth one was enough." This time, Fitzgerald did not inflate his price.

Hemingway heard and responded to the cry for help in this letter. Exasperating as Fitzgerald could sometimes be, Hemingway still felt a real warmth toward him. So his letter of September 13 corrected Scott's crying-drunk statement that he had no friends. He should say instead that he had "no friends but Ernest the stinking serial king." Nor should Scott feel bad about his lack of literary production. Everybody lost the early bloom, he assured Fitzgerald. "You lose everything that is fresh and everything that is easy and it always seems as though you could *never* write" again, but that wasn't true, for you had "more metier and you know more" and when you got flashes of the old juice you could do more with them.

Above all Hemingway encouraged Fitzgerald not to give up. Appropriating to himself the position of mentor, Ernest insisted that there was only one thing to do with a novel and that was to "go straight on through to the end of the damn thing." If only Scott's economic existence depended on the novel and not on short stories! As always when sentiment threatened to intrude, Hemingway couched his message of support in invective. "Oh Hell. You still have more stuff than anyone and you care more about it and for Christ sake just keep on and go through with it now and don't please write anything else until it's finished. It will be damned good." The stories weren't whoring at all, just bad judgment. Scott could make enough to live on writing novels.

THE BOUT WITH MORLEY CALLAGHAN

Morley Callaghan, a young Canadian writer, came to Paris in the spring of 1929 and unwittingly drove a wedge between Fitzgerald and Hemingway, the two American writers he was most eager to see and talk to. The trouble came to a climax in a sparring contest with Hemingway late in June, but it had repercussions that lasted until the end of the year and beyond.

Hemingway met Callaghan in 1923 when both were working for the *Toronto Star Weekly*. After a couple of years as roving correspondent in Europe, Hemingway cut a rather glamorous figure in the *Star* newsroom. People were converting his exploits into the stuff of legend. But what most impressed Callaghan was Hemingway's devotion to the craft of writing. "A writer," he said, "is like a priest," for both professions required the same kind of discipline and commitment. Three years younger than Ernest and an aspiring writer of fiction himself, Morley listened with fascination.

Five years later, when Scribner's published Callaghan's short-story collection, *Native Argosy*, Fitzgerald and Hemingway both signaled their approval. "I think he really has it—personality, or whatever it is," Fitzgerald wrote Perkins. He doubted, though, that Morley was "as distinctive a figure as Ernest." The following year, Callaghan came to Paris, and found himself in the middle of the intensely strained relationship between Scott and Ernest. He even wrote a book about it—*That Summer in Paris*—that was published in 1963. One of the few full-scale reports of the Fitzgerald-Hemingway friendship, this memoir is not entirely objective in its rendering of what happened in Paris, summer of 1929. Many years had elapsed to rub away the memories, and as one might expect, Callaghan made sure that he did not come off badly.

When he arrived in Paris, Callaghan had it in mind to renew his acquaintance with Hemingway and to look up Fitzgerald. He admired both writers, and Max Perkins encouraged him to make contact with them. From the start Perkins had been bewitched by Hemingway's tales of bullfights and boxing. He told Callaghan as if it were gospel a yarn about Ernest knocking out the middleweight champion of France. Callaghan knew that was nonsense, that in boxing as in any other sport, the professional would invariably defeat the amateur. In Paris, he was to find out more about Hemingway—and Fitzgerald—in the ring.

One of Callaghan's short stories used a boxing milieu. Hemingway, whose "Fifty Grand" had established his claim as an expert on the sport, decided to find out if Callaghan knew what he was writing about. When Morley and his wife Loretto called on Ernest and Pauline in Paris, Ernest quizzed him about his experience. Yes, he had boxed quite a bit, Morley said. In fact, he was very fast with his hands. Oral assurances were not enough for Hemingway. He insisted that they strap on boxing gloves and maneuver gingerly around the furniture in the rue de Férou apartment. After a while, Ernest was satisfied. "I only wanted to see if you had done any boxing," he said with a grin, ignoring the fact that he had failed to take Morley's word for it. The two men made a date to box the next afternoon at the American Club nearby, as they did on eight or nine other occasions that spring and summer.

As a fighter, Callaghan discovered, Hemingway "was a big rough tough clumsy unscientific man"—big enough and strong enough to clobber Morley in a back-alley brawl. With gloves on and given room to move around, Callaghan was able to hold his own. In boxing together, Ernest usually tried to nail Morley with a solid left hook, while Morley's technique was to slip those punches and deliver jabs with his quick left hand. It was a fair enough match. Hemingway had the power, Callaghan the speed. Often Morley would come home with welts on his arms and shoulders, badges that signified he had avoided taking Ernest's most damaging blows to the head. On one occasion, when he bloodied Ernest's lip with his jabs, Hemingway sucked in the blood and spat it at Callaghan. It was a terrible insult, Morley knew, but Ernest broke the tension by saying solemnly, "That's what the bullfighters do when they're wounded." Then they showered and went off to the Falstaff, where they had a beer or two with proprietor James Charters, himself a former prizefighter.

Perkins told Callaghan that he did not need to stand on formality with Fitzgerald. Just drop in on Scott, he advised; he'll be glad to see you. That's what Callaghan did, and the initial results were not auspicious. As Morley recalled the meeting, he and Loretto stopped by the Fitzgeralds' apartment about nine-thirty one evening just as a taxicab deposited Scott and Zelda at their door. The Callaghans introduced themselves, and were invited inside, where Fitzgerald—much as he had with Glenway Wescott and Michael Arlen—invited a fellow novelist to join him in admiration of Ernest Hemingway. Scott read aloud the passage from *A Farewell to Arms* that he had proposed as an ending, the burst of rhetoric about how the "world" was sure to kill the very good and the very gentle and the very brave. "Isn't that beautiful?" he asked. Well, yes, of course it was, Morley said, but wasn't it also "too deliberate," something of a set piece?

Fitzgerald took offense and began bombarding Callaghan with sarcastic questions. If that passage didn't impress Morley, what would impress him? Would Morley be impressed if Scott stood on his head? He tried to do so, lost his balance, and sprawled flat on his face. On the way home Callaghan decided Fitzgerald must have been drunk. Loretto wasn't so sure she liked the literary life. Her husband had encountered in Paris the two American writers whose work he most respected. One of them had spit at him, and the other one stood on his head.

The next day, Morley wrote a letter to Scott. As he re-created it in *That Summer in Paris*, this note consisted of an apology about coming by without making an appointment ahead of time. He'd only done so because Max Perkins assured him it would be all right. If he and his wife had upset Scott and Zelda in any way, or kept them up, they were sorry.

Callaghan somewhat rearranged the facts in his memoir. The actual letter, which Fitzgerald preserved, was that of a bitter man whose ego has been sorely bruised. It was written the morning after Morley had dropped by the Fitzgeralds' unannounced, for the *second* time. On the first occasion, Scott and Zelda had been tired, having just returned home from the theater, but Morley nonetheless left the manuscript of his as yet unpublished novel, *It's Never Over*, for Fitzgerald to read. He was understandably eager to hear what Fitzgerald thought of the book, and had gone to their apartment the previous night to find out.

"Your frank opinion of the book is honestly appreciated," Morley wrote. "It was what I wanted. If I had caught you at any other time I would have been the poorer for it. *Please don't think I resent the way you told me the novel was rotten.* [Italics added.] It would have been much easier for you to have said that it was a nice piece of work, and so I am grateful to you." Elsewhere in the letter, however, the injured Callaghan could not maintain this high-minded tone. He summarily refused an invitation to lunch with the Fitzgeralds. "It was very kind of you to ask us, but, if I remember correctly, I made it almost impossible for you to do otherwise." Perhaps they might see each other "sometime" at one of the cafés, he commented, before concluding with a final angry sentence. "And I am sure you'll understand why we can not have lunch together on Wednesday."

This letter provoked an extraordinary reaction from Fitzgerald. According to Callaghan, he sent three separate *pneumatiques* in an attempt to make amends, and he and Zelda turned up at Morley and Loretto's apartment with the same goal in mind. "Never in my life," Morley recalled, "had anyone come to me so openly anxious to rectify a situation." It was a pattern with Fitzgerald: he did outrageous things to alienate people, and then went to great lengths to repair the damage. He could not stand to have others think badly of him.

In any case, the Callaghans and Fitzgeralds continued to see each other, and Morley continued to box with Ernest. Gradually it became clear that he was caught in the middle of the estrangement between Fitzgerald and Hemingway about the apartment. Scott and Zelda had only recently arrived in Paris, and had not yet made connections with the Hemingways. Whenever Morley saw Scott, he was bombarded with questions about Ernest. Had the Callaghans seen the Hemingways? Oh, really, and how often? Why didn't Morley arrange a get-together for the three couples? Ernest failed to respond to such overtures when Morley advanced them. Furthermore, he instructed Callaghan not to reveal his address. He told Morley, as he had written Perkins, that he was afraid Scott would cause a drunken disturbance and get them kicked out of the place. There seemed to be more to it than that, Callaghan thought, "some other hidden resentment." Naturally, he felt awkward about his role as middleman. Scott and Ernest were supposed to be great friends, and here he was in the anomalous position of trying to bring them together. Fitzgerald was particularly eager to see Ernest and Morley box. On the day he finally did, it turned out disastrously.

Callaghan and Hemingway wrote differing interpretations of what happened that June afternoon. These agreed only on the basic fact that Fitzgerald, asked to serve as timekeeper, let a round go too long and Hemingway fell to the canvas. In Callaghan's account, Scott and Ernest showed up at his door together in the best of humor but entirely sober, with Hemingway carrying the gloves. At the American Club, Scott listened attentively to his instructions. Ernest and Morley were fighting three-minute rounds, with one minute of rest in between. He was to call "time" at the end and beginning of each round. But Fitzgerald was caught up in the drama of the occasion, and—Morley thought—shocked to see Ernest's mouth bloodied by one of his jabs. Consequently he forgot to consult his watch, and as the round wore on, Callaghan stepped inside of one of Hemingway's roundhouse swings, caught Ernest flush on the jaw, and knocked him down, "sprawled out on his back."

Only then did an alarmed Fitzgerald cry out, "Oh, my God! I let the round go four minutes." Hemingway, who was not badly hurt physically, would have none of it. "If you want to see me getting the shit knocked out of me," he savagely told Scott, "just say so. Only don't say you made a mistake." As Callaghan recalled, a number of thoughts raced through his head at this outburst. Was the animosity in Scott or in Ernest? Did Ernest resent Scott for helping his career? Did Scott resent Ernest in some way? What he could see for sure was that Fitzgerald was every bit as distraught as Hemingway was angry. For weeks Scott had wanted to see them box and when he did, it brought on this crisis.

Before the afternoon was over, Fitzgerald managed to compound his error. Hemingway and Callaghan resumed their boxing after a brief intermission, and this time Scott was meticulous about his timekeeping. When Callaghan half tripped on the edge of a wrestling mat and went down on one knee, Fitzgerald called out "One knockdown to Ernest, one to Morley." The remark, obviously meant to mollify Hemingway, only made things worse. "[I]f I had been Ernest," Morley wrote, "I think I would have snarled at [Scott], no matter how good his intentions were."

Hemingway sent his version of that bout to Max Perkins in August, during his summer sojourn in Spain. "You would not believe it to look at him," he wrote of

Callaghan, who was overweight and something of a dandy in his dress, "but he is a *very* good boxer." On the day in question, Ernest said, he had an extensive lunch with Scott and John Peale Bishop at Prunier's, lobster thermidor and "several bottles of white burgundy," followed by a couple of whiskeys. He could hardly see Morley when they started boxing, but he thought he could go hard for a minute at a time, and they agreed on *one-minute* rounds with *two minutes* of rest, Scott keeping time. Fitzgerald let the first round go three minutes and forty-five seconds—"so interested to see if I was going to hit the floor!" That did not happen, for although Morley was fast and really knew how to box, he could not hit hard. Ernest, terribly tired, did slip and fall down, pulling a tendon in his left shoulder. Later they resumed boxing, and he managed to sweat the alcohol out of his system. (In telling the story to Arthur Mizener in 1951, Ernest expanded on Scott's incompetence. As timekeeper, he asserted, Fitzgerald had let the round "go *thirteen* minutes"!)

That might have been the end of the affair, were it not for Hemingway's developing celebrity. In November, a third version of the match at the American Club made its way into the daily newspapers. This particular account, which originated in the *Denver Post* and traveled east to Isabel Patterson's gossipy literary column in the *New York Herald-Tribune*, put Ernest in the worst possible light. He had been sitting at the Dôme in Paris, telling one and all that Callaghan knew nothing about boxing. Hearing about this, Morley challenged him to a bout and before "a considerable audience" knocked him cold in a matter of seconds. The unidentified "amateur timekeeper" was so flustered that he forgot to count Hemingway out, and a critic in the audience had to do so.

As soon as Callaghan—now back in Toronto—read this story, he sent a correction to Patterson. He had boxed with Hemingway the previous summer, but they'd never had an audience and he had never knocked Ernest out. Once, it was true, they'd had a timekeeper, and if there "was any kind of a remarkable performance that afternoon the timekeeper deserved the applause." Before his letter of correction was printed, Callaghan got a cable that infuriated him: "HAVE SEEN STORY IN HERALD TRIBUNE. ERNEST AND I AWAIT YOUR CORRECTION. SCOTT FITZGERALD." And the cable came collect! He immediately posted an angry letter to Fitzgerald in Paris. There was no need for him to have rushed in to defend Hemingway. Only a son of a bitch would send such a cable without waiting to see what Morley would do. He assumed that Scott was "drunk as usual when he sent it." Callaghan also wrote Perkins about the cable, and Max set about trying to calm down his authors.

There ensued an outpouring of correspondence between these four principals. *December 12, 1929, Hemingway to Fitzgerald*, obviously written after the insistence decided better not send." The letter to Callaghan was sent in care of Scribner's, and if it was still there Max should hold on to it for him. Ernest also sent a cable asking Perkins not to relay his letter to Callaghan, but to no avail—it had already been forwarded.

Mid-January 1930, Callaghan to Hemingway, in receipt of the January 4 invitation to duke things out, and with a show of belligerence himself, pointing out that he could not in good conscience transfer the epithets he'd used to Scott. Since Ernest had compelled Scott to send the cable, Morley would have to come up "with a whole fresh set of epithets" for him.

January 21, 1930, Fitzgerald to Perkins, thanking him for the documents "in the Callaghan case. I'd rather not discuss it except to say that I don't like him and that I wrote him a formal letter of apology. I never thought he started the rumor and never said nor implied such a thing to Ernest."

February 21, 1930, Hemingway to Callaghan, admitting he'd over-reacted and that he'd not intented to mail his January 4 letter yet still insisting that he could knock out Morley in five two-minute rounds if they used small gloves.

Late February, 1930, Callaghan to Hemingway, saying he did not think Ernest could knock him out but it was all right with him if Ernest wanted to think so, and meanwhile why not disarm?

The clear loser in the boxing match between Callaghan and Hemingway was Fitzgerald. He angered Hemingway by letting the round go on too long and later, by not letting the whole sorry incident fade away. He may have hoped to redeem himself in Ernest's eyes by sending the cable to Callaghan demanding a correction, but only succeeded in arousing Morley's ire and further humiliating himself.

Looking back on his acquaintance with the two men in Paris, Callaghan essayed a psychological comparison between them. Both Scott and Ernest were "extraordinarily attractive men." One difference was that Fitzgerald had a knack for making himself look worse than he was, while no matter what Hemingway did, he managed to emerge in a favorable light. At the end of his memoir, Callaghan illustrated his own point. If there is a villain in *That Summer in Paris*, it is surely Ernest Hemingway. Yet Callaghan maintained in closing that the Hemingway he knew in Paris, the author of *A Farewell to Arms*, was "perhaps the nicest man" he ever met—"reticent...often strangely ingrown and hidden with something sweet and gentle about him." His tragic flaw, Callaghan speculated, may have been his capacity "for moving others to make legends out of his life," a fault as nearly debilitating "as Scott's instinct for courting humiliation from his inferiors."

—✳—

two men had discussed the infamous boxing match and after Scott had sent the cable—*at Hemingway's instigation*—to Callaghan. "I know you are the soul of honor," Ernest assured Scott. "If you remember I made no cracks about your time keeping until after you had told me over my objections for about the fourth time that you were going to deliberately quarrel with me." Sore as he was about the whole thing, he had never accused Scott of time juggling, only asked if he "had let the round go on to see what would happen." That sort of thing often occurred with amateur timekeepers. At the time, he reminded Fitzgerald, he placed no importance on the incident, instead praising Morley for knocking him around. It was only when he read Callaghan's "lying boast" that he became angry.

Hemingway, obviously, felt that the knockout story had originated with Callaghan. From the context of his letter, it is apparent that Fitzgerald was deeply disturbed by the whole incident, and by its unfortunate aftermath. After recounting a yarn about dirty tricks in the prize ring, Ernest returned to his reassurances. "It was only when you were telling me, against all my arguments and telling you how fond I am of you, that you were going to break etc. and that you had a need to smash me as a man etc. that I relapsed into the damn old animal suspicion But...I believe you implicitly."

December 17, 1929, Perkins to Fitzgerald, enclosing the letter he got fro' Callaghan and the note he sent to the *Herald-Tribune*, along with news of he the rumor got started through a reporter named Caroline Bancroft who worl for the Denver paper.

December 27, 1929, Perkins to Hemingway, telling about a lunch du which Callaghan told Max he didn't think *he* could last through the "heart-b ing round" when Scott got distracted and forgot to call time.

January 1, 1930, Fitzgerald to Callaghan, a "dignified, half-formal" apologizing for his "stupid and hasty" telegram and assuring Morley he suspected him of starting the rumor.

January 4, 1930, Hemingway to Callaghan, revealing that Scott the cable "at [Ernest's] request and against his own good judgment." T was entirely his fault, Hemingway insisted, adding belligerently that i' wanted to transfer to him the epithets he applied to Scott he expected to States in a few weeks and would place himself "at your disposal any pl there is no publicity attached."

January 10, 1930, Hemingway to Perkins, thanking him for h December 27 and saying that Pauline "mailed by mistake a letter [h Callaghan [the one quoted immediately above] and then, on Scott's

ROILING THE WATERS

Throughout the fall months of 1929, when both of them returned to Paris after summers elsewhere on the Continent, Scott continued to advise Ernest and to attempt to guide his career. But his advice was no longer wanted, and no longer particularly helpful. At best his suggestions created tension in their relationship. At worst they threatened to break it off entirely.

With *A Farewell to Arms* a prospective best-seller, Ernest was again in demand among American agents and publishers. Harold Ober pressed his interest in representing Hemingway, and assumed that Fitzgerald could help bring Ernest into the fold. Early in the year, Ober wrote Fitzgerald about a volume of the best modern short stories the Modern Library planned to publish. Ober thought Fitzgerald ought to be represented in the book, which was to include work by Sherwood Anderson, Joseph Conrad, E.M. Forster, D.H. Lawrence, Katharine Mansfield, and Somerset Maugham, but Scribner's balked at the proposal. Couldn't Scott change their minds? And couldn't he deliver as well a story each from his friends Ernest Hemingway and Ring Lardner? Fitzgerald promised to talk to Max Perkins about it; he felt sure that Bennett Cerf at the Modern Library could count on something from him. *Great Modern Short Stories*, published in 1930, included Fitzgerald's "At Your Age" and Hemingway's "The Three-Day Blow," neither of which ranked with the best of their work, and nothing from Lardner.

In September, Ober severed his connections with the Paul Reynolds agency, and struck out on his own. Ober had been Fitzgerald's agent from the start, and telegraphed Scott to come along with him. "YOU OWE REYNOLDS NOTHING. I WILL GLADLY MAKE YOU ADVANCES WHEN NEEDED STOP TO AVOID INTERRUPTION WORK PLEASE CABLE ME AUTHORIZATION TO CONTINUE." Then Ober immediately went on to request that Fitzgerald "PERSUADE HEMINGWAY TO SEND STUFF THROUGH YOU TO ME."

Fitzgerald stuck with Ober, a decision made easier by a letter from Reynolds saying that since Ober had handled Scott's work all along it was only fair that he should go on handling it. But Reynolds did not give up so easily on Hemingway, who had resisted signing up with any agent. Without telling Ober, who "they knew perfectly well...had been discussing Hemingway['s]" situation with Fitzgerald, Reynolds and his son tried to negotiate sale of a Hemingway story to *Collier's*—and so to earn status as his agents. An angry Ober asked Scott to intervene with Ernest on his behalf and against the machinations of the Reynoldses. "If there is any way you can steer [Hemingway] my way," he wrote Fitzgerald October 8, "I should appreciate it. I know he thinks a great deal of your advice."

Fitzgerald forwarded this letter to Hemingway, along with a marginal note declaring that he would stay out of the battle over Ernest's work in future, now that he didn't "need any help." In further communication with Ober, he scolded his agent for not moving more quickly to sign up Hemingway. It had been "foolish to let him slide so long as he was so obviously a comer." One way to get Ernest's attention, Fitzgerald proposed in mid-November, was to negotiate a motion picture sale for $20,000 or more. But he cautioned Ober to keep his name out of any communications with Hemingway: "[Y]ou see my relations with him are entirely friendly & not business & he'd merely lose confidence in me if he felt he was being hemmed in by any *coalition*."

Though Fitzgerald more or less kept his distance on the agent front, he remained actively—and at times annoyingly—involved in Hemingway's professional relations with Scribner's, particularly with respect to *A Farewell to Arms*. Scott managed to dishearten Ernest about sales of the novel, for example, despite its obvious success in the marketplace. He also incited Hemingway to seek higher royalties from the book than he had contracted for, and even to become involved in its advertising.

A week after publication of *A Farewell to Arms* on September 27, Hemingway wrote a discouraged letter to Perkins. His mood was largely attributable to authorial postpartum blues, with Fitzgerald helping the melancholy along. He'd always figured, Ernest wrote Max, that if you wrote good books they would sell a certain amount and someday you could live on what they brought in. But Scott told him that was "all bunk—[t]hat a book only sells for a short time and that afterwards it never sells and that it doesn't pay the publishers even to bother with it." (Time was to prove how wrong Fitzgerald was about this, both as regards Hemingway's books and his own.) Writing and publishing books was "just a damned racket like all the rest of it," Ernest said. The only thing he'd gotten out of *Farewell* was disappointment. At least he had earned some money for the magazine serial. Now the book itself had to make money, so that he could support the family his father had so abruptly left behind.

Fitzgerald predicted the novel would sell more than 50,000 copies, and it did considerably better than that. On October 15, after an anxious Hemingway wrote and wired him for a report, Perkins cabled that the first printing of 30,000 copies was sold out and two more printings of 10,000 each had been run.

Prospects looked good, or would have done so except for the stock market crash. The day after Black Tuesday, Perkins wrote Fitzgerald that sales of *Farewell* had reached 36,000 and that no book "could have been better received" by the critics and the public. (Actually, several of the early reviews were negative.) The "only obstacle" he could see to a really big sale was that the collapse of the market could have "a very bad effect on all retail business, including that of books." For the moment Scott refrained from passing on this alarming bit of news to Ernest, but he did urge him to seek a 20 percent royalty once sales went beyond a certain figure. He'd had that arrangement with Scribner's for *his* books, Fitzgerald pointed out.

The issue emerged in Perkins's November 12 letter to Hemingway. The editor began with a report that *Farewell* had been leading the best-seller lists ever since publication, except for one week when it was edged out by *All Quiet on the Western Front*. Sales had reached 45,000, and a total of 70,000 copies had been printed, with paper on hand for another 20,000. But all that success had made Hemingway an extremely desirable commodity, and rumors were rampant in the publishing industry that he was dissatisfied with Scribner's. Offers might have been coming Ernest's way, and Max acknowledged that Scribner's was hardly in a position to ask him to refuse them unless they were willing to make equal offers themselves. If Ernest wanted $25,000 right now, for example, they would gladly advance it to him. Finally, Perkins got to the royalty question.

Things were not the same as they were when they'd first published Fitzgerald, Perkins asserted. Costs were higher, discounts were deeper, and most publishers felt that a 20 percent royalty was too high, that 15 percent was about all a book could bear if it was to be heavily advertised. Still, if Hemingway demanded a 20 percent royalty, even from the first copy sold, they would probably pay it "and face a loss, if necessary." Perkins suggested an alternative that would be fair both to author and publisher. When the six months' royalty report was due, they would be able to calculate the profit that *Farewell* had generated, and could then revise the terms of the contract retroactively.

Hemingway replied that he had no intention of trying to "bid up" his price "It was only when Scott asked me what my arrangements were for a big sale that I mentioned it to you." He was still upset about the barracks language that had been cut out of the novel, feeling that he'd lost his integrity in permitting such excisions. He'd had no interest in the book since, other than as something to "sell by God and fix up my mother and the rest of them." He was setting up a $50,000 trust fund for his mother. An outside source—probably Pauline's uncle Gus—

had promised $30,000 for that purpose, and he'd need $20,000 from Scribner's against royalties after the first of the year.

Perkins did not wait six months, or even until the end of 1929, to amend the royalty rate in Hemingway's contract. Sales continued to soar, and publishers continued to stir up harmful rumors about Ernest's supposed discontent with Scribner's. On December 10, Perkins wrote Hemingway that the contract had been revised. In talking it over with Charles Scribner, Max suggested 17 1/2 percent after 25,000 copies and 20 percent after 45,000, but Mr. Scribner said, "No, 20% after 25,000" and that was to be the rate. If Ernest had any objections, he had only to let Max know. As of that date, about 60,000 copies had been sold.

Fitzgerald was reluctant to relinquish his role as savvy inside adviser to Hemingway. In mid-November, while Ernest was on a trip to Berlin to see his German publisher, Scott came by the rue de Férou apartment and confronted Pauline with Max Perkins's warning about the possible downturn in sales of *Farewell* owing to the stock market crash. He was obviously alarmed, Pauline became alarmed, and when Ernest got back to Paris he joined in the general alarm. But Fitzgerald also suggested a solution: a new advertising campaign to keep sales humming along. In two letters to Perkins—the first of them unsent— Ernest presented that idea.

If sales started to fall off, he wrote, Scott's notion was that Scribner's "should start advertising the book as a love story—which it certainly is as well as a war story." There were other war books on the shelves—Remarque's *All Quiet*, in particular—that might crowd *Farewell*, so the thing to do was to emphasize how it differed. In the letter he decided not to send, Hemingway submitted three separate samples of copy Perkins could use to "hammer" away on his novel as a love story. One of these read as follows:

> There's more than
> War in
>   A Farewell to Arms
> It is
> The Great Modern Love Story

It made him sick to write such stuff, Hemingway admitted, but he pleaded necessity. "You sell the intelligent ones first. Then you have to hammer hammer hammer on something to sell the rest." In the letter he actually sent Perkins, written after a two-day cooling off period, Hemingway advanced Fitzgerald's great modern love story angle but refrained from submitting sample copy for the advertising department. Scott may well have over-reacted, Ernest speculated, as in fact he had. *Farewell* continued to sell at a splendid pace.

Three years earlier Fitzgerald had functioned admirably behind the scenes in guiding Hemingway to Scribner's. Now he only succeeded in engendering anxiety in Ernest and stirring up trouble for Max. In writing to Perkins, Hemingway articulated his irritation at his friend's behavior. He apologized for bothering Max "about the sale stopping," but Scott had come by in some alarm and since he knew "so much more about the financial side of writing" Ernest had become disturbed also. "Am damned fond of Scott and would do anything for him but he's been a little trying lately."

Une Soirée Chez Mademoiselle Stein

Hovering in the background—always there and nearly always mute—was the demon of literary rivalry. It emerged one early December evening at Gertrude Stein's party. Hemingway's admiration for Stein had cooled considerably over the years. By 1928, he was telling Fitzgerald that Stein had not known a moment's unhappiness with her work since she took up "not making sense." And in "My Own Life," a satirical 1927 *New Yorker* piece, he described how he had been banned from Stein's gatherings when he graduated from being her pupil to a writer in his own right. The maid had beaten him about the head with a bicycle pump to keep him away, he wrote, and when he persisted Stein nailed the door shut and posted an attack dog. Hemingway was eager to minimize the importance of Stein's influence on his work. Making fun of her was an amiable way to accomplish that.

It must have been particularly galling, then, when Fanny Butcher in her *Chicago Tribune* review of *A Farewell to Arms*—the review that would have been read by his relatives and friends in and around Oak Park—hailed him as a genius on the one hand and on the other described him as "the direct blossoming of Gertrude Stein's art." He found out directly what Stein thought of his novel during her party in December.

She asked Hemingway to bring Fitzgerald and Allen Tate along to the Wednesday evening gathering. "She claims you are the one of all us guys with the most talent, etc. and wants to see you again," he wrote Scott. At the appointed time, Ernest showed up with a party of nine: the Fitzgeralds, the Hemingways, the Tates (Caroline Gordon), John Peale Bishop and his wife Margaret, and Ford Madox Ford. Stein used the occasion to present a lecture on American literature, tracing the path of greatness from R.W. Emerson through Henry James to the present site of genius, her own flat on the rue de Fleurus.

Afterwards, she told Ernest that she thought *Farewell* was fine when he was inventing, and not so good when he started remembering. When Fitzgerald joined the conversation, Stein went on to remark that his "flame" and Ernest's were very different. According to *The Autobiography of Alice B. Toklas*, the concept of a writer's flame came from Hemingway himself. Supposedly, he said that "I turn my flame which is a small one down and down and then suddenly there is a big explosion. If there were nothing but explosions my work would be so exciting nobody could bear it." On this particular evening, it seemed clear to Hemingway that Stein preferred Fitzgerald's flame to his. Scott refused to see the point, and on their walk home badgered Hemingway relentlessly about her remark.

The next morning, very much as usual, a note of apology arrived from Fitzgerald, and Hemingway took advantage of his hangover to answer at once. He hadn't been annoyed at anything Scott said the night before, only by his refusal "to accept the sincere compliment" Stein was paying him. Instead, Scott had insisted on trying to convert her praise "into a slighting remark." He also seemed determined to interpret her cryptic comment about their differing flames into a preference for Hemingway, when Ernest felt sure that she meant Scott "had a hell of a roaring furnace of talent" and he had a small one. Why Fitzgerald chose to interpret Stein's observation in this way was a question that invited still other questions. Was he really so modest about his own abilities that he could not believe her admiration was sincere? Or was he fearful that by accepting her praise at face value he would damage Hemingway's pride and so earn his enmity?

The hypothetical "flames" stuff was "pure horseshit" anyway, Ernest maintained in his letter. As writers he and Scott started along "entirely separate lines," and the only thing they had in common was the desire to write well. Between serious writers there could be no sensible talk about superiority. They were all in the same boat. Competition "within that boat—which is headed toward death—[was] as silly as deck sports are." This extremely sensible and dispassionate discourse came, as Fitzgerald knew, from one of the most competitive persons on the face of the earth. In every endeavor—from bicycle riding to drinking bouts—Hemingway tried his utmost to prevail. Where his artistic reputation was concerned, he tried, if possible, even harder.

Thus it was not especially surprising that Hemingway went on in this letter — after declaring in no uncertain terms there could be no competition between them — to compare their situation to the most famous competitive event in all literature. "Gertrude wanted to organize a hare and tortoise race," Ernest asserted (actually, the idea of such a race came from him and not from her), "and picked me to tortoise and you to hare and naturally, like a modest man and a classicist, you wanted to be the tortoise." Indeed Scott did, and a few years later, when he was working on the galleys of *Tender Is the Night*, he reverted to this metaphor in a letter to Maxwell Perkins. He was taking great pains with his revisions of the novel, Fitzgerald acknowledged, but that was his way of working. After all, he told Perkins, he was a plodder. "One time I had a talk with Ernest Hemingway and I told him, against all the logic that was then current, that I was the tortoise and he was the hare, and that's the truth of the matter, that everything that I have ever attained has been through long and persistent struggle while it is Ernest who has a touch of genius which enables him to bring off extraordinary things with facility."

Scott then declared that he himself had "no facility," contradicting the widely held view that he wrote too easily and without adequate conscientiousness. In fact, Fitzgerald became increasingly reluctant to stop revising his fiction as he grew older, increasingly unwilling to go into print with less than his very best. And the drafts of Hemingway's stories and novels reveal from the first a similar pattern of careful and crucially important alterations. In that sense, both Scott and Ernest were tortoising along.

In his studies of the two writers, biographer and critic Matthew J. Bruccoli consistently held that Fitzgerald "did not regard writing as competitive." Certainly in the early years of their friendship, Fitzgerald was extraordinarily generous toward Hemingway and selflessly admiring of his work. Even then, however, people were always drawing contrasts between them. Christian Gauss, the Princeton dean who befriended such undergraduate writers as Fitzgerald, Wilson, and Bishop, looked up Scott in Paris during 1925. After a brief meeting with him and Hemingway, Gauss placed the two young authors at opposite ends of the color spectrum. "Without disrespect to him I put Hemingway down on the infrared side and you on the ultra-violet. His rhythm is like the beating of an African tom-tom — primitive, simple, but it gets you in the end." Fitzgerald belonged at the other end of the spectrum. "You have a feeling for musical intervals and the tone-color of words which makes your prose the finest instrument for rendering all the varied shades of our complex emotional states."

Scott could hardly have been displeased by Gauss's judgment, which obviously tilted in his favor. But once Ernest became an established figure and his own career languished, the comparisons were not always so flattering. Scott read or heard what other commentators had to say about himself and Ernest, and sometimes echoed their sentiments in his letters and notebooks. In 1931, for example, Gorham Munson in the *Bookman* bluntly called attention to his failed promise. "Mr. Fitzgerald has not published a novel since 1925 and his vogue has been succeeded by the vogue of Mr. Ernest Hemingway." In a letter of his own, Fitzgerald repeated Munson's point in Munson's language: "I was silent for too long after Gatsby, and then Ernest's vogue succeeded mine."

Fitzgerald would have had to be a saint not to harbor some resentment about this shift in their public reputation. According to Margaret Egloff, a young psychiatrist who became Scott's intimate friend during 1931, he felt that Hemingway "had more success and publicity than was deserved." He had given Ernest a leg up, and thought that he was ungrateful. Among other things, Egloff glossed a dream of Fitzgerald's which ended in a wartime scene, an indication — she believed — of Fitzgerald's "sense of the fight to the death between men for supremacy" and of his "competitiveness with Hemingway."

Over a period of time, Hemingway and Stein took turns deprecating each other in print. She had been his mentor once, a circumstance he wished to disavow. He had done her the favor of pushing for publication of *The Making of Americans*, an instance of indebtedness she was equally anxious to repudiate. Besides, her companion Toklas was jealous of her "weakness for Hemingway." In her *Autobiography of Alice B. Toklas*, Stein depicted him as a careerist wearing the mask of a dedicated artist, as a basically fearful man given to shows of false bravado, and as "90% Rotarian," among other slurs. Hemingway fired a few salvos in her direction before the publication of the *Autobiography* in 1933, and continued the assault in *Green Hills of Africa* (1935) and, most viciously, in the posthumously published *A Moveable Feast*. Hemingway's acidulous portrait of Stein in that memoir was very nearly as ill-spirited as the one he drew of Fitzgerald. Each of them occupied three chapters in the book.

Not Hemingway but Stein was degradingly careerist, according to *Feast*. During the three or four years when they were good friends, Ernest wrote, he never heard Gertrude speak well "of any writer who had not written favorably about her work or done something to advance her career except for Ronald Firbank and, later, Scott Fitzgerald." Fitzgerald's work she always liked, as did Alice Toklas.

But Hemingway's strongest blows in *Feast* were reserved for Stein's lesbianism. Gertrude as advocate instructed him that lesbians were not at all like male homosexuals. The act male lovers committed was "ugly and repugnant and afterwards they are disgusted with themselves." They ended up taking drugs and were always changing partners and never happy. Women making love to each other, on the other hand, did nothing that was disgusting or repulsive "and afterwards they are happy and they can lead happy lives together." Unconvinced, Hemingway asked about a particularly notorious lesbian. Stein assured him that she was an exception, she was "truly vicious, so she can never be happy except with new people. She corrupts people." Did he understand? Ernest was not really sure. "There were so many things to understand in those days and I was glad when we talked about something else."

In a very short chapter, Hemingway described how it ended with Gertrude Stein. On a lovely spring day, he walked through the Luxembourg Gardens with the horse chestnut trees in blossom and children playing on the gravelled walks. The indoor atmosphere of the Stein-Toklas flat at 27 rue de Fleurus proved, by contrast, to be both unnatural and—in contradistinction to Gertrude's pronouncements on the subject—disgusting. The maidservant gave him a glass of *eau-de-vie* and asked him to wait. Miss Stein would be right down. As he waited, he heard "someone" (the name Alice B. Toklas never appears in *A Moveable Feast*) speaking "as I had never heard one person speak to another; never, anywhere, ever."

"Then Miss Stein's voice came pleading and begging, saying, 'Don't, pussy. Don't. Don't, please don't. I'll do anything, pussy, but please don't do it. Please don't. Please don't, pussy.'"

Hemingway swallowed his drink and got out of there. That was the way his friendship with Stein finished, although he "still did the small jobs, made the necessary appearances, brought people that were asked for and waited dismissal with most of the other men friends when that epoch came and the new friends moved in."

To shock and appall Hemingway, the overheard conversation at Gertrude Stein's must have been something. He lived most of the 1920s in Paris, and was well acquainted with the gay and lesbian demi monde. Ezra Pound, for example, introduced him to Natalie Barney, a rich American patroness of the arts who "had a salon at her house on regular dates and a small Greek temple in her garden." Many American and French women who could afford it kept salons in those days, he wrote in *A Moveable Feast*, and he decided early on that they "were excellent places for him to stay away from." Though he eschewed the salons,

Ernest nonetheless formed close friendships with lesbians like Stein and Sylvia Beach, who were in their different ways his benefactors. So too, for a time, was Robert McAlmon.

The Slanderers

McAlmon was a young American writer-dilettante who had, in 1921, made a marriage of convenience with Annie Winifred Ellerman, a British heiress who wrote under the pen name of Bryher. Living in Paris in order to pursue his art, the bisexual McAlmon used money he got from his wife to establish a small press, Contact Editions. He met Hemingway in the winter of 1923, and traveled to the bullfights in Spain with him that summer, accompanied by Bill Bird, another Parisian with a limited edition press. Bird's recollection is that Hemingway was "outrageously insulting" to McAlmon during the Spanish trip. Nonetheless, McAlmon's Contact Editions brought out *Three Stories and Ten Poems*, Ernest's first book publication, late in the year. (The following year, Bird published *in our time*, Hemingway's second.)

According to *Being Geniuses Together*, his immodestly titled memoir of 1938, McAlmon was not impressed when he first met Hemingway. At times, he wrote, Ernest presented "a deliberately hard-boiled and case-hardened" facade, yet on other occasions he played "the hurt, soft, but fairly sensitive boy trying to conceal hurt, wanting to be brave...and somehow on the defensive...He approached a cafe with a small-boy, tough-guy swagger, and before strangers of whom he was doubtful, a potential snarl of scorn played on his large-lipped, rather loose mouth." This invidiously worded description, it should be noted, was composed after the demise of their friendship.

Hemingway sent McAlmon to Perkins with a letter of introduction in October 1929. McAlmon's "best stuff" dealt with homosexuality and was "quite unpublishable," Ernest thought. But there were some other good stories, and despite McAlmon's being "a damned gossip" he could be very intelligent, had been unjustly treated, and ought to "be published if only to take him out of the martyr class."

Perkins accordingly took McAlmon to dinner, and on October 30 wrote Fitzgerald about that evening. Ernest was only trying to help McAlmon find a publisher, Max pointed out, yet as soon as McAlmon started talking he unleashed a series of libelous remarks about Hemingway as a man and a writer. Max cautioned Scott to keep the whole sorry business confidential. "This is absolutely between you and me."

He knew all about McAlmon, Scott replied in mid-November. He was "a bitter rat" who had failed as a writer and was trying to "fortify himself by tying up to the big boys like Joyce and Stein" and despising everyone else. A few years earlier, McAlmon had assured Ernest that Scott "was a fairy—God knows he shows more creative imagination in his malice than in his work." Next he told Callaghan that Ernest was a fairy. "He's a pretty good person to avoid."

There the matter might have rested if Fitzgerald had been able to maintain silence. On December 9, unfortunately, he had dinner at the Hemingways and "while drunk" told Ernest about McAlmon's slandering him to Perkins. The next day, a furious Hemingway wrote Perkins asking for any particulars he could provide about McAlmon's rumors. The only ones he knew about for sure were "(1) That Pauline is a lesbian (2) That I am a homosexual (3) That I used to beat Hadley and as a result of one of these beatings Bumby was born prematurely." From Scott, he had learned about McAlmon telling Callaghan that Ernest was homosexual, along with the further intelligence that he knew it was true because Ernest made a pass at him in Spain.

He'd sat at dinner the previous night, cold sober and madder than hell, listening to an hour of more of "that sort of thing" from Scott, Ernest told Max. "If it's all the same with you," he sarcastically added, "I would rather you wrote me when you hear stories about me—not Scott." There was no point in reproaching Fitzgerald for a breach of confidence. He was "the soul of honor" when sober, and when drunk "no more responsible than an insane man."

"There should be a limit to what lies people are allowed to tell under jealousies," Ernest wrote. Now that things had gone too far, he would have to take corrective action. Beating up McAlmon would give him no pleasure as he was so pitiful. He would get more satisfaction from beating up Callaghan "because of his boasting [presumably, about knocking Hemingway out] and because he is a good enough boxer." Five days later, Hemingway wrote Perkins again assuring him that his anger directed against McAlmon and Callaghan was only "personal anger." He would do nothing to hurt them as writers, but he could and would "handle [his] personal business with them (only hope I won't have to do any time in jail for making it thorough)."

Hemingway did not have to do any jail time, although according to barman James Charters he did knock down McAlmon outside his saloon. There was no confrontation with Callaghan. In two separate letters, Perkins tried to calm the waters. McAlmon reminded him of a once promising newspaper reporter who disparaged the accomplishments of another who had gone on to become a brilliant correspondent. It was a case of "rather malicious envy" and directed not only at Ernest, for McAlmon also "belittle[d] Scott as a writer." People like that were always "depreciating" others, Max pointed out, and it was only because Ernest had played the friend to McAlmon that he mentioned his behavior. And Callaghan, Max maintained, was really a good fellow.

That fall, oddly enough, the expatriate Edward Titus challenged McAlmon and Callaghan to a literary contest. Each of them was to write an *au courant* story about two well-known homosexuals for publication in Titus's *This Quarter*. McAlmon did not complete his story, but Callaghan did. His "Now That April's Here" told about one of the gay men leaving the other for a woman, with the abandoned fellow being consoled by a character based on McAlmon. Hemingway was not in on the contest, but he did write a story for *This Quarter*— probably composed in early 1930—on a curiously similar theme. His "The Sea Change" dealt with the painful situation of a man whose female lover leaves him for another woman.

In his notebooks, Fitzgerald wrote that "I really loved him, but of course it wore out like a love affair. The fairies have spoiled all that." The reference, clearly, was to Hemingway, and the love he spoke of involved a manly bond that did not admit of a physical basis. Among the fairies whose malicious talk "spoiled" things was, surely, Robert McAlmon. At least McAlmon did not make the leap from his assertion that Fitzgerald and Hemingway were homosexuals to the assumption that they were lovers. That accusation came from Zelda.

From the first there had been a degree of animosity between Zelda and Ernest. She regarded him as "bogus" and a "poseur," and was irritated by his show of masculinity. No one could be "as male as all that," she thought. With reason, she regarded Hemingway as a sponger who took advantage of her husband's generosity. She also resented the attachment between the two men that was beyond her capacity to control or sever.

Hemingway claimed that he became aware of Zelda's mental instability as early as the summer of 1926, when she confidentially asked him, as if sharing a great secret, "Ernest, don't you think Al Jolson is greater than Jesus?" But the worst thing about Zelda, as she is portrayed in *A Moveable Feast*, was that she seemed determined to keep Scott from doing his work—both through encouraging him to drink and through arousing his jealousy.

Clever though he was in the game of courtship, Fitzgerald held strongly conventional views of sexual morality. When Zelda slept with him before they were married, it had the effect of making him forever suspicious of her fidelity. He took up the issue directly in an article he published in the spring of 1924 on "Why Blame It on the Poor Kiss if the Girl Veteran of Many Petting Parties Is Prone to Affairs after Marriage?" Fitzgerald optimistically concluded that girls who engaged in considerable pre-marital petting, having already discovered that there was more than one man in the world, were "less liable to cruise" after marriage in order to find that out. Fitzgerald needed reassurance on this score at least as much as his readers, for during the early years of their marriage, Zelda made a practice of flirting outrageously with his friends. Then he was devastated by her affair with Édouard Jozan, only a few months after his article had appeared. These circumstances helped to account for Scott's impertinently asking Ernest, at their first meeting, whether he and Hadley had slept together before their wedding. Fitzgerald really wanted to know. Was this the way of the world, or had he taken a recklessly promiscuous wife?

By the fall of 1929, there was not much left of their extremely close, if always difficult, marriage. For a number of years, according to a handwritten note among his papers, Scott and Zelda managed to get past the rough spots through late-night talks. "I have often thought," he wrote, "that those long conversations...[which] began at midnight and lasted till we could see the first light [of] dawn that scared us into sleep, were something essential in our relations, a sort of closeness that we never achieved in the workaday world of marriage." But those talks stopped "somewhere in Europe," as did their conjugal relations.

In her account of what went wrong with their marriage, Zelda traced two concurrent patterns of alienation—Scott's neglect of her and her growing attachment to her ballet teacher. During the summer of 1928 in Paris, Zelda recalled, she "began to like Egorova." Yet when she told Scott she was "afraid that there was something abnormal in the relationship," he only laughed. The trouble got worse in 1929, as she absorbed herself in her ballet lessons and Scott continued to neglect her. He came into her room only once the whole summer, but she no longer cared. He spent his time drinking, while she "became blindly involved" with Egorova and couldn't so much as walk out the door unless she'd had her lesson. Twice Scott left her bed saying, "I can't. Don't you understand?" She didn't. Zelda didn't lack for prospective lovers. "[T]here was the Harvard man who lost his direction, and when I wanted you to come home with me you told me to sleep with the coal man." And she could think of three other "solutions" in Paris, in addition to "the whole studio."

At the ballet studio, the potential or real lovers were women. As Hemingway observed in *A Moveable Feast* (though he miscalculated the year), that was the time that Zelda "was making him jealous with other women." When they went to parties, Scott was afraid to pass out and afraid to have Zelda pass out. "[T]he way things were going," Ernest wrote, "[Scott] was lucky to get any work done at all." Zelda recalled a couple of such instances. At a dinner given by Nancy Hoyt—a novelist and the sister of poet Elinor Wylie—the hostess "offered her services" but Zelda refused and turned back to the studio. During another party Dolly Wilde, the niece of Oscar Wilde and a lesbian with a cocaine habit, made a pass at Zelda when she was drunk, an incident that infuriated Scott.

The Fitzgeralds went at least twice to Natalie Barney's lesbian salon. They visited the studio of lesbian artist Romaine Brooks, who specialized in portraits of men in women's attire and vice versa. Brooks's painting of the notorious Miss Barney showed her brandishing a whip. Zelda described her studio as "a glass-enclosed square of heaven swung high above Paris." It did not look anything like that to Scott, who was getting his first real exposure to the gay and lesbian sub-culture of Paris. In *Tender Is the Night*, he palpably expressed his disgust with that world.

By the time of her mental collapse in April 1930, Zelda had fallen in love with the "cool and white and beautiful" Egorova. She was going through hell, Zelda wrote Scott from the first of the sanitariums that were to house her for the rest of her life. She could not sleep, and could not understand why God should have allowed her to undergo such torture, "except that it was wrong, of course, to love my teacher when I should have loved you. But I didn't have you to love—not since long before I loved her." The image of her ballet teacher would not be exorcised. Zelda painted a portrait of Egorova and displayed it at her 1934 show in New York. It was the one painting, she warned Scott, that she did not want sold.

Within two months' time after her breakdown, Zelda was hospitalized in three different institutions in France and Switzterland. At each of them she told the same story about her husband. He was a homosexual, in love with Ernest Hemingway. The accusation incensed Scott. In order to dissuade her, he had a notion "to write a letter to the Paris Herald to see if any human being except yourself and Robert McAlmon has ever thought I was a homosexual." Zelda remained adamant. "You said you did not want to see me if I know what I know. Well, I do know."

What she knew—or thought she knew—emerged after a dinner party at the Hemingways' in 1929. "We came back to the rue Palatine and you, in a drunken stupor told me a lot of things that I only half understood; but I understood the dinner we had at Ernest's. Only I didn't understand that it mattered." After he fell into bed that night, Scott had mumbled "No more, baby" in his sleep, which Zelda took as a lover's remark directed toward Ernest.

Whatever its origin, Zelda's charge struck a nerve. "The nearest I ever came to leaving you," he wrote her, "was when you told me you thought I was a fairy in the rue Palatine." Later, he became convinced that her delusions about him derived from an attempt to implicate him in her own tendencies. As he pointed out to Zelda, her "first accusation about Ernest occurred exactly one month after the Dolly Wilde matter." The very idea of homosexuality filled Fitzgerald with loathing. "Fairies," he commented in one of his notes, represented "[n]ature's attempt to get rid of soft boys by sterilizing them." At the same time, he knew that there were things about him—especially his fine-featured appearance—that might persuade others to believe Zelda's "stinking allegations and insinuations." As a young man he was twice cast as a chorus girl for Princeton Triangle shows. Once, on his own, he dressed up in drag to attend a dance at the University of Minnesota. These youthful cross-dressings were all in good fun, but the joke had lost its savor by the time he reached and passed his thirtieth birthday. When people told him he looked like someone else, he observed in 1935, the someone else usually turned out to be a homosexual.

The Fitzgeralds stayed in Europe through all of 1930 and most of 1931, when Dr. Oscar Forel at the Prangins clinic near Geneva decided it would be all right for her to return to the United States. The Hemingways sailed for Key West in January 1930, before Zelda's collapse. But they returned the following year for a summer in Spain, and a mid-September visit to Paris. There, according to Hemingway's recollection in *A Moveable Feast,* he and Scott met for the last time in the city of light where their friendship had been formed, and grown incandescent, and dimmed.

The brief chapter, "A Matter of Measurements," consists of an extended anecdote about Fitzgerald's sexual insecurities. According to Scott, Zelda told him 1) that he never satisfied her sexually, and 2) it was because his penis was too small. Over lunch at Michaud's, he asked for Hemingway's expert opinion about the adequacy of his equipment. By way of reassurance, as Ernest told the story, he escorted Fitzgerald to the men's room for a discourse on the visual effects of foreshortening and then to the Louvre where he could make comparisons with the statuary. "You're perfectly fine," Ernest told Scott. It was just that Zelda was trying to destroy him.

The story sounds like a fabrication, and the fact that Hemingway told it in various versions in various places contributes to that suspicion. Yet Edmund Wilson's diary of 1932 confirmed that Scott was worried about sexual inadequacy (alcohol must have been a contributing factor), and John Peale Bishop contributed the information that on at least one occasion Fitzgerald confessed his doubts about the size of his penis to a female dinner partner. So even if, as seems likely, Hemingway invented the stage business about the men's room and the Louvre, it is probably true that Fitzgerald told him about this example of psychological castration at home. In his cups, he was liable to say almost anything to anyone—and in Hemingway he had the best audience of all.

It is interesting, in this connection, to note what Scott did not tell Ernest. He said not one word to him about Zelda's allegation that they were lovers. It was one thing to indict Robert McAlmon for slander, and another to damn his own wife.

CHAPTER 6

LONG DISTANCE

> "Madame, it is always a mistake to know an author."
> —ERNEST HEMINGWAY, *Death in the Afternoon*

> I avoided writers very carefully because they can
> perpetuate trouble as no one else can.
> —F. SCOTT FITZGERALD, *The Crack-Up*

The Hemingways bought a house in Key West in January 1931, and soon thereafter began a pattern of spending winters and springs in Florida and the warmer months in the high country of the American West. That way, Ernest could indulge his passion for fishing and hunting while working regularly on whatever book was in process. The Fitzgeralds limped back to Montgomery in the fall of 1931, intending to settle down in the comfortable environment of Zelda's hometown. The plan did not work out. In letters written at the hospitals where her schizophrenia waxed and waned, Zelda repeatedly invoked a vision of a home of their own—in one version "a little house with hollyhocks and a sycamore tree and the afternoon sun imbedding itself in a silver tea-pot...with Scottie running about somewhere in white, in Renoir." The Fitzgeralds never owned a home of their own, anywhere, anytime. For the rest of his life, Scott did his work in a series of rented homes and apartments and hotel rooms.

Fitzgerald and Hemingway were on the same continent during most of the 1930s, then, and there was often talk of getting together on one Gulf Stream outing or another, but none of these came to pass. The bloom was off the friendship. Their correspondence trailed off, except in moments of crisis or when one or the other had published a book. Often they communicated through Perkins, who served as a willing go-between. In cross-correspondence—what they had to say about each other, to others—Hemingway became increasingly intolerant and unsympathetic toward his old friend, while Fitzgerald struggled gamely to preserve the illusion of what had once been the closest of relationships. In the last year of his life, he set down the sorry record in an autobiographical note. He and Ernest met only four times during the decade: once in 1931 (the infamous "measurements" meeting), once in 1933, twice in 1937. "Four times in eleven years (1929-1940)," he commented. "Not really friends since '26."

Fitzgerald was thirty-five years old when they came back from Europe, and the generations were tumbling over on schedule. In January 1931, Scott's father died, and he made a melancholy journey to the funeral in Maryland. After long silence, Ernest wrote him a letter of commiseration in mid-April, combining deepest regrets about Zelda's "rotten time" with a recommendation that Scott turn his father's death to proper literary account. "I'm sorry you had a trip to U.S. on such sad business. Hope to read your acct. of it between board covers rather than in Post. Remember us writers have only one father and one mother to die. But don't poop away such fine material."

The cruelly worded warning was right on the mark, for Fitzgerald did try to express his feelings about his father's death in an indifferent story called "On Your Own." Ober was unable to place the story with the *Saturday Evening Post*, or anywhere else. Scott resurrected a phrase from the rejected tale to use "between board covers" in *Tender Is the Night*. Dick Diver like Fitzgerald returns to the States for the funeral of the father who has taught him much about decency and honor, and there, in the cemetery among the graves of the early settlers, utters farewell to the past. "Good-by, my father—good-by, all my fathers."

The elegy might also have served for the passing of Judge Anthony Sayre, Zelda's father, in November 1931. By that time, Scott was in Hollywood on assignment from Irving Thalberg at Metro-Goldwyn-Mayer to rewrite a screenplay of *Red-Headed Woman* as a vehicle for Jean Harlow. Fitzgerald stayed in California for five weeks, finished the job, and was back in Montgomery for Christmas with $6,000 in his pocket. This would buy him time, he felt sure, to buckle down on his novel. "Am replanning it to include what's good in what I have, adding 41,000 new words & publishing," he wrote Perkins in January. "Don't tell Ernest or anyone—let them think what they want—you're the only one who's ever consistently felt faith in me anyhow." Scott now was centering his thinking on the story of Dick and Nicole Diver's troubled marriage, with glimpses along the way of the Parisian demimonde, the psychiatric sanitariums of Switzerland, the seemingly charming life of the rich on the Riviera, and the distinct whiff of political and economic upheaval in the air.

The Fitzgerald who wrote *Tender Is the Night* in 1932 and 1933 was a very different person from the one who had started work on *The Boy Who Killed His Mother* in 1926—older, wiser, more deeply hurt, and infinitely more aware of the wider world.

Talking with Zelda's doctors, he acquired a layman's understanding of Freud and Jung. Reading Spengler and Yeats, he learned that the West was in decline and the center could not hold. Above all, it began to seem that Marx was right, and that capitalism must soon give way. Had he gone over to communism like Bunny Wilson? Ernest asked Scott. If so, he was much too late. Ernest had undergone his own flirtation with Communism in 1919-1921, and now had put it behind him. Still, he added, he supposed "everybody has to go through some political or religious faith sooner or later."

Scott was in fact highly interested in Marxist ideas at the time. While he was in Hollywood, he persuaded Zelda to read M. Ilin's *New Russia's Primer*, a simplified description of the Soviet Five-Year Plan written for schoolchildren. She and Scottie had "a long bed-time talk about the Soviets and the Russian idea," Zelda wrote Scott in Hollywood. She also advanced a highly sensible program of her own, and sought her husband's endorsement by an appeal to Hemingway's authority. "We *must* reduce our scale of living," she said. It would be easier if they could start from a lower base. That, she pointed out, was "sound economics and what Ernest and most of our friends do." Despite his developing political-economic consciousness, Fitzgerald was loath to change his extravagant spending habits.

Outlining his "General Plan" for *Tender Is the Night* early in 1932, Scott emphasized the revolutionary background. His novel, he wrote, should "[s]how a man who is a natural idealist, a spoiled priest, giving in for various causes to the ideas of the haute bourgeoisie, and in his rise to the top of the social world losing his idealism, his talent and turning to drink and dissipation." In order to cure his wife of her illness, this man (Dick Diver) was to pretend to a belief in the current order he did not hold, "being in fact a communist-liberal-idealist, a moralist in revolt." After his private collapse, Diver was to send "his neglected son into Soviet Russia to educate him."

Much of this outline was scrapped before Fitzgerald was through with his novel, but not—significantly—his implicit condemnation of the rich, and particularly of the Warren family, from the crooked grandfather to the degenerate father and the daughters who use their sexual power (Nicole) and financial means (Baby) to dominate and mistreat others.

Zelda was also at work on a novel. She had written several articles and stories during the 1920s, which were usually published under false colors as the joint work of F. Scott and Zelda Fitzgerald or under her husband's byline alone. His name on the piece commanded a higher price. During her sixteen months at Prangins clinic in Switzerland, she wrote "sixteen or twenty short stories" to release the artistic energy that had previously gone into ballet. Most of these were never published—Scott thought that they were unprofessional, "about as interesting as the average high-school product and yet all of them 'talented.'" Restored to the familiar surroundings of her childhood, Zelda shifted from stories to a novel about a young Southern girl who goes off to Europe with her philandering husband and discovers herself as a ballet dancer.

Zelda emerged psychologically intact from the crisis of her father's death, but suffered a relapse early in 1932 while working hard on her novel. In February Scott took her to the Phipps clinic at Johns Hopkins in Baltimore. Though undergoing treatment, she continued to write, and in four weeks time finished the first draft of the novel. Scott must have felt embarrassed that Zelda had accomplished so much, so fast. But her book as it was then fashioned needed considerable editing—among other things, she had named her heroine's unsympathetic husband Amory Blaine, the name of the hero of *This Side of Paradise*. Scott worked with her on that task, eventually sending the revised script to Perkins in mid-May along with some promotional comments. Zelda's book, which was to be called *Save Me the Waltz*, was "a good novel now, perhaps a very good novel." Scott went on to compare her work to that of Hemingway and Thomas Wolfe, two writers Perkins was editing. Zelda's novel was more "the expression of a powerful personality," like [Thomas Wolfe's] *Look Homeward, Angel,* than the work of a finished artist like Ernest Hemingway. It should appeal to the thousands of readers interested in dancing. The book was "*about something* & absolutely new, & should sell.*"

But Fitzgerald also had a touchy issue to deal with. Hemingway had told him once he would never publish a book in the same season with him, "meaning it would lead to ill-feeling." Now that promised to happen with Ernest's book about bullfighting, *Death in the Afternoon,* and with Zelda's novel, both coming out in the fall. If he saw Ernest, Scott advised, *"Do not praise [Zelda's novel], or even talk about it to him!"* Even though there was no possible conflict between the two books, Ernest would expect Max's "entire allegiance." Besides, Scott pointed out in considerable understatement, there "has always been a subtle struggle between Ernest & Zelda," and it would be better not to risk "curiously grave consequences—curious, that is, to un-jealous men like you and me."

Fitzgerald's warning came too late. Perkins had already written Hemingway with the news that he had seen Zelda's novel—it was initially sent directly to Max, without any editing or commentary from Scott—and that there were some good things in it. "If you ever publish any books by any wives of mine," Ernest wrote back, "I'll bloody well shoot you." *Death in the Afternoon* was published September 23, 1932. The reviews ranged widely, and the book had a decent if not spectacular sale. *Save Me the Waltz* was published exactly two weeks later, on October 7, 1932. The reviews were poor, and despite Fitzgerald's predictions the book did not sell. Max sent Ernest a copy of Zelda's novel, which he "found to be completely and absolutely unreadable." He offered to forward it to anyone Max could think of who might be able to read it.

One of the reasons Perkins wanted to publish *Save Me the Waltz* was the hope that Zelda might turn out to be "a writer of popular books" and through her earnings rescue the Fitzgeralds from their precarious financial condition. Over the years of waiting for Scott's next novel, Max confided to Ernest, Scribner's had advanced him so much that it was impossible to imagine his making "anything out of a novel even if it were a great success." But if Zelda could begin to make money, Perkins thought, "they ought to get into a good position where Scott could write."

In this and other letters of the early 1930s, Perkins was manifestly trying to include Hemingway in his concern about Fitzgerald's various troubles. In effect, he was asking Ernest to commiserate with him in his distress, and on occasion to participate in schemes to relieve Scott's woes. Until the end of 1929, Hemingway willingly accepted complicity with Perkins in this task. In correspondence he chided Scott for writing stories instead of novels, but the harsh message was softened by the clear and sometimes explicit assumption that Scott was an important writer and what he did with his talent therefore mattered. By 1932, however, Hemingway had renounced the role of rehabilitating Fitzgerald.

Yes, Scott had been his benefactor, but as always he was eager to discharge the debt and move on. And yes, Scott had once been his best friend, but those days were over, brought to an end by Fitzgerald's series of personal and social blunders during 1929: making a mess of timekeeping in the bout with Callaghan, spilling the beans to Vallombrosa, abasing himself by misinterpreting Stein's observations, tipsily revealing the worst of McAlmon's slanders, and interposing himself as editor, agent, adman, and all-around nuisance with regard to *A Farewell to Arms*. It seemed very much as if Scott were bent on alienating Ernest's affections. Certainly his behavior had that effect.

In his letters to Perkins, therefore, Hemingway adopted an increasingly callous attitude toward Fitzgerald. "Poor old Scott," he'd remark by way of dismissing the subject, and then move on to more important matters. "Poor old Scott" was no longer his problem. "Listen," he wrote Perkins by way of signing off on any future obligation, "you have troubles, and they are real troubles, and Scott has bad troubles, and I have had some troubles and if Mr. Thomas Wolfe lives long enough, great writer though he should be, he will have plenty of troubles too but I get my work done in spite of all troubles and when it is done to hell with it being bitched by somebody else's troubles." And to John Dos Passos later that month, kidding Dos's "camera eye" technique in *U.S.A.* and denigrating Fitzgerald: "Writing a fine book about Scott Fitzgerald oddly enough. Very interesting and instructive. Am going to have a camera eye looking up a horse's ass and newsreels of you singing in Chinese and give a drink of hot kirsch to every customer." And again to Max Perkins in July, in reply to Max's letter about seeing Fitzgerald in Baltimore, in fine spirits but not looking well: "Poor old Scott—He should have swapped Zelda when she was at her craziest but still saleable back 5 or 6 years ago before she was diagnosed as nutty—He is the great tragedy of talent in our bloody generation."

During this period, Hemingway was not alone in wanting to limit his relations with Fitzgerald. Scott also managed to antagonize two other men he greatly admired, H.L. Mencken and Edmund Wilson.

Even before they came to Baltimore, Fitzgerald had wired Mencken for advice about "the biggest psychiatrist at Johns Hopkins for nonorganic nervous troubles." Once living there, he looked up the Menckens socially. There was a "somewhat weird evening" at La Paix, the Fitzgeralds' rented house outside the city where Zelda, on outpatient basis, struck the sage of Baltimore as "palpably only half sane." Mencken's wife, Sara, spooked by the dinner party, vowed never to return. Later Scott got into the disconcerting habit of dropping in on the Menckens, usually uninvited. He still stood in awe of Mencken, whom he had regarded as a kind of literary god in the earliest days of his writing career. For his part Mencken took an interest in Fitzgerald as yet another literary acquaintance who was ruining himself with drink. "[L]iquor sets him wild," he noted, "and he is apt, when drunk, to knock over a dinner table, or run his automobile into a bank building." Joseph Hergesheimer, in nearby West Chester, reported that Fitzgerald caused a sensation "by arising at the dinner table and taking down his pantaloons, exposing his gospel pipe." When an "always plainly tight" Scott began to propose taking Sara and Menck for automobile rides with himself at the wheel, they decided to bar him from the house. They were both fond of him, but he was making himself impossible.

With Wilson, another man he regarded as his intellectual superior, Fitzgerald's behavior followed a different but equally offensive course. After passing a certain point of alcoholic consumption, Scott would alternate needling his friends with even more annoying expressions of admiration. He would abase himself before Wilson, for example, characterizing himself as a vulgarian sitting at the feet of the scholar. Then he would switch to insulting remarks, adding, "Can't take it, huh?" if Bunny came back at him. All this struck Wilson, admittedly "a hard guy to get along with" himself, as "high school (Princeton University) stuff" they should dispense with, now that they were well into their thirties. In a 1950 letter to Fitzgerald biographer Arthur Mizener, Wilson downplayed this tension between them as "due to a misunderstanding on my part, my own self-confidence at the time being probably in as bad shape as his." But Scott's needling-praising technique was damned irritating, and not uncommon at this stage of his life. John Bishop was subjected to this treatment, he told Wilson, and Bunny himself had seen Fitzgerald do it with Hemingway.

DINNER AT THE AURORA

In January 1933, Fitzgerald went on a "terrible bat" in New York, and in the midst of it arranged for a dinner meeting with Hemingway and Wilson. The effects were disastrous. All three men did some drinking in advance. Ernest arrived in a horse-drawn carriage, announcing that he wanted to do something for the horse, after attempting to justify the death and disemboweling of horses during bullfights in *Death in the Afternoon*. In great good spirits, he sang a bawdy Italian song for the waiters at the Aurora restaurant. Scott was already drunk when Wilson arrived, and immediately began to jibe at him. "Where's Mary Blair?" he demanded. Mary Blair was Wilson's first wife, whom he had divorced years earlier. Wilson was then grieving for his second wife Margaret Canby, who had died in an accident a few months before.

With Ernest, Scott took a stance of abject hero worship. "Hemingway was now a great man," Wilson reported, "and Scott was so much overcome by his greatness that he embarrassed me by his self-abasement." He was looking for a woman, Scott declared, and Ernest told him he was in no shape for one. Well, he was done with men, anyway, Scott said. Hemingway told Wilson to ignore that comment, for he and Scott sometimes joked around about homosexuality. Then he told Fitzgerald "not to overdo it." As the evening deteriorated, Fitzgerald laid his head on the table, then lay on the floor pretending to be unconscious but actually listening to the conversation and "from time to time needling his hero, whose weaknesses he had studied intently, with malicious little interpolations." From time to time Wilson or Hemingway escorted him to the men's room, to hold his head while he vomited. Finally, Ernest and Bunny returned Scott to his hotel room at the Plaza. Wilson stayed on to hear what Fitzgerald might have to say as he sobered up, but Scott simply undressed and put himself to bed and stared at Bunny "with his expressionless birdlike eyes."

The next day, as was his wont, Scott called both of his dinner companions to apologize. When Wilson mentioned the cold eye Fitzgerald had fixed him with, Scott belligerently said, "No confidence, eh? Well, you'll have to learn to take it." Ernest assured Scott he would not mention the incident to Max Perkins, but Fitzgerald brought it up anyway in a letter to Max regretting that he had violated "a custom of many years standing" by not telephoning him during his New York trip. By return mail, Perkins let Fitzgerald know that there was no need for such explanations. He had called Max up after all, leaving a message when he was out, and Max had called back, missing connections with Scott at the Plaza. It was the least of the things he would have liked to forget about that trip.

"I came to New York to get drunk and swinish and I shouldn't have looked up you and Ernest in such a humor of impotent desperation," Fitzgerald wrote Wilson a month later. "I assume full responsibility for all unpleasantness— with Ernest I seem to have reached a state where I half bait, half truckle to him... Anyhow, plenty of egotism for the moment." In his notebooks years later, he was inclined to absolve himself of much of the blame. "Very strong personalities must confine themselves in mutual conversation to very gentle subjects," he generalized. "[I]f they start at a high pitch as at the last meeting of Ernest, Bunny and me, their meeting is spoiled. It does not matter who sets the theme or what it is."

After the dinner at the Aurora, Hemingway wrote Perkins that he didn't know whether Scott was going to "ever come out of this thing." He seemed so "damned perverse." Of course it wasn't easy to get your work done properly, but that didn't account for Scott's "wanting to fail—it's that damned, bloody romanticism." What he really needed to do was to grow up—and dry out. "I wish to Christ I could see him sober," Ernest concluded. A few weeks later, he wrote Perkins speculating that the only things that might make Scott a writer again would be 1) Zelda's death, or 2) his stomach giving out so he couldn't drink. Worst of all, Scott was now cultivating his failure. "He's gone into that cheap Irish love of defeat, betrayal of himself, etc."

Ernest did nothing to bolster Scott's confidence—quite the contrary. In "Homage to Switzerland," which appeared in the April 1933 *Scribner's* magazine, he took a satirical swipe in a fictional conversation at the subject matter of Fitzgerald's magazine fiction. Were the Berlitz students a wild lot? a traveling American asks his Swiss waitress, who has been studying languages. "What about all this necking and petting? Were there many smoothies? Did you ever run into Scott Fitzgerald?"

"Homage to Switzerland" was one of the lesser stories in *Winner Take Nothing*, Hemingway's collection that was published in October 1933. By this time, Wilson had apparently decided, on the basis of the dinner at the Aurora and other signals, that the way to motivate Fitzgerald was to appeal to his rivalrous instincts vis-à-vis Hemingway. After reading an advance copy of *Winner Take Nothing*, he wrote Scott congratulating him on at last completing *Tender Is the Night*, which was then scheduled for January-April 1934 serialization in *Scribner's* magazine, to be followed by book publication. Although the best of the stories in Hemingway's new collection were "excellent," Wilson said, he still advised Fitzgerald—not once but twice—that "now is your time to creep up on him." The subtext of that particular image was anything but reassuring. As Wilson saw the literary contest, Hemingway was obviously in the lead and Fitzgerald could only gain on him through stealth.

Wilson was correct in thinking that the issue of comparative standing was on Fitzgerald's mind. Late in September 1933, he unveiled to Perkins his plan "to prevail upon the [newly formed] *Modern Library*, even with a subsidy, to bring out *Gatsby* a few weeks after the book publication of [*Tender*]." He would share in the cost of the subsidy, if needed. Fitzgerald felt that Scribner's business department had taken a short-sighted view of the importance—to the firm as well as to the author—of his literary reputation. "As for example," he went on, "a novel of Ernest's in the *Modern Library* [*A Farewell to Arms* came out in a Modern Library edition in May 1932] and no novel of mine, a good short story of Ernest's in their collection of the Great Modern Short Stories and a purely commercial story of mine." He added two ingratiating remarks. First, he assured Max that he would be easier to deal with than Ernest when it came to making cuts in *Tender* for serial publication. Second, he would deliver the final manuscript to Scribner's in a month's time. *"Please do not have a band as I do not care for music."* Fitzgerald's reputation was indeed on the wane. Athough *The Great Gatsby* appeared as he wished in a Modern Library edition in September 1934, there was only one printing, of 5,000 copies.

MISSED CONNECTIONS

Fitzgerald had a great deal riding on *Tender*, his first novel in nine years. Initially he considered a preface that would try to account for the long gap. After all, there had been scarcely a week during that period when someone didn't ask him for a report on when his new book would be finished. But he scotched that plan, and counseled Perkins to play down the "At last, the long awaited..." approach in advertising. Above all he wanted to differentiate his novel from his formulaic happy-ending stories in the *Saturday Evening Post*. He cautioned Perkins not to "use the phrase 'Riviera' or 'gay resorts'" in ad copy. It would be much better to point out that "after a romantic start, a serious story unfolds"—advice that Scribner's followed in writing the book-jacket description of the novel. He was also dead set against any kind of personal ballyhoo or publicity. "The reputation of a book must grow from within upward, must be a natural growth," he maintained, and *Tender Is the Night* perfectly illustrated his point. Undervalued in its own time, it has grown to rank, with *Gatsby*, as the work on which Fitzgerald's critical reputation most securely rests.

In a letter to John Peale Bishop the week before publication of *Tender*, Fitzgerald discoursed on the distinction between his two great novels. The intention of the two books was "entirely different." *Gatsby* was a *dramatic* novel, a kind of "tour de force" demanding sharply drawn dramatic scenes. *Tender* was a "philosophical, now called psychological novel," with material so "harrowing and highly charged" that he deliberately refrained from pointing it up emotionally. That was particularly true of the "dying fall" ending that Hemingway had "developed to me, in conversation." In *Tender*, he was covering a far wider canvas than in *Gatsby*, a novel with a strict time sequence and a tightly knit plot line. It was like comparing a sonnet sequence with an epic.

Fitzgerald may have counseled against ballyhoo, but could hardly prevent his publishers from seeking endorsements from illustrious literary figures. Hemingway was not one of them; wisely, neither Scott nor Ernest supplied blurbs for each other's books. For endorsements, Scribner's turned instead to Gertrude Stein, who had praised *Gatsby* in her autobiography, and to T.S. Eliot.

In February 1933, Eliot came to Baltimore to lecture at Johns Hopkins, and a meeting was arranged with Fitzgerald. Scott stayed sober for the afternoon and evening they spent together. "I read him some of his poems and he seemed to think they were pretty good," Fitzgerald wrote Wilson afterwards. He liked Eliot, who had just ended a devastating marriage, but thought he seemed "very broken and sad and shrunk inside." Eliot's manner reminded him of what Stein said about Hemingway: that he was "one of those tall men who are always tired." In any case, Eliot proved willing when asked for a word of praise about Fitzgerald. Scribner's printed his comment on the front flap of the book jacket for *Tender*: "I have been waiting for another book by Mr. Scott Fitzgerald with more eagerness and curiosity than I should feel towards the work of any of his contemporaries, except that of Mr. Ernest Hemingway." A fine encomium but for the galling comparison at the end.

Scribner's also used a laudatory phrase from Eliot on the back of the book jacket, quoting his comment—in a 1925 letter to Fitzgerald—that he regarded *Gatsby* as "the first step forward in the American novel since Henry James." Scott sent off a letter to Eliot in London disavowing complicity in the gaffe. "I regret terribly that they used a line from a personal letter of yours on the jacket," he wrote. "I know how I would feel if anyone used as publicity what I had written in a personal letter."

Still, the technique of praise by reference to another eminence—Fitzgerald compared to James—was one that Scott himself used in a letter of introduction composed on the same day he wrote Eliot in England. The introduction was intended to help a young man named Charles (Bill) Warren land a job in Hollywood. Warren "has shown a remarkable talent for the theatre in writing, composing and directing two shows" in Baltimore, Fitzgerald observed. His gifts were "amazingly varied," and he should soon fit in and rise close to the top in motion pictures. "[I]n fact," Fitzgerald added as a clincher, "I haven't believed in anybody so strongly since Ernest Hemingway." Thanking Fitzgerald for his letter of introduction a few months later, Warren pointed out that the "little line of yours about 'haven't been as interested in anyone since Hemingway' has had the desired effect every time."

With so much at stake, Fitzgerald revised his novel tirelessly right up to publication day. Busy with the galleys in March, he wrote Perkins that he couldn't help making changes. As "a serious man" he was determined to struggle over every line he published, and if the last-minute alterations cost money, Scribner's could charge them to his account. Later in the year, when he was working on proofs for his 1935 book of stories *Taps at Reveille*, he confessed that a pile of proofs had the same effect on him that a covey of partridge did on Hemingway. He couldn't leave them alone. Perkins tried to forestall him from excessive tinkering with the stories, and from omitting some of the best of them— "The Swimmers" and "One Trip Abroad," for example—which had been raided to supply passages in *Tender Is the Night*. By way of argument, Max pointed out that Hemingway had sometimes used the same phrases in both story and novel. That was not justification enough for Fitzgerald, who was no longer willing to let Hemingway occupy the high literary ground. Ernest "might be able to afford a lapse in that line," Scott wrote, but he could not. "Each of us has his virtues and one of mine happens to be a great sense of exactitude about my work."

"I'm so glad all the good people liked your book," Zelda wrote her husband shortly after *Tender* came out. That was an exaggeration, for the reviewers varied widely in their assessments. Among the most favorable was Gilbert Seldes, who thought the novel so intense that he had to put it down in order "to stop, to think and to feel." Among the least was Fanny Butcher, who labeled the book "a brilliant failure." *Tender Is the Night* sold reasonably well, for a book published in the trough of the depression. During April and May the book ranked tenth on the *Publishers Weekly* best-seller lists. Criticism focused less on its subject matter—the life of rich expatriates on the Riviera—than Fitzgerald had feared, with one notable exception. Philip Rahv in the *Daily Worker* acknowledged that the novel portrayed the collapse of the haute bourgeoisie, "dying in hospitals for the mentally diseased, in swanky Paris hotels and on the Riviera beaches." At the same time, however, he thought that Fitzgerald discerned "a certain grace" in the last gasps of the leisure class. Why write about them at all? "Dear Mr. Fitzgerald," Rahv concluded in politically doctrinaire fashion, "you can't hide from a hurricane under a beach umbrella."

A number of reviewers were put off by the novel's structure, and particularly by its opening on the Riviera with Rosemary's adoring and romantic depiction of Dick and Nicole Diver's world. This beginning, many felt, made Diver's subsequent downfall hard to accept, and hard to credit. Fitzgerald suspected they were right, and in his notes sketched out a plan for reorganizing the novel along chronological lines.

Most of Fitzgerald's literary friends weighed in with praise for *Tender*. The most perceptive of these appreciations came from John Dos Passos, who admitted that he'd been "enormously thrown off by the beginning" but realized later how establishing that glamorous facade was necessary before showing how it was being eroded by its intrinsic amorality and the social and economic currents of the time. Zelda also noted the revolutionary thrust of the novel. "The book is grand," she wrote Scott. It was very moving to witness "characters *subserviated* to forces" stronger than themselves and "succumbing to the purpose of a changing world." Both Fitzgeralds understood that her history of mental instability supplied *Tender* with much of its authenticity. Scott went so far as to take portions of her troubled letters and assign them to Nicole Diver. It was his material, after all, and he was the professional writer, or so at least he argued in a confrontation with Zelda in May 1933. At that time, and despite the failure of *Save Me the Waltz*, she was contemplating a novel dealing with her schizophrenia. Her doctors thought this was a topic she should avoid, for the sake of her health. Scott thought so too, and not only for that reason.

In February 1934, Zelda suffered another relapse, and was sent to Craig House in Beacon, New York. With dancing and writing more or less forbidden to her, she had turned her attention to painting. Scott arranged a show of her work—thirteen paintings and fifteen drawings—at Cary Ross's gallery in New York from March 29 to April 30, 1934, to overlap publication of *Tender*. Ernest came to see her show, she wrote Scott from Craig House. There was no word from him about Scott's novel.

Although Hemingway delayed letting Fitzgerald know what he thought of *Tender Is the Night*, he freely expressed his opinion to others. He wrote Gerald Murphy, for example, that the book was marred by "too much bloody flashy writing." And he unburdened himself to Max Perkins at length. Perkins had written Hemingway in advance of publication to say that he thought Fitzgerald would "be completely reinstated, if not more" by his novel. When Scott was through with all the revising, Max believed he "would have a genuine masterpiece in its kind." Ernest did not think so.

"Scott's book...has all the brilliance and most of the defects he always has," he wrote Max after finishing the novel. The two most serious defects, in

Hemingway's view, were that Fitzgerald did not really understand people, and that he did not invent enough. In *Tender Is the Night*, Scott started with Gerald and Sara Murphy as models for the Divers, and did a marvelous job of catching "the accent of their voices, their home, their looks." But he invested them with a romantic aura, and knew nothing about them emotionally. "[Y]ou do not learn about people," Ernest pointedly added, by asking them questions such as "Did you sleep with your wife before you married her?" Instead of inventing, Hemingway maintained, Fitzgerald had "made the story conform to the few wows he had saved up out of his life." This was the wrong way to go about writing fiction. In making his argument, Ernest alternated deprecatory remarks about Scott with reflections on the theory of literature.

> The trouble is that he wouldn't learn his trade and he won't be honest. He is always the brilliant young gentleman writer, fallen gentleman writer, gent in the gutter, gent ruined, but never a man. If he is writing about a woman going crazy he has to take a woman who has gone crazy [Zelda]. He can't take one woman [Sara] who would never go crazy and make her go... If he is writing about himself going to hell as a man and a writer he has to accept that and write about that. He can make it all up and imagine it all but he has to imagine it truly...[i]f he wants it to be literature. You can make up every word, thought, and action. But you must make them up truly. Not fake them to suit your convenience or to fit some remembered actions. And you must know what things are about. He misunderstands everything. But he has this marvellous talent, this readability, and if he would write a good one now, making it all up, he could do it. But using actual stuff is the most difficult writing...Making it all up is the easiest and the best.

"Did you like the book?" Fitzgerald finally wrote Hemingway on May 10. "For God's sake drop me a line and tell me one way or the other." Either way, Ernest couldn't hurt his feelings. Scott simply wanted an intelligent opinion to get "the reviewers' jargon" out of his head. Then, as if to provoke an unfavorable response, he went on to criticize *Winner Take Nothing*. As a collection, it had neither the surprise nor the unity of *In Our Time*, and it did not contain "*as large a proportion* of first-flight stories" as *Men Without Women*. It would have been better to hold the book for more material, so that its "sheer bulk" might atone for its inferiority to Hemingway's earlier collections.

"I liked it and I didn't like it," Hemingway reported in a letter of May 28. A major difficulty, as he saw it, was that Dick and Nicole Diver were obviously fashioned after the Murphys at the beginning, but by the end had segued into fictionalized versions of Scott and Zelda. In arguing the point, Hemingway adopted his characteristic stance as expert. "You can take you or me or Zelda or Pauline or Hadley or Sara or Gerald but you have to keep them the same and you can only make them do what they would do. You can't make one be another." Invention was "the finest thing" but it didn't work if you made up something that would not actually happen. There were some "wonderful places" in the novel, and no one could write better, but Scott "cheated too damned much in this one."

He'd "always claimed" Fitzgerald couldn't think, Hemingway continued, but backed down from that generalization to a more specific charge. A long time ago, he wrote, Scott "stopped listening except to the answers to your own questions." Seeing and listening were the writer's stock in trade. Scott could still see well enough, but he wasn't listening. The novel "was a lot better than I say," Ernest conceded. "But not as good as you can do."

Hemingway proceeded with a barrage against Fitzgerald's failings that, depending on one's point of view, could be construed either as bracing critiques or downright insults. First came the "masterpiece" issue, in combination with a jibe at Fitzgerald's popular fiction for the magazines. Scott simply had to write, and not worry "about what the boys will say nor whether it will be a masterpiece." He himself produced one page of masterpiece to ninety-one pages of shit, and tried to put the shit in the wastebasket, Ernest said. Scott felt he had to "publish crap to make money to live," but that was all right so long as he wrote as well as he could on his novels and forgot about creating masterpieces. He didn't think "well enough to sit down and write a deliberate masterpiece."

Next Ernest turned his attention to what he regarded as Scott's unseemly wallowing in his misfortunes. Here as throughout the letter, Hemingway's advice came in the form of a directive from on high. "Forget your personal tragedy," he commanded Fitzgerald. "We are all bitched from the start and you especially have to be hurt like hell before you can write seriously. But when you get the damned hurt use it—don't cheat with it." Neither of them were tragic characters. "All we are is writers and what we should do is write."

Before signing off, Hemingway went on to take swipes at Fitzgerald's wife and his drinking. "Of all people on earth you needed discipline in your work and instead you marry someone who is jealous of your work, wants to compete with you and ruins you." He was oversimplifying, Ernest admitted, but he thought

Zelda was crazy the first time he met her, and Scott "complicated" matters by being in love with her. Then too, he was "a rummy" but no more a rummy than James Joyce and most good writers were. The thought inspired Ernest to finish on a note of encouragement. "But Scott, good writers always come back. Always." What's more, Scott was a much better writer now than he had been a decade before, when he thought he was so marvellous.

The letter ended in a glow of good feeling. Ernest was "damned fond" of Scott and wished they had a chance to talk. Scott had been "so damned stinking" in New York (at the dinner with Wilson) that they didn't get anywhere. Still, they'd "had good times talking" in the past. In his comments on *Tender*, he'd left out commentary on its "good parts," for Scott knew how good they were. What's more, Ernest agreed with Scott about *Winner Take Nothing*. He'd wanted to hold off publication until he had more stories, himself. Almost as an afterthought, he appealed to Fitzgerald's long-standing practice of promoting his career. Scott had Hollywood connections, he knew. "What about The Sun also and the movies? Any chance?"

Fitzgerald replied at once to Hemingway's letter. He took exception to Ernest's views on "composite characters" like Dick and Nicole Diver—a point he was to expand upon in correspondence with John Peale Bishop and Sara Murphy—and confessed that he'd committed a literary "burglary" by adopting Ernest's concept of an emotionally subdued ending for *Tender*. He thanked Hemingway for his letter, which was "damned nice." And he too wished they might talk face to face. Perhaps it was true that he no longer listened. "But I listen to you and would like damn well to hear your voice again."

In writing her husband from Craig House, Zelda proposed that he should invite Ernest to visit him in Baltimore. He had "more room than people in the house," she pointed out, now that she was no longer in residence. Scott issued no such invitation, but a number of meetings between the two men were suggested during 1934 and 1935. In December 1934, for example, Arnold Gingrich at *Esquire* was planning to visit Hemingway in Key West, and go fishing with him on his new 38-foot boat, the *Pilar*. Gingrich proposed bringing Fitzgerald along, and Hemingway okayed the idea. At the last minute, Fitzgerald canceled by telegram: SEEMS IMPOSSIBLE TO GET DOWN THIS WEEK AND I CERTAINLY REGRET IT. HAD SO MANY THINGS TO TALK TO YOU ABOUT.

According to Fitzgerald, his mother's illness prevented the trip. In reality, Scott did not want to face Ernest in an environment where he would feel out of his depth. The following month, it was Perkins who suggested bringing

Fitzgerald along when he came to Key West to read the typescript of Hemingway's *Green Hills of Africa*. This time, Hemingway discouraged the notion. It would be better to see Fitzgerald after he'd finished revisions on the book, Ernest wrote Max. Scott's literary judgments were "deplorable." As ever the peacemaker, Perkins wrote Fitzgerald after his trip to Key West that "Hem was quite mad" when he didn't bring Scott with him. Late in February, he passed on to Hemingway Scott's claim that he'd been "on the absolute wagon for a month" and felt fine. It would be a miracle if Scott could really quit drinking, Max realized, but a note from Ernest might help.

The prospect for a reunion improved after Hemingway wrote Perkins in April that he was having second thoughts about Scott's novel. "How is Scott?" Ernest wrote. "I wish I could see him. A strange thing is that in retrospect his *Tender is the Night* gets better and better. I wish you would tell him I said so." Max passed on the good words to Fitzgerald, who pasted them in his scrapbook. "Thanks for the message from Ernest," Scott wrote back. "I'd like to see him too and I always think of my friendship with him as being one of the high spots of my life. But I still believe that such things have a mortality, perhaps in reaction to their very excessive life, and that we will never again see very much of each other." So it worked out, even though Max continued to propose a foregathering of his two authors. He'd like to see Ernest, Scott responded on May 11, but only "under the most favorable of circumstances." At that moment, Zelda was in "very bad condition" and his own mood reflected hers. Two days later, however, Scott wired Ernest that he could make a three-day stay at Key West if that didn't interfere with his plans. By way of setting the ground rules for his visit, he added, NOT UP TO ANYTHING STRENUOUS PROBABLY RESULT OF TEETOTALLING SINCE JANUARY. The timing was off. Pauline wired back that Ernest was in Bimini.

In December Hemingway sent Fitzgerald a macabre invitation. He began with a discussion of illness—Zelda's continuing troubles, Scott's bad liver and heart and lungs, his and Scott's mutual insomnia—before firing his opening salvo. "You put so damned much value on youth it seemed to me that you confused growing up with growing old," he observed. Still, Ernest admitted, Scott had taken so much punishment he had no business trying to tell him anything.

Now that the revolution was heating up in Cuba, Ernest had a specific proposal in mind. Scott had been complaining to him of his illnesses and misfortunes. All right, then: if Scott really felt blue, he should get himself heavily insured and come down to Key West and Ernest would take him to Cuba on his boat and see to it that he got killed. His family would be provided for and he wouldn't have to write any more and Ernest would write him a fine obituary. "[W]e can take your liver out and give it to the Princeton Museum, your heart to the Plaza Hotel, one lung to Max Perkins and the other to George Horace Lorimer. If we can still find your balls I will take them...to Antibes and have them cast into the sea off Eden Roc and we will get MacLeish to write a Mystic Poem to be read at that Catholic School...you went to." Then he ventured on such a poem himself, to be titled "Lines To Be Read At the Casting of Scott FitzGerald's balls into the Sea from Eden Roc." Get that insurance, pal, he repeated, in a curious echo of his father's preparations for death. "If they won't give you health or life insurance get accident insurance."

Such was the kind of thing Ernest expected to pass for good-natured raillery. He finished with an exclamatory "Merry Christmas!" and signed himself "Yours always affectionately." Scott did not go to Key West, or on Ernest's boat to Cuba. They would not meet again until 1937. During the interim, Fitzgerald's life and career touched bottom. There were times when he wished he were dead.

In talking with Fitzgerald and Hemingway in 1925, Dean Gauss from Princeton brought up the issue of early indebtedness. Fitzgerald admitted that British author Compton Mackenzie strongly influenced *This Side of Paradise*, and Hemingway acknowledged that Sherwood Anderson's *Winesburg, Ohio* had been his first model. Both agreed that they had to pay for whatever help they'd gotten from others and then proceed to find their own voice. "It was like consulting a psychiatrist," Gauss wrote. "If you were to go on your own, you soon had to wean yourself of such outside direction." Ernest had paid Anderson off, somewhat brutally, in *The Torrents of Spring*. But Gertrude Stein was still around, and still asserting her importance in shaping his work.

Since the summer of 1933, when Gertrude Stein's *Autobiography of Alice B. Toklas* was serialized in the *Atlantic*, Arnold Gingrich had been urging Hemingway to respond to her accusations that he had been "formed" as a writer by her and Anderson ("they were both a little proud and a little ashamed" of their handiwork) and that he was both fragile and "yellow," like some of the flatboat men on the Mississippi Mark Twain had written about. Gingrich pressed the point when Stein and Toklas came to the United States for an extended lecture tour in late 1934. Hemingway was writing informal and wide-ranging "letters" for *Esquire* every month, anyway. Why not take a whack at Gertrude in one of them? It would make "a sure-fire piece" for the magazine.

With a show of restraint, Hemingway said no. He'd heard Stein on the radio, he wrote Gingrich in mid-November, and she sounded "so God awful" that a counterattack would be "like socking a dummy or a ghost." He knew all her weak spots, and there was "a certain damned fine feeling of superiority" in knowing he could finish her off at any time and still not doing it. Besides, he didn't like "to slam the old bitch around" when she was having such a fine time being lionized in the United States.

In fact Ernest was not so magnanimous as all that. In his introduction to James Charters's (Jimmie the Barman's) memoirs of Montparnasse, published in July 1934, he expressed his pronounced preference for honest saloons over the literary salons of "legendary women." And in a passage for *Green Hills of Africa*, which was to be published the following year, he repeated a conversation between himself and Pauline about Gertrude Stein. Once she had been talented. Now she was all "malice and nonsense and self-praise....Woman of letters. Salon woman. What a lousy stinking life." In the same book, he turned the issue of influence upside down. It was not that she had "formed" him, but the other way around. Stein never could write dialogue, until she learned how to do it from his fiction. "She never could forgive learning that and she was afraid people would notice it, where she'd learned it, so she had to attack me." Stein had been all right until she went through menopause, Hemingway wrote both Gingrich and Perkins. Then, suddenly, she lost "all sense of taste" and couldn't tell a good picture from a bad one, or a good writer from a lousy one.

When Stein's memoir appeared, Fitzgerald called Perkins to ask whether Hemingway was "bothered" by her slurs against him. A little bit at first, Max replied, putting it mildly. But Scott was only human, and could not help being pleased by Stein's prediction in the *Autobiography* that he would be read long after "his contemporaries" were forgotten. In his notebooks, Fitzgerald used one of her aspersions against Hemingway as a spur for his own ambitions. "I want to write scenes that are frightening and inimitable. I don't want to be as intelligible to my contemporaries as Ernest who as Gertrude Stein said, is bound for the Museums. I am sure I am far enough ahead to have some small immortality if I can keep well."

So, when Stein wrote him that she and Toklas would be in Baltimore over the holidays, and that she "liked a lot" of *Tender Is the Night*, Fitzgerald invited them to Christmas Eve dinner. A curious exchange of presents ensued. When Scottie came down to greet the guests, Gertrude apologized for not bringing her a Christmas gift. "I did not know I was to see you," she explained. Undaunted, Scottie asked if perhaps Stein might not have something in her pocket—and was pleased when the visitor produced a pencil and presented it to her. "I shall keep this as a souvenir," the fourteen-year-old girl announced solemnly.

Zelda was also on the scene, on overnight leave from Sheppard and Enoch Pratt hospital. During the evening, she showed Stein some of her recent paintings. When Gertrude expressed an interest, Scott immediately proclaimed that she must accept as a gift any two of them she liked. That was fine with Gertrude, who chose two paintings, but Zelda drew the line. Scott pointed out that Gertrude had been exceedingly kind to him, and that when she hung Zelda's work in her Paris salon, it might make her famous. That was not her husband's gift to make, Zelda made clear. He could give Stein everything he owned, but she couldn't have those paintings. In the end, Gertrude took a canvas with her, but it was not one of the two she selected. A few days later, Scott assured Stein in a letter that Zelda had been given "a tangible sense of her own existence" when Gertrude liked two of her paintings well enough to want to own them. In his usual fashion, he also apologized for having, himself, been "somewhat stupid-got with the Christmas spirit."

In 1934 alone, Fitzgerald twice invoked Hemingway's name in articles for *Esquire*. "F. Scott and Zelda Fitzgerald," as authors of "Auction—Model 1934," recall that their treasured Lalique turtle "held the white violets the first night Ernest Hemingway came to our house"—an occasion that even Zelda, who probably wrote the piece, must have felt worth noting. "Sleeping and Waking," Fitzgerald's powerful December 1934 essay on insomnia, began with the observation that for a long time he thought Hemingway's 1927 story "Now I Lay Me" constituted the last word on the subject.

The primary example of Fitzgerald's continuing obsession with Hemingway, however, came in the form of "Philippe, Count of Darkness," the historical novel he embarked upon immediately after *Tender Is the Night*. The book, which was never completed, was to recount the adventures of a French nobleman modeled on Hemingway. This medieval novel "shall be the story of Ernest," Fitzgerald declared in his notebooks, where he also articulated his ambitions for this work-in-progress: "Just as Stendhal's portrait of a Byronic man made *Le Rouge et le Noir*, so couldn't my portrait of Ernest as Philippe make the real modern man?" He completed four installments of the novel, which were published in *Redbook*. In the first three, Philippe battles the Normans for the land his father bequeathed to him, survives a dangerous encounter with King Louis the Stammerer, brutally disposes of a number of enemies, and woos women with masterful dominance—an almost invincible warrior-hero. In the fourth episode, however, Philippe is weakened by his love for the Lady Griselda, a witch who exerts her power over him—a plot development that suggests his hero worship of Hemingway may have been waning.

Fitzgerald knew a good deal about French history, and did considerable research for "Philippe." But the results were less than satisfactory. In the first place, the exploits of the hero were not credible. Second, and more important, the dialogue was written in an unintentionally comic patois mixing medieval formality with modern slang. The four installments, all written in 1934 and 1935, read as poorly as anything Fitzgerald wrote. Nonetheless, he twice proposed going back to them late in 1938, either as (when rewritten) the leadoff item for a new collection of stories or (when fleshed out considerably) as a full-scale novel. He was reluctant to give up on a project he had devoted so much time to.

There is no evidence that Hemingway read these stories, or that he knew Philippe was fashioned after himself. Fitzgerald understood, of course, and was also concerned about a possible conflict between his medieval book and what Hemingway was then writing. Late in 1934 he quizzed Perkins about Ernest's next novel, and was relieved to find that it was not to be the story about the Crusades Hemingway once spoke to him about. "I would hate like hell for my 9th century novel to have to compete with *that*," he commented.

The Question of Influence

Students of literature are notorious for finding improbable connections between authors and their works. It is a consequence, probably, of too much indoor cogitation and not enough exercise. Eureka! the dedicated think, as they consign their revelations to the paper that will prove their brilliance. Usually the result is an arid intellectual exercise that convinces no one but the writer of the many ways, many, that X influenced Y. Books, as Emerson warned in "The American Scholar," "are for the scholar's idle times."

This is not to say that writers do not influence each other. Of course they do. T.S. Eliot, who knew what he owed to Dante and Spenser and Shakespeare, made the point cogently:

> Someone said: "The dead writers are remote from us because we know so much more than they did." Precisely, and they are that which we know.

Eliot's own history proved the point. The shadow of "The Waste Land" falls across both *The Great Gatsby* and *The Sun Also Rises*, as across much of the modern literary landscape.

Among contemporaneous writers, the issue becomes more complicated and controversial. Loyalists are liable to disavow indebtedness on the part of "their author." Matthew J. Bruccoli, the leading authority on the life and work of F. Scott Fitzgerald, has declared that "[n]either Hemingway nor Fitzgerald influenced the other's writing." Bruccoli points out, rightly, that the two men wrote in "utterly dissimilar" styles: Fitzgerald the more lyrical and traditional, Hemingway in a vocabulary not much beyond Basic English and with the understatement Eliot advocated in his doctrine of the "objective correlative." Fitzgerald could evoke emotional reactions through the magical sound of his particular voice on the page. Hemingway aimed to let the concrete suggest the ineffable, to "put down what really happened in action; what the actual things were which produced the emotion that you experienced."

The difference between them as writers may be measured in the conclusions to their greatest novels. Each book ends with the death of a principal figure. At the end of *The Great Gatsby*, Nick Carraway has made a last trip to the dead protagonist's "huge incoherent failure of a house." In a powerfully charged poetic voice, he—and Fitzgerald through him—calls up a vision of the promise of America.

> Most of the big shore places were closed now and there were hardly any lights except the shadowy, moving glow of a ferryboat across the Sound. And as the moon rose higher the inessential houses began to melt away until gradually I became aware of the old island here that flowered once for Dutch sailors' eyes—a fresh, green breast of the new world. Its vanished trees, the trees that had made way for Gatsby's house, had once pandered in whispers to the last and greatest of all human dreams; for a transitory enchanted moment man must have held his breath in the presence of this continent, compelled into an aesthetic contemplation he neither understood nor desired, face to face for the last time in history with something commensurate with his capacity for wonder.
>
> And as I sat there, brooding on the old unknown world, I thought of Gatsby's wonder when he first picked out the green light at the end of Daisy's dock. He had come a long way to this blue lawn and

his dream must have seemed so close that he could hardly fail to grasp it. He did not know that it was already behind him, somewhere back in that vast obscurity beyond the city, where the dark fields of the republic rolled on under the night.

Gatsby believed in the green light, the orgastic future that year by year recedes before us. It eluded us then, but that's no matter— tomorrow we will run faster, stretch out our arms further....And one fine morning—

So we beat on, boats against the current, borne back ceaselessly into the past.

Past and future and present merge in the imagery of this reflection, and are mirrored in the changes of tense of the final two brief paragraphs. A man's reach must exceed his grasp, Browning wrote. Fitzgerald wanted us to feel that there was something magnificent in Gatsby's quest for the unattainable—and unworthy—object of his dreams. And he did it with his extraordinary gift for evocative language.

At the end of *A Farewell to Arms*, Hemingway lets clipped dialogue and a fade-out paragraph convey Frederic's desolation. Controlled fury emerges from the persistent negations of his conversation with the doctor, and pathos from his despairing attempt to commune with the dead Catherine. He is angry and he is alone and nothing will ever be the same again.

Outside the room, in the hall, I spoke to the doctor. "Is there anything I can do to-night?"

"No. There is nothing to do. Can I take you to your hotel?"

"No, thank you. I am going to stay here a while."

"I know there is nothing to say. I cannot tell you—"

"No," I said. "There is nothing to say."

"Good-night," he said. "I cannot take you to your hotel?"

"No, thank you."

"It was the only thing to do," he said. "The operation proved—"

"I do not want to talk about it," I said.

"I would like to take you to your hotel."

"No, thank you."

He went down the hall. I went to the door of the room.

"You can't come in now," one of the nurses said.

"Yes I can," I said.

"You can't come in yet."

"You get out," I said. "The other one too."

But after I had got them out and shut the door and turned off the light it wasn't any good. It was like saying good-by to a statue. After a while I went out and left the hospital and walked back to the hotel in the rain.

Gertrude Stein and Christian Gauss were right in concluding that the two young authors, both twenty-nine when they finished these novels, burned with different flames and drew from opposite ends of the color spectrum. Yet they *did* influence each other in demonstrable and important ways.

Fitzgerald was highly sensitive to the echoes of Hemingway he heard on every side. In his October 1933 memorial essay on Ring Lardner, he commented that Ring's many imitators "lifted everything except the shirt off his back—only Hemingway had been so thoroughly frisked." And in critiquing Bishop's novel *Act of Darkness*, he called attention to "the tremendous power of certain stylists." He detected traces of Hemingway's cadence in Bishop's writing, and cautioned him against letting borrowed language "cradle his ideas." He had found from his own experience, Scott said, that it was much better to cut such passages and substitute "something that *is* yourself."

When he was working hard on the last stages of *Tender Is the Night*, Fitzgerald was particularly aware of the danger of lapsing into Hemingwayesque patches. Directly to Hemingway, he talked about "pieces and paragraphs" Ernest had written that he "read over and over." He'd had to stop doing so for fear that Hemingway's "particular rhythms were going to creep in on mine by process of infiltration. Perhaps you will recognize some of your remarks in *Tender*, but I did every damn thing I could to avoid that."

The manuscripts of Fitzgerald's novel testify both to the "awful pull" he felt toward Hemingway's style, and his determined efforts to resist it. In the draft of one scene, for example, Fitzgerald initially wrote, "Dick and Mrs. Spears [Rosemary's mother] sat in the Cafe des Allies in Cannes. It was August now and all the leaves were dusty and the sparkle of the mica was dulled and dusty on the baked ground. A few gusts of a mistral from farther down the coast seeped through the Estoril and rocked the fishing boats in the harbor, pointing their masts here and there at the featureless sky. The waiters sweated working in the shade." In the margin, next to the sentence about August and its repetition of "dusty," he wrote "Hemmingway." What Fitzgerald was hearing in his own prose, Alan Margolies has suggested, was the beginning of *A Farewell to Arms*. "Troops went by the house and down the road and the dust they raised powdered the leaves of the trees. The trunks of the trees too were dusty and the leaves fell early that year and we saw the troops marching along the road and the dust rising and leaves, stirred by the breeze, falling and the soldiers marching and afterward the road bare and white except for the leaves."

In revision, Fitzgerald tried to erase the similarity. He eliminated the second "dusty" and the leaves and dropped the sentence about the sweating waiters. In still other passages, he warned himself against imitative language, inserting "Hem" above a sentence he deleted, remarking "Beware Ernest in this scene," and, again, "Now cheerful cafe scene but remember to avoid Hemmingway." At another place in his drafts, Fitzgerald invoked Hemingway's name and the most widely quoted passage in *A Farewell to Arms*. Dick Diver is thinking about a female patient of his, an artist who is tortured by eczema (as was Zelda). Not for her, he reflects, "the frontiers of consciousness." That kind of exploration "was for peasants, with big thighs and thick ankles who could take punishment as they took bread and salt, take it on every inch of flesh until the word pride was distorted and meaningless, like those words honor and glory and sacrifice that Hemingway speaks of as having been made meaningless in the war." In his manuscript, Fitzgerald placed three question marks in the margin of that last clause. In the book as published, he kept the business about the peasants, but omitted the reference to Hemingway and to Frederic Henry's condemnation of empty patriotic rhetoric.

If Fitzgerald was generally successful in fighting off Hemingway's influence, there is at least one instance where I think Ernest borrowed directly from Scott. In "The Rich Boy," Fitzgerald's story that ran as a two-parter in *Redbook* for January and February 1926, the protagonist Anson Hunter is visiting Paula Legendre—a woman who was once in love with him but who has subsequently found happiness in her marriage to Peter Hagerty. Hagerty returns home about eleven P.M. after having a drink with a friend. "Do you want to see our family gymnastic stunt?" she asks Anson.

> "Yes," he said in an interested voice.
> "All right. Here we go!"
> Hagerty picked her up easily in his arms.
> "This is called the family acrobatic stunt," said Paula. "He carries me up-stairs. Isn't it sweet of him?"

"Yes," said Anson.

Hagerty bent his head slightly until his face touched Paula's.

"And I love him," she said. "I've just been telling you, haven't I, Anson?"

"Yes," he said.

"He's the dearest thing that ever lived in this world, aren't you, darling? ... Well, good night. Here we go. Isn't he strong?"

"Yes," Anson said.

"You'll find a pair of Pete's pajamas laid out for you. Sweet dreams—see you at breakfast."

"Yes," Anson said.

This scene resonates strongly with the end of *The Sun Also Rises*. Jake Barnes has come to Madrid at the behest of Lady Brett Ashley (AM RATHER IN TROUBLE, she'd wired him). On arrival Jake must listen to her go on and on about her affair with Pedro Romero. The situations are much alike, and so is the language the authors employ to communicate emotion. Both Anson and Jake are forced into hearing about their lady love's intimate relationship with another man. And in each case, curt replies—for Hemingway, the monosyllables occasionally shade off into silence—are used to suggest how deeply the protagonist is hurt. In *Sun*, Jake comes to Brett's hotel, puts his arms around her, and kisses her, sensing as he does so that she has something on her mind. She begins to tell him how devastated she feels about having to send the young bullfighter Romero away.

"He shouldn't be living with any one. I realized that right away."

"No."

"Oh, hell!" she said, "let's not talk about it. Let's never talk about it." (*First and second mentions of a proposal Jake welcomes.*)

"All right."

(*Resuming.*) "It was rather a knock his being ashamed of me. He was ashamed of me for a while, you know."

"No."

"Oh, yes. They ragged him about me at the cafe, I guess. He wanted me to grow my hair out..."

....

"What was it about being in trouble?"

"I didn't know whether I could make him go, and I didn't have a sou to go away and leave him. He tried to give me a lot of money, you know. I told him I had scads of it. He knew that was a lie. I couldn't take his money, you know."

"No." (*Beginning to grasp that Brett called on him to rescue her, financially.*)

"Oh, let's not talk about it. There were some funny things, though. Do give me a cigarette." (*Third proposal not to talk, immediately recanted.*)

I lit the cigarette. (*And said nothing.*)

"He learned his English as a waiter in Gib."

"Yes."

"He wanted to marry me, finally."

"Really?"

"Of course. I can't even marry Mike."

(*Lightening up.*) "Maybe he thought that would make him Lord Ashley."

"No, it wasn't that. He really wanted to marry me..."

(*Trying flattery.*) "You ought to feel set up."

"I do. I'm all right again. He's wiped out that damned Cohn."

"Good."

....

"I'm thirty-four, you know. I'm not going to be one of those bitches that ruins children."

'No." (*Monosyllabically.*)

"I'm not going to be that way. I feel rather good, you know. I feel rather set up."

"Good."

She looked away...Then I saw she was crying...I put my arms around her.

"Don't let's ever talk about it. Please don't let's ever talk about it." (*Fourth and fifth times.*)

"Dear Brett."

"I'm going back to Mike." I could feel her crying as I held her close. "He's so damned nice and he's so awful. He's my sort of thing."

She would not look up. I stroked her hair. I could feel her shaking. (*Silence.*)

"I won't be one of those bitches," she said.

"But, oh, Jake, please let's never talk about it." (*Sixth such proposal.*)
(*Silence.*)

The woman in charge of the hotel will not let Jake pay Brett's bill. Romero had taken care of it. Over a couple of pre-prandial martinis, Brett brings up the affair once more. It is then that Jake warns her, "You'll lose it if you talk about it." At lunch he drinks enough wine to stun an ox.

The scene in "The Rich Boy" has been incorrectly cited as an example of *Hemingway's* influence on *Fitzgerald*. The critic who made that mistake was probably led astray by Fitzgerald's letter about having to stop reading Hemingway to avoid imitating him, and by his mention, in *The Crack-Up*, of Hemingway's "infectious style." Yet chronology makes it clear that the influence worked the other way around. Fitzgerald wrote "The Rich Boy" during his stay in Capri in the winter of 1925, before he even met Hemingway, and the story was published as a two-parter in *Redbook* for January and February 1926. Close as they were, there is every reason to suppose that Ernest read Scott's story in manuscript during the fall of 1925, when he was at work on *Sun*. Fitzgerald did not read *Sun* until June 1926.

For the most part, Hemingway kept quiet about stylistic debts to Fitzgerald. There was at least one exception to the rule. In his 1950 novel *Across the River and Into the Trees*, Hemingway's Colonel Cantwell—en route to his beloved Venice—comments, "They were coming up on Mestre fast, and already it was like going to New York the first time you were ever there in the old days when it was shining, white and beautiful. I stole that, he thought." The theft was from Fitzgerald's 1932 essay "My Lost City." There he described the enchantment that the "tall white city," the "whole shining edifice" of New York had once provoked in him, and in a forlorn cry calls out for a return of what is forever past: "Come back, come back, O glittering and white."

CHAPTER 7

AFTERNOON OF AN AUTHOR

> It is in the thirties that we want friends. In the forties
> we know they won't save us any more than love did.
> — F. SCOTT FITZGERALD, *Notebooks*

Advised by his doctors to take the mountain air for his health, Fitzgerald spent much of 1935 and 1936 in the salubrious surroundings of western North Carolina, and particularly in Asheville. The weather may have been good for his lungs, but the rest of his life bottomed out in a descent that was still ongoing when he wrote the confessional "Crack-Up" essays during November 1935. He was troubled by his tuberculosis and alcoholism, by Zelda's worsening condition, and by his sense of himself as a man.

In April 1935, Fitzgerald wrote Mencken a curious letter. In the course of delivering a message of consolation for the death of his wife, Sara, Scott told Mencken—a generation older than himself—how important his support had been.

> We have both lived too deeply in our own generation to have much
> communication except with a mutual respect, but that you accepted
> me as an equal...settles something that has been haunting me about
> my relations with men ever since my tacit break with Earnest
> Hemingway. I suppose like most people whose stuff is creative fiction
> there is a touch of the feminine in me (never in any sense tactile—I
> have always been woman crazy, God knows)— but there are times
> when it is nice to think that there are other wheelhorses pulling the
> whole load of human grief and despair.

Here Fitzgerald is making at least two points. First, he felt insecure in his relationships with male companions, and the "tacit break" with Hemingway—following so closely on the accusations from McAlmon and Callaghan—had made him question his own masculinity. Mencken's acceptance of him as a writer and a man had given him some reassurance along these lines. Second, he felt a still stronger connection with Mencken in their "mutual grief," as fellow wheelhorses beset by the worst of misfortunes.

Living at the Grove Park Inn in Asheville in the summer of 1935, Fitzgerald continued his run of bad luck. The hotel itself was beyond his means, and he soon added to his expenses by hiring Laura Guthrie as his secretary-amanuensis. He also exercised his considerable charm on her, producing a "fierce" infatuation that drove her "nearly crazy" with thoughts of him. Guthrie, a divorcee whose nominal job at the Grove Park Inn was to read the palms of wealthy guests, kept a journal during the course of that eventful summer, recounting almost everything that Fitzgerald said and did. He talked about Zelda and his fear that he was to blame for her terrible condition. He drank vast quantities of beer, "almost to the exclusion of eating food, because his stomach hurts then, and he has to get the alcoholic stimulation to keep himself at his work." He explored the borders of sexuality. "Women don't give me a kick," he said, trying her out. "I am a fairy. What are you? Are you like that?" And he talked incessantly of Hemingway.

"Ernest Hemingway is his best friend and he admires him extravagantly—both in a literary way and as a man," Guthrie recorded, adding a number of direct quotes she'd scribbled in her notes. "We are Damon and Pythias," Fitzgerald said of a friendship he knew had foundered. Then he went on to implied comparisons: "Ernest is the best writer in the U.S.A. today." "I used to want to be the best damn writer in the U.S.A. I still do."

Hemingway had achieved the heights, and he was still climbing, a ranking Fitzgerald reiterated in a note he himself made during a visit with novelist James Boyd at Southern Pines. "Dorothy Parker once said that Ernest Hemmingway could make a six-day bicycle race interesting to a Mother Superior, or words to that effect—the present writer has no claim to such talent, but..."

One of Guthrie's duties was to accompany Fitzgerald to nightspots in and around Asheville. They whiled away the time one night by creating a "genius" chart, in which Fitzgerald classified the great men and women of the time—both those he had known and those he knew of—on a scale ranging from "16" to "29." He may have adopted this numbering system from the game of cribbage, where

29 is the highest score a player can make on any given hand. Fitzgerald awarded three women the highest ranking: writers Willa Cather, Edith Wharton, Edna St. Vincent Millay. Six men qualified for 29s: inventors Thomas Edison and Guglielmo Marconi, industrialist Henry Ford, and writers Hemingway, Mencken, and Theodore Dreiser. Hemingway's name he wrote at the very top.

"I've simply got to arrange something for this summer that will bring me to life again," Fitzgerald wrote Max Perkins in mid-April 1935. What he arranged was an affair with Beatrice Dance, a young married woman from San Antonio who was also staying at the Grove Park Inn. The affair lasted seven weeks, from mid-June to early August, when her husband and doctor broke it off. "I gather [Scott's] been having some kind of what's called a love-affair.—But I guess not serious," Perkins wrote Hemingway on August 30. He didn't like the idea, Max went on, but at least it wouldn't "hurt his writing or his health, like gin. Might even help." Ernest agreed, with emasculating qualifications. "Imagine a love affair would help Scott if he has anything left to love with and the woman isn't so awful that he has to kid himself too much."

The affair was no casual summer romance as Perkins and Hemingway assumed. Beatrice Dance, anything but awful, fell very much in love with Scott, and he was revived by the intensity of her passion. "You are the loveliest human being I have ever known," he wrote her when the affair ended. "I love you—you are crystal clear, blown glass with the sun cutting always very suddenly across it...Goodbye, goodbye, you are part of me forever." In Hollywood a few years later, he told Sheilah Graham that he'd been in love with Beatrice. She was the first woman to make him forget Zelda.

In the aftermath of the affair, Fitzgerald abandoned the beer and ale regimen he'd been following all summer and went back to gin. Sticking to malt beverages was supposed to cut down on his alcohol intake, but it did not have that effect. "Beer ran down his throat like a waterfall runs down a rock," Guthrie noted in her journal, "but with more disastrous effects." His mind wandered, and he couldn't finish telling stories aloud, much less get them down on paper. The switch to gin made matters worse. "Being tied to an alcoholic whether as secretary, nurse, or wife," Guthrie concluded, was the hardest work in the world.

On Friday the 13th of September, she cleaned up the mess in Fitzgerald's room, packed his dirty clothes in a suitcase, helped him get dressed, and accompanied him to the desk in the lobby while he checked out. Debilitated as he was, appearances still counted. Then they took a taxicab to the hospital's alcoholic ward, where she deposited him and escaped. There were to be several such drying-out periods during the following year. A few months earlier, Laura Guthrie had been consumed by her feelings for Fitzgerald. On the day she turned him over to the hospital nurses, she remarked in her journal, "I never felt less in love with a man in my life."

Later that month, after Fitzgerald returned to Baltimore, Perkins sent him the latest news of Hemingway. Ernest had come through New York, and would not return to Key West until the weather cooled down. His safari book, *Green Hills of Africa*, was scheduled for publication on October 25, and Max was worried about its reception. The critics, and to a lesser extent the public, seemed to have turned against Hemingway after the lukewarm reception of *Death in the Afternoon* and *Winner Take Nothing*. In effect, Max was asking Scott to sympathize with Ernest's travail, much as he did when summoning Hemingway to share in his distress about Fitzgerald. "Every writer seems to have to go through a period when the tide runs against him strongly," Perkins pointed out. From that point of view it was probably just as well that the anti-Hemingway tide was running when Ernest "was writing books that are in a general sense minor ones." *Green Hills of Africa* belonged in that category.

Green Hills provided an account of Ernest's 1933 safari to Africa with Pauline and Key West friends Charles and Lorine Thompson under the guidance of white hunter Philip Percival. As with *Death in the Afternoon*, the book also offered Hemingway the opportunity to discourse on any number of unrelated subjects. One such topic was the present state of American literature. In addressing it, Ernest on three occasions made damning remarks about Scott. The first— and worst—of these, had to do with cowardice among writers. Archie MacLeish "had the most charm" and they'd had good times together. "But he was really a coward so you were never completely comfortable with him just as he was never completely comfortable with himself." John Dos Passos, though "perhaps a little over-married," was as brave as a buffalo. Fitzgerald, like MacLeish, "was a coward of great charm. I wondered why the cowards all had so much charm."

The passage about cowardice was deleted from the manuscript, but two other slurs directed at Fitzgerald's reputation made it into print. He did not use Fitzgerald's (or anyone else's) name, but the context makes it clear that he had Scott in mind. Hemingway held forth on what writers need—talent, discipline, "an absolute conscience"—and on the forces that "destroy" them, especially money. "[O]ur writers when they have made some money increase their standard of living and they are caught. They have to write to keep up their establishments, their wives, and so on, and they write slop." Ernest further cited "two good writers" who were ruined because "they have read the critics and they must write masterpieces. The masterpieces the critics said they wrote. They weren't masterpieces, of course. They were just quite good books. So now they cannot write at all. The critics have made them impotent."

On the day after publication of *Green Hills*, Perkins went over the immediate reaction in a letter to Fitzgerald. On balance, he thought the reviews were favorable, particularly the first-rate one in the Sunday *New York Times* supplement. The unfavorable ones, Max believed, were motivated by the "prevalent idea," at the bottom of the depression, that writers should concern themselves with "troubles of the day" rather than hunting expeditions. In fact, most of the major reviewers disliked the book. "Just another safari." "It used to be pretty exciting, sitting down to read a new book by Hemingway, but now it's damn near alarming." "[F]ew fine and no extraordinary passages, and large parts of it are dull." Most tellingly, Edmund Wilson observed that Hemingway was "beginning to be imposed upon by the American publicity legend which has been created about him." Among the principal figures in his books, the pontificating Hemingway of *Green Hills* was "his own worst-drawn character" and "his own worst commentator. His very prose style goes to pot."

Such responses drove Hemingway into a state of depression, and he was displeased when Fitzgerald wrote him six weeks after the appearance of the book that he too hadn't much liked it. That letter has been lost, but it probably reflected the views Scott expressed to Perkins: that he had been put off by the "calendar of slaughter" and the "sad jocosity" of Ernest's references to Pauline as "P.O.M." or Poor Old Mama. "Was delighted from your letter to see you don't know any more about when a book is a good book or what makes a book bad than ever," Ernest wrote in reply to the critique. Scott reminded him of "a brilliant mathematician who loves mathematics truly and always gets the wrong answers to the problems."

In the rest of this December 16 letter, however, Hemingway went out of his way to make amends. He was damned fond of Scott and hoped they would soon have a chance to talk. He'd started up to see him in Asheville but family duties kept him away. The more he thought about it, the better *Tender* seemed. Still, Fitzgerald's comments must have stung. Writing Dos Passos the next day, Ernest complained about Scott's "very supercilious letter" about how bad *Green Hills of Africa* was. (Fitzgerald did not, apparently, raise the issue of why Hemingway had chosen to attack him in the book.) "Goddamn it," Ernest told Dos, "that is a *good* book. I'm not a goddamned patriot about my stuff and can tell good from bad and that is a good book." The swearing and protestation made it sound as though he were trying to convince himself.

— ✳ —

"The Crack-Up" and the Crack in "Snows"

After a fallow few months in Baltimore, Fitzgerald returned to the mountains to take stock of a badly diminished life. It had become painfully evident that Zelda would not recover from her illness. She was kept under close supervision at Sheppard-Pratt as she alternated between a catatonic state and an "intense suicidal mania." Scott's own health was deteriorating as well. His energy was flagging. He had trouble sleeping. His drinking forced him to the hospital. He was strapped for funds, and could no longer write the formulaic boy meets girl, boy loses girl, boy wins girl back yarns that for so long had kept him financially afloat.

This time, Fitzgerald stayed not in the elegant Grove Park Inn but at the pedestrian Skylands hotel in Hendersonville. He brought with him a mantra suggested by *Esquire*'s Gingrich, who was buying short pieces from him for one-tenth of what his stories had brought in a few years before. In order to escape his writer's block, Gingrich suggested, Scott was to repeat "I can't write stories of young love for *The Saturday Evening Post* because I can't write stories of young love for *The Saturday Evening Post* because..." and so on. Holed up in Hendersonville and living on the cheap, he wrote the "Crack-Up" articles that amply demonstrated *why* he couldn't go on writing stories of young love.

In his elegiac essay about Ring Lardner two years before, Fitzgerald regretted that his friend had not lived up to his promise as a writer. One reason was that Lardner resisted expressing his innermost thoughts and feelings in his work. Scott suggested to him once that he should write something "deeply personal," but Ring refused out of reticence and modesty. The unfortunate consequence was that Lardner "got less percentage of himself on paper than any other American of the first flight." It was a mistake Fitzgerald wanted to avoid. For *Esquire*, during the middle 1930s, he turned out a series of autobiographical essays. The best-known of these were the three "Crack-Up" pieces that ran early in 1936: "The Crack-Up" (February), "Pasting It Together" (March), and "Handle with Care" (April).

The articles set out to explore Fitzgerald's "dark night of the soul," to come to grips with his depression. By the standards of confessional memoirs at the end of the century, the account of his breakdown seems less than candid. Much is withheld.

Zelda's illness is not mentioned, and the essays bring up drinking only in order to rule it out as a cause of Fitzgerald's problems. The only character is the enervated and somewhat cynical persona of F. Scott Fitzgerald, at the end of his rope.

Fitzgerald does not use much concrete detail in these essays, nor does he supply much by way of narrative. There are a few anecdotes, but mostly he talks about his feelings—normally a sure-fire recipe for producing boredom. Yet the "Crack-Up" essays elicited an extraordinary reaction among readers at the time of publication, and continue to generate considerable power two generations later. One quality keeping the essays alive is Fitzgerald's gift for communicating how he feels through metaphor. He is like a cracked plate, Fitzgerald tells us, not to be brought out for company but good enough to "hold crackers...or go into the ice box under left-overs." He is an emotional bankrupt who has overdrawn on his resources. He is a beggar holding "the tin cup of self-pity." He is an ineffectual soldier "standing at twilight on a deserted range, with an empty rifle in [his] hands and the targets down." He is a little boy left home alone at night.

In the last of the three essays, these comparisons become progressively more self-demeaning. Finally, Fitzgerald warns that he has hung a *"Cave Canem"* sign above his door. "I will try to be a correct animal though, and if you throw me a bone with enough meat on it I may even lick your hand." He will no longer squander his emotions as in the past. He will adopt a serviceable if insincere smile to deal with everyday encounters. He will become "a writer only," and so—with luck—survive the storms ahead. In good part, he has been reduced to this depleted condition because he has no real self of his own, having borrowed so much of his personality from others. His "intellectual conscience," for example, derived from Wilson (duly identified) and his "artistic conscience" from another source who was, manifestly, Ernest Hemingway.

Fitzgerald got a lot of mail in response to the "Crack-Up" articles. Old friends counseled him to cheer up. Fans encouraged him to keep writing. His professional colleagues, however, were generally dismayed. Perkins thought the essays might be taken as signaling the end of a career. Ober feared they would compromise his attempt to secure Fitzgerald a job in Hollywood. On a wider scale, Dos Passos objected to Scott's concentration on his own troubles as the depression continued and fascism flourished in Europe. "Christ, man," he objected, "how do you find time in the middle of the general conflagration to worry about all that stuff?"

Ernest did not write Scott directly about his confessional essays, but let others know how he felt. After reading the first installment, he wrote Dos Passos that he'd been trying to cheer Fitzgerald up through his letters—including, presumably, the one about casting his balls in the sea, if he had any balls left—but that he hadn't been able to. "See the reason now. He's officially cracked up." As for Fitzgerald's ills, "Max says he has many imaginary diseases along with, I imagine, some very real liver trouble."

After the second essay appeared, Ernest wrote Max at substantial length. The *Esquire* pieces "seem to me to be so miserable," and there was another one coming. He'd always known Scott couldn't think, but he did have "a marvellous talent and the thing is to use it—not whine in public." Hemingway went on to generalize that "people go through that emptiness many times in life and come out and do work."

In this letter, too, Ernest included two disparaging comments about Fitzgerald that were often repeated in his correspondence. First, his lack of courage: "If Scott had gone to that war that he always felt so bad about missing, he would have been shot for cowardice." Second, his failure to grow up: "It was a terrible thing for him to love youth so much that he jumped straight from youth to senility without going through manhood." It seemed "rotten" to criticize Scott after all he'd gone through, Ernest acknowledged. "Maybe the Church would help him." Work definitely would help, but only honest, noncommercial work. "I wish we could help him," Ernest concluded.

Perkins noted in reply that Fitzgerald had recently appealed to him for money, and he supposed he would give it to him. The important thing was to get him back on his feet and at his desk. As always on the lookout for the bright side, Max propounded the theory that a truly hopeless man would not have written the first two *Esquire* articles. If he really felt that bad, he would not have been able to talk about it. Scott was only forty, he mentioned in closing [actually, still 39]. It was "absurd for him to give up." Following the appearance of the final essay, Ernest told Max he wished Scott "would pull out of that shamelessness of defeat." They were all bound to die. Why quit before then? Was Scott trying to make a career out of "being through"? Then he reverted to the cowardice theme. Fitzgerald, he wrote, had "something in common" with Max Baer, the heavyweight boxer who (Hemingway thought) had taken a dive against Joe Louis to avoid being beaten up.

Writing Sara Murphy in March 1936, Fitzgerald remembered the awful "*suddenness*" with which the Murphys' son Baoth had died from spinal meningitis the previous year. He had gone through nothing quite like that, but he was writing her as a fellow sufferer of misfortunes. It was different with Ernest, who had "managed to escape the great thunderbolts." This was not entirely true. Hemingway's father's suicide administered one such shock, and his father bequeathed to him the painful legacy of depression. Ernest was susceptible all his life to terrible bouts of what he called "the black ass." With them came periods when he behaved with extraordinary cruelty to almost everyone he knew, himself included if you take into account his long list of self-inflicted injuries. The late 1930s were one such period. His work was being panned, his marriage to Pauline was falling apart, and he lost all tolerance for former friends like Archibald MacLeish and John Dos Passos and, most notably, Scott Fitzgerald.

In June 1936 Arnold Gingrich went down to Bimini to join Hemingway in another of his deep-sea fishing outings. There he met Jane Mason, the beautiful young wife of Pan Am's man in Havana and possibly, at the time, Hemingway's lover. Gingrich liked Jane a great deal—twenty years later they would get married—and started talking to her about his admiration for Fitzgerald. He "draws the finest and purest tone from the English language of any writer now alive," Gingrich said. Mason shushed him. "We don't say things like that around here," she said. Members in good standing of the Hemingway camp were not to praise Fitzgerald.

While Ernest had not written Scott directly about what he regarded as the deplorable "Crack-Up" essays, he let him know instead in "The Snows of Kilimanjaro," his story in the August 1936 *Esquire*. Hemingway's cruelly insensitive comment about Fitzgerald in that story breached the boundaries of personal and professional courtesy, and effectively shattered the cracked plate of their friendship. The passage, occurring midway through the story, recorded the thoughts of the narrator about the rich.

[They] were dull and they drank too much, or they played too much backgammon. They were dull and they were repetitious. He remembered poor Scott Fitzgerald and his romantic awe of them and how he had started a story once that began, "The very rich are different from you and me." And how some one had said to Scott, Yes, they have more money. But that was not humorous to Scott. He thought they were a special glamorous race and when he found they weren't it wrecked him as much as any other thing that wrecked him.

This heartless passage derived from two sources. The first was Fitzgerald's "The Rich Boy," where *his* narrator expounds on the situation of the very rich as a group before going on to deal with the specific case of Anson Hunter.

Let me tell you about the very rich. They are different from you and me. They possess and enjoy early, and it does something to them, makes them soft where we are hard, and cynical where we are trustful, in a way that, unless you were born rich, is very difficult to understand. They think, deep in their hearts, that they are better than we are...Even when they enter deep into our world or sink below us, they still think they are better than we are. They are different.

The other, unattributed source was a luncheon Hemingway and Perkins had in New York with the quick-witted Irish writer Mary Colum. Ernest began talking about his contacts with the wealthy folk in Bimini who fished and partied off their yachts. He was getting to know the rich, he said. "The only difference between the rich and other people," Colum instantly responded, "is that the rich have more money." The remark rather belittled Hemingway, who had been waxing expansive. In "The Snows of Kilimanjaro" he transferred the put-down to Fitzgerald.

Perkins reported the Hemingway-Colum exchange in an August 1936 letter to his intimate friend Elizabeth Lemmon. To take Colum's comment and use it against Fitzgerald struck him as "contemptible," Max said. He used no such judgmental language in correspondence with Scott or Ernest, however. In fact, he did not even let Fitzgerald know of the luncheon conversation.

Upon reading "The Snows of Kilimanjaro" in *Esquire* (the issue also contained Scott's "Afternoon of an Author," an autobiographical account of a writer unable to work because of a loss of vitality), Fitzgerald objected at once in a brief letter to Hemingway.

Dear Ernest:
Please lay off me in print. (*Direct, and to the point.*) If I choose to write *de profundis* sometimes it doesn't mean I want friends (*still friends, then?*) praying aloud over my corpse. No doubt you meant it kindly (*how could that have been?*) but it cost me a night's sleep. (*Only one night: I'm tougher than you think.*) And when you incorporate it (the story) in a book would you mind (*gently, gently*) cutting my name?
It's a fine story—one of your best—(*absolutely true, and under the circumstances insightful and generous*) even though the "Poor Scott Fitzgerald etc." rather (*putting it mildly*) spoiled it for me.

Ever Your Friend (*despite all*)
Scott

Riches have never fascinated me, unless combined with the greatest charm or distinction. *(Setting the record straight.)*

Hemingway replied to this letter, but his response has been lost or destroyed. As Fitzgerald told Beatrice Dance, in his response Ernest "rather resentfully" agreed to omit Scott's name when the story was republished in a book. Hemingway also commented that since Fitzgerald had been exposing his private life so "shamelessly" in *Esquire*, he figured it was "open season" on him. At that point, Scott said, he wrote Ernest "a hell of a letter that would have been sudden death for somebody the next time we met" and then—in an access of self-control—decided to tear it up.

Ernest was quite "as nervously broken down" as he was, Scott added, "but it manifests itself in different ways. His inclination is toward megalomania and mine toward melancholy." The megalomania he noted in Hemingway ("a psychopathological condition in which delusional fantasies of wealth, power, or omnipotence predominate") was real enough, but so was *Ernest's* very real melancholia ("a mental disorder characterized by severe depression, apathy, and withdrawal").

Hemingway told Max Perkins that Fitzgerald "was sore" because he'd used his name in "Snows." "He has only been writing those awful things about himself since Feb. in Esquire but if I took issue with his analysis of his proclaimed break-up he gets sore." For five years, Ernest said, he hadn't written a line about anybody he knew because he was so sorry for them all—an inaccuracy, considering *Green Hills of Africa*—but time was running short and he "was going to cease being a gent and go back to being a novelist." This observation, Hemingway must have realized, paraphrased Fitzgerald's resolution in the final "Crack-Up" essay to stop trying to be good or kind or thoughtful and to concentrate instead on becoming a writer only.

Hemingway was not entirely through keeping "anybody he knew" out of his fiction. In a draft of "Snows," Hemingway's protagonist is reminiscing about his days in Paris. "And there in the cafe as he passed was Malcolm Cowley with a pile of saucers in front of him and a stupid look on his potato face talking about the Dada movement with a Roumanian who said his name was Tristan Tzara." Before publication in *Esquire*, however, Hemingway deleted Cowley's name and substituted "that American poet." An element of professional calculation may have contributed to that decision. Cowley was an influential critic and literary editor of the *New Republic*. His name came out. "Poor Scott Fitzgerald" stayed in.

Looking back on Hemingway's insult in "Snows" two months later, Fitzgerald confessed to Perkins that somehow he loved "that man, no matter what he says or does," though his patience had been sorely tried. But he went on to make an attack of his own against Ernest's recent work. "No one could ever hurt him in his first books but he has completely lost his head and the duller he gets about it, the more he is like a punch-drunk pug fighting himself in the movies."

Did Fitzgerald think of the very rich as a "special glamorous race"? And why did Ernest determine, all of a sudden, that this was one of the things that "wrecked" Scott? Earlier he had attributed Fitzgerald's troubles as a writer to a number of causes. Zelda was jealous of his work and tried to emasculate him. Scott could not control his drinking. He wrote slop for money. He was stalled by critical over-praise and the sense that he must write masterpieces. He couldn't think. He didn't listen. He fell in love with the idea of failure. He loved youth so much he never grew up. And so on. In "Snows" for the first time Hemingway cited Fitzgerald's "romantic awe" of the rich as yet another principal cause of his crack-up.

Context helps to explain why. "The Snows of Kilimanjaro" tells the story of Harry, a failed writer, and his rich wife, Helen. In marrying Helen, the writer chose security and comfort over his career, and what happened to him subsequently was very much like what happened to Fitzgerald's Dick Diver in *Tender Is the Night*. He fell into a pattern of too much drinking and too much travel and not enough work. In Africa on safari with his wife (as Ernest and Pauline Hemingway had been in 1933), Harry contracts gangrene and dies, after thinking back on all the stories he had not written. The rotting away of his leg symbolizes the rot in his soul. As much as any story ever written, "The Snows of Kilimanjaro" illustrates how the very rich are different from other people and how they can "wreck" writers. It constitutes a cautionary tale directed at Hemingway himself. Harry rather cynically reflects, as Ernest must have done after leaving Hadley for Pauline, that he had "traded on" his talent. "It was strange, too, wasn't it, that when he fell in love with another woman, that woman should always have more money than the last one?" In singling out Fitzgerald as a writer destroyed by admiration for the rich, Hemingway was transferring the guilt implicit in his own story.

In doing so, moreover, Hemingway chose to ignore what Scott had written on the subject. In the second "Crack-Up" essay, he thought back to the summer of 1919, when Zelda "closed out" their engagement on the basis of common sense. "It was one of those tragic loves doomed for lack of money," and though Fitzgerald wrote a novel and so made it come out all right, "it came out all right for a different person." The man who married the girl in the spring of 1920 "would always cherish an abiding distrust, an animosity, toward the leisure class—not the conviction of a revolutionist but the smouldering hatred of the peasant." Since that time, Fitzgerald had never been able "to stop thinking that at one time a sort of *droit de seigneur* might have been exercised to give one of [his rich friends] my girl." He distrusted the rich, yet worked for money "to share their mobility and the grace that some of them brought into their lives."

In his fiction as well, Fitzgerald consistently repudiated the rich for their callousness toward others (Anson Hunter in "The Rich Boy"), for leaving the dead and destroyed behind them as they took their leave (Tom and Daisy Buchanan in *The Great Gatsby*), and for using up and discarding lesser mortals (Nicole and Baby Warren in *Tender Is the Night*). The "mobility and grace" of the very rich might merit emulation, but not their morals.

The fact is that both Fitzgerald and Hemingway were simultaneously attracted and repelled by the world of the very rich. In "The Short Happy Life of Francis Macomber," a companion safari story to "Snows," Ernest chronicled the sudden coming-of-age of a wealthy playboy and his seemingly accidental murder by his wife, who would have preferred that he remain arrested in his cowardly boy-man status. In *To Have and Have Not*, he sketched the rich yacht people anchored off Key West as immoral, exploitative, sexually conflicted, alcoholic, and generally to be avoided. Most notably, he excoriated the wealthy in *A Moveable Feast* for helping to break up his marriage to Hadley, a union he tended to idealize after the breakup. In their youthful innocence, Ernest wrote, he and Hadley did not learn soon enough "about the good, the attractive, the charming, the soon-beloved, the generous, the understanding rich who have no bad qualities and who give each day the quality of a festival and who, when they have passed and taken the nourishment they needed, leave everything deader than the roots of any grass Attila's horses' hooves ever scoured." So much for the Murphys. And so much and more for John Dos Passos, the "pilot fish" who led them to their prey. (Actually, as Gerry Brenner discovered from the drafts of the posthumously published *A Moveable Feast*, Hemingway intended to moderate this attack on the rich.)

Despite such pronouncements in his fiction, Hemingway in his private life was if anything more involved with the wealthy than was Fitzgerald. Only the very rich had the time to pursue those outdoor sports that meant so much to Ernest: hunting the high country, fishing the deep seas, going to bullfights in Spain or on safari to the Serengeti. And as he grew older and more famous, Ernest became a more desirable object of their social patronage. The very rich inhabited a different world, Hemingway understood. But he maintained that he could go into their country as he would enter any foreign country, and emerge unharmed.

Getting Hemingway to remove "poor Scott Fitzgerald" from "The Snows of Kilimanjaro" was not as easy as Perkins assured Fitzgerald it would be. In fact Ernest contemplated compounding his attack in the months after his story appeared in *Esquire* and Scott asked him to lay off. In early drafts of *To Have and Have Not*, written at that time, Ernest engaged in some extraneous literary gossip. Harry Crosby was a terrible writer who should have killed himself sooner. The homosexual Hart Crane, another suicide, had an unfortunate proclivity for picking up the wrong sailors. About Fitzgerald he put down what he had been saying in letters to Perkins and others: he was all charm and talent with no brains, and had gone straight from youth to senility without stopping at manhood. All of these slurs, together with other passages that obviously libeled Dos Passos (another friend Hemingway had turned against), were cut out before publication.

Fitzgerald did not know about these derogatory reflections, but he *was* worried that Hemingway might not follow through on his promise to delete the reference to himself in book publication of "Snows." It was hard to imagine that Ernest retained "any friendly feeling" toward him at all, Scott wrote Max Perkins in March 1937. But he reminded Perkins that Hemingway had agreed to the change in copy "if the story should come in with me still in it." Not to worry, Max wrote back. He'd spoken to Ernest a while back, and his feelings toward Fitzgerald were "far different from what you seem to suspect." Ernest had "some queer notion" that the reference in "Snows" would give Scott a "jolt" and be good for him. "Anyhow, he means to take it out."

"Thanks for the word about Ernest," Scott answered. "Methinks he does protest too much."

A year later, Fitzgerald took up the issue once more. He sent Perkins a letter he'd received that showed "how a whole lot of people interpreted Ernest's crack" in "Snows." The story had since appeared, without alteration, in *The Best Short Stories 1937*, a collection edited by Edward J. O'Brien. Scott gathered that Ernest could not help that, but then gave vent to his developing indignation. In the fall, Scribner's was planning to publish Hemingway's *First Forty-nine Stories*. "[D]o keep in mind that he has promised to make an elision of my name. It was a damned rotten thing to do, and with anybody but Ernest my tendency would be to crack back. Why did he think it would add to the strength of his story if I had become such a negligible figure? This is quite indefensible on any grounds."

When Hemingway's amended copy for the book came in, late in August, it included some minor changes in the passage but otherwise simply reduced "poor Scott Fitzgerald" to "poor Scott." In mild protest Perkins elaborated on why it would be better if "his name could come out altogether." If people did not recognize "Scott" as Fitzgerald (though he was identified as a writer in the following sentence), "it might as well be some other name." And if they did so identify him, it might take them out of the story for a moment and into thinking about Fitzgerald instead. He'd shown the passage to two people who thought Scott might still feel bad about it, "being very sensitive." It would be good if his name could come out. But they could talk about it when Ernest came to see him during the week ahead.

At that meeting, apparently, Hemingway agreed to take "Scott" out and replace him with "Julian" (the name, by the way, of the suicidal and alcoholic protagonist of John O'Hara's 1934 novel *Appointment in Samarra*). Nor did Perkins tell Fitzgerald of Ernest's halfway measure of changing "Scott Fitzgerald" to "Scott." In a September 1 letter to Scott, Max discoursed on the omnibus Hemingway volume coming out. Titled *The Fifth Column and the First Forty-nine Stories*, it was to include Ernest's new play about the Spanish Civil War, all of his previously collected stories, and four new stories. "One of the new stories is 'The Snows of Kilimanjaro' and you are not in it," Max reported, as if to suggest it had been no trouble at all to get rid of his name. The O'Brien *Best Stories* collection, he added, had nothing to do with Scribner's (it was published by Houghton Mifflin) and he hadn't known it contained "Snows" until after it came out. Max did not say that Ernest surely did know the *Best Short Stories 1937* would contain "Snows." Or that, since the volume was not published until May 1937, Hemingway had time enough to delete the reference to Fitzgerald, if he wished.

In February 1939, Fitzgerald wrote Max commiserating about Thomas Wolfe's unflattering portrait of him in *The Web and the Rock*. Wolfe's making a villain out of his former editor and friend was "astonishing." By way of softening the blow, Scott mentioned Ernest's "sharp turn" against him, a turn that seemed to have a "pointless childish quality—so much so that I really never felt any resentment about it." Looking back on the episode in 1951, Hemingway exhibited no regret whatever. "Poor Scott," he wrote Fitzgerald biographer Arthur Mizener, "and didn't he know that the man in The Snows of Kilimanjaro would have spoken of him, or thought of him, exactly as he, Scott, would have mentioned actual things, cars and places?" Except, of course, that he, Scott, was not an inanimate object like a Ford or a Chevrolet.

"Poor Scott Fitzgerald" was corrected to "poor Julian" in the fall of 1938. Over the years, a legend about an exchange of views on the very rich between Fitzgerald and Hemingway has grown up and become an apocryphal part of literary history. In his notebooks, Fitzgerald wrote, "They have more money. (Ernest's wisecrack.)" When editing *The Crack-Up*, Edmund Wilson included a number of entries from Fitzgerald's notebooks, including that one. In a footnote, Wilson incorrectly explained that "Fitzgerald had said, 'The rich are different from us.' Hemingway had replied, 'Yes, they have more money.'" Lionel Trilling repeated "the famous exchange" in one influential essay, and Harry Levin did in another. So the story has come down to us that the discussion about the very rich—as told in "Snows"—really took place between Fitzgerald and Hemingway, and that Hemingway got the better of it by making the "more money" wisecrack.

There was such a discussion, and in it Mary Colum one-upped Hemingway, not Hemingway Fitzgerald. And even in "Snows," Ernest did not claim credit for the "Yes, they have more money" line, assigning it to an unspecified "someone." (In an early draft of "Snows," Hemingway gave the retort to his protagonist Harry, a fictionalized version of himself.) In the construction of legends, truth cannot compete with fiction.

Last Encounters

In the "Crack-Up" essays, Fitzgerald purported to tell about "a self-immolation" that left him purified and able to face the future, albeit with less energy and enthusiasm than in the past. He had touched bottom, the articles seemed to promise, and was on his way up. This prognosis was premature. Fitzgerald's summer of 1935 in Asheville was disastrous. The summer and fall he spent there in 1936 were worse.

For one thing, Zelda's condition had deteriorated, and Scott had given up hope for her full recovery. In April 1936 he transferred her from Sheppard-Pratt hospital in Baltimore to Highland hospital in Asheville. She weighed only eighty-nine pounds at the time. During the previous three months of "intense suicidal mania," she had tried to strangle herself and to throw herself in front of a passing train. At Highland she came under the care of Dr. Robert Carroll, a forceful director who believed in a regimen of rigidly controlled diet and lots of exercise. To some degree, Zelda responded. She seemed happier, and made no further attempts to kill herself. Instead she began an extended period of religious delusion, believing herself in direct contact with God and almost everyone else headed for an afterlife in hell. Zelda's entire appearance had changed from that of the flirtatious strawberry blond Scott had fallen in love with. Her facial planes had thickened and her skin coarsened in the six years since her breakdown. She rarely smiled, and in photographs looked dour and dull-eyed. When Scott went to see her, the meetings often ended in anger and coldness. "I am sorry," she poignantly wrote him after one such failure of a visit, "that there should be nothing to greet you but an empty shell... I love you anyway—even if there isn't any me or any love or even any life."

Financially and professionally, Fitzgerald continued to slide downhill. In 1935 he made about $17,000 from his writing. In 1936 the figure dropped to $10,000, less than in any year since he started his career in 1920. He could no longer produce stories that would draw several thousand dollars from high-circulation magazines. Liquor was part of the problem, but so was his "emotional bankruptcy." As he commented in a March 1933 essay, he could find plots anywhere—a thousand of them in any criminal law library—but they wouldn't work for him. He had to "start out with an emotion—one that's close to me and that I can understand." By the middle 1930s, he no longer possessed the emotional power to generate short fiction. There seemed less weather than in his youth, he wryly observed in his notebooks, and "practically no men and women at all."

The "Count of Darkness" stories represented an attempt at finding salable subject matter, but they were too remote from his own experience to succeed. The "Gwen" stories about father-and-daughter conflicts originated closer to home, but lacked the punch of his earlier fiction. The *Saturday Evening Post* bought a few of them, and then cut Fitzgerald off as a contributor, for good.

Broke though he was, Fitzgerald stayed at the Grove Park Inn from July to December 1936. He was desperate, and he was drinking heavily. A minor disaster occurred in July when he broke his shoulder diving into the resort's pool; the bone fractured, he insisted, before he hit the water. Worse troubles lay ahead. Fitzgerald had a revolver, and fired it off in an apparent suicide attempt. Thereafter the Inn refused to allow him to remain as a guest unless he was in the care of a trained nurse. Dorothy Richardson was hired to take on this task, which mostly involved trying to control Scott's drinking. The two of them were in his room when an enterprising *New York Post* reporter named Michel Mok came to interview Fitzgerald on September 24, 1936, his fortieth birthday. It turned out to be one of the most devastating interviews in the history of journalism.

Mok's story appeared the following day in the *Post*, under the headline "The Other Side of Paradise: Scott Fitzgerald, 40, Engulfed in Despair." It was the "Crack-Up" articles, of course, that led Mok to pursue Fitzgerald, and during the interview Scott continued to exhibit the same kind of obsession with his own decline that characterized the *Esquire* pieces. "The poet-prophet of the post-war neurotics observed his fortieth birthday yesterday," Mok wrote. He was trying to come back from "the hell of despondency" but there was "obviously little hope in his heart." Mok let description unveil Fitzgerald's condition: "his jittery jumping off and onto his bed, his restless pacing, his trembling hands, his twitching face with its pitiful expression of a cruelly beaten child." He made frequent trips to the highboy which contained a bottle. Each time he poured a drink, he would look appealingly at his nurse and ask, "Just one ounce?" As he grew more expansive, he poured a drink with a cavalier "Much against your better judgment, my dear" for the nurse's disapproving look.

"A series of things happened to papa," Fitzgerald said, commandeering Hemingway's Papa nickname for himself. "So papa got depressed and started drinking a little." It was a case of "[o]ne blow after another, and finally something snapped." In the course of a long and disjointed conversation, Fitzgerald rambled on about his father, about his Army service, about his brief stint in advertising, about his early years as a writer. The "jazz-mad, gin-mad generation" he helped to invent had ended in calamity. "Some became brokers and threw themselves out of windows. Others became bankers and shot themselves... And a few became successful authors." Fitzgerald's face twitched. "Successful authors!" he cried. "Oh, my God, successful authors!" He stumbled to the highboy for another drink.

Fitzgerald also compared himself to two such successful authors. "A writer like me," he said, "must have an utter confidence, an utter faith in his star. It's an almost mystical feeling." Thomas Wolfe and Ernest Hemingway had that kind of confidence, Scott said. He'd once had that feeling too, before losing it "through a series of blows, many of them my own fault." He also praised Hemingway for scolding him about the "Crack-Up" essays. "My best friend, a great American writer—he's the man I call my artistic conscience in one of the *Esquire* articles— wrote me a furious letter. He said I was stupid to write all that gloomy personal stuff."

Fitzgerald did not, however, mention Hemingway's egregious insult in "The Snows of Kilimanjaro." And when he read Mok's ruinous interview, he wired Ernest for his assistance. IF YOU EVER WANTED TO HELP ME YOUR CHANCE IS NOW, he telegraphed, going on to say that Mok's interview put him "in an absurd position" and "cut" on him "directly and indirectly." After some delay, the message reached Hemingway in Cooke City, Montana. He telegraphed Fitzgerald immediately. DEAR SCOTT PLEASE WIRE ME WHAT YOU WANT ME TO DO STOP HAVEN'T SEEN INTERVIEW STOP...WILL DO ANYTHING I CAN AS ALWAYS ERNEST. By the time this telegram reached Scott, his rancor had abated. WIRED UNDER IMPRESSION THAT YOU WERE IN NEW YORK NOTHING CAN BE DONE AT LONG RANGE AND ON COOLER CONSIDERATION SEEMS NOTHING TO BE DONE ANYHOW THANKS BEST ALWAYS SCOTT. Just what Scott thought that Ernest, had he been in New York, might have done is unclear—perhaps look up Mok and punch him out. The cry for help, in his humiliation, was clear enough.

Perkins and Ober, who had vested interests in Fitzgerald's career, were horrified by the interview in the *Post*. In sending along Scott's first telegram, Max wrote Ernest that it "seemed as if Scott were bent upon destroying himself." When a man put himself in the care of a trained nurse, it was time to despair of him. And Scott had been foolish to trust a reporter. As printed, his story "gave you the impression of a completely licked and very drunk person, bereft of hope, acquiescing in his ruin." Fortunately, he added, "hardly anybody reads the New York Post." That consolation went by the boards when *Time* magazine reprinted Mok's interview on October 5.

On that same day, Fitzgerald wrote Ober rationalizing his behavior. He had a fever of 102 and the reporter appealed to his better instincts by claiming to have a relative afflicted with mental trouble, so Scott talked more freely than he should have done. (Later he was to claim, incorrectly, that Mok pieced together fragments from the "Crack-Up" articles instead of reporting what he said and did.) When he read the story in the *Post*, he told Ober, "it seemed about the end" and so he swallowed "four grains" of morphine, "enough to kill a horse. It happened to be an overdose and almost before I could get to the bed I vomited the whole thing and the nurse came in and saw the empty phial and there was hell to pay for a while and afterwards I felt like a fool."

Fitzgerald was in better shape when Marjorie Kinnan Rawlings, another Scribner's author, came to visit him at the suggestion of Max Perkins. Scott seemed exhilarated and sure of his future, she recalled years later. He had "gone astray with his writing, but was ready to go back to it in full force." Rawlings was impressed by two other things about Fitzgerald. Although not interested in her or her writing, he "turned on his charm as deliberately as a water-tap" for her benefit. And he spoke of Hemingway with affection and with another quality that puzzled her. "It was not envy of the work or the man, it was not malice." She decided it was irony, and akin to the irony with which he set out to charm her. In this exercise, Fitzgerald resembled Dick Diver at the end of *Tender*, knowingly pretending affection for Mary North Minghetti, a woman he despised.

Fitzgerald suffered another blow to the ego in print within months. This was administered by his old friend John Peale Bishop in "The Missing All," an article in the Winter 1937 issue of the *Virginia Quarterly Review*. Bishop organized his essay around the contrasts between Hemingway and Fitzgerald, as prime examples of the "Younger Generation" in American literature. In this comparison, Hemingway emerges as an admirable figure—both as a man and a writer—and Fitzgerald as something of a lightweight.

Bishop begins, logically enough, with first meetings. Ezra Pound took him around to see Hemingway in Paris in 1922, when Ernest and Hadley—still childless—were living in a fifth-floor walkup on the rue Cardinal Lemoine. Hemingway was then still sending dispatches to the *Toronto Star Weekly*, but Pound, always quick to jump, had read and admired some of his first unpublished stories and thought that Bishop, as a poet and aspiring fiction writer himself, should meet the young correspondent. Hemingway opened the door: "a stalwart, smiling, good-looking young man" with a pronounced limp. When they left, Pound told Bishop that the limping young man been wounded fighting with the Italians during the war and "left four days for dead." This gross exaggeration provided early evidence of Hemingway's capacity to inspire legends.

Fitzgerald and Bishop met in the fall of their freshman year at Princeton, 1913, and started a conversation about their literary interests. Scott "was pert and fresh and blond, and looked, as some one said, like a jonquil." Not much of a student, he "left Princeton without a degree and without much of an education." He and Bishop talked books: "those I had read, which were not many, those Fitzgerald had read, which were even less, those he said he had read, which were many, many more." At times Bishop sounds affectionate toward his Princeton friend, but the tone throughout is one of casual superiority.

It was in their attitudes toward writing that Bishop drew his sharpest distinction between Hemingway and Fitzgerald. According to Bishop, Hemingway "developed a perfect consciousness of his craft" in Paris because of his innate honesty and incorruptible subjugation to his art. In his discipline and dedication, he was a direct descendant of Flaubert. His accomplishment promised to earn him a place in American literature. His work had both historical and literary importance.

By way of contrast Bishop stressed Fitzgerald's role as social historian. During the 1920s he made himself into "the embodiment of youth's protest against the inhibitions and conventions of an outworn morality." But his implicit program of freedom vs. repression degenerated like the Jazz Age itself into license rather than liberty, and the long hangover that followed. "One can scarcely say that he thinks," Bishop observed of Fitzgerald. Like Rosemary in *Tender Is the Night*, he was "Irish and romantic and illogical." His great subject was first love, and its interconnection with money.

Bishop began the transformation of the "poor Scott Fitzgerald" passage in "Snows" into a celebrated literary anecdote. Here is his version of what Ernest had written, six months before:

> "The rich are not as we are." So began one of [Fitzgerald's] early
> stories. "No," Hemingway once said to him, "they have more money."

In this form, the anecdote was only halfway complete. It was not a direct conversation between Scott and Ernest yet, for "The rich are not as we are" still emanates from a *story* of Fitzgerald's. But the "some one" of "Snows" who responds with the wisecrack had already undergone a metamorphosis into Hemingway himself.

Bowdlerized as it was, the reference was important to Bishop's argument. What he did, in effect, was to provide a rational explanation for Hemingway's remark that Fitzgerald was wrecked by his "romantic awe" of the very rich. According to Bishop, Scott was a victim of his belief that the rich were a race apart. Inasmuch as he shared this misperception with the country at large, it made him an ideal "historian of the period." But it also led to personal disillusionment. Like Gatsby, Bishop maintains, Fitzgerald "remained an intruder in the moneyed world; he admired it and would have liked to be a part of it; and yet with every passing year it becomes more difficult to face it. He has learned the price of everything, and is not a cynic, but a moody sentimentalist who gives himself a very bad time." For Bishop, who had of course read the "Crack-Up" essays, Fitzgerald represented a sad case. He accordingly felt sorry for Scott. And perhaps because he had known him when he was young and foolish and looked "like a jonquil," he could not envision that his Princeton classmate was, like Hemingway, a writer for the ages.

Fitzgerald was hurt by Bishop's essay, the more so because it came from a longtime friend whose career he had vigorously promoted. It was a rotten return, he thought, "for ten years or trying to set him up in a literary way." In the May 1940 letter to Perkins where he wrote those words, Scott linked John Bishop's disloyalty with "Ernest's crack in 'Snows'" (and Harold Ober's decision to stop advancing him money) as a betrayal of friendship. He followed with a curious and revealing passage.

> Once I believed in friendship, believed I could (if I didn't always) make people happy and it was more fun than anything. Now even that seems like a vaudevillian's cheap dream of heaven, a vast minstrel show in which one is the perpetual Bones.

To earn friends, Fitzgerald manifestly believed, you had to make them happy, and for a long time it "was more fun than anything" when he could do so. In the last year of his life he came to see how demeaning it was to play the clown for the entertainment of others.

Scott and Ernest met twice in two months in the summer of 1937. These were brief encounters, not extended reunions. What was over was over. Fitzgerald continued to speak of the friendship as if were still flourishing, as a way of purchasing respect through association. To a lesser degree, so did Hemingway. He came through New York on one trip associated with his activities on behalf of the Loyalists in Spain, and stopped off to visit Perkins at his home. Ernest demanded a telephone at once, announcing that he had "to talk to Scott. He's the only person in America worth talking to."

During the late 1930s, Ernest devoted much of his time and energy to fighting fascism, which was threatening to take over Spain as it had Germany and Italy. He raised money for the cause, and twice traveled to the front during the Spanish Civil War as a correspondent and propagandist. In Madrid, he lived openly with Martha Gellhorn, the writer who was soon to supplant Pauline and become his third wife. With Joris Ivens, he helped to film *The Spanish Earth*, a propaganda film designed to arouse Americans in the battle against fascism as the war escalated and spread.

On June 4, 1937, Hemingway spoke at the second American Writers' Congress in Carnegie Hall. The evening was sponsored by the League of American Writers, a group made up of well-intentioned liberals and doctrinaire Communists. MacLeish was moderator, and the three featured speakers were

Hemingway, Ivens, and Earl Browder, secretary of the Communist Party, U.S.A.

The hall was jammed and hot as Hemingway nervously began his talk about why writers needed to join the cause. Fascism was the only system that would not allow them to tell the truth; unless they spoke now, they would be silenced. It was the speech of the meeting. The audience came to see Hemingway, and though he sweated and stammered at first, he pleased most of them. The novelist Dawn Powell was something of an exception. Ernest's message, as she construed it, was that "war was pretty nice and a lot better than sitting around a hot hall and writers ought to all go to war and get killed and if they didn't they were a big sissy."

Whether Fitzgerald actually attended the writers' congress is unknown. But he and Hemingway did get together sometime during that New York visit. Probably Scott took the train from Baltimore to see Ernest. This meeting produced no fireworks. On the day after the Carnegie Hall gathering, he wrote Hemingway from the train going south. "It was fine to see you so well & full of life, Ernest...All best wishes to your Spanish trip—I wish we could meet more often. I don't feel I know you at all."

A month later Fitzgerald took the long transcontinental train trip to California, where Harold Ober had negotiated a contract for Scott to work for Metro-Goldwyn-Mayer. He had barely arrived when Hemingway and Ivens blew into town to raise funds for Loyalist war relief. According to a letter Robert Benchley wrote his wife, he and Fitzgerald and Hemingway had "a warm and good-humored" lunch together on July 11. The following day, Ernest screened *The Spanish Earth* (with his own voice doing the narration) for some of Hollywood's elite. Fitzgerald was invited to the showing, but there is no firm record that he and Hemingway even talked that evening. (Lillian Hellman, in her unreliable memoir *An Unfinished Woman*, spun a yarn about Scott driving her to a party that Dorothy Parker gave afterwards and being afraid to go in to confront Ernest directly.)

The following day, Scott telegraphed Ernest, THE PICTURE WAS BEYOND PRAISE AND SO WAS YOUR ATTITUDE. He went into greater detail in a letter to Perkins. "Ernest came like a whirlwind, put Ernst Lubitsch the great director in his place by refusing to have his picture prettied up and remade for him a la Hollywood at various cocktail parties." In his notebooks, Fitzgerald wrote, somewhat mysteriously, "Ernest Hemingway and Ernst Lubitsch—Dotty 'We're all shits.'" This suggests that it may have been at Dorothy Parker's party that Hemingway put Lubitsch down, eliciting a cynical remark from the often cynical Parker. Ernest's mission was wildly successful, Scott told Max. "He raised $1000 bills won by Miriam Hopkins fresh from the gaming table, the rumor is $14,000 in one night." But there was also a noticeable change in Hemingway's demeanor. "I felt he was in a state of nervous tensity, that there was something almost religious about it." Scott and Ernest never saw each other again.

AMBIVALENT TO THE END

A month later, in the confines of Perkins's office at Scribner's, Hemingway's temper boiled over. During the interim, Max had written Ernest approvingly about Scott's fresh start in Hollywood. Everyone there seemed impressed by the change in him, and Max's pockets were full of money from the weekly check Fitzgerald sent as payment on his debt. To conclude, Perkins dug a sidelong elbow at Fitzgerald's lamentations in the "Crack-Up." Everything might turn out for the best, he wrote, if Scott "will only begin to dramatize himself as the man who came back...." This time, however, the dramatics came from Ernest and not from Scott.

Hemingway had long been simmering with anger for Max Eastman, a left-wing litterateur he initially met—and liked—while covering the international economic conference in Genoa in 1922. In a June 1933 *New Republic* review of Hemingway's book on bullfighting, Eastman directed a few *ad hominem* thrusts at Ernest. Titled "Bull in the Afternoon," the belated review speculated that Hemingway must lack the "serene confidence" that he was "a full-sized man." Why else would he continue to proclaim his red-blooded masculinity? "Come out from behind that false hair on your chest, Ernest," he advised. Some heated correspondence ensued, involving MacLeish and Perkins as well as Hemingway and Eastman. As usual Perkins poured oil on the troubled waters, assuring Ernest that the article didn't amount to anything. As Hemingway saw it, Eastman had accused him of impotence, and he was determined to exact revenge.

More than four years later, on the afternoon of August 11, 1937, he had his opportunity. When Ernest entered Perkins's office, there was Eastman talking to Max about a new edition of his *Enjoyment of Poetry* anthology. Hemingway and Eastman shook hands amicably enough, but the trouble soon began. A smiling Hemingway ripped open his shirt to expose a chest "hairy enough for anybody." All three men laughed. Then he reached over and opened Eastman's shirt, revealing a chest "as bare as a bald man's head." Further laughter, now a bit tense. Perkins was contemplating unbuttoning his own shirt—at least he could come in second, he figured—when Ernest stopped smiling and suddenly demanded of Eastman, "What do you mean by accusing me of impotence?" He hadn't done that at all, Eastman insisted, and by way of proof picked up a collection of his work lying on Perkins's desk and showed Ernest the reprinted "Bull in the Afternoon" piece. Hemingway was less than delighted to see this attack on him preserved between book covers. After some debate over who should read the piece aloud, Ernest snatched the book from Perkins's hands and slapped Eastman across the face with it. Eastman rushed at Hemingway and the two large men tumbled to the floor, upsetting books and papers from Perkins's desk as they fell. The editor, who was fearful that Hemingway might "kill" Eastman, grabbed the man on top only to discover that the one on the bottom, grinning up at him in absolute equanimity, was Ernest.

There the fracas might have ended had not Eastman written an account of what he regarded as his victory and read it out to friends at a dinner party. The word spread at once, and the story appeared in the evening papers on Friday, August 13. As a full-fledged celebrity, anything about Hemingway qualified as news, particularly if it served to undermine his public image. This was not man bites dog, but close: the older, hardly athletic Eastman had apparently bested the rugged outdoor man of action in a wrestling match. The following day, as he was embarking for Europe aboard the *Champlain*, Ernest presented his own version of the encounter to the *New York Times*. Eastman's claim that he had thrown him to the floor was nonsense. In fact, Eastman jumped at him "like a woman, clawing...with his open hand" and Ernest held him off, not wanting to hurt him. Now, however, he was ready to issue a challenge. He was eager to fix Eastman so he wouldn't give any statements to the press for a while. If Eastman took his fighting prowess seriously, Ernest told the *Times*, let him waive "all legal claims to damages," and he would put up $1,000 for any charity Eastman favored. "Then we'll go into a room and he can read his book to me... The best man unlocks the door."

With that, he sailed off to Spain, and the war, and Martha Gellhorn at the Hotel Florida in Madrid.

Reading about this dustup in the papers, Fitzgerald first wrote Perkins asking what really happened. Was Ernest "on a bat"? Had Eastman run off to Shanghai with Pauline? In any case, he felt "damn sorry" for Hemingway after his own recent "taste of newspaper bastards." Once Perkins provided the details, Scott commiserated with him about Ernest's decline—assuming the role usually occupied by Hemingway feeling sorry for him. He was amused by Perkins's account, but the fact remained that "Ernest did exactly the same asinine thing that I knew he had it in him to do when he was out here" in Hollywood. His discretion "must have been at a low ebb" or he would never have trusted the reporters at the boat. Scott laid the blame on what he thought of as Ernest's somewhat deranged psychological condition. "He is living at the present in a world so entirely his own that it is impossible to help him, even if I felt close to him at the moment, which I don't." Still he liked Ernest so much that it made him wince when imbeciles could "dig at him and hurt him. After all, you would think that a man who has arrived at the position of being practically his country's most eminent writer, could be spared that yelping."

Fitzgerald's feelings about Hemingway grew increasingly ambivalent during his last years in Hollywood. When Scott came through New York in the winter of 1938, sober and solid, he told Max Perkins that he thought of Hemingway as "the most dynamic personality" in the world, or anyhow in the country. Max relayed this news to Ernest, who responded that he never wanted to be dynamic, only a writer, and that at that particular moment he was "in such an unchristly gigantic jam of every bloody kind...that it's practically comic." His marriage to Pauline was on the rocks, for one thing. And the reception of *To Have and Have Not*, published in October 1937, had been anything but favorable.

Like Fitzgerald, Hemingway had gone a long time between novels, eight years having elapsed since *A Farewell to Arms* appeared in 1929. He had hardly been fallow in the interim, but neither his nonfiction books, on bullfighting and Africa, nor the story collection *Winner Take Nothing* did much to advance his reputation. *To Have and Have Not* did still less.

The book cobbled together several long stories about Harry Morgan, a poor working stiff trying to make a living off his boat in Key West. As a "have-not," Morgan is driven into dangerous and illegal activities to support his family. His desperate struggle is pointedly contrasted with the immoral behavior of the "haves" who idle away their time on yachts in the harbor. Dying at the end of the novel, Morgan reflects that "One man alone...ain't got no bloody fucking chance." It was as close to an overt political statement as anything in Hemingway's work, and his novel was greeted by Communist critics as the work of "a great artist and a brave one, brave enough to risk not writing a masterpiece once in a while, big enough to see the thing through." Sinclair Lewis, on the other hand, took a jaundiced view of Hemingway's message "that all excellently educated men and women are boresome and cowardly degenerates, while un-lettered men engaged in rum running and the importation of Chinese coolies are wise and good and attractive." Edmund Wilson called it Hemingway's "Popeye the Sailor" novel.

What made Ernest seem particularly "dynamic" in the late 1930s was his adventuring as a correspondent in the Spanish Civil War. Fitzgerald was of two minds about this—at once admiring and suspicious of Hemingway's motives. In April 1938, Perkins wrote Scott that Ernest had gone back to Spain yet again, for the good reason that he "couldn't reconcile himself to seeing it all go wrong over there—all the people he knew in trouble—while he was sitting around in Key West." From the ship, Hemingway sent Perkins a letter that sounded as if he might not survive this trip to the wars. In this farewell communication, Max said, Ernest "especially mentioned" Scott. Fitzgerald replied that he was touched by Hemingway's "premonitory last word, and fascinated, as always, by the man's Byronic intensity"—Byron having been another writer who thought that he could change the course of history through his actions. He had been reading Ernest's dispatches from Spain in the *Los Angeles Times*, Scott added, but there had been none the last three days. He kept hoping "a stray Krupp shell hasn't knocked off our currently most valuable citizen."

In a fragmentary play script among his papers, Fitzgerald placed Heming-way in the same category with movie actor Errol Flynn as flamboyant partici-pants in the Spanish Civil War. The last time Flynn was in Spain, one character remarks, "he got wounded with some window plaster and Hemingway says that country isn't big enough to hold them both." In pursuing the Loyalist cause, Fitzgerald implied, Hemingway was also pursuing celebrity. In conversation, he told his secretary Frances Kroll that Ernest went to the war in order to prove him-self to himself. It occurred to her that Scott, confined to his desk in Hollywood, might have envied Ernest in the field with a beautiful companion at his side in Martha Gellhorn.

At the same time, Fitzgerald continued to rank Hemingway among the greatest of modern writers. In dispensing advice to young people who aspired to the craft, he consistently singled out Hemingway as a model for them to emulate. Frances Turnbull of Baltimore sent him a story, and Scott returned it with the comment that she hadn't dug deep enough into her emotional life. Look at Dickens, he recommended, who recycled his childhood abuse and starvation into *Oliver Twist*. Or at Hemingway's first stories in *In Our Time* that "went right down to the bottom of all that he had ever felt or known." Willingness to invade one's most private feelings was the price of admission to the profession.

215

In his regular letters of instruction to daughter Scottie at Vassar, Fitzgerald posed questions she was to answer about various books and poems, *A Farewell to Arms* notably among them. It was not surprising that she decided to write a paper about Hemingway. In December 1938, Scott wrote her that he didn't have time to "dig you up stuff about Ernest" and advised her that she could learn a lot about him from reading *In Our Time*. Writing Morton Kroll, secretary Frances's younger brother, Fitzgerald listed a number of "great English classics" he should read, including only two by living writers: Hemingway's *Farewell* and Joyce's *Dubliners*. Thomas Wolfe was not really in the same league, he told Scottie. Wolfe beautifully recapitulated what Walt Whitman said, but unlike Joyce and Eliot and Hemingway, he had "nothing really new to add."

In effect, Fitzgerald accepted the judgment of Bishop—and many others at the time—that Hemingway was bound for the favorable judgment of posterity, despite his unsuccessful works of the 1930s. Scott could not help comparing his own career to Ernest's, and speculating on what the future might bring. In December 1938, for instance, he asked Perkins if what "was left" of his reputation wasn't being allowed to slip away. "Since the going-out-of-print of [*This Side of Paradise*] and the success (or is it one?) of the [*Fifth Column and the First Forty-nine Stories*]," he felt "somewhat neglected." Perkins raised the prospect of an omnibus volume including *Paradise*, *Gatsby*, and *Tender*, but made it clear that would have to wait until Fitzgerald wrote a new "major book." Meanwhile, the Modern Library was resisting proposals to bring out an edition of *Tender*.

Fitzgerald's prospects looked dim, particularly as contrasted to Hemingway's. It was discouraging. "I don't write any more," he told Thornton Wilder in 1937. "Ernest has made all my writing unnecessary." And in what may be the most often-quoted phrase on the Hemingway-Fitzgerald relationship, Scott put his particular spin on the issue of comparative standing. "I talk with the authority of failure—Ernest with the authority of success. We could never sit across the same table again." The observation said a great deal about both writers, and about the current of competition in American culture dictating that there could be no winners without losers.

The Protestant ethic, derived from the Puritans, held that to succeed was to prove one's virtue. The good would prosper, the bad go to ruin. This doctrine maintained a firm grip on the muscular Christianity of Oak Park, where Ernest Hemingway grew up. His boyhood pastor was the father of Bruce Barton, pioneer advertising man and author of the best-selling *The Man Nobody Knows*, in which Jesus returns to life as a champion capitalist. Without entirely accepting the gospel of wealth in such an extreme form, Hemingway absorbed the basic creed and drove himself for the success—measured both in money and in fame—that would validate his existence.

With Fitzgerald, the situation was skewed by a number of factors. He was brought up Catholic, for one thing. And his father, a failure in business, was a romantic Southerner, who taught his only son to embrace the lost cause of the South. Young Scott was also on the side of Bonnie Prince Charlie and Mary Queen of Scots. Invariably he cheered for the underdog, for the small animals in their losing war against the larger ones. His fiction reflected that way of thinking. As he wrote in "Early Success" (October 1937), from the beginning "[a]ll the stories that came into my head had a touch of disaster in them—the lovely young creatures in my novels went to ruin, the diamond mountains of my short stories blew up, my millionaires were as beautiful and damned as Thomas Hardy's peasants."

These disastrous endings did carry a certain authority, for in depicting (and even in cultivating) failure, Fitzgerald was very much in the American grain. Flowing counter to the idea of success and with its own substantial power was the idea of failure as fulfillment. The Christian paradox of the defeated as victor resonates powerfully in our collective consciousness. As Emily Dickinson suggested in her poem beginning "Success is counted sweetest/ By those who ne'er succeed," only those who failed could properly understand or appreciate success. Fitzgerald was constitutionally drawn to the notion, as one critic put it, that nothing succeeds like failure. Swimming in the same waters, the two writers were carried along on competing currents.

Other Fitzgerald notes of the late 1930s dealt with the collapse of his friendship with Hemingway. "Ernest—until we began trying to walk over each other with cleats," he wrote, probably taking more blame than he should have for rough treatment. A more cynical comment evoked with bitterness the days when he devoted so much time and energy to promoting Hemingway: "Ernest would always give a helping hand to a man on a ledge a little higher up." A three-word cryptic note read "Bald Hemingway characters"—probably a comment on the lack of description Ernest provided in introducing major figures in his fiction. In a much longer note, Scott set down a semi-hilarious account of Hemingway as celebrity:

Ernest Hemingway, while careful to avoid cliches in his work, fairly revels in them in his private life, his favorite being "Parbleu!" ("So what?"—French), and "Yes, We Have No Bananas." Contrary to popular opinion, he is not as tall as Thomas Wolfe, standing only six feet five in his health belt. He is naturally clumsy with his body, but shooting from a blind or from adequate cover, makes a fine figure of a man. We are happy to announce that his work will appear in future exclusively on United States postage stamps.

A well-meaning British writer, turning out a script for television about the lost generation of the 1920s, took this satire seriously and had Hemingway spouting "Parbleu" and "Yes, We Have No Bananas" all over Paris and the Riviera. (Fortunately, the film was not made.) It is the only instance where Fitzgerald, albeit privately and rather subtly, called Hemingway's bravery into question, in the comment about "shooting...from adequate cover."

Fitzgerald worked hard to learn the movie business, in order to clear his debts and support Zelda's care and Scottie's schooling. As his young colleague Budd Schulberg commented, "he didn't just take his $1,500 a week and run." But the lyricism that freshened his fiction on the page did not translate well to motion pictures. He became increasingly frustrated as very little that he wrote made it onto the screen, and he began to go on binges. M-G-M let his contract lapse at the end of 1938. He was back on his own, trying to make his living with stories for the magazines, but his knack for writing popular fiction had vanished. To make ends meet, he resumed his old policy of asking Harold Ober for advances. At first Ober complied, but early in July he said no. He knew about Fitzgerald's benders, and he could not sell the stories Fitzgerald was writing. It was a business decision. On a personal level, the Ober family continued to provide a home away from home for Scottie, while her father was in California and her mother institutionalized in North Carolina.

In a March 1939 letter to Perkins, Ernest confessed that he "always had a very stupid little boy feeling of superiority about Scott like a tough durable little boy sneering at a delicate but talented little boy." He asked Max to convey his "great affection" to Scott and wondered if it were "really all over" with him as a writer. He hoped not, after seeing in retrospect how "excellent" most of *Tender* was. When Ober withdrew his support, it must have seemed very nearly over for Fitzgerald. The one good thing about the financial crisis was that it inspired Fitzgerald to undertake another novel. He had learned a good deal about the movies and the people who made them. He had formed a long-term relationship with gossip columnist Sheilah Graham as lover and companion, and as an insider she too had much to teach him. In midsummer he started work on *The Last*

Tycoon, his unfinished novel about Hollywood, and on his own entered into negotiations with *Collier's* to publish the book as a serial. Even though this deal fell through, Fitzgerald kept going. Perkins reported to Hemingway that Scott was indeed at work on a new novel, though he would not reveal the subject matter. Fitzgerald was cranking hard on *Tycoon* when he died.

As Fitzgerald's fortunes declined, Hemingway's prospered. He shaped his experiences in Spain into *For Whom the Bell Tolls*, published in October 1940. The book was a whopping financial success. Max Perkins wrote Scott that the Book-of-the-Month Club had selected Ernest's novel, assuring a substantial sale. It was "[t]he stamp of bourgeois approval," though Ernest would hate to think of it that way. He was about to be divorced and to marry Martha Gellhorn, Perkins added. Scott wrote back that it would be odd to think of Ernest "married to a really attractive woman" and predicted, correctly, that the pattern of this marriage was liable to be different "than with his Pygmalion-like creations" Hadley and Pauline. To Zelda, he relayed the news about the Book-of-the-Month. "Do you remember how superior [Ernest] used to be about mere sales?" he asked her.

Hemingway sent Fitzgerald a copy of *Bell*, inscribed "To Scott with affection and esteem." As he was reading it, Scott reported to Zelda that the book had been sold to the movies for over a hundred thousand dollars and that Ernest would earn $50,000 from the Book-of-the-Month Club in addition. "Rather a long cry from his poor rooms over the saw mill in Paris." Zelda heard the indignation in Scott's voice, but did not entirely share it. "Though I am vaguely resentful of Ernest's success (his work being neither as meritorious nor as compelling as your own), I am also glad." His success represented "at least a casual passing acknowledgement" of the "writer's faith." She hadn't read the book herself. All five copies at the lending library were out.

Directly to Hemingway, Fitzgerald offered only praise of *For Whom the Bell Tolls*. "It's a fine novel," he began, "better than anybody else writing could do." He accurately isolated a number of the book's high points. "The massacre [of the Fascists in Pilar's village] was magnificent and also [El Sordo's] fight on the mountain and the actual dynamiting scene." While he was at it, Fitzgerald told his old friend how much he liked *To Have and Have Not*. "[P]aragraphs and pages" in that book ranked "right up with Dostoevsky in their undeflected intensity." Scott, who had learned not to criticize anything in Ernest's writing, was not entirely candid in these statements. But he ended his letter on a note of absolute sincerity. In congratulating Hemingway on the commercial success of *Bell*, he wrote that he envied him "the time it will give you to do what you want."

As he wrote those words, Fitzgerald had only seven weeks left to live.

To Zelda, to his notebooks, to Budd Schulberg, Scott confided less complimentary views of *For Whom the Bell Tolls*. It was not as good as *Farewell*, he wrote Zelda. The novel would please the average reader, he supposed, but it didn't "seem to have the tensity or the freshness nor has it the inspired poetic moments" of *Farewell*. In his weekly letters to Zelda at this time, Scott repeatedly mentioned his struggles over the composition of *The Last Tycoon*. He was "living in" the book, he wrote her. His room was "covered with charts" just as it had been for *Tender*. But he was having trouble with the "character-planting phase," because he "felt people...less intently" than he once had. At his age, it was difficult to "remember emotionally." In his final word to Zelda about Ernest and *Bell*, Scott was speaking for himself as well: "I suppose life takes a good deal out of you and you never can quite repeat."

In his notebooks, he took an even harsher view of Hemingway's novel about the Spanish Civil War. It was "a thoroughly superficial book," he observed, with "all the profundity of [Daphne Du Maurier's best-selling] *Rebecca*." On the phone one night with Schulberg, Fitzgerald talked "for anyway forty minutes" about the "dreadful" depiction of Maria and the love interest in *Bell*.

In his last months, Fitzgerald had a hard time entertaining positive thoughts about Hemingway. Ernest was among those he had in mind when, in a mid-October letter to Perkins, he alluded to "dear friends" who had been referring to him as "poor old Scott" for almost a decade. One night that fall, he took Frances and Morton Kroll to dinner and over the wine spoke disparagingly of Hemingway. Ernest owed a lot to Stein and Pound for their early criticism, Scott said. There was nothing admirable about his trips to Spain and Africa, either. He sought out adventure because he needed to demonstrate his manliness. Besides, he was running out of material.

On the day he was struck down by a fatal heart attack—Saturday, December 21—Scott and Sheilah were talking about the war raging in Europe. Sooner or later, he predicted, the United States was going to have to get involved. If *The Last Tycoon* turned out to be a success, he told Sheilah, he'd like to go to Europe to write about the war. "Ernest won't have that field all to himself, then."

On the same day, Bill Warren—the young theatrical genius Scott had introduced to Hollywood—wrote Scott a letter from back east. In his financial extremity, Scott had asked Warren to repay a loan. Warren responded apologetically that he couldn't do so right away, but would send the money soon. "And I hope with everything I've got," he added, "that the novel you are working on is

It. I hope it does for you what his did for that Hemmingway. That obscenity." The letter Fitzgerald wrote Warren has not surfaced, but it must have contained besides a request for reimbursement some remarks 1) on *Tycoon* in progress, 2) on the success of *Bell*, and 3) on Scott's disillusionment with "Hemmingway" (Warren reproduced Fitzgerald's spelling), the man who had transmuted himself from closest friend to most hurtful former friend.

Ernest did not go to Scott's funeral. "I thought of telegraphing you [in Key West] about Scott," Max Perkins wrote him a week later, "but it didn't seem as if there were any use in it, and I shrank from doing it." Max went on at some length about Scott's will. The estate would not be cleared up for some time, and meanwhile Perkins and others were going to make sure Scottie had the funds to finish college. "There is no use talking about Scott now."

For fifteen years Max had been writing Ernest about Scott—and, to a lesser degree, Scott about Ernest. He had discharged that duty as best he could. No longer would he use Hemingway as a sounding board for his ideas about reforming Fitzgerald's drinking or spending habits, or enlist him as an ally in coaxing Fitzgerald back from despondency into full-scale production. *There was no use talking about Scott now.*

CHAPTER 8

ALCOHOLIC CASES

First the man takes a drink,
Then the drink takes a drink,
Then the drink takes the man.
— Japanese saying

On *Comedy Central*'s August 26, 1998, "Daily Show," Craig Kilborn reported that
Ernest Hemingway's posthumously published *True at First Light* contained an account
of his supposed "marriage," when on safari in Africa, to a young native girl. This news
inspired Kilborn to comment that when Scott Fitzgerald heard about Hemingway's
eighteen-year-old African "bride," he demanded an eighteen-year-old bottle of Scotch.

The punch line from Kilborn derived from the prevailing public perception of
the two famous writers: Hemingway a macho adventurer, Fitzgerald an indoor drunk.

There are alcoholics and alcoholics. Liquor is no respecter of persons, as a
visit to any Alcoholics Anonymous meeting quickly reveals. The people who rise
to announce, "My name is _____, and I am an alcoholic" are truck drivers and
schoolteachers, business executives and door-to-door salesmen, panhandlers
and artists, housewives and professional women. What they have in common is
the misery that drinking has brought them. The horrific stories they tell run to a
pattern. At one stage or another in their lives, they were taken drunk.

FITZGERALD'S CASE

Fitzgerald became an alcoholic in his late twenties, and for the rest of his
lamentably short life never quite shook free of the malady. The story of his

friendship with Hemingway has been full of talk about his drinking—talk from Ernest, from Max Perkins, from Harold Ober, and above all from Scott himself, as he variously minimized or claimed victory over the demon that possessed him.

By the time Scott and Ernest met in 1925, Fitzgerald's "cafard"—as John Cheever, another alcoholic writer, called it—had taken over control of his being. The most striking thing about Scott's drinking, Ernest thought, was that he got drunk after imbibing so little. It was "hard to accept him as a drunkard, since he was affected by such small quantities of alcohol." Hemingway converted drinking—like most endeavors—into a competitive sport. In his view, holding one's liquor was a test of manhood—a test that Scott failed at their first meeting and kept failing on serial occasions thereafter. "Fitzgerald was soft," he told an interviewer in 1960. "He dissolved at the least touch of alcohol."

Hemingway himself loved to drink and from his earliest years in Europe made it an essential part of each day's activity. He had a vast capacity for the stuff—perhaps owing in some degree to his six-foot, two-hundred-pound frame—but eventually liquor had its debilitating way with him. He was a functioning alcoholic for many years before drink took the man.

There was always a trace of the theatrical in Fitzgerald's drinking. As a boy he sometimes pretended to be drunk, reeling around a streetcar for the entertainment of its passengers. His *Ledger* recorded his first serious intoxications, "Tight at Susquehana" in April 1913 when still in prep school, "Tight in Trenton" in October 1913 as a Princeton freshman, "Passed out at dinner" celebrating election to the Cottage Club in March 1915. During his college years he often bragged about his drinking. "Pardon me if my hand is shaky," he wrote a girlfriend, "but I just had a quart of sauterne and 3 Bronxes." Very probably, he hadn't. His friends at Princeton did not think of him as a lush, and suspected him of playing the clown.

In Zelda Sayre, he found a companion who liked drinking—and exhibitionism—as much as he did. When she broke off their engagement in the summer of 1919, he went on a three-week bender in New York that is vividly described in *This Side of Paradise*. Once they were married, Scott and Zelda became mutually notorious for their behavior when on a party—leaping fully-clothed into the Pulitzer fountain outside the Plaza Hotel, rolling champagne bottles down Fifth Avenue at dawn. Published in the newspapers, these exploits established them as the prototypical Jazz Age couple, in rebellion against the mores and standards of the older generation. Though he was conservative—even puritanical—about matters of sex, Fitzgerald eagerly accepted the role of the defiant young man. In a letter to a friend back in St. Paul, he repudiated a pallid career as a merchant or politician, envisioning himself instead as following in the footsteps of such "drunkards and wasters" as "Shelley, Whitman, Poe, O. Henry, Verlaine, Swinburne, Villon, Shakespeare."

From the earliest days of their marriage, the Fitzgeralds' outrageous behavior courted trouble. Usually their spontaneity and charm and good looks would win people over, but not always. A month after their marriage and the publication of *This Side of Paradise*, they went down to Princeton for house party weekend. Scott introduced Zelda as his mistress, acquired a black eye during a scuffle in Harvey Firestone's car, and was summarily suspended from membership in the Cottage Club. Fitzgerald, always sensitive to social slights, was bitterly hurt. In a poem memorializing the occasion, Edmund Wilson (who had accompanied the Fitzgeralds to Princeton) put Scott's sins into perspective:

Poor Fitz went prancing into the Cottage Club
With his gilt wreath and lyre,
Looking like a tarnished Apollo with the two black eyes
That he had got, when far gone in liquor, in some unintelligible fight,
But looking like Apollo all the same, with the sun on his pale yellow hair;
And his classmates who had been roaring around the campus all day
And had had whiskey, but no Swinburne,
Arose as one man and denounced him
And told him that he and his wife had disgraced the club and that he
    was no longer worthy to belong to it
(Though really they were angry at him
Because he had achieved great success
Without starting in at the bottom in the nut and bolt business).

By 1921, in his twenty-fifth year, Fitzgerald's drinking escapades had developed into something far more damaging than high old times. What had started out as gay irresponsible partying turned destructive. He and Zelda rented a house in Westport, presumably to escape the continual alcoholic haze of New York. But "Fitzgerald vanished into the city on two- and three-day drunks, after which neighbors would find him asleep on the front lawn. At dinner parties, he crawled around under the table, or hacked off his tie with a kitchen knife, or tried to eat soup with a fork." Once he drove his car into a pond, deliberately. He shocked new acquaintances by introducing himself as "F. Scott Fitzgerald, the well-known alcoholic." His behavior became increasingly unfunny. As he con-

Gerald Murphy at Yale, Sara Murphy at 19— the elegant star-crossed couple who befriended both writers. (*Photo courtesy of Corbis/Bettmann*)

The handsome Edward Fitzgerald with his beautiful boy Scott, Christmas 1899. (*Photo courtesy of the Fitzgerald Papers at the Princeton University Library*)

Mollie Fitzgerald, who doted on son Scott, with outrageous hat and penetrating gaze. (*Photo courtesy of the Fitzgerald Papers at the Princeton University Library*)

Young Scott Fitzgerald in prep school, 1911. (*Photo courtesy of the Fitzgerald Papers at the Princeton University Library*)

Ginevra King at 17—she broke Scott's heart, and some others as well. (*Photo courtesy of the Fitzgerald Papers at the Princeton University Library*)

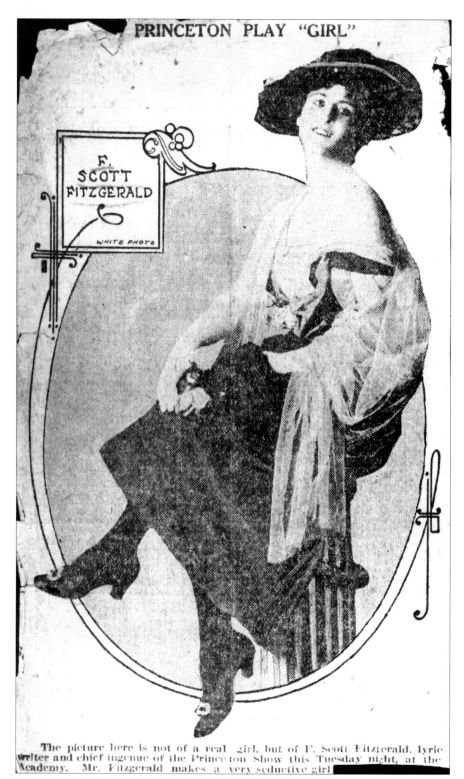

PRINCETON PLAY "GIRL"

F. SCOTT FITZGERALD

WHITE PHOTO

The picture here is not of a real girl, but of F. Scott Fitzgerald, lyric writer and chief ingenue of the Princeton Show this Tuesday night, at the Academy. Mr. Fitzgerald makes a very seductive girl

Scott as a "showgirl" for the Princeton Triangle Club, 1915. (*Photo courtesy of the Fitzgerald Papers at the Princeton University Library*)

Zelda Sayre in February 1920, shortly before her marriage to Scott Fitzgerald. (*Photo courtesy of the Fitzgerald Papers at the Princeton University Library*)

Fitzgerald in the early 1920s, with remarkable eyes that looked blue to some and green to others, and a mouth that "worried" Hemingway. (*Photo courtesy of the Fitzgerald Papers at the Princeton University Library*)

Zelda, Scottie, and Scott Fitzgerald in the Luxembourg Gardens, Paris, ca. 1925.
(*Photo courtesy of the Fitzgerald Papers at the Princeton University Library*)

Fitzgerald in the early 1930s, as he labored to finish *Tender Is The Night*. (*Photo courtesy of the Fitzgerald Papers at the Princeton University Library*)

Scott with Sheilah Graham in California, ca. 1939. (*Photo courtesy of the Fitzgerald Papers at the Princeton University Library*)

fessed in a letter, he "couldn't get sober long enough to tolerate being sober."

Fitzgerald in his cups became alternately belligerent and maudlin. He and Zelda began to quarrel, in large part because of her flirtatiousness and his fear of what might happen when *she* was intoxicated. In May 1921 they again attempted to quiet the hectic pace with a geographical change—this time, a trip to Europe. Shortly before leaving, Zelda goaded him into a brawl, in which Scott—at a mere five feet seven and 140 pounds—was clobbered by a professional bouncer.

The European trip did not change their style of life. On return they went to St. Paul to await the birth of their only child, Scottie, where Fitzgerald wrote Perkins a discouraged letter lamenting five months of loafing. *The Beautiful and Damned* was in press, but Scott commented that his next novel, "if I ever write another, will I am sure be black as death with gloom." He would like to sit down with half a dozen chosen companions and drink himself to death, he added. If it weren't for Zelda, he would disappear for a few years: "[s]hip as a sailor or something and get hard."

The public reputation he was constructing as a rebellious Jazz Age playboy stood at odds with the image he was hoping to establish of a serious and dedicated writer. It did not help when his friend Thomas Boyd reported in the *St. Paul Daily News* that Fitzgerald "had been sequestered in a New York apartment with $10,000 sunk in liquor and that he was bent on drinking it before he did anything else." Luckily Edmund Wilson sent Scott a pre-publication draft of the extended article he was writing on him for the January 1922 *Bookman*. There were a number of slurs in that rather patronizing piece that Scott might have objected to, but the only thing he asked Wilson to change was the emphasis on drinking.

"Now as to the liquor thing—," he wrote Wilson, "it's true, but nevertheless I'm going to ask you to take it out...the legend about my liquoring is terribly widespread and this thing would hurt me more than you could imagine—both in my contact with the people with whom I'm thrown—relatives and respectable people [especially Zelda's parents, who "never miss *The Bookman*"]—and, what is much more important, financially." Wilson cut most of his copy on Fitzgerald's drinking.

In their restless careering about, Scott and Zelda next fetched up in Great Neck, Long Island. Fitzgerald's play *The Vegetable* went into production, and they saw a lot of the theatrical crowd and of Ring Lardner, with whom Scott consumed "oceans of Canadian ale." In his *Ledger* for July 1923, Fitzgerald recorded the pattern of his days: "Intermittent work on novel. Constant drinking." After the failure of his play, and a fallow period in his writing, Fitzgerald wrote Perkins that he realized how much he'd "deteriorated" in the previous three years, spending time "uselessly, neither in study nor in contemplation but only in drinking and raising hell generally." Still, he felt he had "an enormous power" in him, and proved it by writing his masterful *The Great Gatsby* in 1924.

With that task behind him, Scott's trouble with the bottle began again. In Rome, he was beaten by the police after a drunken argument—an incident he wove into Dick Diver's downfall in *Tender Is the Night*. He and Zelda "sometimes indulge[d] in terrible four-day rows that always start with a drinking party," he wrote John Bishop early in 1925. When he met Hemingway at the Dingo in Paris and ignominiously passed out, the probability is that Fitzgerald was in the midst of a drinking cycle lasting for several days.

In his *Moveable Feast* account of their trip to Lyon, Hemingway carefully distinguished his own drinking habits from those of Fitzgerald. "In Europe then," he explained, "we thought of wine as something as healthy and normal as food and also as a great giver of happiness and well being and delight." He took wine or beer with his meals as a pleasant and perfectly natural part of everyday life. For Fitzgerald, on the other hand, the consumption of liquor only served to make him drunk. In his judgment, Scott simply couldn't handle booze. Yet on the day of their driving trip, as Hemingway recalled it, the two of them consumed five bottles of Macon in the car. As the expert in these matters, Ernest uncorked the bottles as needed and passed them to Scott. Drinking from the bottle "was exciting to him as though he were slumming or as a girl might be excited by going swimming for the first time without a bathing suit."

By early afternoon Fitzgerald became convinced that he was suffering from congestion of the lungs and they stopped for the night at a hotel. There they drank three double whiskey sours apiece before going down to dinner. Scott told Ernest about Zelda's affair with the aviator Édouard Jozan at St. Raphael so clearly that Hemingway "could see the single seater seaplane buzzing the diving raft and the color of the sea and the shape of the pontoons and the shadow that they cast and Zelda's tan and Scott's tan and the dark blonde and the light blond of their hair and the darkly tanned face of the boy that was in love with Zelda." Ernest drank most of a carafe of Fleurie while Scott was on the telephone with Zelda, and when he came back to the table they ordered a bottle of Montagny, "a light, pleasant white wine of the neighborhood," with their dinner. Scott ate very little, and passed out after sipping at one glass of the wine.

Considering the amount of alcohol he had imbibed that day and evening, this was not surprising. But it surprised Hemingway. He decided that anything Scott drank would first over-stimulate him and then poison him, and he resolved to cut all drinking to the minimum the following day. He would tell Scott that he, Ernest, could not drink because they were getting back to Paris and he "had to train in order to write." This was not true, for Hemingway's sole rules on the subject were "never to drink after dinner nor before [he] wrote nor while [he] was writing." But it would keep Fitzgerald from the liquor that acted on him like a poison.

During the months ahead, Ernest and Hadley were to discover just how much of a nuisance Fitzgerald could be when he was on a party. "The six o'clock in the morning drunk," Hadley called him. He and Zelda would turn up at the Hemingways' apartment at outlandish hours, and do foolish things like unraveling a roll of toilet paper from the top of their stair landing. At first Ernest let them in when they came to call. He found it interesting, Hadley thought, to watch an alcoholic demean himself. Later, when the Fitzgeralds' disturbances threatened to get them kicked out their apartment, Hemingway became increasingly intolerant of their drunken misbehavior. Hadley shared her husband's impression that Scott simply couldn't handle liquor. He "would take one drink and pretty soon he'd turn pale green and pass out." But hadn't he and Zelda been consuming alcohol all night before they paid their early-morning call on the Hemingways and took that "one drink"?

By the mid-1920s, liquor was beginning to determine the course of Scott Fitzgerald's life. Excessive drinking was ruining his marriage and affecting his ability to work. The talent was extant, but his dedication to the task dwindled steadily under the influence of the bottle. And worst of all, for someone who lived for the approval of other people, Fitzgerald's outrageous behavior when intoxicated was alienating those he most cared about—including Ernest Hemingway and Gerald and Sara Murphy.

The etiology of alcoholism is a notoriously complicated subject. It is a disease traceable to hereditary factors, some maintain: in Fitzgerald's case that makes some sense, for his father had a drinking problem. Chemistry causes the malady, others hold. In this connection, a number of biographers (and one psychiatrist) have attributed Fitzgerald's troubles to hypoglycemia, a condition in which the body produces an excess of insulin and a craving for sugar that alcohol can supply. But the most authoritative and knowledgeable biographer, Matthew J. Bruccoli, concluded that there was no medical evidence to support such a diagnosis. According to Dr. William Ober, a pathologist who examined Fitzgerald's medical records, "[h]e did not drink because his blood sugar level was low; he drank because he was a drunkard. 'Drunkard' is the old-fashioned term for alcoholic, and, as we know today, it is an addiction, a form of escape for people with inadequate personalities, people with deep-seated insecurities, people with unresolved intra-psychic conflicts (often sexual but by no means always so), as well as people...who use it to drown out the still small voice of self-reproach."

Dr. Ober's reasoning nicely fits the case of F. Scott Fitzgerald, who was handicapped by social insecurity and drank in order to cover it up. John Dos Passos, a firsthand observer of Fitzgerald's antics at Antibes in the mid-1920s, speculated that he was not always as intoxicated as he seemed to be, and that he put on his drunk and disorderly performance "because he had never learned to practice the first principles of civilized behavior." Lacking any sure sense of himself, he played two roles: Prince Charming and Peck's Bad Boy. Fitzgerald could be "quite irresistible" when he set out to charm, and quite impossible when he switched into his naughty boy routine. His mother had forgiven him all such misbehavior. His contemporaries, even the long-suffering Murphys, were less tolerant.

During the summer of 1926, Fitzgerald went out of his way to antagonize Gerald and Sara. He ruined their party for Hemingway by throwing ashtrays and crawling around like a dog. During another party at the Murphys' elegant Villa America, he threw a fig at a titled female guest, smashed the Venetian glassware, and punched both Gerald and Archie MacLeish. While Scott was rude beyond imagining, Zelda liked to take risks. She threw herself down a flight of stone steps one night when Scott paid undue attention to the dancer Isadora Duncan. She insisted on making dangerous dives from the cliffs, and dared Scott into following her lead. In their car, on the winding roads above the Mediterranean, they were a menace to themselves and everyone on the road. The Murphys were exceptionally fond of the Fitzgeralds, and exceptionally understanding. But their patience was not infinite, and on occasion they exiled Scott and Zelda from their circle for specified periods of time.

The Fitzgeralds sailed back to the States in December 1926, alighting at Ellerslie mansion outside Wilmington. In the year-end summary of his *Ledger*, Scott excoriated himself. "Futile, shameful useless... Self-disgust. Health gone."

In his journals or in correpondence, Fitzgerald took himself to task for his drinking. In public pronouncements, he was much less willing to do so. Writing Hemingway in September 1929, for example, he characterized his "drinking manners" as worse than those of the lowest bistro boy. But he adopted a far more light-hearted approach in "A Short Autobiography," a piece he wrote for the *New Yorker* that year. The "autobiography" takes the form of an annual diary. Listed under each year were the particular alcoholic beverages he remembered drinking, and where. The first and last entries were:

1913

The four defiant Canadian Club whiskeys at the Susquehanna in Hackensack.

1929

A feeling that all liquor has been drunk and all it can do for one has been experienced, and yet—*"Garçon, un Chablis-Mouton 1902, et pour commencer, une petite carafe de vin rose. C'est ça—merci."*

He could not treat his drinking so cavalierly after Zelda collapsed in the spring of 1930. One after another of the doctors who treated her urged Scott to give up alcohol in order to facilitate her recovery. Fitzgerald's letters to these doctors provided a remarkable record of the rationalization and denial symptomatic among alcoholics.

Summer 1930, to Dr. Oscar Forel (italics Fitzgerald's):

"My work is done on coffee, coffee and more coffee, never on alcohol."

"It was on our coming to Europe in 1924 and upon her urging that I began to look forward to wine at dinner—she took it at lunch, I did not... *The ballet idea was something I inaugurated in 1927 to stop her idle drinking after she had already so lost herself in it as to make suicidal attempts."*

"Two years ago in America I noticed that when we stopped all drinking for three weeks or so, which happened many times, I imme-diately had dark circles under my eyes, was listless and disinclined to work...*I found that a moderate amount of wine, a pint at each meal made all the difference in how I felt."*

"Wine was almost a necessity to me to be able to stand her long monologues about ballet steps, alternating with a glazed eye toward any civilized conversation whatsoever."

"To stop drinking entirely for six months and see what happens, even to continue the experiment thereafter if successful—only a pig would refuse to do that. Give up strong drink permanently I will. Bind myself to forswear wine forever I cannot...*the fact that I have abused liquor* is something *to be paid for with suffering and death perhaps but not with renunciation*...I cannot consider one pint of wine at the day's end as anything but one of the rights of man."

"Is there not a certain disingenuousness in her wanting me to give up all alcohol? Would not that *justify her* conduct completely to her-self and prove to *her relatives, and our friends that it was my drink-ing that had caused this calamity, and that I thereby admitted it?"*

To sum up Fitzgerald's points, the problem was Zelda's, not his. She started him drinking in the first place, and later became so boring about the ballet that he had to continue. He did not drink when he was working. *Not* drinking was bad for his health. He would give up hard liquor, but not the wine he deserved at the end of the day. If he had abused liquor in the past, he'd suffered enough for it. And if he stopped drinking, wouldn't that make him the villain of the piece?

> March 1932, to Dr. Mildred Squires:
> "...if the situation continues to shape itself as one in which only one of us two can survive, perhaps you would be doing a kindness to us both by recommending a separation."
>
> "Perhaps fifty percent of our friends and relatives would tell you in all honest conviction that my drinking drove Zelda insane—the other half would assure you that her insanity drove me to drink. Neither judgment would mean anything. The former class would be composed of those who had seen me unpleasantly drunk and the latter of those who had seen Zelda unpleasantly pyschotic. These two classes would be equally unanimous in saying that each of us would be well rid of the other—in full face of the irony that we have never been so desperately in love with each other in our lives. Liquor on my mouth is sweet to her; I cherish her most extravagant hallucination."

In the context of suggesting that it might be better if he and Zelda separated, Scott acknowledged his weakness for drink as complementary to her schizophrenia. They were terribly dependent on each other's illness.

> Spring 1932, to Dr. Mildred Squires (after Zelda finished *Save Me the Waltz* and sent it to Max Perkins):
> "You will see that same blind unfairness in the novel. The girl's love affair is an idyll—the man's is sordid—the girl's drinking is glossed over (when I think of the two dozen doctors called in to give her 1/5 grain of morphine on a raging morning!), while the man's is accentuated."

According to Scott, Zelda was the *really* serious abuser of alcohol in the family.

Spring 1933, to Dr. Adolf Meyer:

"When you qualify or disqualify my judgment on the case, or put it on a level very little above hers on the grounds that I have frequently abused liquor I can only think of Lincoln's remark about a greater man and heavier drinker than I have ever been—that he wished he knew what sort of liquor Grant drank so he could send a barrel to all his other generals.

"This is not said in any childish or churlish spirit of defying you on your opinions on alcohol—during the last six days I have drunk *altogether* slightly less than a quart and a half of weak gin, at wide intervals. But if there is no essential difference between an overextended, imaginative, functioning man using alcohol as a stimulus or a temporary *aisment* and a schizophrene I am naturally alarmed about my ability to collaborate in this cure at all."

"The witness is weary of strong drink and until very recently he had the matter well in hand for four years and has it in hand at the moment, and needs no help on the matter being normally frightened by the purely physical consequences of it. He does work and is not to be confused with the local Hunt-Club-Alcoholic and asks that his testimony be considered as of prior validity to any other."

"I can conceive of giving up all liquor but only under conditions that seem improbable—Zelda suddenly a helpmate or even divorced and insane. Or, if one can think of some way of doing it, Zelda marrying some man of some caliber who would take care of her, *really* take care of her."

In summary, Fitzgerald protested that Dr. Meyer should trust his judgment and not Zelda's. He used liquor as a stimulus for his work and/or to ease the pressures of the day, but was no ordinary hunt-club drunk. He could even imagine quitting entirely, but only if the real problem, embodied in Zelda and her illness, were removed. As with Dr. Squires a year earlier, Fitzgerald sounded as if he would welcome such a resolution, no matter how it was achieved.

May 1933, Zelda and Scott in discussion with Dr. Thomas R. Rennie:

Scott: "I am perfectly determined that I am going to take three or four drinks a day." If he stopped, he told Dr. Rennie, "[Zelda's] family and herself would always think that that was an acknowledgment that I was responsible for her insanity."

Zelda, asked by Scott what caused him to think he had ruined his life (he meant her mental illness): "I think the cause of it is your drinking. That is what I think is the cause of it."

The issue joined between them, with Scott maintaining the high ground because of his so-far less debilitating disease.

THE FICTIONAL EVIDENCE

A reader of Fitzgerald's fiction who knew nothing at all about his life might logically conclude that the author was a habitual drinker. Why else would he bring up the subject so often and create so many alcoholic characters? The tendency was apparent from the beginning. In *This Side of Paradise*, Fitzgerald's autobiographical protagonist goes on an extended bender like the one Scott himself underwent after rejection by Zelda. Still more striking was the portrayal of Anthony Patch's alcoholic ruin in *The Beautiful and Damned*. Anthony's descent into alcoholism is conveyed with convincing authenticity. Near the end of the novel, he gets into a fight with his wife Gloria and stalks out of their apartment. "He's just drunk," Gloria tells an observer, who cannot believe it—he had seemed absolutely sober. But that's the terrible mundane way of it, Gloria explains. "[H]e doesn't show it any more unless he can hardly stand up, and he talks all right until he gets excited. He talks much better than he does when he's sober. But he's been sitting here all day drinking."

In *The Great Gatsby*, Gatsby himself is never drunk and the narrator Nick Carraway rarely so, but the book is saturated with liquor. In this novel, drinking can lead to hilarious consequences, as when an inebriated guest tries to drive a car shorn of one of its wheels. "No harm in trying," he mumbles. Or it can alter perceptions, as happens to Nick during the late-night party at Muriel's apartment in New York. Or it will lighten the atmosphere, as when a tray of cocktails floats into view. The entire novel is structured around a series of parties, in a faithful recollection of the Fitzgeralds' days on Long Island. But in Nick's view and that of the author who stands behind him, the pervasive drinking of the characters causes nothing important to happen. The tinkling of glasses simply functions as background.

As his own condition worsened, Fitzgerald increasingly turned to alcoholics and their troubles for the subject matter of his stories and novels. Zelda's collapse and the doctors who challenged him to help her (and himself) by giving up drinking were obviously reflected in two stories of 1931, "Babylon Revisited" and "A New Leaf." Charlie Wales, the protagonist of "Babylon Revisited," looks back on the boom years of too much drinking. One wintry night, when his wife was flirting with another man and he was drunk, he locked her out of their Paris apartment—and she contracted pneumonia and died. Now he has stopped drinking, except for one invariable drink every day, and wants to lead a healthy and responsible life. Yet there remains some question whether Wales has really reformed. On the one hand, he has come to understand the meaning of the word "dissipate"—to make nothing out of something. Yet at the same time he returns compulsively to the places where he indulged in that dissipation. On the one hand, he believes in character and wants to jump back a whole generation "and trust in character again." On the other hand, he is inclined to parcel out his guilt for the tragic death of his wife to the general debauchery of the times or simply bad luck. In depicting a likable and yet highly suspect reformed alcoholic, Fitzgerald may have been expressing some of his own ambivalence on the subject. Or confessing that in his periods of drunkenness he had in effect locked Zelda out in the cold.

In the person of Dick Ragland in "A New Leaf," he painted his most convincing portrait of a man destroying himself through drink. The story is narrated by Julia, and the reader is asked to share both her initial enchantment with Dick and her subsequent visceral distaste for him. Authentically enough, alcohol produces in him a Jekyll to Hyde transformation. In his charming Dr. Jekyll role, Ragland "was a fine figure of a man, in coloring both tan and blond, with a peculiar luminosity to his face. His voice was quietly intense; it seemed always to tremble a little with a sort of gay despair; they way he looked at Julia made her feel attractive." He is also honest and forthcoming about what led to his troubles, and here Fitzgerald patently seems to be speaking through his created character. "I found that with a few drinks I got expansive and somehow had the ability to please people, and the idea turned my head. Then I began to take a whole lot of drinks to keep going and have everybody think I was wonderful."

Julia falls in love with this version of Dick, and is ready to marry him despite his reputation as a drunk. But at another meeting it is Mr. Hyde who appears. "His face was dead white and erratically shaven, his soft hat was crushed bunlike on his head, his shirt collar was dirty, and all except the band of his tie was out of sight...His whole face was one long prolonged sneer—the lids held with difficulty from covering the fixed eyes, the drooping mouth drawn up over the upper teeth, the chin wabbling like a made-over chin in which the paraffin had run—it was a face that both expressed and inspired disgust."

In those two descriptions, Fitzgerald vividly demonstrated the drastic effects of alcoholism. It is impossible to believe that in observing his own decline he did not share a measure of Dick Ragland's self-disgust.

1932 was not, for Fitzgerald, an auspicious year. "Drinking increased. Things go not so well," he wrote in his *Ledger* for September. But he was not fully prepared to condemn drunks in his fiction. Both Dr. Forrest Janney (in "Family in the Wind") and Joel Coles (in "Crazy Sunday") emerge as basically sympathetic figures. They may be alcoholics (Dr. Janney assuredly is), but Fitzgerald asks us to like them.

The situation with Dick Diver was much the same. Especially in the opening section, *Tender* built Diver up as immensely charming. When he later suffers his downfall, we are apt to ascribe it to factors other than his drinking— the influence of too much Warren money, for example. Fitzgerald shows the drinking and its effects, as on the night in Rome when the drunken Dr. Diver brawls with the police and spends the night in jail. Fitzgerald did not want to deprive his hero of all dignity, however, and carefully revised the final scene of the novel to make his hero less obviously intoxicated. In its final two drafts, the novel ended with Diver drunk. In one version, he falls on his face; in another, he is helped away by a waiter Baby Warren sends to assist him. In the published book, Diver drinks enough to be "already well in advance of the day," and sways a little as he stands up to bless the beach, but requires no assistance in keeping his feet.

Tender was unusual in dividing its alcoholism between Dick Diver, a primarily admirable figure, and poor Abe North, who is assigned the cruder attributes of the drunkard and killed off in absentia. "To give a full, convincing picture of Diver's alcoholism," Thomas Gilmore has proposed, "might have been as intolerably painful to Fitzgerald as fully accepting his own."

More or less desperate for material, Fitzgerald drew on his own drying-out periods in undistinguished stories like "Her Last Case" (November 1934) and "An Alcoholic Case" (1937). And during his last two years, he turned out a number of stories about Pat Hobby, a Hollywood hack writer. Hobby has so many things wrong with him, including womanizing and perpetual lying, that the fact that he is a lush is often obscured. "Pat Hobby's College Days," however, comments indirectly on Fitzgerald's own drinking. In the story, Pat attempts to sell an idea for a college movie to a committee from the University of the

Western Coast. He prepares himself with a slug from the half-pint bottle he invariably carries. But Hobby's sales pitch is ruined when his secretary is ushered into the room with "a big clinking pillow cover" containing empty whiskey bottles. Shortly before writing this story, Fitzgerald had disastrously drunk himself out of a film job at the Dartmouth Winter Carnival. And in fact he assigned his Hollywood secretary the task of disposing of his empties.

In correspondence, Fitzgerald often admitted his drinking problem while attributing it to causes beyond his control. Two letters of late 1934 illustrate the pattern. His *Ledger* for June of that year revealed for the first time that he had suffered episodes of delirium tremens, an acute and sometimes fatal descent into disorientation and hallucination, and that he required a trained nurse to look after him. No word of this was conveyed to Maxwell Perkins or Harold Ober—his two most important and valuable professional supporters—in communications mailed that November and December. Fitzgerald brought up the subject of his drinking with Perkins only to rationalize it away. "I know you have the sense that I have loafed lately but that is absolutely not so. I have drunk too much and that is certainly slowing me up. On the other hand, without drink I do not know whether I could have survived this time." Fitzgerald also pleaded extenuating circumstances to Ober, who unlike Perkins had reproached him about drinking. "[T]he assumption that all my troubles are due to drink is a little too easy," he wrote. His domestic difficulties—Zelda's illness—were also to be considered, and the ebbing away of his literary reputation, and the pleurisy he'd come down with on a trip to Bermuda. In previous years he may have been guilty of self-indulgence. Lately the gods had simply not smiled on him.

Throughout his career Fitzgerald supplied his editor and agent with intermittent and seemingly sincere bulletins about quitting. The basic message was that he could stop drinking any time, or even better, that he *had* gone on the wagon—for six weeks, for three months if you didn't count Christmas, for February and March of 1933. In May 1935 he went so far as to tell Arnold Gingrich of *Esquire* that he thought his prose looked "rather watery" and he planned to "quit drinking for a few years." The very fact that he kept making these reassurances was the best reason not to believe them, and it is doubtful if Fitzgerald's periodic announcements of sobriety persuaded anyone—least of all himself. In his notebooks, he rather cynically observed that when "anyone announces to you how little they drink, you can be sure it's a regime they've just started." And one that would not last.

The notebooks, in fact, contain Fitzgerald's most candid and confessional observations about alcohol and its effects on him. "Drunk at 20, wrecked at 30, dead at 40. Drunk at 21, human at 31, mellow at 41, dead at 51," one entry reads. If he'd taken his first drink at thirty-five instead, he commented in a 1937 letter, he might have progressed "to a champagne-pink three score and ten." During his last years, he carried around a portfolio of photographs showing the grisly effects of alcohol on various human organs. "Drinking is slow death," he warned Robert Benchley. "Who's in a hurry?" Benchley responded.

This was witty, but Fitzgerald had passed the point where drunkenness seemed amusing. Another note conveyed his awareness that misbehavior when intoxicated was destroying him socially. "Just when somebody's taken him up and is making a big fuss over him he pours the soup down his hostess's back, kisses the serving maid and passes out in the dog kennel. But he's done it too often. He's run through about everybody, and there's no one left." He could apologize all day long, but when there were too many apologies on too many mornings-after, the people he'd offended stopped listening.

Somewhere during the mid-1930s Fitzgerald become convinced that he needed to drink in order to write. He had not believed that at the start. In a 1922 interview with Tom Boyd, he expressed his conviction that liquor was "deadening to work." He could understand drinking coffee for the stimulation, but not whiskey. By March 1935, this position had been modified. In a letter to Perkins, Fitzgerald asserted that "a short story can be written on a bottle, but for a novel you need the mental speed that enables you to keep the whole pattern in your head and ruthlessly sacrifice the sideshows as Ernest did in 'A Farewell to Arms.'" Organizing a long book or revising it with "the finest perceptions and judgment" did not "go well with liquor." He would give anything if he "hadn't had to write Part III of 'Tender Is the Night' entirely on stimulant" and could have one more crack at the novel "cold sober." "Even Ernest," he added, had commented about sections that were needlessly included, "and as an artist he is as near as I know for a final reference." In a postscript, Scott maintained that he hadn't had a drink for six weeks and hadn't felt "the slightest temptation as yet."

Basically Scott was making three points about drinking and the creative process in this letter. The most obvious one was that you could not afford to let alcohol shut down the rational left side of the brain when working on a long book. At the same time, he now believed that *short stories* could be written when drinking and that liquor could serve as a *stimulant* rather than a depressant. Putting those propositions together, he arrived at the conviction that drinking was necessary to his work, or at least to the short fiction by which he earned his livelihood. "Drink heightens feelings," he told Laura Guthrie in Asheville that summer. "When I drink, it heightens my emotions and I put it in a story...My stories written when sober are stupid...all reasoned out, not felt." It was a conviction he held until the end of his life. In 1940 he convinced Frances Kroll that for him alcohol was a stimulant, and that he required "the medicinal lift" it gave him.

Once he'd arrived at that rationalization, Fitzgerald was in thrall to drink. James Thurber, another writer afflicted by alcohol, detected the self-justifying process that provided Fitzgerald with multiple reasons for drinking. "Zelda's tragedy, his constant financial worries, his conviction that he was a failure, his disillusionment about the Kingdom of the Very Rich, and his sorrow over the swift passing of youth and romantic love." All those reasons put together, Thurber believed, were not as harmful to Fitzgerald as the conviction that "his creative vitality demanded stimulation" from liquor. He had to drink in order to write. He had to write in order to live. He would not live long if he continued to drink.

One evening in May 1978, sitting in a bar appropriately enough called "Gatsby's" in Georgetown, I got to talking with Scottie Fitzgerald about her father's drinking. She proposed a two-question test to determine an alcoholic. Did liquor have a drastically unhealthy effect on one's life? Did one's personality change as a result of drinking? In the case of F. Scott Fitzgerald, she'd decided that the answer to both questions was yes. When sober he was a thoughtful and gentle and kind, if somewhat over-solicitous, father. When drunk, he became "a totally different person...not just gay or tiddly, but *mean*."

Scottie had reason to know. He embarrassed her dreadfully at the December 1936 tea dance in Baltimore that father and daughter planned together. In the preparatory stages, Fitzgerald was humorous and helpful, but he drank too much at the dance and insisted on weaving around the dance floor with some of Scottie's young friends. She resolutely ignored his gaffe and refused all offers of sympathy from her peers. It could have been worse, she knew. Her father could have become angry or combative. Once he had slapped her for interrupting his writing. Another time he threw an inkwell past her ear.

During his Hollywood years, Fitzgerald's worst behavior emerged in connection with the women in his life—Scottie somewhat, Zelda and Sheilah Graham to a far greater degree.

Scott twice accompanied Zelda on holidays approved by her doctors at

Highland hospital, in April 1938 and April 1939. Each outing ended disastrously. In 1938, according to the account Fitzgerald sent her doctors, he "added to the general confusion [of their visit to Virginia Beach] by getting drunk, whereupon she adopted the course of telling all and sundry that I was a dangerous man and needed to be carefuly watched." She convinced everyone on the corridor of their hotel that he was a madman, and turned the trip into "one of the most annoying and aggravating experiences" of his life. He sobered up the second he put Zelda on the train back to Carolina, Scott maintained.

Zelda's spring holiday the following year provided further evidence that the chemistry between them had turned toxic. For whatever reasons—he too was on holiday, not working, and must have felt at least a modicum of guilt for conducting a long-term affair with Sheilah in Hollywood—Fitzgerald went on a bender whenever he saw his wife. This time they journeyed to Cuba, where Scott was beaten up while trying to stop a cockfight, and to New York, where he ended up in the hospital for detoxification. Zelda went back to Asheville alone, and covered for him with her doctors. For that enabling kindness, he was truly grateful. "You are the finest, loveliest, tenderest, most beautiful person I have ever known," he wrote her a few weeks later. They never saw each other again.

Scott met Sheilah Graham within two weeks of his arrival in Hollywood in July 1937. A month later they had become lovers, and remained intimate companions for the last three and a half years of his life. For much of that time Fitzgerald was on his best behavior. He knew that his reputation as a drinker preceded him, and managed to stay sober for extended periods. But his demon would only stay stoppered up for so long before pouring out in terrible binges. By this time, the personality change that alcohol produced in him had become spectacular—and the blonde and beautiful Sheilah became its victim.

In her memoir *Beloved Infidel*, Graham vividly portrayed both sides of the Fitzgerald she came to know. The man she fell in love with was engaging and gallant, sending notes of endearment and standing up for her against the real and fancied detractors she attracted in her role as gossip columnist. Sheilah was a kind of female Gatsby, who changed her name and reconstructed her past on the way toward achieving a successful independent life. She had grown up in a working-class British family, and her education ended in a London school for orphans. As a remedy, Scott devised a "College of One" wherein he set lessons in literature and history and quizzed her on what she had learned. He was the amiable and loving professor, she his eager student. It was an idyll of sorts.

Then there was Fitzgerald drunk. He demanded to know how many men

Graham had slept with—as Dick Diver in *Tender Is the Night* demanded of the actress Rosemary Hoyt. She didn't know what to say. She was twenty-eight, she'd been on the stage in England. Finally she came up with eight as a "nice round figure." Fitzgerald was shocked, and intrigued, and then overcome with jealousy. He called her his "paramour" in public, he called her a slut in private, on the back of her framed picture he scrawled "Portrait of a Prostitute." This alcoholic Fitzgerald also became physically dangerous, threatening her and then himself with his pistol. Gingrich met Sheilah in Chicago where she was recording a nationwide radio show on the movies. Scott, on one of his binges, accompanied her and challenged the executive in charge to a fight. Sheilah drew Scott aside, whereupon he abusively turned upon her. "The son of a bitch bit my finger" were the first words Gingrich heard her utter.

Probably the most ruinous drinking bout of Fitzgerald's life came in July 1939, when he broke down on the job at the Dartmouth Winter Carnival. He did irreparable damage to his career on that occasion by presenting himself in a soddenly incoherent state to producer Walter Wanger. Assisted by Sheilah Graham and Budd Schulberg, Scott once again landed at Doctors Hospital in New York for a three-day drying-out period. Ober got wind of the incident, decided to stop advancing Fitzgerald funds, and wrote him a letter explaining why. In a fit of pique, Scott replied that he had indeed "lived dangerously" and might very well have to pay for it, "but there are plenty of other people to tell me that and it doesn't seem as if it should be you." Back in Hollywood, few producers were inclined to take a chance on someone as unreliable as Fitzgerald. He feared that there was an unofficial blacklist against him, he wrote agent Leland Hayward in January 1940. There were only three days while he was on salary in motion pictures when he "ever touched a drop," he insisted. "One of those was in New York and two were on Sundays." Although this was untrue, Fitzgerald did manage to scale back his drinking in the last year of his life.

One precipitating factor was a climactic blowup with Sheilah in October 1939. In the aftermath, Scott wrote an abject letter appealing to her maternal instincts. "I want to die, Sheilah, and in my own way. I used to have my daughter and my poor lost Zelda. Now for over two years your image is everywhere. Let me remember you up to the end which is very close. You are the finest. You are something all by yourself. You are too much something for a tubercular neurotic who can only be jealous and mean and perverse." Acknowledging some of his ills—the ones that might elicit sympathy—Fitzgerald could not bring himself to declare his alcoholism. Sheilah took him back, but could not persuade him to join

Alcoholics Anonymous. He wasn't a joiner, he told her. Besides, "AA can only help weak people...The group offers them the strength they lack on their own."

By way of demonstrating his own strength, he continued to work steadily on *The Last Tycoon* even after *Collier's* rejected a proposal to serialize the novel. He did not stop drinking entirely. Frances Kroll disposed of the bottles he did not want anyone else, Sheilah included, to see. It seemed to Frances that drinking "was not important" to Fitzgerald when he had a major project, like the writing of *The Last Tycoon*, to complete.

Did Fitzgerald's drinking kill him? As a single cause, probably not. But liquor certainly undermined his health, just as it undermined his career and his relationships. And it was undoubtedly a contributing factor to the heart attack that struck him down in Sheilah Graham's ground-floor apartment on Saturday afternoon, December 21, 1940. He was forty-four years old. Dorothy Parker, who came to view his body at the mortuary, looked down at his unlined face and terribly wrinkled hands and gave him a much-quoted send-off. "The poor son of a bitch," she said. In his notebooks, Fitzgerald wrote an epitaph of his own: "Then I was drunk for many years, and then I died."

HEMINGWAY'S CASE

Hemingway was a late-blooming alcoholic, and did not regularly make the public displays of himself that characterized Fitzgerald's histrionic drunkenness. As a result, we know much less about his drinking than about Scott's. Still, Hemingway's letters and his fiction, and the testimony of his friends and doctors, make it possible to trace the course of his drinking life.

Still more than for Fitzgerald, Hemingway regarded drinking as an act of rebellion against conventional mores. He was brought up in a teetotalling household, and in a suburban community which prided itself on maintaining old-fashioned values. It was not surprising that he—and his fictional counterparts—went out of their way to defy convention. In his first letter back home after his wounding in Italy, written on his nineteenth birthday, Ernest adopted an aggressively upbeat tone. He was in a peach of a hospital, there were about eighteeen nurses for four patients, the surgeon was one of the best in Milan, he hoped to be back driving in the mountains by August. In short, there was nothing for his parents to worry about, or at least nothing associated with his injury. At the end of his letter,

Ernest appended a stick figure drawing of himself, lying prone with 227 wounds in his legs. Issuing from his mouth was a cartoon balloon, reading "gimme a drink!" That phrase, which must have shocked his parents, declared his independence from them on the subject of drinking. He was letting them know that in Italy, serving as a volunteer in the war, he had learned—and earned the right—to drink.

In fact Hemingway drank so much in the hospital, enlisting nurses and orderlies as his agents to secure his supply of liquor, that he got into trouble with the head nurse. The episode is re-created in fictional form in *A Farewell to Arms*, where the obtuse and straitlaced Miss Van Campen discovers Frederic Henry's cache of brandy bottles and accuses him of drinking in order to induce jaundice and so delay his return to the front. Even Agnes von Kurowsky, the nurse he'd fallen in love with, warned Ernest, good-naturedly enough, not to "lap up all the fluids at the [G]alleria" when she was transferred away from Milan.

From the beginning, Ernest had a prodigious capacity for alcohol. In correspondence with fishing buddies from Walloon Lake and friends from the ambulance corps, he repeatedly boasted about his intake. "Lately I've been hitting it up," he wrote Bill Smith in December 1918, "about 18 martinis a day." Back in the States six months later, he told Howell Jenkins that he'd established "the club record" in a drinking bout in Toledo: "15 martinis, 3 champagne highballs, and I don't know how much champagne then I passed out." Hemingway converted drinking like almost everything else into a competitive sport, and valued companions who could compete with him in their consumption of alcohol. Drinking together established a kind of camaraderie.

In this spirit, he wrote John Dos Passos in April 1925 about their mutual friend and co-writer Donald Ogden Stewart. The previous summer, they had all gone to the bullfights in Spain. Now Stewart was claiming to have outdrunk Dos Passos, Hemingway said, but this was nonsense. "Somebody has got to put that cheap lecturer in his place. He's claiming to be a drinker now. Remember how he vomited all over Pamplona? Drinker? Shit." In fact Stewart was one of Hemingway's favorite drinking companions, as *The Sun Also Rises* illustrated. In that novel, Stewart served as the model for Bill Gorton, who spends a hilarious evening with Jake Barnes in Paris and later goes fishing with him prior to the fiesta. There the two of them make fun of various sacred cows of middle-class America, including prohibition. "Well," Jake says. "The saloon must go." "You're right there," Bill agrees. "The saloon must go, and I will take it with me."

For Hemingway, getting drunk represented good fun, and also served as a test of manhood. "I like to see every man drunk," he observed in 1923. "A man does not exist until he is drunk." In every possible way, Fitzgerald failed to meet his standards. With his limited tolerance for alcohol, he could not qualify as a worthy drinking companion. And when he did get drunk, he made a nuisance of himself instead of contributing to the high spirits of the occasion.

Ernest liked his wives to drink along with him, for that way his own drinking seemed less like an aberration. All of them—with the exception of Martha Gellhorn— learned to keep him company with the bottle. Even Agnes, who had previously never touched liquor, knocked back a couple of whiskeys to please him. Hadley showed "considerable promise" as a drinker from the start. During their years in Paris, she developed an iron constitution of her own. As a regular practice, they each consumed a bottle of wine with lunch, followed by aperitifs before dinner and another two bottles with the meal. They figured that they could burn off the effects of the alcohol with regular exercise, in hour-long walks around Paris or hikes in the mountains.

For many years, this regimen seemed to work for Hemingway. He drank a great deal, and was able through vigorous exercise to counteract unpleasant after-effects. In an August 1929 letter to Maxwell Perkins, he expounded on this process. They had both heard about famous drinkers of the past, he wrote, but those three- and four-bottle men "were living all the time in the open air—hunting, shooting, always on a horse." Living that way, you could "drink any amount." The fresh air would oxidize the alcohol. For himself at that time, living in Paris and at his desk most of the day, boxing in the gym enabled him to sweat the liquor out of his system. Soon thereafter, Hemingway moved to Key West where he could spend more of his time outdoors on the water, and test his dubious "fresh air" theory by drinking still more.

Fond of the bottle Hemingway assuredly was. During the middle and late 1930s, he celebrated the wondrous effects of liquor in his correspondence and in his published writing. In *Green Hills of Africa* (1935), he meets an Austrian intellectual in Africa who cannot understand why Hemingway should place so much importance on drinking. It had always seemed a weakness to him, the Austrian said. "It is a way of ending a day," Hemingway objected. "It has great benefits. Don't you ever want to change your ideas?" He elaborated on those benefits in a letter to Ivan Kashkin, a young Russian critic who admired Hemingway's writing. "I notice you speak slightingly of the bottle," Ernest observed, and went on to explain why Kashkin was wrong to do so.

I have drunk since I was fifteen and few things have given me more pleasure. When you work hard all day with your head and know you must work again the next day what else can change your ideas and make them run on a different plane like whisky? When you are cold and wet what else can warm you? Before an attack who can say anything that gives you the momentary well being that rum does? I would as soon not eat at night as not to have red wine and water.

Alcohol, in short, was essential to his work and his well-being, as indispensable as food or shelter—and a source of great pleasure.

Having praised whiskey and rum and red wine to Kashkin, Hemingway went on to deliver a remarkable encomium to absinthe in *For Whom the Bell Tolls* (1940). According to the protagonist Robert Jordan, who is fighting a guerilla war in Spain, absinthe had the power to bring back the happiest memories of happier times. One cup of it

took the place of the evening papers, of all the old evenings in cafes, of all chestnut trees that would be in bloom now in this month, of the great slow horses of the outer boulevards, of book shops, of kiosques, and of galleries...and of being able to read and relax in the evening, of all the things he had enjoyed and forgotten and that came back to him when he tasted that opaque, bitter, tongue-numbing, brain-warming, stomach-warming, idea-changing liquid alchemy.

He could still drink vast quantities without drastic consequences, Ernest bragged in a February 1940 letter to Perkins. He'd gotten drunk the night before, he admitted. "Started out on absinthe, drank a bottle of good red wine with dinner, shifted to vodka in town...and then battened it down with whiskys and sodas until 3 A.M. Feel good today. But not like working." In fact the liquor was making inroads, changing not only "ideas" but actions. At a fortieth birthday party given for him in Cuba on July 21, 1939, Hemingway got completely drunk and behaved very much like Fitzgerald at the Murphys' a decade and a half earlier. He threw his host's clothes out the window, and began breaking his Baccarat crystal glasses.

Writing Fitzgerald during those years, Hemingway made it clear that he regarded drinking as something that could be controlled by an act of will. He scolded Scott for getting "stinking drunk" during their 1933 dinner with Wilson and for humiliating all three of them with his combination of excessive praise followed by vicious insult. He assumed that Fitzgerald acted that way deliberately. Why didn't he put a stop to it?

Ernest *thought* that he could quit drinking at any time, but *knew* he didn't want to. The trouble was, as he wrote Archibald MacLeish in December 1943, that throughout his life "when things were really bad he could take a drink and right away they were much better." While serving as a war correspondent in Europe two years later, he wrote his fourth wife Mary Welsh that he hadn't had any liquor for two days. "[Y]ou'll be happy to know that I am all the same without it as with it—think maybe steadier and better—although I have loved it, needed it, and many times it has saved one's damned reason, self-respect, and whatall...We always called it the Giant Killer and nobody who has not had to deal with the Giant many, many times has any right to speak against the Giant Killer." He reiterated the point in a 1950 letter to Arthur Mizener contrasting his drinking habit with Fitzgerald's. "[A]lcohol, that we use as the Giant Killer, and that I could not have lived without many times; or at least would not have cared to live without; was a straight poison to Scott instead of a food."

The Giant Hemingway had in mind, almost certainly, was the depression that periodically overtook him—an inherited malady that started early and that he was never able to escape. When Hemingway repeatedly praised alcohol for its ability to "change ideas," he meant that it could at least temporarily shut down the darkness. As early as "The Three-Day Blow," a story of 1924, he celebrated liquor for its ability to make things seem "much better." In that story, Nick gets drunk and manages to dispel his unhappiness at having broken up with his girl-friend. Under the influence, "the Marge business was no longer so tragic. It was not even very important." How he would feel the next day was another matter, but he could always call on alcohol to perform its magic in the ongoing cycle. What was true of the character Nick Adams in 1924 came to pass for his creator a quarter of a century later. By that time, according to Ernest's son Patrick, his father would succumb to depression whenever he was deprived of liquor.

In 1949, Hemingway wrote magazine writer A.E. Hotchner that drinking was "fun, not a release from something," an assertion that flatly contradicted the need to kill the Giant letter he had written MacLeish six years earlier. There was a reason why he had arrived at this opinion, as the letter to Hotchner went on to reveal. Those who needed drink as "a release from something," he explained, got to be rummies. He had spent much of his life straightening out rummies and all of his life drinking, but since writing was his true love he never got "the two things mixed up." Scott Fitzgerald was one of the rummies he had in mind. Reading *Tender Is the Night*, he claimed, he could tell precisely when Fitzgerald started hitting the bottle. He could spot it in Faulkner as well. He himself would never let drinking "mix up" or contaminate his writing.

This was a classic case of denial, for Hemingway did need alcohol as "a release" from his depression. Moreover, his writing was affected by liquor—and had been since the books of the 1930s on bullfighting in Spain and big-game hunting in Africa in which, as Edmund Wilson observed, he seemed to be engaged in "a deliberate self-drugging." By 1949, when Lillian Ross wrote her long profile of him in the *New Yorker*, Ernest was manifestly in the grip of alcoholism. Ross followed him around New York for a couple of days, as he exhibited various signs of his addiction. He drank heroic amounts of booze, held forth on any number of subjects in a sub-literate patois, and—most tellingly— put on an exhibition of grandiosity by comparing himself, favorably, with great writers of the past. Ross's portrait contributed to the legend of Hemingway as a man of action—no pantywaist aesthete, he—who downed world-record draughts as regularly as he attended wars. In the 1950s, guidebooks to Europe started list-ing his favorite watering holes as places for travelers to visit—Harry's Bar in Venice, the Ritz in Paris, Chicote's in Madrid. There are other famous saloons in this hemisphere associated with Hemingway, notably Sloppy Joe's in Key West and the Floridita in Havana, the home of the Papa Doble, or double daiquiri. All became tourist destinations because Ernest Hemingway drank there.

This part of the legend reached its nadir in *Across the River and Into the Trees*, Hemingway's talky novel about fifty-year-old Colonel Richard Cantwell and Renata, his nineteen-year-old Italian mistress. Most of the major characters in Hemingway's novels were drinkers, but Cantwell outdid the rest. Tom Dardis kept track of one day's consumption by Cantwell in *The Thirsty Muse*, his groundbreaking study of drinking among twentieth-century American authors. Upon arrival in Venice one afternoon, the colonel warms up with two gin and camparis, three very dry double martinis, and three even dryer Montgomerys (martinis made fifteen parts gin to one part vermouth). At dinner, he shares a bot-tle of Capri Bianco, two bottles of Valpolicella, and two bottles of champagne with his adoring young lover. He takes along another bottle of Valpolicella to drink in the gondola where he makes love to Renata at least twice. The next morning, Cantwell wakes up at first light without a trace of a hangover.

On the surface, this catalogue of the colonel's consumption—more than a quart of alcohol over the space of six or seven hours, without losing mental or sex-ual powers—seems almost comical in its excess. Who could believe it? What Dardis suggests, however, is that in *Across the River and Into the Trees* Hemingway was in substance portraying reality as he then knew it. He was him-self fifty years old, in love with Adriana Ivancich, a nineteen-year-old Venetian, and—according to his Cuban doctor, José Luis Herrera Sotolongo —always drunk. "If you keep on drinking this way," Herrera Sotolongo warned Ernest, "you won't even be able to write your name." It was a bad time in the marriage as well, for Ernest and Mary were constantly fighting. At one stage the doctor removed all guns from the Hemingways' house. They were threatening to shoot each other.

At the end of their African safari in 1953-1954, Hemingway was badly wounded in two plane crashes. A number of newspapers incorrectly reported that he had been killed, but his injuries were so severe that he turned to the Giant Killer for relief.

His oldest son Jack came to visit Ernest at his *finca* in Cuba in 1955, and the two men got drunk together. Hemingway decided that they should reduce the population of buzzards around the place. Armed with shotguns and pitchers of martinis, they mounted to the tower above his workroom and started blazing away. After three pitchers and much hilarity, Ernest called a cease-fire and they repaired to the main house. Mary slammed her door, disgusted by the wholesale slaughter. Father and son continued their drinking as they viewed Ernest's print of *Casablanca*. "Isn't the Swede beautiful?" Ernest asked Jack, who responded that in his eyes too Ingrid Bergman looked "really, truly...beautiful." Her beauty was too much for them, in their maudlin state, and they both dissolved in tears. That drunken afternoon, Jack remembered, was the closest he'd ever felt to his father.

At about the same time, Hemingway formed an epistolary friendship with the great art connoisseur Bernard Berenson at Villa i Tatti outside Florence. Ernest's "rambling and affectionate" letters must have been written under the influence of alcohol, the eighty-nine-year-old Berenson intuited. He looked forward to Hemingway's impending visit "with a certain dread." He was afraid that Ernest in the flesh might prove "too overwhelmingly masculine" and that he might expect Berenson "to drink and guzzle with him." The visit did not take place. Ernest became ill in Venice and did not make the journey to Florence.

During the last decade of his life, Hemingway was often ill. In November 1955, for example, he came down with an attack of hepatitis. Herrera Sotolongo put him on a daily ration of two ounces of whiskey, one in the morning and one in the afternoon, that Ernest adhered to for a time. He also did some reading about hepatitis in a book, *The Liver and Its Diseases*. He underlined a number of passages in the book, including one that told him what he wanted to hear, that "the apparent connection between hepatic fibrosis and alcoholism can more easily be explained as a result of malnutrition than as a consequence of alcohol." Good diet and exercise could prevent cirrhosis, Dr. Herrera Sotolongo also believed, and that was what he prescribed. Hemingway suffered another attack of viral hepatitis, but did not develop cirrhosis of the liver.

Soon he resumed drinking heavily. According to A.E. Hotchner, in 1956 Ernest drank Scotch or red wine nightly, and "was invariably in bad shape when finally induced to go to his room." Daytimes, he sat for hours rooted in one position, "sipping his drinks and talking, first coherently, then as the alcohol dissolved all continuity, his talk becoming repetitive, his speech slurred and disheveled." The verbal picture captured Hemingway in the worst of condition, immobilized by drink. For many years, Hemingway had been able to handle liquor and continue to function, but no longer. He could still boast to Hotchner that he had "been drunk 1,547 times in [his] life, but never in the morning." And he could still wake up and declare that he'd gone "five rounds with Demon Rum last night and knocked him on his ass in one fifty-five of the sixth." But he could not make it to lunch without some restorative tequila or vodka. He had crossed "the great divide," as Gingrich put it, "between great drinkers and great drunks." In March 1957 Dr. Jean Monnier, the ship's doctor on the *Ile de France,* instructed Hemingway that painful though it might be, in order to survive he had to "*stop drinking alcohol.*" This Ernest could not do. Staying cold sober made him dull. He felt like a racing car without oil.

In his book *Alcohol and the Writer*, Dr. Donald W. Goodwin asserts that there was reason to believe that Hemingway was diagnosed as a manic-depressive during his stay at the Mayo Clinic in 1961. He underwent shock treatment there, and—seemingly better—was sent home to Ketchum, Idaho, where he killed himself early on the morning of July 2. He had many things wrong with him, physically. He suffered from high blood pressure, liver and kidney disease, diabetes mellitus, and hemochromatosis. His cholesterol count was 380. His liver bulged out against his body, George Plimpton said, "like a long, fat leech." Mentally, he had become paranoid, convinced that various federal authorities were on his trail and that those who pretended to be friends were plotting against him. Alcohol contributed to many of these conditions, as it played a role in interaction with the worst condition of all, the depression that drove him to place the shotgun against his head and trip both barrels.

"One problem with heavy drinkers," Goodwin observes, "is that they become depressed and one never knows whether drinking causes the depression or depression causes the drinking. Psychiatrists agree that a heavy drinker must stop drinking before a diagnosis can be made." Well, Hemingway stopped drinking during the last months of his life and then committed suicide. This makes it possible to conclude, without much conviction, that it was the depression that caused the alcoholism that relieved the depression as it worked its own insidious deadly way into the system. In a family beset by suicides—Ernest's father's, his own, his brother's, at least one sister's, his granddaughter's—the suggestion is strong that Ernest Hemingway took his own life because he was depressed. For many years alcohol offered him temporary relief from his attacks of the "black ass," while in the long run exacerbating his mental and physical woes. Hemingway died a ruined writer and a desperately sick man, convinced that life was not worth the living. In large part, that conviction derived from the Giant Killer.

A WRITERS' DISEASE

In his *Natural History of Alcoholism*, Dr. George Vaillant defined alcoholism as a disease in which "loss of voluntary control over alcohol consumption becomes a necessary and sufficient cause for much of an individual's social, psychological, and physical morbidity." The way in which the disease developed and its outward manifestations varied markedly from one person to another, as in the cases of Fitzgerald and Hemingway. But there can be no doubt that both of them were in the grip of alcohol, and could not shake free of it short of the grave. In their misfortune, they joined a host of American writers of the early and middle twentieth century. Alcoholism among these writers, Goodwin asserted, constituted an "epidemic." Among others the roster includes E.A. Robinson, Dreiser, Stephen Crane, London, Hart Crane, O'Neill, Lardner, Lewis, Faulkner, Wolfe, Millay, Parker, Benchley, Thurber, O'Hara, Steinbeck, Hammett, Chandler, Cummings, Roethke, Berryman, Tennessee Williams, Inge, Capote, Saroyan, Aiken, Kerouac, Agee, James Jones, Lowell, Jarrell, Sexton, Cheever, Stafford, and Carver. Excessive drinking, it seemed clear, was an occupational hazard. According to Goodwin only bartenders had higher rates of alcoholism than writers.

One reason for the epidemic was the epidemic itself. If all these great writers were drunks, didn't it follow that you had to drink to be a great writer? Fitzgerald embraced that notion when he challenged a correspondent to "name a single American artist except James & Whistler [both of whom lived in England] who didn't die of drink." American culture came to expect such self-destruction from its artists. As the poet Donald Hall expressed it, "[t]here seems to be an assumption, widely held and all but declared, that it is *natural* to want to destroy yourself." This pernicious doctrine encouraged young writers to emulate the

Berrymans and O'Neills and Fitzgeralds by drinking themselves into insensibility while "consumers of vicarious death" sat on the sidelines and applauded. The applause, Hall felt, should be reserved for writers who survived. Self-destruction was no sure sign of genius, and genius no excuse for self-destruction.

A number of other explanations have been offered for the phenomenon of the drunken writer in America. Goodwin presented several of them in *Alcohol and the Writer*.

"Writing is a form of exhibitionism; alcohol lowers inhibitions and prompts exhibitionism in many people. Writing requires an interest in people; alcohol increases sociability and makes people more interesting. Writing involves fantasy; alcohol promotes fantasy. Writing requires self-confidence; alcohol bolsters confidence. Writing is lonely work; alcohol assuages loneliness. Writing demands intense concentration; alcohol relaxes." Most of these motivating factors seem to fit Fitzgerald's case better than Hemingway's, particularly the release from inhibitions (the "stimulus" of liquor) and the access of sociability.

Alcohol's effect on social relations constituted the first of the three reasons Malcolm Cowley cited for drinking among writers. Cowley's observations carry a certain authority, for as a poet, critic, and editor, he had an unusually wide acquaintance among the century's greatest writers. His three "special reasons," in abbreviated form, were: 1) "Writers are probably shyer, on the average, than members of other professions...and at the same time they are more eager to establish direct personal communications. Alcohol serves, or appears to serve, as a bridge between person and person." 2) "Writing is an activity that involves a high degree of nervous tension, and alcohol is a depressant that helps to soothe the nerves." 3) "For many writers drinking becomes part of the creative process. They drink in order to have visions, or in order to experience the feeling of heightened life that they are trying to convey...or in order to get in touch with their subconscious minds...or in order to overcome their excessive obedience to the inner censor, or simply in order to start the flow of words." Or, the cynic is tempted to add, for almost any other reason that will give them leave to drink.

The novelist Walker Percy, himself a doctor, presented yet another problem confronting writers: the problem of "reentry" after exaltation. "What goes up must come down. The best film of the year ends at nine o'clock. What to do at ten? What did Faulkner do after writing the last sentence of *The Sound and the Fury*? Get drunk for a week. What did Dostoyevsky do after finishing *The Idiot*? Spend three days and nights at the roulette table. What does the reader do after finishing either book? How long does his exaltation last?"

As the questions make clear, "reentry" poses difficulties for everyone. In Percy's formulation, these are "most spectacular" for writers, who "seem subject more than most people to estrangement from the society around them, to neurosis, psychosis, alcoholism, drug addiction, epilepsy, florid sexual behavior, solitariness, depression, violence, and suicide." They retreat into art, as Einstein did into science, "to escape the intolerable dreariness of everyday life." But the escape can never be complete. As Percy posed the dilemma, "How do you go about living in the world when you are not working at your art, yet still find yourself having to get through a Wednesday afternoon?"

Combining physiological and psychological thinking, Percy arrived at a persuasive account of "Why a Writer Drinks."

He is marooned in his cortex. Therefore it is his cortex that he must assault. Worse, actually. He, his self, is marooned in his left cortex... Yet his work, if he is any good, comes from listening to his right brain, locus of the unconscious knowledge of the fit and form of things. So, unlike the artist who can fool and cajole his right brain and get it going by messing in paints and clay and stone...there sits the poor writer, rigid as a stick, pencil poised, with no choice but to wait in fear and trembling until the spark jumps the commissure. Hence his notorious penchant for superstition and small obsessive and compulsive acts such as lining up paper exactly foursquare with desk. Then, failing in these frantic invocations and after the right brain falls as silent as the sphinx—what else can it do?—nothing remains, if the right won't talk, but to assault the left with alcohol, which of course is a depressant and which does of course knock out that grim angel guarding the gate of Paradise and let the poor half-brained writer in and a good deal besides. But by now the writer is drunk, his presiding left-brained craftsman-consciousness laid out flat, trampled by the rampant imagery from the right and a horde of reptilian demons from below.

For all these many reasons, then, writers turn to alcohol. But there are those who turn back, too, among them in recent times John Cheever and Raymond Carver. In fall 1973 they were colleagues and alcoholics together at the University of Iowa's writers workshop. Carver used to drive Cheever to the liquor store so they could be there when it opened. Neither of them took the cover off his typewriter the entire autumn. But somehow Cheever stopped drinking, sobered up, wrote *Falconer*, and received the homage due him before his death in 1982. Carver quit in 1978, and survived for ten more productive years. "Don't weep for me," he told his friends when he was dying. He'd lived ten years longer than he expected, and those years were "*all* gravy."

The novelist and newspaperman Pete Hamill wrote about his alcoholism in his 1994 memoir, *A Drinking Life*. In his boyhood, he used to go to Gallagher's saloon with his father. Billy Hamill was the star of the place, singing Irish songs and commanding the attention and admiration of the other drinkers. "This is where men go," Pete thought, "this is what men do." Unlike his father he did not sing, but he knew how to tell stories, and he told a lot of them in one saloon or another that served as his nightly home away from home—and wife and children. In December 1973, he was standing at a bar making epigrams and telling jokes and repeating lines that had gotten laughs from others when it suddenly struck him that he "was performing [his] life instead of living it." If this was a play, he wanted a better part. Hamill quit drinking then, and to help him stick to that decision adopted a mantra: "*I will live my life from now on, I will not perform it.*"

When people asked him why he didn't drink, he'd say, "I have no talent for it." Sober, he found he had more time for his family and for his writing. And he no longer had to spend the hangover days lacerating himself for crimes and misdemeanors of the night before. "No more apologies for stupid phone calls, asinine remarks, lapses in grace." In Hollywood, he met out-of-work directors and screenwriters and actors, all ruined by booze. He could not help thinking of "some of the final tortured stories by Scott Fitzgerald," another alcoholic of Irish heritage, another histrionic drunk, another chronic apologizer. He felt "a surge of pity" for him, struck down in his early forties. But pity is not strong enough for what Fitzgerald left undone and what Hemingway could no longer do as drink took over their lives. We cannot know exactly what was lost— only that the loss was immense, and irrecoverable.

Whoever won the battle between Scott and Ernest for writer of his generation, they both lost the war to alcoholism.

CHAPTER 9

THAT PRONE BODY

> Defend me from my friends; I can defend myself
> from my enemies.
> —CLAUDE LOUIS HECTOR, Duc de Villars

> Mr. Hemingway's piercing jabs at that prone body.
> —SCOTTIE FITZGERALD

The complicated relationship between Fitzgerald and Hemingway falls logically into three distinct stages. During the first stage, lasting from their meeting in Paris in May 1925 through the end of 1926, they were very close companions who saw each other often and wrote warmly to each other when apart. Fitzgerald as the more experienced writer took the lead in cementing their friendship. He campaigned to deliver Hemingway to Scribner's and Maxwell Perkins, he wrote a laudatory review of *In Our Time*, he loaned Hemingway money and support as needed, and he made valuable suggestions for tightening up the opening of *The Sun Also Rises*.

The relationship cooled in the period from 1927 to 1936, as Hemingway's star ascended and Fitzgerald's began its decline. Bridling at his role as beneficiary of Fitzgerald's advice and guidance, Ernest became increasingly abrasive in his comments about Scott and his weaknesses, among them feeling sorry for himself, selling out his talent, succumbing to drink, and allowing Zelda to dominate him. The crowning blow came in *Esquire*'s August 1936 publication of "The Snows of Kilimanjaro," with its gratuitous reference to "poor Scott Fitzgerald" as a writer wrecked by his idolization of the very rich.

After that time and until Fitzgerald's death in December 1940, the friendship was effectively over, though both men used Perkins as a go-between to obtain news about each other and Fitzgerald, in particular, made frequent comments about Hemingway in his correspondence and notebooks.

Handy as it is in summarizing the relationship, this three-stage division does not take account of what happened after Fitzgerald's death. What becomes clear, in reading through Ernest's correspondence (some of it, like his letters to Charles Scribner, only recently opened), is that Hemingway repeatedly and systematically denigrated Fitzgerald during the two decades remaining to him, and that these attacks were occasioned or at least intensified by the posthumous revival of Fitzgerald's reputation. The revival began with the publication of *The Last Tycoon* in 1941, continued with *The Crack-Up*, *The Portable Fitzgerald*, and the Armed Services edition of *The Great Gatsby* in 1945, and reached its climax with four books of 1950 and 1951. Two of these—*The Stories of F. Scott Fitzgerald*, selected by Malcolm Cowley, and Cowley's revised version (following Fitzgerald's notes) of *Tender Is the Night*—made the body of his work more widely available to readers. The other two—Budd Schulberg's novel *The Disenchanted* and Arthur Mizener's biography *The Far Side of Paradise*— aroused an extraordinary degree of interest in Fitzgerald's unhappy life.

Ten days after Fitzgerald's death, Perkins wrote Hemingway that he was "trying to think of some way that something could rightly be done to bring his writings forward." The most obvious course was to bring out his novel about Hollywood, since it was going well when he died and "might have vindicated Scott completely." The trouble was that the novel was "very far from being finished." A few weeks later, Perkins wrote his friend Elizabeth Lemmon to the same effect, adding that he was interested in "getting Hem or Bunny Wilson to write some sort of memoir of him."

Apparently Perkins did not ask Hemingway to write such a piece at this time. Edmund Wilson took over as editor and introducer of *The Last Tycoon*, which was brought out in an omnibus volume also containing *The Great Gatsby* and five of Fitzgerald's major stories. In opposition to Perkins, Wilson wanted to include the "Crack-Up" articles, Fitzgerald's letters to his daughter, selections from his notebooks, and tributes to Scott that he had solicited for the *New Republic*. Perkins did not want to see "those terrible cracked plate pieces from *Esquire*" in a Scribner's book. Such a miscellaneous book would be bad for Fitzgerald's reputation, he felt. Besides, it wouldn't sell. In the light of these objections, the idea for such a book was set aside for the time being.

Early in April Perkins wrote Hemingway that a plan had been worked out about Scott's Hollywood novel. The book ran to 37,000 words only, and had not been revised. The final third had not even been written. Nonetheless *The Last Tycoon* broke "wholly new ground" for Scott, had its share of magical moments, and deserved to be published. So Scribner's decided that Bunny Wilson should edit the unfinished novel, and contribute an introduction that covered Scott's career as a writer. With *Gatsby* and the stories, Perkins thought, the volume would constitute an omnibus of Fitzgerald's "best writings in fiction."

He hoped Bunny Wilson would "not knife Scott in that [introduction] he is going to write," Ernest replied. In fact Wilson was a less than ideal editor, for he regarded himself as Fitzgerald's intellectual superior and did not hesitate to change copy and rearrange scenes. Still, in the foreword he gave *The Last Tycoon* a favorable sendoff as "Fitzgerald's most mature piece of work" and "far and away the best novel we have had about Hollywood." Reviewers echoed those lines, and several took the occasion to reassess Fitzgerald's career as a writer. "If only he had lived, if only his constitution had served him better," John Chamberlain commented in *Harper's*, "what fiction he might have done! As it is, he was the best of the lot—and I, for one, can't understand why more useful sermons have not been preached over his grave." Stephen Vincent Benét, in the *Saturday Review of Literature*, thought that *The Last Tycoon* showed Fitzgerald working at the height of his powers. "You can take off your hats now, gentlemen," he concluded, "and I think perhaps you had better. This is not a legend, this is a reputation—and, seen in perspective, it may well be one of the most secure reputations of our time."

To put it mildly, Hemingway did not agree. "There are very fine parts" in the novel, he acknowledged in a November 1951 letter to Perkins, "but most if it has a deadness that is unbelievable from Scott." The part about Stahr was very good. You could recognize Irving Thalberg (the charismatic producer upon whom Fitzgerald modeled his hero Monroe Stahr), "his charm and skill, and grasp of business, and the sentence of death over him." But the women in the novel were "pretty preposterous," he thought, for Scott really didn't have "any knowledge of people." In the things between men and women, "the old magic was gone." As far as it went, Hemingway's criticism was right on the mark. By far the most effective sections of *Tycoon* depict Stahr commanding every facet of the movie-making process, and dealing brilliantly with actors, directors, writers, and cameramen. In contrast, the love story involving Stahr and Kathleen seems pallid and unconvincing. But Hemingway had only begun his adverse criticism.

At this stage in his letter, Ernest introduced a metaphor that he was to return to time and again by way of denigrating his onetime best friend. "He still had the technique and the romance of doing anything, but all the dust was off the butterfly's wing for a long time even though the wing would still move up until the butterfly was dead." The dead butterfly led to Scott's death in life, as Hemingway went on to describe it. He died "inside himself" when he was thirty to thirty-five years old, and his creative powers died "somewhat later." His heart died in him in France (the Jozan episode, presumably) and the rest of him "just went on dying progressively after that."

As to Wilson's contribution, Hemingway observed that he had done a creditable job of "explaining, sorting, padding and arranging" the fragmentary novel Fitzgerald left behind. But he disapproved of the "very poor selection" Wilson had made among Fitzgerald's stories. Specifically, he thought "The Rich Boy" "profoundly silly" and "The Diamond as Big as the Ritz" "simply trash."

Perhaps inspired by the butterfly metaphor, Ernest tried out two others in his disparagement of *The Last Tycoon*. Reading the book, he said, was "like seeing an old baseball pitcher with nothing left in his arm coming out and working with his intelligence for a few innings before he is knocked out of the box." That comparison at least gave Fitzgerald credit for trying before failing. The other, more devastating metaphor contained no such ameliorative touch. Scott's book reminded him of "a slab of bacon on which mold had grown. You can scrape off the mold, but if has gone deep into the meat, there is nothing that can keep it from tasting like moldy bacon."

In his final remarks, Hemingway tried to soften these blows to Fitzgerald's corpus, if not (as Scottie thought) to his corpse. "If [*If!*] I sound deprecatory about Scott, remember I know how good he is and was only criticizing Wilson's selections and his posthumous work." In dealing with literature, Ernest observed, it was best to speak frankly and critically.

Fitzgerald not only left *The Last Tycoon* unfinished at his death, but— according to Hemingway—even if Scott had lived longer he never would have finished it. It was a point he made first to Perkins, citing as evidence Fitzgerald's "preposterous outline" for the final stages of the book, and then to Charles Scribner, who became his in-house confidant at Scribner's following the death of Perkins in 1947. The "worst symptom" of a writer emerged when he began to show his work-in-progress or read it aloud or "Make the Gigantic Outline," Ernest wrote Scribner in August 1948. Scott would not have completed *Tycoon* "in 1,000 years. I know it and you know it, but who the hell else knows it?" The following year, Hemingway suggested that Fitzgerald had behaved dishonestly in trying to sell *Tycoon* to the magazines in its incomplete form, "giving samples here and there like a mining prospector with a salted mine."

Edmund Wilson exhibited his famously fractious personality in the course of editing *The Last Tycoon* for Scribner's. He and Perkins differed on the issue of what should accompany Fitzgerald's fragmentary novel in a book. Wilson not only wanted the volume to include a collection of letters, notebook entries, and essays by and about his former Princeton companion, he also wanted to reprint *Tender Is the Night* and some of Fitzgerald's slight Pat Hobby sketches from *Esquire*. It was impractical to include *Tender*, Perkins pointed out: it would make the book too long. He also balked at using the Pat Hobby stories. "I know you to be an immovable man when you have made a decision," he wrote Wilson, "but I truly do not think the Pat Hobby stories are good enough for this book." They were "not much more than anecdotal," and Scott would not "have wanted them in a book"—certainly not in a book of his best work, including *Gatsby* and a selection of his best stories. Wilson has been given a good deal of credit for rebuilding Fitzgerald's reputation, but in this instance as in others, it was Perkins who was functioning as Scott's posthumous guardian and protector.

Following Fitzgerald's death, obituary writers were virtually unanimous in depicting him as an author whose star had risen and fallen during the 1920s. When the Jazz Age "petered out, as much from emptiness as anything else," commented the *Providence Journal*, "he, too, petered out—tragically and completely." Westbrook Pegler delivered a vicious diatribe against those days in his nationally syndicated column. Fitzgerald's passing reminded him "of a queer band of undisciplined and self-indulgent brats who were determined not to pull their weight in the boat and wanted the world to drop everything and sit down and bawl with them." A more restrained but still sniffy *New York Times* editorial acknowledged that Fitzgerald had captured "the life and times of a certain section of our society" during the days after World War I, but lamented that he had not since grown up. The obituary in *Time* magazine was so bent on tying Fitzgerald to the Jazz Age that it mentioned only his two early novels, ignoring both *The Great Gatsby* and *Tender Is the Night*. It was as if Herman Melville had been memorialized as the author of *Typee* and *Omoo*, never mind *Moby-Dick*.

In short, Fitzgerald was a back number, and some readers must have been surprised to discover that he was still alive enough to die in December 1940. The previous year, a young and highly literary Budd Schulberg was startled when asked to work with Fitzgerald on the Dartmouth Winter Carnival movie. He'd supposed that Scott was dead and gone.

Maxwell Perkins may have been the best friend F. Scott Fitzgerald ever had. During Scott's lifetime Max did him the considerable honor of continuing to believe in him through long and distressing periods of alcoholic silence. And immediately after his death, Perkins set about to rescue Fitzgerald's reputation from the casual dismissals in the newspapers and magazines. He struck this note vigorously in two February 1941 letters to Wilson. "[W]hat we must do," he wrote Wilson, "is to show the world in so far as we can by what we publish, that Scott was very much beyond the boundaries of the Jazz Age, with which his very success at the start identified him." His object was to bring out writings of Fitzgerald "which would demonstrate irresistibly that he was far more important, far more the distinguished and significant writer, than the public in general thinks him to be; that he vastly transcended the Jazz Age kind of writing with which they associate him." The public never fully understood, Perkins believed, that Fitzgerald's early fiction "cut both ways": that he saw the excesses of the Jazz Age even as he seemed to be glamorizing them. "Pegler didn't seem to have any hint of that in his mind." His aim, Max said, was "to reveal the living writer, not the dead man."

In his "immovable" fashion Wilson could not be deterred from his plan to reprint Fitzgerald's "Crack-Up" essays, together with various other material, in book form. Perkins, who thought that Scott over-dramatized his depressed state in the "Crack-Up," remained opposed to this idea, and in due course, Scribner's turned down Wilson's proposal for such a collection. He then shopped the idea elsewhere, to Princeton University Press, to the Colt Press in San Francisco, to Houghton Mifflin, and to New Directions, which brought out *The Crack-Up* in 1945 and has kept it in print ever since.

There were certain roadblocks Wilson had to surmount in order to get this book published. For one thing, James Laughlin at New Directions objected to his procedure, as editor, of choosing selectively among Fitzgerald's notebooks. "Fitzgerald is not your concession," Laughlin insisted to Wilson. "He belongs to the world." As Laughlin saw it, Wilson's trust was to present "an untampered-with version" of what Fitzgerald left behind. "How would you like to have somebody scissoring your notes when you were dead?" The implied attack on his integrity infuriated Wilson, who wrote Fitzgerald's executor John Biggs that Laughlin had "a mental age of about 14 and is considered by those who know him to be on the verge of dementia praecox."

This dispute was smoothed over when Laughlin agreed, in the contract, not to change any of Wilson's editorial decisions. Another hurdle was surmounted when Wilson persuaded Scottie Fitzgerald to permit publication of the book, over the objections of Perkins and Harold Ober. But there was still Hemingway to deal with.

Wilson intended to print letters by Fitzgerald referring to Hemingway in his miscellaneous volume, as well as some of Scott's comments about Ernest in his notebooks. Bunny had reason to fear that Ernest might object, so all of these references were dispatched to Hemingway's lawyer Maurice Speiser for approval. In reply, Hemingway wrote Speiser that he had "no objection to Wilson publishing any non-libellous letters by Scott Fitzgerald." He added that if Wilson was considering editing Fitzgerald's letters that he had a hell of a lot of them in Paris and Key West. He "cared for Scott so much and respected the good that was in him and understood the causes of his trashiness, when he was trashy, and the real causes of his crack-up, which [could] not yet be published." But he thought that publication of these letters was "premature" until a real study could be written which would truly portray "the whole tragedy of Scott and Zelda."

What Hemingway was saying, between the lines, was that he knew much more about Fitzgerald than Scott's Princeton companion Wilson—and that he rather resented Bunny turning Scott's manuscripts into his private "concession." When Perkins wrote Ernest in February 1944 that he too had some wonderful letters from Scott, Hemingway advised him to hang on to them rather than "letting Bunny Wilson pee them away in his malicious little driblets." Wilson had not even asked him for one of his letters from Scott, Ernest pointed out. He and Max should both save their letters, and then get out a good book on Fitzgerald and his letters. He knew Scott, "through some periods, better than anyone, and would be glad to write a long, true, just, detailed...account" of those years. Then they could get John Peale Bishop to edit the letters. Bishop was unfailingly "kind, impersonal, and disinterested," while Wilson was "usually twisting the facts to cover some expressed error of critical judgment...or some prejudice or lack of knowledge or scholarship." Wilson was "the great false-honest, false-craftsman, false-great-critic of our exceedingly sorry times."

Nonetheless Ernest asked Max to send him a copy of *The Crack-Up* in advance of its August 1945 publication date. "I feel badly not to write anything about Scott when I knew him, possibly, the best of any of them," he observed. But he could not "write anything true" as long as Zelda was alive, just as he could not write about his own family with his "bitch of a mother still able to read." Then he proceeded to level his guns against Fitzgerald. *Tycoon* was really a mock-up "to draw advances on." Scott "was almost completely uneducated." He did everything wrong, and for a time it came out all right. "But geometry always catches up with you."

Ernest invited Max to share his disaffection. "I always feel that you and I can talk truly about Scott because we both loved him and admired him and understood him. Where other people were dazzled by him we saw the good, the weakness and the great flaw that was always there"—the cowardice, the dream world about football and war. Next time, Hemingway said, he'd write "what was good in [Fitzgerald]. But we take it for granted people should be good. And in a horse, a regiment, a good writer I look for what is wrong. Take it for granted they are good or would not be looking at them." The next time, when Ernest would write about what was good in his old friend, did not come to pass.

For the most part, Hemingway's correspondence with Charles Scribner following Perkins's death concentrated on professional matters, in author-to-publisher fashion. But occasionally, and more or less gratuitously, Ernest would insert a jibe about Fitzgerald—whose reputation, of course, depended to a considerable degree upon the house of Scribner. Late in 1948, for example, he reported that he had been given an Italian award "so old and decrepit" that Charlie could now refer to his wife Mary as "Lady Mary." He would assume no title himself, Hemingway said. "Mister" was good enough for him. Then he added, as an afterthought: "Poor Scott, how he would have loved it."

In August 1949, Hemingway linked Fitzgerald with another famous Scribner's author in a double-barreled blast. Sometimes, he wrote Scribner apropos of nothing, he thought of "Scott and his ideas of GLAMOUR and they seem ridiculous. Also that over-grown Little Abner, THOMAS WOLFE, and his mother." Ernest next wrote at considerable length about how Zelda had unmanned Scott by telling him his "equipment was insufficient." Ernest tried to reassure Scott by looking in mirrors and at statues in the Louvre—the same story Hemingway was to present in fleshed-out form as "A Matter of Measurements" in *A Moveable Feast*. But Scott could not be reassured, for he had sunk into a "lace-curtain Irish slough of despond" and never got out of it except to borrow money for a book he knew he couldn't finish.

In a final paragraph, Ernest apologized for talking tough about Scott and proceeded to a veritable masterpiece of faint praise. "But what a lovely writer he was, within his ignorance and lack of education, and his adoration of the rich. He should have been a spaniel," summoning up an image of Fitzgerald as lapdog fawning before the rich. On second thought, though, Hemingway decided that Fitzgerald "did not rate" to be a cocker and even less a springer, like his own much-loved Black Dog.

In a somewhat similar letter of May 1951, Ernest disparaged the posthumous idealization of Max Perkins. "Please bury Max's ghost for keeps," he wrote Scribner, and along with it any idea that he or Wolfe (who died in 1939) or

Fitzgerald were gods. "Max was Max with five daughters and an idiot wife. Tom Wolfe was a one book boy and a glandular giant with the brains and the guts of three mice. Scott was a rummy and a liar and dishonest about money with the in-bred talent of a[n]...easily frightened angel." As an editor, Hemingway correctly pointed out, Perkins never touched his copy, aside from removing an obscenity here and there. But he did not call attention to Max's greatest quality as an editor: that he befriended and encouraged and supported the authors he worked with, including Hemingway as well as Fitzgerald and Wolfe. Ernest did not observe the convention of speaking well of the dead. Inasmuch as they could no longer feel pain, they needed less protection than the living. Besides, as he commented in 1959, "a son of a bitch live is a son of a bitch dead."

Hemingway also dropped derisive comments about Fitzgerald into his extensive correspondence with Malcolm Cowley of the late 1940s and early 1950s, commencing with discussions in advance of Cowley's laudatory "A Portrait of Mister Papa" for *Life* magazine's January 10, 1949, issue. "Can remember Scott, on 5th avenue, telling me what a great football player he would be if he could only play now when he really knew and understood the game," Hemingway said in a September 1948 letter. But Scott, "a basic coward," would not cross the street in traffic, even though Ernest told him a good broken field runner "would sift through traffic anytime with perfect confidence and without danger. I was only a lineman but traffic no bother me Dr. Will cross through it going backwards anytime if you will pay me or make a bet. And not worry." At the same time, he pointed out in a subsequent letter, Hemingway had "no illusions" that he had been or could be a great football player. Those were "the sort of daydreams Scott and John O'Hara had about twelve."

As the Fitzgerald revival heated up in the early 1950s, Cowley expatiated on the vagaries of the literary stock market. Fitzgerald Common, down for so long, was on the rise at last. With his extraordinary competitiveness—you couldn't take a bike ride with Hemingway without getting into a race—Ernest could not avoid seeing fellow writers as rivals, and doing what he could to cut the ground from under them. Wolfe and O'Hara and Faulkner came in for this kind of treatment, but Fitzgerald bore the brunt of it. In his correspondence, Hemingway characteristically deflected attention from Fitzgerald's often wonderful writing to his shortcomings as a human being and the trials of his far-from-wonderful life. So too, in their way, did Budd Schulberg's autobiographically oriented novel *The Disenchanted* and Arthur Mizener's biography *The Far Side of Paradise*, with its emphasis on Scott's dissipation.

Motivated by admiration for Fitzgerald's writing, Cowley was determined to do just the opposite—to "do right by Scott" by leaving out "the sensational passages that the movies and television are excited about" and instead treating Fitzgerald as he deserved, "just as a writer." In this spirit, Cowley first edited a collection of Fitzgerald's best short stories, and then embarked on a revised version of *Tender Is the Night*. He had as his mandate for this venture Scott's own notes about telling the story of the novel chronologically rather than starting *in medias res* on the beach at Antibes. Cowley was eager to get Hemingway's reaction to this reorganized *Tender*, and that stimulated a flurry of correspondence between the two men.

From the start Ernest had reservations about the revised novel. *Tender Is the Night* was the one novel of Fitzgerald's that he invariably praised—"a damned beautiful and most sad book," as he wrote Cowley in July 1951. He rather liked the complicated time line of the original, and was not sure he wanted to see the novel tampered with. In explaining why, he reiterated the butterfly comparison and tried out another from the insect world. "Scott had, most of all, charm and in this book more than any other. I think there is a danger in over-dissecting charm just as you don't really understand the butterfly any better by rubbing the dust from his wings...Scott had nearly as much logic as a hawk moth around a lantern."

In September Hemingway launched a full-scale assault on authors of then-popular novels about World War II, including James Jones, Irwin Shaw, and Norman Mailer. All of them, he said, would have been frightened out of their wits if they'd been in the Hürtgen forest campaign he went through as a war correspondent. As for Fitzgerald, he was poorly educated and suffered from spells of unbelievably bad taste. He caught the surface of characters but in *Tender* he mixed up himself and Zelda with Gerald and Sara Murphy as models for Dick and Nicole Diver. "How could he ever know people except on the surface when he never fucked anybody, nobody told him anything except as an answer to a question and he was always too drunk late at night to remember what anybody really said?" Drink ruined him, along with "Zelda, and cowardice, and ambition and love of earning money...."

When he read the revised *Tender Is the Night* in November, he responded immediately that in straight chronological order the book lost "the magic completely." There was no secret and no mystery, and "all sense of a seemingly magical world (the world of Sara and Gerald Murphy) being destroyed by something...unknown is lost." Once again, Hemingway reverted to the butterfly trope. The revision of Fitzgerald's novel was "just like taking the wings off a butterfly and arranging them so he can fly straight as a bee flies and losing all the dust that makes the colors that makes the butterfly magical in the process." He understood that Cowley was only developing Fitzgerald's idea for changing the novel, but felt confident that if he'd had the opportunity he would have been able to talk Scott out of it. None of this was important, he added, "unless everything is important in writing."

In this same letter, Hemingway made it clear that he was not pleased by the ongoing efforts to restore Fitzgerald's reputation. "You and Edmund Wilson tidy Scott up," he told Cowley, "and he becomes a sort of Henry James of the twenties."

When Arthur Mizener contacted Hemingway in the course of research for his Fitzgerald biography, Ernest sounded more than willing to cooperate. He couldn't send Mizener any of the Fitzgerald letters he'd asked for—they'd become rat and roach food in the muggy Key West climate, he feared—but otherwise he offered to "help any way I can on Scott."

In the several letters he wrote to Mizener, Ernest's assistance took the form of a series of insults about Scott. He ridiculed his Walter Mitty–like dreams of glory, for example. Fitzgerald was always talking about playing football again, or going to war for the first time, but he lacked the requisite courage. As a combat soldier, Hemingway asserted, he "would probably have been re-classified or shot for cowardice." Fitzgerald was "fragile Irish instead of tough Irish" and had no discipline. He would "quit at the drop of a hat" and if necessary go out and borrow someone's hat to drop.

One of Hemingway's techniques for putting Fitzgerald down was to follow a favorable comment with a damning contradiction: the "yes, but" approach. When sober Scott could be a charming companion, he told Mizener, *but* he had an embarrassing tendency to hero-worship. "I loved Scott very much," he declared, *but* "he was extremely difficult with that situation he got himself into and Zelda constantly making him drunk because she was jealous of his working well." Bunny Wilson and John Bishop were good friends from Princeton, *but* "they never saw much of him when he was at his best, which was over a short time." Scott had "a very steep trajectory and was almost like a guided missile with no one guiding him."

Hemingway repeated his tale about Fitzgerald's sexual insecurity for Mizener, and added that Scott "never slept with any girl except Zelda" until she "went officially crazy." Patently, Hemingway's goal was to belittle Fitzgerald in the eyes of his first biographer, just as he had done with Perkins and Scribner and Cowley—all of them in a position to advance or retard the revival of Scott's reputation. "Poor Scott," Ernest wrote Mizener, "how he would have loved all this big thing about him now." He never had any respect for him "except for his lovely, golden, wasted talent." Scott was "romantic, ambitious, and Christ, Jesus, God knows how talented." But he was also generous without being kind, and completely uneducated. If Scott were still around, Ernest would be glad to let him read everything he said about him. He would never say such things behind his back.

For Mizener's benefit, Hemingway did a brief and unflattering run-through of Fitzgerald's published works. *Tender Is the Night* was the best of his books, despite its inconsistencies. *The Great Gatsby* "was ok with reservations." None of the stories were great but the best, Ernest guessed, were "Babylon Revisited" and "The Rich Boy" (which he had called "profoundly silly" a decade earlier). *This Side of Paradise* was comic. And he couldn't read *The Beautiful and Damned*. "[W]ho the hell said they were beautiful and what the hell were they damned by?" The Italian soldiers he'd known on the Basso Piave may have been damned but it didn't seem to him that "you were necessarily damned because you made a little money." Mizener had picked a tough subject to write about in Fitzgerald, he observed, and by his standards one hardly worth the effort.

Despite his own critical remarks about Fitzgerald, when *Life* ran a selection from Mizener's biography on January 15, 1951, that called attention to a number of Scott's problems, and particularly his drinking, Hemingway attacked it as unforgivable grave-robbing. "I'd kill a guy for money if times were bad enough, I guess," he wrote Harvey Breit. "But I don't think I could do that." Directly to Mizener he wrote that he would rather clean sewers, be a bouncer in a bad whorehouse, or pimp for a living than to sign such an article. Mizener's letters tricked him into thinking he was "a straight guy," he told Cowley. "Poor Scott: what robes, or shroud, he had were torn and sold by very strange people." Both Mizener and Schulberg (in whose *The Disenchanted* Fitzgerald appeared as the alcoholic screenwriter Manley Halliday) were "swine." Cowley was a decent man but "that Schulberg-Mizener Axis could well be hanged, head down, in front of any second rate garage." When the *New York Herald-Tribune*'s Sunday book review asked him for a list of books he liked, Hemingway came up with "*Longevity Pays: The Life of Arthur Mizener* by F. Scott FitzGerald [sic] and *The Schulberg Incident* by F. Scott FitzGerald [sic, again]."

Hemingway's virulent feelings about these books, and particularly Mizener's, did not on the surface make much sense. In a "Foreword to Scott" passage cut from *A Moveable Feast* by his widow, Mary, and Scribner's editor L.H. Brague, Jr., Hemingway claimed that "[o]ther people have written about him and did not know him, but I tried to help in the parts about him that I knew, telling them of his great generosities and kindnesses." The seven letters to Mizener contain no account whatever of such generosities and kindnesses. In *The Far Side of Paradise*, Mizener may over-emphasize Fitzgerald's drunken behavior, but for mean-spiritedness his biography cannot compete with the comments in Hemingway's correspondence with him.

What troubled Ernest most about the success of Schulberg's and Mizener's books was that they promised to encourage unwanted invasions of *his* privacy. By mid-century the Hemingway legend had taken hold of the public imagination. He had dwindled into a celebrity who could not travel to Italy without photographic coverage in the newspapers and magazines, or come to New York without an obligatory mention in Leonard Lyons's *New York Post* column. To avoid this sort of attention, Mary Hemingway reported, she and Ernest used to duck out of hotels by back doors and service entrances. These were annoyances. Longer studies that delved deeper into his past were far more threatening.

Ernest cooperated with Cowley for his *Life* portrait in 1949, and was reasonably satisified with the result. The next year, he also cooperated with Lillian Ross for her *New Yorker* profile, and this time emerged as a rather foolish and self-important figure who spoke in pidgin English and drank enormous quantities of champagne. What was really troubling him in May 1951, however, was the impending threat of a psychologically oriented book from Philip Young. In writing Cowley at that time, he made the connection between Young's book-in-progress and Mizener's biography. "The Mizener formula on grave-robbing Scott Fitzgerald was a money-maker. So every publisher wants to follow it. But Scott is dead and through very good luck I am not." As a consequence he planned to make "a cold, hard fight" against publication of Young's book. Cowley discouraged Hemingway from pursuing such a policy. It was probably a losing battle, he pointed out, and not worth the effort. Besides, Young's was basically a book of literary criticism, although he psychoanalyzed from the fiction.

Reluctantly, Hemingway gave up the battle to suppress, and was infuriated when Young's *Ernest Hemingway* came out in 1952, advancing a Freudian "wound theory" to account for most of his life and work. Still, he blamed Mizener for preparing the way. Letters were pouring in from would-be biographers, he told Cowley. Several of them commented "that they admired Arthur Mizener's book on F. Scott Fitzgerald and please send them all available details and any unpublished material about my life." In attacking Mizener and Schulberg as grave robbers, Hemingway was not so much defending Fitzgerald as defending himself against having his life closely examined while he was living it.

Ernest may also have wanted to keep under wraps the family propensity to depression, most obviously manifested in his father's suicide. In writing Cowley, he specifically objected to the revelation of Zelda's mental illness, and its possible effect on Scottie Fitzgerald. "Do you think it is fair to a girl that Mizener, for money, should publish that her mother was a schizophrenic?"

After his experience with Young, Hemingway was wary about Charles Fenton's book dealing with his apprenticeship as a writer—the years from 1916 to 1924. In Fenton's favor were the disarming letters he wrote, and the fact that he'd been a newsman and flown with the R.A.F. in World War II. But Ernest became annoyed when Fenton dug up juvenilia he'd written in Oak Park, and when he swallowed whole the tall tales of veteran reporter Lionel Moise who'd worked with Ernest on the *Kansas City Star*. At one stage, he ordered Fenton to "cease and desist" looking into biographical detail. He'd promised cooperation on his early career as a newspaperman, but that was as far as he would go. "It is an invasion of privacy to have some one following everywhere you have been or lived as though the FBI were on your tail." Philip Young had given him his word that his book was "neither biographical nor psychoanalytical. I suppose taking a man's word is old-fashioned." After considerable delay, Fenton's book was published in 1954. With Young and Fenton in mind, Ernest complained that he was fed up with "chicken English instructors constituting themselves detectives and writing about your life and getting it all wrong but bringing in so many people and places that you are deprived of making stories, by their intrusions, because you would expose yourself to libel suits." When they do the sort of job Mizener did on Fitzgerald "*in your lifetime* they destroy all possibility of your writing your own Remembrance of Things Past when Albertine was really a girl and not your chauffeur." He made the same point to Carlos Baker, who published an influential book of criticism about Hemingway's fiction in 1952. He didn't want any biography written when he was alive, Ernest insisted. Nor did he want dates and hotel registers uncovered: too many people were involved, both whores and nice girls.

Hemingway's jaundiced attitude toward the Fitzgerald revival of 1950-1951 may have been exacerbated by the unfavorable reception of *Across the River and Into the Trees*, his novel published in September 1950. Long on talk and short on plot and character development, that book marked the nadir of Hemingway's literary career. A few reviews dodged the obvious faults of *Across* to celebrate Hemingway's wider accomplishment. John O'Hara, in the *New York Times Book Review*, called Ernest "the most important author living today, the outstanding author since the death of Shakespeare." But most of the judgments deplored the book as trivial, lamentable, and distressing—so egregiously bad as to be embarrassing.

With his own reputation skidding, Ernest had additional reason to oppose the elevation of Fitzgerald's. Yet his epistolary jabs at Scott's prone body continued after he earned critical and popular acclaim for *The Old Man and the Sea*, the novella presented in its entirety to the readers of *Life* on September 1, 1952— and to two generations of schoolchildren since that time. Nor did they stop after Hemingway achieved the pinnacle of recognition with the award of the Nobel prize for literature two years later.

To take but two examples, Hemingway went out of his way to denigrate Fitzgerald in correspondence with Charles Poore in March 1953 and with Harvey Breit in August 1954. Poore was assembling material for *The Hemingway Reader* and planned to include a sizable chunk of *A Farewell to Arms*. Ernest wrote him his oft-told story about Scott's foolish suggestion for the end of that novel: specifically, that he thought it should end with Frederic Henry getting word of the Allied victory at Belleau Wood. Poore wanted to include this anecdote in the *Reader*, but pointed out that the chronology was wrong. The novel ended early in 1918, months before the battle at Belleau Wood. Of course this was true, Hemingway acknowledged in his March 1953 letter to Poore—though he did not admit that the mistake as to timing (since he invented the tale) was his and not Fitzgerald's. At this point, Hemingway backed down on the shaky grounds of his affection for Scott. Better skip the anecdote, he advised Poore. "Scott was a good friend of mine. He could not stay the course for many reasons. But I have never written about him except the one reference in 'The Snows of Kilimanjaro' and I would hate to have a slighting reference now."

There were slighting references aplenty in his letter to Breit the following year. Breit was beginning work on a stage adaptation of Schulberg's *The Disenchanted* and asked Hemingway for his insights about Fitzgerald, the model for the leading character in that novel. Despite his previous diatribes about grave robbing, Ernest saw no objection to Breit's doing a play about Scott, who was "in the public domain now." Then he followed with a series of deprecatory comments about Fitzgerald, presumably to guide Breit as he fleshed out his character for the stage.

Eager to establish his authority, Hemingway told Breit that he knew Fitzgerald much better than Budd Schulberg, who had written his biographical novel on the basis of his trip to Dartmouth with Scott and a few other meetings in Hollywood. "I knew him for a long time and under all circumstances and was his hero which is a job you can have any time." In similarly sarcastic tone, Ernest leveled his customary charges against Zelda for unmanning Scott sexually, for her jealousy of his work, and for being "completely crazy," but revealed—for the first time, I believe—the information that "she was unfaithful to him first with a young French naval flying officer."

When it came to Scott's drinking, Ernest also supplied some fresh stories (which may or may not have been invented) to undergird his usual derogatory comments. Not only did Scott have no tolerance for alcohol, for example, but—and this was new—he "enjoyed passing out cold too because it made him the center of attention. Without meaning to be he was a terrific exhibitionist and as time went on he became a nastier and nastier drunk." Hemingway provided two specific examples of this nastiness. The first occurred in Paris, when he and Hadley were living above the sawmill on rue Notre-Dame-des-Champs. Fitzgerald, drunk, came to see the Hemingways and let his daughter Scottie pee-pee just outside the landlord's door. Very politely, the landlord came out and told Scott there was a toilet under the stairs that the child could use.

"I know there is, you son of a bitch," Scott said. "And I'll take you and shove your head in it."

There were "hundreds and hundreds like that," Ernest wrote. They would go out to dinner together and Scott would insult people so that Hemingway had to intervene "to keep him from being beaten up." One night he'd had to bribe the doorman at the Plaza "to square something really awful Scott had done." Scott seemed "to love to be humiliated and, of course, to humiliate whoever he was with...At the start he used to be terribly contrite afterwards. Finally he didn't remember." To do Fitzgerald one sentence worth of justice, Ernest added that he "was always generous and he could be so damned nice sober."

Hemingway figured that most of what he had to say about Fitzgerald wouldn't help Breit much in writing a play about Scott in Hollywood, when he may have been very different from the time he knew him best. Still, he offered a possible scene from his own experience. "When I first knew him he was very good looking in a too pretty way and every time he took a drink his face would change a little and after four drinks the skin would be drawn and it would look like a death's head. I guess you could do that in a play with lighting." His friendship with Fitzgerald wasn't all as "sour" as he'd made it sound, Ernest commented before closing. "Sometimes it was funny. But it never was sound. I knew him better than anybody did then, I guess."

Most of these accusations against Fitzgerald—or the Fitzgeralds, one should say—were revived in *A Moveable Feast*, which Hemingway wrote during the late 1950s. A few, like the urinary insult to the landlord, were not. Whether in print or out—and Hemingway did not intend his correspondence to be published—this letter to Harvey Breit represented the single cruelest communication about Fitzgerald he ever put down on paper.

Poor Butterfly

> I am bothered by my tendency to metaphor, decidedly
> excessive. I am devoured by comparisons, as one is by life,
> and I spend my time doing nothing but squashing them.
> —Gustave Flaubert

As a device for invective, David Worcester points out in *The Art of Satire*, metaphor is superior to direct statement, for it "opens the gates to imagination and suggestion...Whereas a man can harden himself before a torrent of abuse and shrug it off, his dignity can hardly survive a good [Samuel] Butlerian simile." In addition, a metaphor or simile has the advantage of allowing the reader or listener to participate by drawing his own deductions.

Hemingway like Flaubert was beset by a predilection for metaphor, particularly when he was writing satire. That happened often, starting with his earliest days in journalism. In dispatches to the *Toronto Star Weekly*, he repeatedly deflated the high and mighty, or anyone he found pompous or pretentious, with targets ranging from the grandstanding mayor of Toronto to the scum of Greenwich Village "skimmed off and deposited in large ladles" on the cafés of Montparnasse to Benito Mussolini "the biggest bluff in Europe." He may well have learned the effect of the devastating metaphor from his mother, who on his twenty-first birthday compared her love for him to a bank account on which he had overdrawn.

When Hemingway wanted to say something particularly malicious, he often couched the insult in metaphor. He was especially fond of the "if this, then that" construction. If his brother Leicester had been a magazine, he once commented, he'd think twice before renewing his subscription. Edmund Wilson had so many leaks in his integrity that if he were an aqueduct, he'd be dry. His marriage to Martha Gellhorn failed because her vaginal operation produced a two-car garage while he had only one car to park. His idyllic marriage to Hadley was cut to pieces by rich sharks led to their prey by a pilot fish he leaves unnamed in *A Moveable Feast* but recognizable as former friend John Dos Passos.

In his assault upon Fitzgerald, Hemingway used several such dehumanizing metaphors. A month after belittling him as a "spaniel" in a letter to Charles Scribner, Ernest tried out another comparison. Scott was "a good writer punched full of holes," ready to sink like a destroyer because of "three holes along the water line with nobody checked out on how to patch them." Or, in another military trope, he was like an unguided missile who came crashing to earth on a "very steep trajectory."

On occasion Hemingway turned to the world of sport for demeaning similes. In his lack of capacity for alcohol, Fitzgerald reminded him of a glass-jawed boxer who couldn't take a punch—and in his supposed cowardice, of the heavyweight fighter "Maxie Baer" who had entirely lost his nerve. Reading *The Last Tycoon* was like seeing an old baseball pitcher with a dead arm working a few innings before being knocked out of the box. Scott "tried to be a better writer than he was and he threw the ball over the grandstand."

All of these metaphors appear in Hemingway's correspondence, where—most frequently of all—he likened Fitzgerald to a butterfly. In *A Moveable Feast*, he settled on that single analogy, though only after essaying yet another in a passage cut from the manuscript. Written in pencil, it begins in 1931, when Scott was thirty-five-years-old. After two crossed-out beginnings, Hemingway started with "I had not seen them for a year and Scott, as always, looked older." There followed one of Hemingway's most telling and vicious metaphors about Fitzgerald. "He showed his age, month by month, as perceptibly as cut flowers do each day and now, at thirty-five, if he had been in a vase in your house you would have thrown him out long ago." Scott had written "so freely, so lovingly, so romantically and so inaccurately" about his youth, Ernest observed, that it was time for someone else to write about his middle age, "which commenced the year he was thirty." Unlike the other unpublished sections of the memoir Hemingway left behind at his death, this fragment of the manuscript was closed by Mary Hemingway for twenty-five years.

The butterfly metaphor dominates the italicized epigraph introducing *A Moveable Feast*'s three chapters on Fitzgerald:

His talent was as natural as the pattern that was made by the dust on a butterfly's wings. At one time he understood it no more than the butterfly did and he did not know when it was brushed or marred. Later he became conscious of his damaged wings and of their construction and he learned to think and could not fly any more because the love of flight was gone and he could only remember when it had been effortless.

Hemingway worked hard on this passage, making two significant deletions before letting it stand as above. One of these, which originally appeared after "brushed and marred," read: "He even needed someone as a conscience and he needed professionals or normally educated people to make his writing legible and not illiterate." Hemingway, who was perfectly aware that Fitzgerald had referred to him in "The Crack-Up" as his "artistic conscience," crossed out this derogatory sentence.

The other omitted section came at the end of the published epigraph. "In the meantime, thinking well and fairly conscious of its worth, he had written The Great Gatsby. Tender Is the Night is a better book written in heroic and desperate confusion. It was the failure of these...He was flying again and I was lucky to meet him just after a good time in his writing if not a good one in his life." In this case, the deleted passage tended to put Fitzgerald in a favorable light. In reducing the epigraph to a single elegant comparison, Hemingway cut both a nasty comment and one that recognized Scott as a "heroic" and accomplished writer.

The butterfly metaphor remained, with all its connotations. Hemingway had introduced this motif repeatedly in correspondence, but artfully reshaped it for A Moveable Feast. In print, he likened Fitzgerald's talent not to a *butterfly* itself nor the *flight* of the butterfly nor the insect's *wings* nor even the *dust* on those wings, but to the *pattern* the dust made. The pattern, which made the butterfly beautiful, was also highly perishable. Ernest might have stated directly that Scott's talent was fleeting or ephemeral or incredibly fragile, but the metaphor said it for him more effectively.

The comparison also served to call Fitzgerald's masculinity into question, abetting Hemingway's delineation of Fitzgerald on the next page as a man "who looked like a boy with a face between handsome and pretty" and with "a delicate long-lipped Irish mouth that, on a girl, would have been the mouth of a beauty." When Vladimir Nabokov, a great writer who was also an expert lepidopterist, described the transformation from caterpillar to pupa to butterfly, he assigned each stage its own gender: the caterpillar was a *he*, the pupa an *it*, and the butterfly a *she*. In Spanish the word *mariposa* for butterfly is often used interchangeably with *maricon* for homosexual, as Hemingway, who spoke demotic Spanish well, must have known. In English too, butterflies flit, as in demeaning slang do gay men.

A Moveable Feast has been called, accurately enough, a "triumphal banquet of self-celebration, a feast of victims." The parade of victims who stagger through the pages of Hemingway's book of reminiscence include Gertrude Stein, Ford Madox Ford, Ernest Walsh, and others in addition to Fitzgerald, the most severely wounded. In this wickedly funny book, the humor comes at the expense of those who were Ernest's benefactors when he was starting out in Paris in the 1920s. For every fault singled out and satirized, Hemingway by implication assumes the opposite virtue. It is, finally, too much to believe. Hemingway was right to warn the reader, in his preface, that it might be wise to regard the book as fiction rather than fact.

In the final scene involving Fitzgerald, Hemingway recounted a post–World War II conversation with Georges, the *chasseur* at the Ritz bar during the '20s when Scott did some of his most notorious drinking there. People were forever asking him about "Monsieur Fitzgerald," Georges says, but he could not remember him at all. This was odd, since he remembered everybody from those days. Who was this Fitzgerald, Georges wanted to know. Was he a good writer? Did he come to the Ritz often? Perhaps, if Hemingway wrote about him, Georges might be able to bring him to mind. This anecdote, which nicely diminished Fitzgerald, appears to have been apocryphal. In 1957 a graduate student at the Sorbonne interviewed Georges for her doctoral dissertation. He said he remembered Fitzgerald very well indeed.

In collecting examples for a book called *The Cutting Edge*, Louis Kronenberger had difficulty locating effective sharp-edged satirical pieces. Most of them went too far, he found. They were "much oftener disagreeable, or enraged, or obscene, or vitriolic than wittily crushing or brilliantly lethal." By a curious paradox, the assailants did harm to themselves in the course of disparaging others. The poisoned dart turned into a boomerang.

Many readers of *A Moveable Feast*, like the critic Jacqueline Tavernier-Courbin, have come to feel that way about an author who systematically presented almost everyone else as badly flawed and himself as "virtually perfect." When the chapters on Fitzgerald in that book are considered in combination with Hemingway's ill-spirited letters during the 1940s and 1950s, the sole sensible conclusion to arrive at is that Ernest did considerable harm to his own reputation while attempting to damage Scott's. Only two very great writers could have survived those darts, those boomerangs.

CHAPTER 10

THE SPOILS OF POSTERITY

What artists call posterity is the posterity of the work of art.
—MARCEL PROUST, *Remembrance of Things Past*

The victor belongs to the spoils.
—F. SCOTT FITZGERALD, *The Beautiful and Damned*

The object in the game of Monopoly is to squeeze the competition into insolvency. The winner ends up with all the valuable property, the losers are bankrupted. In a world where such games are played in earnest, legislatures try to rein in monopolists while widespread admiration goes to those who evade the rules to ride triumphantly above fallen competitors. Winning is a national obsession, as a weekend watching sports on television will prove. The "Just win, baby" mantra that Al Davis taught his gladiators on the Oakland Raiders was more than advice; it was a command. In baseball, our National Pastime, players do their best to get the umpire to make mistakes in their favor. Fair play doesn't count. Nice guys finish last.

As William James observed near the beginning of the century, "the exclusive worship of the bitch-goddess SUCCESS...is our national disease," and in the United States success has meant making money or becoming famous. This is the standard for the artist as well as for the tycoon or the athlete, *during his lifetime*. Thereafter the artist faces another and more demanding court of judgment, where it will be decided if the work merits the attention of succeeding generations. Out of every hundred writers who achieve a measure of financial success and/or recognition while alive, only one or two will be judged worthy for the pantheon.

"Who do you like best?" people ask about great writers. "Who is better? Who will last?" The three apparent winners in the American literary competition as the twentieth century winds down are William Faulkner, F. Scott Fitzgerald, and Ernest Hemingway, in no particular order beyond this alphabetical one. That's the way it looks at this writing, but things change.

This is one reason friendships between writers are so unstable. "Literary friends walk on eggshells," Richard Lingeman, biographer of Theodore Dreiser, commented, for "the demons of jealousy, envy, competitiveness" are forever lurking—usually in the shadows, sometimes more overtly. Lingeman had in mind Dreiser and H.L. Mencken, who had the gall to say frankly what he thought of Dreiser's writing. "To H.L Mencken, my oldest living enemy," Dreiser inscribed one of his books. The eggshell comment also applies to Hemingway and Fitzgerald, once the closest of friends, who moved sharply apart under the pressure of rivalry. "Scott was crazy about immortality etc. and I was very fond of him even though he was a horse's ass," Ernest wrote Harvey Breit as the Fitzgerald revival was heating up in July 1950. But of course he too was concerned about the favorable judgment of posterity. What else was there to work for?

The hope of recognition beyond the grave motivates most artists. Even the greatest are liable to wonder whether their accomplishment deserves the attention of future generations. On his deathbed, Leonardo da Vinci is supposed to have posed a melancholy question: "Tell me if anything ever was done." And especially in America, given the cultural imperative of winning at all costs, the artist may look around him and regard the success of others as a threat to his own standing in the halls of judgment. There are so few niches, and so many competitors.

So it was that Ernest Hemingway took every opportunity to downgrade both of his principal rivals for preeminence in the literary sweepstakes: not only Fitzgerald but Faulkner as well. The battle was joined in the spring of 1947 when Faulkner did some informal ranking of contemporary American writers during a talk at the University of Mississippi. The best of them, he said, were Wolfe, Dos Passos, Caldwell, Hemingway, and himself. In that elite category, he placed Wolfe at the top for his courage in taking risks—including clumsiness and even dullness—in "shooting the works." He had achieved the most "splendid failure." Hemingway he placed at the bottom of the list, for unlike the others—Faulkner said—he lacked the courage to go out on the limb of experimentation.

The story got in the papers, and when Ernest read it he blurred the issue by taking Faulkner's remarks as a personal insult. He enlisted Buck Lanham, who had seen him under fire in World War II, to testify to his physical courage. Buck loyally wrote Faulkner that he thought Ernest "the most courageous man" he had ever known, in war or in peace. Thereupon Faulkner apologized to Hemingway. He was "just making $250" in doing his talk, and did not think he was speaking for publication. In direct communication with each other, neither writer openly addressed the sensitive subject of ranking.

In 1952, Faulkner had another opportunity to express his opinion of Hemingway's work, and once again he managed to infuriate his rival. Breit, at the *New York Times*, conceived the bright idea of getting Faulkner, who had just received the Nobel prize for literature, to review *The Old Man and the Sea*. He wouldn't know how, Faulkner said, but then sent Breit a "statement" about Hemingway and the situation of the writer. "A few years ago," Faulkner wrote, Hemingway said that writers "should stick together, just as doctors and lawyers and wolves do." That observation had more wit than truth in it, Faulkner thought, "since the sort of writers who need to band together...resemble the wolves who are wolves only in pack, and, singly, are just another dog." Hemingway himself was not that kind of writer, Faulkner pointed out. In fact, he needed the protection of the pack least of all. Breit passed on Faulkner's letter to Hemingway, who chose to misconstrue it as an attack on himself as "just another dog." In his own Nobel prize acceptance speech, two years later, Hemingway said almost exactly what Faulkner had been saying in his statement—that a writer had to work alone. Writers' organizations might "palliate" the loneliness but were unlikely to improve the writing.

In his own correspondence, Hemingway frequently disparaged Faulkner and his books. Faulkner could have his "Octonawhoopoo" or "Anomatopoeio" county. He felt cramped in any county. Faulkner's 1954 *The Fable* was full of phony religiosity; it was not even good night soil, only "impure diluted shit." All you needed to write five thousand words a day like that was a quart of whiskey, the loft of a barn, and a total disregard of syntax. He started calling Faulkner "Old Corndrinking Mellifluous." When a collection of Faulkner's hunting stories was published in 1955, Ernest sent a message via Breit that he would have been more impressed if Faulkner hunted animals that ran both ways. In his 1959 "The Art of the Short Story," Hemingway took credit for promoting Faulkner's reputation in Europe many years earlier "because he never had a break then and he was good then." Now, however, it was different. "Very good writer," he said by way of summing him up. "Cons himself now. Too much sauce." Faulkner had written "a really fine story" called "The Bear" that Hemingway would be proud to have done. "But you can't write them all, Jack."

— ✳ —

BEJEWELED BY BUNNY WILSON

According to the conventional standards of success in America, Fitzgerald died a failure. The high-paying magazines would no longer buy his stories. The Modern Library took *The Great Gatsby* out of circulation. His books were *not* out of print, as has been widely reported—Scribner's had six of them in the warehouse, but they weren't selling. Fitzgerald's last royalty check, in August 1940, was for the unlucky sum of $13.13, and represented the sale of forty copies. Most of those he bought himself. "[M]y God I am a forgotten man," he wrote Zelda in March 1940.

He had been famous, early in his career, as a romantic playboy who chronicled the rebellion of the well-to-do younger generation against the convenional mores of their elders. Fitzgerald not only wrote about that generation, but was regarded as its representative figure. Newspaper accounts of the early 1920s concentrated on his personal appearance, as if he were a movie actor. "His eyes were blue and clear, his jaw was squared..., his nose was straight and his mouth, though sensitive looking, was regular in outline. His hair, which was corn colored, was wavy." These were the features Americans associated with beauty, "but there was a quality in the eye with which the average mind [was] unfamiliar." Recitations of his striking good looks—the blue-green eyes, "the thatch of curly, canary hair, sliced down the middle"—were often accompanied by photographs and reports on the gay and carefree life he and his beautiful young wife were pursuing. Still in his twenties, F. Scott Fitzgerald had become a celebrity, and not a celebrity—as one commentator observed—to whom much deference need be paid. Like Jay Gatsby, he had the knack of inspiring tall tales about himself. "He was an old man; he was a young roué; he was a typical westerner, who wore a big sombrero; he was a college youth, who wrote only when completely spifficated on absinthe and gin." Finally, and most tellingly, he "was a bad influence on the country"—a reckless youth who had a great deal of growing up to do. In his influential *Main Currents of American Thought* (1930), Vernon Louis Parrington wrote him off as "[a] bad boy who loves to smash things to show how clever he is, a bright boy who loves to say smart things to show how clever he is—a short candle already burnt out."

There has always been a contradiction—or "disconnect," in the present idiom—between Fitzgerald as a man and as an author. The beautiful bad boy side of his personality, which continues to generate admiration even as it invites scorn, stands in sharp opposition to the hard-working professional who observed

275

in one of his last letters that "[w]hat little I've accomplished has been by the most laborious and uphill work, and I wish now that I'd never relaxed or looked back—but said at the end of *The Great Gatsby*: 'I've found my line—from now on this comes first. This is my immediate duty—without this I am nothing.'" Instead, he had embarked on a decade of dissipation (one of his late stories is called "The Lost Decade"), and only in his final years in Hollywood did he begin to recover a sense of himself as "a writer only."

The image of Fitzgerald as youthful playboy continues to influence popular thinking about his short unhappy life, and it has been joined in the public imagination by a conception of him as an artist in spite of himself. As Joseph Epstein concluded in an insightful essay, Fitzgerald "has been judged something like a lucky genius as a writer and an almost pure disaster as a man." No one is more responsible for this view of him than Edmund Wilson.

The two men met at Princeton, where Bunny Wilson—a class ahead of Fitzgerald—was editor of the *Nassau Literary Magazine*. He first appears in Fitzgerald's *Ledger* in March 1915, at a time when Wilson was heavily editing Scott's material before running it in the *Lit*. They also collaborated that year on the Triangle Club's "The Evil Eye," Wilson writing the book and Fitzgerald contributing the lyrics. The two undergraduates were radically different people. Wilson, with a large head surmounting his stocky body, was sternly rational in thought and already a practicing intellectual. The radiantly handsome Fitzgerald knew much less about literature, which he approached spontaneously and intuitively. In 1916 Wilson and John Peale Bishop, another undergraduate who was unusually widely read, deflated the relatively shallow and unlettered Fitzgerald in a satirical poem about his career at Princeton.

> I was always clever enough
> To make the clever upperclassmen notice me;
> I could make one poem by Browning,
> One play by Shaw,
> And part of a novel by Meredith
> Go further than most people
> Could do with the reading of years;
> And I could always be cynically amusing at the expense
> Of those who were cleverer than I
> And from whom I borrowed freely,
> But whose cleverness

Was not of the kind that is effective
In the February of sophomore year...
No doubt by senior year
I would have been on every committee in college,
But I made one slip:
I flunked out in the middle of junior year.

This poem displayed two emotions that motivated almost everything Wilson wrote or said about Scott Fitzgerald. As Fitzgerald's intellectual and moral superior, Bunny looked down on him with an air of condescension. But he also envied him his "cleverness"—or, to use a more generous term, his talent.

"My relations with Scott were somewhat embarrassed by my position of seniority and mentorship at college, from which he never recovered." So Wilson summarized their friendship in a 1962 letter to Morley Callaghan, omitting to mention that he too had difficulty recovering from his initial assumption of superiority. When Fitzgerald sent him the manuscript of *This Side of Paradise* to read, immediately after its acceptance by Scribner's in the fall of 1919, Wilson responded with a brutally frank letter. He liked the "pretty writing and clever dialogue" (the adjectives undercutting the praise), acknowledged that "some of the poems and descriptions are really exceedingly good" (singling out for admiration what was least important, and in those double adverbs at the end revealing his surprise), and confessed that he'd enjoyed reading the book, since Scott had "the knack of writing readably" (but only a knack, after all).

The rest of the letter laid down a barrage of criticism against Fitzgerald's first novel. It contained so many mistakes it might easily be confused with the recently published *The Young Visitors*, a book supposedly written by a nine-year-old British girl. It read "like an exquisite burlesque of Compton Mackenzie with a pastiche of Wells thrown in at the end." Amory Blaine, the hero, struck Wilson as an "intellectual fake of the first water, and I read his views on art, politics, religion and society with more riotous mirth than I should care to have you know" (if I hadn't only just told you). Scott needed to "tighten up" his artistic conscience and pay more attention to form, "[c]ultivate a universal irony and...read something other than contemporary British novelists." The "history of a young man stuff" had been run into the ground. As in *Paradise*, it merely consisted "of dumping all one's youthful impressions in the reader's lap with a profound air of importance." These criticisms were meant for Fitzgerald's benefit, Wilson maintained. "I feel called upon to give you this advice because I believe you might become a very popular trashy novelist without much difficulty."

There may have been another reason for the apparent bile in this letter to Fitzgerald. Wilson had already begun to establish himself as a leading literary commentator and critic, but must have felt a twinge of envy that Fitzgerald preceded him in getting a novel written and accepted. He rarely could bring himself to say anything positive about Fitzgerald's fiction, without immediately undercutting the praise. That was Wilson's customary pattern, to be sure. As Daniel Aaron, editor of his *Letters on Literature and Politics*, observed, practically every literary friend of Wilson's received "one or more admonishing letters" of this sort; "even an enthusiastic commendation was sure to contain at least a remark or two on an error in fact, a mistake in diction, or some other lapse in style or content. Wilson gladly learned, but he even more gladly taught." The harshness of the criticism Wilson customarily leveled against everyone was only exacerbated, in Fitzgerald's case, by memories of him as a foolish and pretentiously ambitious collegian. Wilson couldn't get that recollection out of his mind long enough to conceive of Fitzgerald's accomplishing anything really important.

Fitzgerald accepted his role as inferior pupil to Wilson's stern tutor, and adopted Wilson's barbs against *This Side of Paradise* as his own. He inscribed a copy of the novel for Mencken as "an exquisite burlesque of Compton Mackenzie with a pastiche of Wells at the end." He also submitted the first draft of his second novel, *The Beautiful and Damned*, to Wilson for revision. What he wanted, Scott wrote, was this kind of criticism:

P. 10x I find this page rotten
P. 10y Dull! Cut!
P. 10z Good! Enlarge!
P. 10a Invert sentence I have marked (in pencil!)
P. 10b unconvincing!
P. 10c Confused!

In response Wilson clarified fuzzy allusions, corrected illogical syntax, and applied his editorial discernment to passages like the following:

So the bottom dropped out of the world and the two people fell into the center of the earth where, presently, they were licked by purgatorial flames. The manna of one century is the hail of the next, and the two had hailstones for food.

Wilson wrote two sentences—in pencil—in the margin. "I don't understand about the manna and the hailstones and in my opinion the whole passage is bullshit" and "Purgatory wasn't supposed to be in the center of the earth and it [contained] no flames." Fitzgerald deleted the paragraph.

In March 1922, Wilson published the single most influential article ever written about Fitzgerald's life and work. As a courtesy, he sent the piece to Fitzgerald in advance of publication, and as a further courtesy agreed to drop his references to Scott's excessive drinking. There was a good deal else that Fitzgerald might have objected to, but did not. As usual, Bunny mingled a few complimentary remarks with a good many derogatory ones. The essay, in the *Bookman*, assessed both of Fitzgerald's first two novels. *This Side of Paradise* possessed "almost every fault or deficiency" a novel could possibly have yet did not commit the unpardonable sin: it did "not fail to live." *The Beautiful and Damned*, Wilson thought, represented an advance over the earlier book, but Fitzgerald remained a "dazzling extemporizer" who had not yet acquired the discipline to "produce something durable."

The emphasis throughout was on what Fitzgerald lacked. In considering the writer himself, Wilson stressed Fitzgerald's Irish and middle-western origins. These had left him *without* qualities that he ought to have had. Scott was "extraordinarily little occupied with the general affairs of the world." He was "not much given to abstract or impersonal thought." He suffered from a "poverty of aesthetic ideas." He lacked "a sound base of culture and taste." His values, deprived of a firm foundation, centered on a "preoccupation with display" and an "appetite for visible magnificence and audible jamboree."

Most significantly of all, Wilson borrowed a metaphor from Edna St. Vincent Millay to begin his portrait of Fitzgerald. To meet him, Millay said, 'is to think of a stupid old woman with whom someone has left a diamond; she is extremely proud of the diamond and shows it to everyone who comes by, and everyone is surprised that such an ignorant old woman should possess so valuable a jewel; for in nothing does she appear so inept as in the remarks she makes about the diamond." Wilson corrected the details of the comparison. Fitzgerald was "no old woman, but a very good-looking young man, nor is he in the least stupid, but, on the contrary, exhilaratingly clever." Yet there was a symbolic truth to the description. "[I]t is true that Fitzgerald has been left with a jewel which he doesn't know quite what to do with. For he has been given imagination without intellectual control of it; he has been given the desire for beauty without an aesthetic ideal; and he has been given a gift for expression without very many ideas to express."

This "jewel" passage is, I think, quoted more often than any other critical comment on Fitzgerald. In it, Wilson pinned his specimen butterfly to the wall—Fitzgerald as artistic naïf, as lucky genius, as an Artist in Spite of Himself—and the characterization has stuck.

Fitzgerald not only accepted Wilson's strictures about himself as a man and a writer, he welcomed them. As he wrote Max Perkins at the time, he thought Wilson's article was "superb. It's no blurb—not by a darn sight—but it's the first time I've been done *at length* by an intelligent and sophisticated man and I appreciate it—jeers and all." He expressed his thanks directly to Wilson, the "shy little scholar of Holder Court" who had already become an influential man of letters. He read Wilson's article with "uncanny fascination," Fitzgerald said. He did not see how he "could possibly be offended by anything in it." What Wilson wrote about him was "pretty generally true." He was guilty of the faults and took "an extraordinary delight in its considered approbation." This sort of bowing and scraping before a man he regarded as his intellectual superior could and did become tiresome over time, but it was entirely characteristic of Fitzgerald. He knew how to humble himself, and seemed to derive satisfaction from the process.

For his part, Wilson thought Fitzgerald had plenty to be humble about. In conversation with the New York literati, he repeatedly made slighting remarks about his Princeton protégé. Burton Rascoe's *New York Herald* "Bookman's Daybook" column for May 26, 1923, reported Wilson's observation that "F. Scott Fitzgerald mispronounces more words than any educated person he knows" and that he spends much of his time composing "idiotic songs" in collaboration with Ring Lardner. In fact Wilson saw a good deal of the Fitzgeralds during the early 1920s, and on one of those occasions *he* and Scott slapped together a humorous song of their own, entitled simply "Dog."

Dog, dog—I like a good dog —
Towser of Bowser or Star —
Clean sort of pleasure —
A four-footed treasure —
And faithful as few humans are!
Here, Pup: put your paw up —
Roll over dead like a log!
Larger than a rat!
More faithful than a cat!
  Dog! Dog! Dog!

And so on. As Wilson saw it, Fitzgerald's talent was best concentrated on the trivial. Only given a mindset of this sort could a normally astute critic like himself have gone so far wrong on *The Vegetable, or From President to Postman,* Fitzgerald's comedy of 1923.

Wilson encouraged and supported Fitzgerald at every stage during composition and production of this play, a parody of the American success story. In a reversal of fortune, a drunken railroad clerk becomes president of the United States, predictably makes a mess of things, and in the end finds happiness as a postman. The characters have no depth and the comedy lacks bite and conviction, but *The Vegetable* displayed Fitzgerald's cleverness and that was enough for Wilson. It was "one of the best things" he'd ever written, Wilson told Fitzgerald, "the best American comedy ever written." He urged Scott to go on writing plays, and with the help of Mary Blair, his actress wife, worked to place the play on Broadway. Wilson stuck to his guns even after the production bombed in Atlantic City. "The Vegetable," he wrote, was "a fantastic and satiric comedy carried off with exhilarating humor...I do not know of any dialogue by an American which is lighter, more graceful or more witty." Graceful, witty, and light: that was the sum of what he thought Fitzgerald capable. Reviewing Scott's story collection *Tales of the Jazz Age* (1922), he compared the author to humorists Lewis Carroll, W.S. Gilbert, and Edward Lear. In the hardcover edition of *The Vegetable* published in 1923, Fitzgerald dedicated the play to "Edmund Wilson, Jr./Who deleted many absurdities/From my first two novels I recommend/The absurdities set down here."

Helpful as Wilson had been in getting *The Vegetable* on the boards, he remained in print a singularly censorious friend to Fitzgerald. In April 1924, he exposed Scott's immaturity and irresponsibility in a *New Republic* essay called "The Delegate from Great Neck." The piece took the form of an imaginary dialogue between F. Scott Fitzgerald, as a representative of the nation's younger generation of writers, and Van Wyck Brooks, the distinguished senior critic. Wilson had been thinking about doing such an article for two years. As he wrote H.L. Mencken in May 1922, it struck him "as ironic that while Fitz and Zelda were reveling nude in the orgies of Westport...Brooks in the same town, probably without even knowing they were there, should have been grinding out his sober plaint against the sterile sobriety of the country." In the dialogue Wilson created between them, Brooks speaks with dignity of his dedication to literature, and Fitzgerald emerges as an intellectually limited young man with a hunger for the immediate rewards of money and publicity. Through Brooks, Wilson was articulating his conviction that Fitzgerald had been swallowed up by a culture of commercialism. Fitzgerald lapsed into the jargon of advertising during their conversation, for example, and discoursed on how difficult he found it to get along on the princely sum (for 1924) of $36,000 a year. To support himself, Fitzgerald added, he had "to write a lot of rotten stuff that bores me and makes me depressed." When Brooks intervenes to ask whether he couldn't live more cheaply somewhere else, Fitzgerald replies, "Nowhere that's any fun."

At the end of their conversation, an exuberant Fitzgerald invites Brooks to attend "a little party" he and Zelda are giving at Great Neck. Gloria Swanson was coming. And John Dos Passos and Sherwood Anderson. And Marc Connelly and Dorothy Parker. And Rube Goldberg. And Ring Lardner. And some dumbbell friends of Scott's from St. Paul. And a man who sings a song called "Who'll Bite Your Neck when My Teeth Are Gone." He'd like "ever so much" to come, Brooks responds, and he'd like to meet all those people, but he cannot accept. He must devote all his free time to writing about Henry James.

Wilson's piece was obviously written to entertain readers of the *New Republic* at the expense of Fitzgerald. Still, the contemptuous portrayal may have had the beneficial effect of awakening Scott to an awareness of the way his frivolous existence impinged on his obligations as an artist. Shortly after publication of "The Delegate from Great Neck," he noted in his *Ledger* the decision, as of April 15, 1924, to go to Europe. There he escaped the partying long enough to write *The Great Gatsby*.

After the Fitzgeralds decamped from Great Neck that summer, they never again lived in the orbit of New York City where Wilson was headquartered. There were only a few meetings thereafter, and the dynamics of the relationship stayed the same. Bunny was the master, Scott the pupil. Revering Wilson's erudition and critical acumen, Fitzgerald deferred to him on literature and politics and other important issues. In "The Crack-Up," he declared Wilson his "intellectual conscience." In 1939, he wrote Wilson that he was "still the ignoramus that [he] and John Peale Bishop wrote about at Princeton." In his notes for *The Last Tycoon*, he set down a proposed dedication: "This novel is for two people — S.F. [daughter Scottie] at seventeen and E.W. [Edmund Wilson] at forty-five. It must please them both." Wilson was one of those he always wanted to please, if only because he so rarely succeeded in doing so. "My one hope is to be endorsed by the intellectually elite," Fitzgerald wrote Max Perkins at the beginning of his career. During his lifetime, the hope went largely unrealized. Fitzgerald's deferential attitude toward Wilson led to the only serious quarrel between them in the fall of 1933, when Bunny objected to playing the "scholar" to Scott's "vulgarian." Like Hemingway, he did not much fancy being hero-worshipped.

A great critic, Wilson yearned to be what he was not: a great novelist. Privately, he was able to recognize Fitzgerald's talent as superior to his own, as in a 1929 letter to Hamilton Basso. "I was re-reading *The Great Gatsby* last night, after I had been going through my page proofs [of the novel *I Thought of Daisy*], and thinking with depression how much better Scott Fitzgerald's prose and dramatic sense were than mine. If I'd only been able to give my book the vividness and excitement, and the technical accuracy, of his!... I think it's one of the best novels that any American of his age has done. Of course, he had to pass through several immature and amateurish phases before he arrived at that one." Of course.

Wilson did not share his admiration for *Gatsby* with Fitzgerald, nor did he express it in print. In his published comments about Fitzgerald's work, qualified praise is outweighed by brutally frank criticism. This pattern was undoubtedly caused, at least in part, by Wilson's resentment of the adulation Fitzgerald commanded from publishers, particularly as it took the form of financial support. His anger boiled over in an October 1938 letter to Perkins, where he reminded him of two previous occasions when Scribner's refused to assist him. "You wouldn't do anything for me on either occasion at a time when you were handing out money to Scott Fitzgerald like a drunken sailor—which he was spending like a drunken sailor." Bunny Wilson would have given his eye-teeth to achieve half of Fitzgerald's reputation as a novelist, Max Perkins observed. Not until Fitzgerald died was Wilson able to regard his writing with an unprejudiced eye.

In *The Crack-Up* Wilson finally did his best for his old Princeton friend. As Marc Dolan perceptively commented in *Modern Lives*, a significant change in Fitzgerald's orientation toward his work occurred in his autobiographical pieces of the mid-1930s, and particularly in the three "Crack-Up" essays of 1936. His previous demands for personal attention gave way to a new demand for attention as "a writer only." "'Look at me,' he had always implicitly proclaimed, but these new texts sang a different refrain: 'Look at my writing.'" In editing the Fitzgerald memorial volume *The Crack-Up*, Wilson did his best to comply with that request.

Very likely it was the shock of editing *The Last Tycoon*, and discovering in the process Fitzgerald's extensive planning for that book, that stimulated Wilson to an understanding that the charming and insignificant undergraduate he had known in college had grown into a mature and accomplished artist. Then in putting together the *Crack-Up* volume, Wilson took it upon himself to help rescue Fitzgerald from his notorious reputation as a Jazz Age playboy—a reputation he had been instrumental in establishing. Fitzgerald was both a popular author *and* an artistic one, he had decided, and it was the artistic one who deserved to last.

"Consequently," as Dolan expressed it, "throughout the editing of [*The Crack-Up*], Wilson remained singularly focused on what he saw as his primary task: the depiction of F. Scott Fitzgerald as a writer rather than a celebrity...." The selections from Scott's notebooks and letters were designed to illustrate the seriousness of Fitzgerald's dedication to his craft. Among the essays, Wilson included only those wherein Fitzgerald addressed his particular problems as a writer, leaving out the casual "advice" pieces of the 1920s about, for example, how former flappers and sheiks could keep their marriages alive. Omitted too was the not entirely lovable Fitzgerald who expounded for the amusement of the readers of the *Saturday Evening Post* on how he had gone broke on $36,000 a year (the very figure Wilson borrowed for his satirical thrust in the *New Republic*). Only two lighthearted autobiographical articles found their way into the volume, and both of these—though sold and signed as the work of "F. Scott and Zelda Fitzgerald"—were written by Zelda. In the other eight essays Wilson chose to reprint in the *Crack-Up* volume, Fitzgerald considered such issues as *the passing* of the Jazz Age and of his youthful excitement about the dreamland of New York City, and his subsequent struggles as a writer: the quest for material, the problem of how much of himself to reveal in his work, the flagging of energy and enthusiasm, the problem of "encore" confronting someone disadvantaged by too much early success.

The title page, with its roster of impressive literary contributors, lent authority to Fitzgerald as a major American writer—a description that few would have applied to him in 1945. Wilson decided on *The Crack-Up* as a heading for the book, followed by several subheadings:

With other Uncollected Pieces,
Note-Books and Unpublished Letters
Together with Letters to Fitzgerald
from Gertrude Stein, Edith
Wharton, T.S. Eliot, Thomas Wolfe
and John Dos Passos
And Essays and Poems by Paul
Rosenfeld, Glenway Wescott, John
Dos Passos, John Peale Bishop and
Edmund Wilson

The letters from luminaries Stein, Wharton, and Eliot all praised *The Great Gatsby*. Eliot's was especially commendatory, with its famous avowal that he thought *Gatsby* "the first step that American fiction has taken since Henry James." The essays about Fitzgerald made up a mixed bag. Rosenfeld's, published in February 1925, confessed a certain surprise at discovering "ideas so mature and poignant and worthy of fine settings" in writing so carelessly and exuberantly undertaken by this "bannerman of the slicker and flapper." Fitzgerald showed tremendous promise but had "not yet crossed the line that bounds the field of art." Wescott's 1941 memorial essay, written for the *New Republic* at Wilson's instigation, lauded Fitzgerald for daring to adopt a confessional stance in "The Crack-Up," but otherwise rehearsed the standard party line on Scott's life and work. "In the twenties, his heyday," Wescott wrote, "he was a kind of king of our American youth" and "[a]side from his literary talent—literary genius, self-taught—I think Fitzgerald must have been the worst educated man in the world" and "[h]e was our darling, our genius, our fool."

Dos Passos put things right in "A Note on Fitzgerald," composed for publication in *The Crack-Up*. Fitzgerald, it was true, lived through the "roaring twenties" and wrote about them. But he was no mere recording machine for the times. In fact, Dos Passos declared, Fitzgerald's best work had the admirable quality "of detaching itself from its period while embodying its period." Now that he was gone, surely it was time to value *Gatsby* and *The Last Tycoon* ("the beginnings of a great novel") as they deserved. "The celebrity was dead. The novelist remained."

Everything in *The Crack-Up* is sandwiched between two reminiscent poems by John Peale Bishop and Edmund Wilson. Bishop's "The Hours," which closes the book, recalls the dazzling Fitzgerald of their youth:

No promise such as yours when like the spring
You came, colors of jonquils in your hair,
Inspired as the wind, when woods are bare
And every silence is about to sing.

None had such promise then, and none
Your scapegrace wit or your disarming grace...

But it also poignantly recorded the despair that overtook Scott during the 1930s.

I have lived with you the hour of your humiliation.
I have seen you turn upon the others in the night
And of sad self-loathing
Concealing nothing
Heard you cry: *I am lost. But you are lower!*
And you had that right.
The damned do not so own to their damnation.

I have lived with you some hours of the night...

Wilson's opening poem, called "Dedication," presents a picture of Fitzgerald at Princeton, but without the glamour. It begins with Wilson doing for this last time what it was he had always done with Fitzgerald: fixing his copy.

Scott, your last fragments I arrange tonight,
Assigning commas, setting accents right,
As once I punctuated, spelled and trimmed
When, passing in a Princeton spring—how dimmed
By this damned quarter century and more!—
You left your Shadow Laurels *at my door.*

The memory takes him back to a day when he unlatched his door at college and found Scott inside:

The pale skin, hard green eyes, and yellow hair—
Intently pinching out before a glass
Some pimples left by parties at the Nass...

An Atlantic storm is raging outside as Wilson writes his dedicatory poem, and the vision of Fitzgerald as self-absorbed juvenile gives way to a mirror image of "hard and emerald eyes" that

...leave us, to turn over, iris-fired,
Not the great Ritz-sized diamond you desired
But jewels in a handful, lying loose:

Wilson may have settled on the jewel image to make amends for the devastating 1922 essay where he stigmatized Fitzgerald as a man given a jewel he did not know what to do with. In the 1945 poem, Wilson by no means discovers that all the stories and novels Fitzgerald left behind are precious stones. That would be to ask more of the critic—to shut down his conviction that the worst deserved mention at least as much as the best—than he was able to grant. So he discovers among his handful of Fitzgeraldian jewels flawed amethysts and shifty yellow opals and tinsel zircons. But also, and for Wilson this was an enormous *but*,

> *Two emeralds, green and lucid, one half-cut,*
> *One cut consummately—both take their place*
> *In Letters' most expensive Cartier case.*

In so celebrating *Tycoon* and *Gatsby*—two emeralds, one half-cut—Wilson went as far as he could go. Although generous with time and energy in editing both *Tycoon* and *The Crack-Up*, in the end he did Fitzgerald's reputation more harm than good through his unshakable condescension.

One difficulty was that Wilson was afflicted by what Perkins called a "Jehovah complex." In the early 1960s, *Punch* lampooned this side of his personality. In this piece, William Shakespeare traveled to Princeton in order to seek Wilson's advice about the play he was working on, *King Lear*. The visit went badly, Wilson reported in his journal:

> That week had already been a hard one for me, teaching Scott Fitzgerald and Ernest Hemingway how to write, and explaining to them about T.S. Eliot and Henry James, so I may have spoken abruptly when Mr. Shakespeare did not seem to get my meaning at once...

Worse yet, Shakespeare did not take Wilson's advice about how to put right the flaws in the play's psychology. "I am beginning to suspect," Wilson concluded, "that some writers are not worth helping, or at least that a stopover in Princeton is not enough for them to absorb all I have to tell them."

Formidably in the right as Wilson considered himself to be, he invariably argued his case with lucidity and logic. He and Fitzgerald were—quite literally—of different minds. In a January 1929 letter to Hemingway, Perkins mentioned that Scott and Bunny were coming in for lunch the next day. The odds were that Scott would steer them to a speakeasy. "The only trouble with him is that in talk he's all over the place. You can never finish up anything you start to talk about. Wilson is thorough in his talk. I'll be glad to see them together."

Here Perkins caught the distinction between them: Wilson rational and closely reasoned, Fitzgerald imaginative and maddeningly inconsecutive. As Eliot said of James (the very writers Wilson was "explaining" about in the *Punch* piece), Fitzgerald "had a mind so fine that no idea could violate it." Eliot meant this as a compliment to James. Immersion in the realm of the rational was, in his view, the greatest danger that artists faced: "instead of thinking with our feelings (a very difficult thing) we corrupt our feelings with ideas." Reading Fitzgerald, we are moved to care about his characters nearly as much as he does, and often we take in a moral as well. But we are not taught or lectured to or reasoned with, as in even the best of Wilson's criticism.

When he first knew Scott, he was a radiant youth, handsome and early rewarded with success. Women were "beglamored" by Fitzgerald, Bunny observed. He seemed to have everything that the American dream could envision. "Youth, beauty, success—" Andrew Hook posed the dilemma, "how many critics are prepared to tolerate such a combination?" It was to be expected that Wilson, and the other critics who followed his lead, should have characterized him as immature and lacking in intellect (as compared to them), and hopelessly devoted to creation of superficial characters in a superficial Jazz Age society. In his 1934 preface to the Modern Library edition of *Gatsby*, Fitzgerald rose up in protest against this kind of dismissal. "I had recently been kidded half haywire by critics who felt that my material was such as to preclude all dealing with mature persons in a mature world. But, my God! it was my material, and it was all I had to deal with." Despite this sensible complaint, and despite the corrective effect of his rise in reputation, the picture of Fitzgerald in the collective mind continues to be that of an extraordinarily good-looking young man who was somehow occasionally visited by genius.

That image has persisted, but did not seize hold on the popular imagination until it was combined with the poignant saga of Scott and Zelda as star-crossed lovers destroyed by the fates as much as by alcohol and schizophrenia. A few documents from Fitzgerald's revival outline the progress of this legend. John Abbot Clark, in his April 1952 "The Love Song of F. Scott Fitzgerald," drew on the Schulberg and Mizener books in a parody of Eliot's J. Alfred Prufrock.

Let us go then, you and I,
When Dartmouth is spread out against the sky
Like a student cracked up on a ski-run.
Oh, damn it, Budd, don't ask, "What is it?"
Let us go and make our visit...

And when I was a youngster, prepping at Newman,
The coach sent me in to play safety,
And I was frightened. And out I came.
In one's room with a book, there you feel free.
I drink, much of the night, and go south in the winter...

And so on, in a series of glimpses showing Fitzgerald in his most foolish and least mature moments.

Mizener's groundbreaking biography was followed by Andrew Turnbull's *Scott Fitzgerald* (1962), by four books from Sheilah Graham, most notably *Beloved Infidel* (1958), and in 1970 and 1971 by Nancy Milford's best-selling *Zelda* and Sara Mayfield's *Exiles from Paradise*. The emphasis in these books shifted from Fitzgerald as artist in spite of himself to the unhappy saga of Scott and Zelda. Russell Baker, in a December 1971 column, blamed his fascination with these proliferating books for his failure to achieve recognition as "Man of the Year" from *Time* magazine. In turning him down (in favor of Richard Nixon), *Time* explained why. In April, Baker read "a new book about the tragedy of F. Scott Fitzgerald," and that impressed the magazine's editors, because they were "literary men." But in May he read "another new book about the tragedy of F. Scott Fitzgerald," in June "a magazine article about the tragedy of F. Scott Fitzgerald," and in October "two new books about the tragedy of F. Scott Fitzgerald."

"The editors agreed that if the Man of the Year was going to read every new manuscript that came along about F. Scott Fitzgerald, he was going to have precious little time to do Man-of-the-Year things."

The wonder is that Fitzgerald has survived this kind of stereotyping to command his place as one of the major literary artists of the century. To achieve a similar level of recognition, Hemingway has had to outlive the deleterious effects of an even greater celebrity.

THE WRITER AS CELEBRITY

When Hemingway shot himself in July 1961, one editorial commented that it was as if "the Twentieth Century itself ha[d] come to a sudden, violent, and premature end." Hemingway was then the most famous writer in the world (as he still is, for that matter), and his passing brought messages of condolence from the Kremlin as from the White House. In the public mind, he existed as a rugged bearded figure known as Papa, better known for his battles with great beasts than for anything he happened to write. People knew a good deal more about what he looked like than about what he wrote (and that, too, is still true).

To a considerable extent, Hemingway was complicit in the formation of this public image. He rejected the concept of the writer as aesthete in favor of the writer as man of action, and went to bullfights and wars in order to prove the point. But much of his celebrity he could not have prevented, for he possessed from the beginning a rare charisma. Archibald MacLeish declared that he had known only two men in his life who could empty the air from a room simply by entering it: Franklin Delano Roosevelt and Ernest Hemingway. In large part, Hemingway simply could not stop people from talking about him.

As Dorothy Parker pointed out in her adoring 1929 profile of the thirty-year-old Hemingway for the *New Yorker*, "[p]robably of no other living being has so much tripe been penned and spoken." Unable to get from Ernest much by way of information about his background, Parker presented some wild rumors about his toughness and athleticism. "About all that remains to be said," she concluded in a passage reminiscent of the tall tales about Jay Gatsby, "is that [Hemingway] is the Lost Dauphin, that he was shot as a German spy, and that he is actually a woman, masquerading in man's clothes." It was odd, too, that as a far-fetched legend, Parker should have come up with Ernest as a woman in disguise, for the single word most associated with Hemingway's public persona is, as everyone knows, *macho*.

In July 1929, an article in a magazine called *Spur* profiled Hemingway at the fiesta in Pamplona. The piece concentrated on description. Hemingway is spotted "at a table against one of the pillars, with a bottle of beer in front of him, and a newspaper folded to the criticism of yesterday's bull-fight, exchanging idle comments with two friends, heedless of the racket that encompasses him...dressed in loose tweeds, his collar is low and soft and his necktie is pulled awry, he is hatless and one foot is thrust into a clumsy woolen carpet slipper. Somehow he cut his foot a day or so ago." Somehow, in fact, Hemingway was constantly injuring himself, and whenever he did it made news.

During the 1930s, as at no other time in his life, Hemingway indulged in presentation of himself (and his ideas about life and love and literature) in his writing, particularly in *Death in the Afternoon* and *Green Hills of Africa*. In a 1933 cartoon, William Steig caught the spirit of his public persona by depicting him holding a rose in his hairy tattooed fist. In the same year, Ernest expressed his legitimate impatience with the garbage spilled onto the page about him by various publicity agents. He got Max Perkins to issue a statement in protest against Paramount's stories about him in connection with the Gary Cooper–Jennifer Jones film version of *A Farewell to Arms*. "Mr. Ernest Hemingway has asked his publishers to disclaim the romantic and false military and personal career imputed to him in a recent film publicity release...While Mr. H. appreciates the publicity attempt to build him into a glamorous personality like Floyd Gibbons or Tom Mix's horse Tony, he deprecates it and asks the motion picture people to leave his private life alone."

The engines of publicity, once started, could not easily be brought to a halt. As a young man crafting a prose style for his time in Paris, Hemingway aimed high, with the prospect of fame driving him. It was his misfortune, as it was Fitzgerald's to a lesser degree, that his pursuit of fame was to have what Leo Braudy in *The Frenzy of Renown* called a "baroquely warping effect" on his life and reputation. Famous people in the twentieth century have characteristically shrunk into celebrities under the klieg lights of the mass media, their achievement ignored as every detail of their private lives comes under intense scrutiny.

To claims that Ernest courted such publicity, Mary Hemingway objected that they frequently dodged contact with reporters and photographers. Yet her husband seemed perfectly willing to exhibit his competitiveness and belligerence in public, as in a 1950 burst of braggadocio to Lillian Ross. "I started out very quiet and I beat Mr. Turgenev. Then I trained hard and I beat Mr. de Maupassant. I've fought two draws with Mr. Stendhal, and I think I had an edge in the last one. But nobody's going to get me into any ring with Mr. Tolstoy unless I'm crazy or I keep getting better." Then he proceeded, for Ross's edification, to denigrate Fitzgerald for his lack of knowledge of prizefighting and football. By this time, the dedicated and hard-working writer of *A Farewell to Arms* (1929), who withheld so much of himself that Dorothy Parker was reduced to making up rumors about him, had apparently deteriorated into a long-winded buffoon capable of thinking *Across the River and Into the Trees* (1950) his very best work.

In January 1954, Hemingway reached the pinnacle of his fame when reports of his premature death were circulated in newspapers around the globe. Twice in three days, planes carrying Ernest and Mary crashed, and in the second case Hemingway very nearly did die of his injuries: a concussion, a ruptured liver, spleen, and kidney, loss of vision in his left eye, loss of hearing in his left ear, a crushed vertebra, a sprained right arm and shoulder, a sprained left leg, paralysis of the sphincter, and first-degree burns on his face, arms and head. Biographer Carlos Baker believed that Hemingway never fully recovered from those injuries, which were severe enough to undercut the pleasure he might have taken in reading his own obituaries. At the end of 1954, he was fully resurrected—in the public mind, at least—by the award of the Nobel prize.

In the time remaining to him, Hemingway could never escape the glare of publicity. He had become a celebrity who was only by the way a writer. Playing the role of Papa Hemingway became a bore and a burden. Then the books began, joining the magazines and newspapers in an intolerable invasion of privacy. In his last paranoid years he became terrified that everyone—the IRS, the FBI, the Immigration and Naturalization Service—was watching him.

It has not been widely realized that Edmund Wilson played a crucially important role in establishing Hemingway's reputation, just as he did with Fitzgerald's. Wilson gave Ernest's career a very early boost and later scolded him for the self-indulgent writings of the 1930s. The young Hemingway initiated the contact between the two of them after reading in Burton Rascoe's "Bookman's Daybook" column that Wilson was amused by the *in our time* sketches Ernest had published in the *Little Review*. On October 11, 1923, he wrote Wilson an ambitious writer's letter mentioning the Rascoe column, sending him a copy of *Three Stories and Ten Poems* (which had been published in a limited edition that summer), and humbly asking for the names of "four or five people to send it to to get it reviewed." Wilson acknowledged receipt of the book and said he might do a note on it for the *Dial*, eliciting from Hemingway flattery—"[a]s far as I can think yours is the only critical opinion in the States I have any respect for," gratitude for Wilson's "offer to help [him] get a book before the publishers," and praise for the helpfulness and insight of Gertrude Stein.

At the time, Hemingway's work had not been reviewed anywhere, or so he thought. In fact, Stein had done a review of *Three Stories and Ten Poems* for the Paris edition of the *Chicago Tribune*, but Hemingway, living in Toronto at the time, did not know that. As he wrote Wilson, "[y]ou don't know anything in Canada." Stein, oddly, preferred the poems to the stories. When he composed his review of both *Three Stories* and *in our time* for the October 1924 *Dial*, Wilson took the more sensible view that "Mr. Hemingway's poems are not particularly important, but his prose is of the first distinction." After pointing out Stein's salutary influence, Wilson turned to *in our time*: "I am inclined to think that this little book has more artistic dignity than anything else about the period of the war that has as yet been written by an American."

Ernest, back in Paris, wrote with thanks for the review. "It was cool and clear minded and decent and impersonal and sympathetic": refreshingly different from "this terrible personal stuff" others were writing about him. Wilson was the only critic he could read when the book being criticized was one he knew something about. Intelligence was "so damn rare." He did not yet know that he was already in Wilson's debt on another account. It was Bunny who recommended his work to Scott Fitzgerald and so introduced Hemingway to his greatest benefactor.

Wilson reprinted these early letters from Hemingway as aspiring writer in *The Shores of Light* (1952), where he took some pride in having written (as he thought) the first criticism of Hemingway's work in print. As Robert Frost said of Ezra Pound, one of the good things about Wilson as critic was that he was not "afraid to jump." Having jumped on Hemingway's bandwagon at the start, Wilson stayed on for some time. As literary editor of the *New Republic*, he wrote Hemingway in January 1927 with his assessment that *The Sun Also Rises* was "a knockout—perhaps the best piece of fiction that any American of this new crop has done" and asking for something from Ernest for the magazine. Hemingway sent along the "Italian sketches" for the May *New Republic*, which were printed that fall as "Che Ti Dice La Patria?" in *Men Without Women*.

In part because of the title—it put Virginia Woolf off, for example—that collection of stories came in for a good deal of criticism. Wilson defended Hemingway in a December 1927 article that took reviewers Lee Wilson Dodd and Joseph Wood Krutch to task. Dodd complained that the characters in Hemingway's stories were "very vulgar people" and "very much alike: bullfighters, bruisers, touts, gunmen, professional soldiers, prostitutes, hard drinkers, dope-fiends." In Hemingway's hands, according to Krutch, the subject matter of literature was reduced to "sordid little catastrophes." It was true that he depicted a world full of suffering, Wilson admitted, but his attitude toward it was subtle and complicated. Wholesale condemnation of his work, like Dodd's and Krutch's, ignored such sensitively realized stories as "Hills Like White Elephants" and "A Canary for One." More importantly, even in the stories dealing with primitive types the "drama almost always turns on some principle of courage, of pity, of honor." Hemingway was best understood "not [as] a moralist staging a melodrama, but an artist exhibiting situations the values of which are not simple."

By way of a more aggressive retaliation, Hemingway wrote a doggerel, "Valentine For a Mr. Lee Wilson Dodd and Any of His Friends who Want It":

Sing a song of critics
pockets full of lye
four and twenty critics
hope that you will die
hope that you will peter out
hope that you will fail
so they can be the first one
be the first to hail
any happy weakening or sign of quick decay.
(All are very much alike, weariness too great,
sordid small catastrophes, stack the cards on fate,
very vulgar people, annals of the callous,
dope fiends, soldiers, prostitutes,
men without a gallus*)
If you do not like them lads
One thing you can do
stick them up your asses lads
My Valentine to you.

*........

What that asterisk stood for was not clear. Hemingway's fury was. Invariably hurt by such critiques, he found that lashing out was one way of relieving the attacks of depression that they brought on. Wilson, at least, was one critic who seemed to understand what he was working at. When Scribner's brought out a new edition of *In Our Time* in 1930, Hemingway recommended to Perkins that Wilson write an introduction, and so he did. Ernest read it while laid up in a Billings, Montana, hospital with a broken arm, and grumbled about some of Wilson's judgments, but did not ask for changes.

Relations between author and critic worsened during the 1930s, as Wilson became increasingly disillusioned about Hemingway's output. He thought "Hemingway's bullfighting book," *Death in the Afternoon*, "was pretty maudlin," Wilson wrote Fitzgerald in March 1933. Two months later the three men had their infamous dinner in New York City, where Hemingway showed signs of grandiosity while Scott alternated between flattering and insulting both of his heroes in his "half-truckle, half-bait" fashion. This was the time, Bunny twice told Scott, to "creep up" on Hemingway. In fact, Fitzgerald did more than that by publishing *Tender Is the Night* in 1934, a book that has lasted longer than anything Hemingway brought out in that decade.

Wilson had his critical say about several of those publications. "*Green Hills of Africa* is certainly far and away [Hemingway's] weakest book," he declared in December 1935. It even made "Africa and its animals seem dull." The Hemingway of *Green Hills* was writing about himself instead of about Africa, and, when he spoke in his own person, he often sounded fatuous or maudlin. Wilson suspected that this failure in self-criticism might be owing to the publicity legend which had been created about Hemingway. "But, in any case, among his creations, he is certainly his own worst-drawn charracter, and he is his own worst commentator."

To Have and Have Not, Hemingway's episodic novel of 1937, Wilson regarded as "lousy," "Hemingway in pieces," his "Popeye-the-Sailor" novel that "from a literary point of view" surpassed even *Green Hills* as the worst one he had written. Nor was Wilson sympathetic to Hemingway's conversion to the cause of the Loyalists during the Spanish Civil War. A reformed Communist himself, Wilson became militantly anti-Stalinist in the late 1930s, and thought that Hemingway was unwittingly circulating the Moscow party line in his writing about the Spanish war. Ernest made four trips to observe the fighting in Spain during 1937 and 1938, and sent back twenty-eight dispatches to the North American Newspaper Alliance (NANA) between May 1937 and June 1938.. These revealed a man willing or even eager to put himself at risk from enemy aircraft, artillery, and rifle fire, in order to report upon and support the Spanish Republicans in their struggle against fascism. A number of his dispatches were collected to make up an entire issue of a left-wing magazine called *Fact*. Wilson characterized them as "inept" in their insistent presentation of Hemingway's courage under fire.

This was too much for Ernest, who sat down and wrote Wilson an exceedingly insulting letter. (It may not have been sent.) He began calmly enough. "You were the first critic to take any interest in my writing and I have always been very grateful and I have always looked forward to reading anything you write about what I publish." He had not authorized the reprinting of his dispatches in *Fact*, Ernest explained, but he was certainly not ashamed of them. He was hired to provide eyewitness accounts of the fighting, and that was what he did. "If you are being paid to be shot at and write about it you are supposed to mention the shooting." Then Hemingway shifted to an *ad hominem* attack on Wilson as a non-combatant.

Someday, he supposed, his children would ask him, "Papa, did you really know Edmund Wilson?"

And he could say proudly, "Children I was as close to him as *that*...We called him Wilson the Incomparable. There was no one like him. Brave, cool, never at a loss what to do."

"What did he do, Papa?"

"He stayed in New York and attacked everybody who went to Spain as a tool of Stalin."

"Wasn't he smart," said the children admiringly.

In the same December 10, 1938, review where he condemned Hemingway's Spanish dispatches, Wilson considered the merits of *The Fifth Column and the First Forty-Nine Stories*. The play, "The Fifth Column," he thought almost as bad as *To Have and Have Not*, but the volume was redeemed by the stories and particularly by such great new ones as "The Short Happy Life of Francis Macomber." The collection of Hemingway's first forty-nine short stories "represents one of the most considerable achievements of the American writing of our time," Wilson summed up, "and ought, as they say, to be in every home."

At the same time, however, Wilson was disturbed by the transformation of Hemingway from a private writer into a celebrity, displayed in "handsome photographs with the sportsman's tan and the outdoor grin, with the ominous resemblance to Clark Gable, who poses with giant marlin which he has just hauled in off Key West." He was thus heartened, like many other critics, by the appearance of *For Whom the Bell Tolls* in 1940. "The big game hunter, the waterside superman, the Hotel Florida Stalinist, with their constrained and fevered attitudes, have evaporated like the fantasies of alcohol. Hemingway the artist is with us again; and it is like having an old friend back." Wilson wrote those semi-ameliorative words in October 1940, but by that time he had already published his most influential essay on Hemingway—one that drove a wedge between them.

"Hemingway: Gauge of Morale" was printed in the July 1939 *Atlantic Monthly*. In this extensive essay, Wilson reconsidered Hemingway's career to date, repeating and elaborating on his distaste for the books of the 1930s. "As soon as Hemingway begins speaking in the first person, he seems to lose his bearings, not merely as a critic of life, but even as a craftsman." Nonetheless, he regarded Hemingway as a major artistic figure who had the capacity—as stories like "Macomber" and "Snows" proved—to recover from his mistakes. Hemingway's greatest achievement, Wilson saw (and however prickly and arrogant he may have been, as a critic Wilson was uncannily often right), was to tune "a marvelous prose" that derived "effects of the utmost subtlety" out of colloquial American speech. In doing so, Ernest had learned from Stein and Anderson and Lardner, but he made the technique peculiarly his own by applying it to a universe charged with pain. For his characters, the condition of life was one of struggle against the odds, ending in defeat. Though destined to lose the struggle, they could manage a kind of moral victory by losing with honor.

To Wilson, it seemed clear that the tensions faced by Hemingway characters confronted the author himself. Yet "if he has sometimes, under the menace of the general panic, seemed on the point of going to pieces as an artist, he has always pulled himself together the next moment." In his closing paragraph, Wilson introduced the Bourdon gauge that gave his article its title. The principle of the gauge, used to measure the pressure of liquids, "is that a tube which has been curved into a coil will tend to straighten out in proportion as the liquid inside it is subjected to an inner pressure." Out of such pressures, if he could stand them, emerged the artist.

When Wilson attempted to reprint this essay in *The Wound and the Bow*, Hemingway did everything he could to stop it. Scribner's contracted to publish the book, but backed down when Ernest vehemently objected. Max Perkins then sent Wilson's manuscript to Houghton Mifflin, where Hemingway raised legal objections before finally retiring from the field. What most bothered Ernest, judging from a 1950 letter to Arthur Mizener, were Wilson's intimations about his psychological difficulties. "I get sick of Bunny Wilson writing about some mysterious thing that changed or formed my life," he wrote to Mizener. "Why doesn't he say what the mysterious thing is? Could it be that my father shot himself? Could it be that I did not care, overly, for my mother? Could it be that I have been shot twice through the scrotum and through the right hand, left hand, right foot and left foot and through both knees and the head?" Luckily, he could console himself with "a beauty picture" of Wilson being kicked in the ass that Perkins had sent him.

As an early discoverer of Hemingway, Wilson had a certain investment in his success. And there can be no question that he admired the prose style Ernest was working toward in the mid-1920s — his dedication to setting down words, as Ford Madox Ford put it, that "strike you, each one, as if they were pebbles fetched fresh from a brook. They live and shine, each in its place." When he encouraged Fitzgerald in 1933 to produce more fiction in the competition with Hemingway, the implicit assumption between them was that Ernest was the more gifted and committed artist. Only after Fitzgerald's death, when he edited the manuscript of *The Last Tycoon* and assembled material for *The Crack-Up*, did Wilson recognize him as an important American writer who did not need to take a back seat to Hemingway. Ernest's spiteful attempt to stop republication in book form of the "Gauge of Morale" essay may have influenced Wilson in arriving at that judgment. By 1942, in any case, he was able to write Gertrude Stein agreeing with her that Scott had a much stronger sense of form than Ernest, "the constructive gift that Hemingway doesn't have at all." He felt sure that some of Fitzgerald's work would last.

Hemingway's suicide in 1961 upset Wilson. Even though Ernest often made a fool of himself, he wrote, his passing made it seem "as if a whole corner of [their] generation had suddenly and horribly collapsed." Wilson also thought it depressing that after encouraging writers to last and get their work done, Hemingway "should have died in such a panicky and undignified way as by blowing his head off with a shotgun." Depressing, but not entirely surprising. "The desperation in his stories had always been real: his most convincing characters are always just a few jumps ahead of death. It is a wonder that this was not more noticed."

Wilson expressed similar thoughts in his 1963 review of Morley Callaghan's *That Summer in Paris*. Mary Hemingway objected to his description therein of Hemingway's life as one of "acute moral strain that gave a sharp edge to sensuous enjoyment, of delusions, euphoric or frightening, that made his personal relations erratic, of deep malaise." To that, she felt sure, Ernest would have said "Rubbish!" He cultivated no "deep malaise," she insisted. In the twenty-five years they had been together, she "never knew him to wake up in the morning any way but happily." That this could not have been true of the last couple of those years hardly lessened her sense that Ernest's ghost had been somehow violated.

The violation took a more overt form in 1966, when A.E. Hotchner, the magazine writer who befriended Hemingway in his late years, published *Papa Hemingway*, with its revelations about the debilitating mental illness that overtook him. Mary sued in an unsuccessful attempt to squelch the book. She told me afterwards that if Ernest had known what Hotch planned to write about him, he would have taken him far out into the Gulf Stream and chucked him overboard for the sharks to feed on.

COMMERCIALIZING THE PRODUCT

Hemingway and Fitzgerald led fascinating and complicated and in the end tragically unhappy lives, and the outpouring of biographical material has kept them both in the public eye. So, too, has the substantial posthumous publication of the novels, stories, letters, and other documents they left behind. In the case of Fitzgerald, there have been several collections of stories, two books of autobiographical essays and fiction, five books of letters, books reprinting his juvenile stories and plays, a book assembling miscellaneous writings by and about him from college days on, his "Notebooks" in book form, his "Ledger" in book form, and so on.

Hemingway's mountain of unpublished and/or uncollected documents rose even higher, and has been quarried for half a dozen full-sized books, including most recently *True at First Light*, about the African safari in 1953 and 1954 and published at his centenary on July 21, 1999. The mining of this material has been so extensive as to arouse a certain amount of controversy among writers and critics. In the November 9, 1998, *New Yorker*, Joan Didion denounced the practice of printing work that Hemingway had not signed off on, with particular attention to the African book. In this case, Ernest left behind some 850 manuscript pages, which were reduced to half that length in the volume as edited by his son Patrick. In *The Garden of Eden* (1987), which has had a tremendous influence on Hemingway's reputation, only about one-third of an amorphous script found its way into book publication. Hemingway set down in his will a specific prohibition against publication of his letters, a clause that was countermanded by the 1981 appearance of an extensive selection from them. But at least those letters were finished, signed, stamped, and mailed. For Didion, as for other writers who have echoed her objections, to publish rough and incomplete matter like *The Garden of Eden* or *The Dangerous Summer* (1985), about bullfighting in Spain, summer of 1959, or *True at First Light* as the work of "Ernest Hemingway" represented a deeper betrayal of confidence. This was work he had not finished, and as an artist he would hardly have wanted to leave it to aftercomers to do the job for him. Except for removing obscenities, no one at Scribner's was allowed to touch his copy. "It is damned hard on Scott to publish anything unfinished any way you look at it," he wrote Max Perkins when he heard about plans to bring out *The Last Tycoon*, "but I suppose the worms won't mind."

And yet for those of us who are eager to read everything available of Fitzgerald or Hemingway or any number of other major writers, such books offer an unexpected opportunity to savor their work anew—or at least a reasonable facsimile of it. They are both highly marketable authors, the necessary victims—or beneficiaries—of their fame. In a culture which increasingly markets writers as it does other consumer goods, it was to be expected that their names should be appropriated to sell not only their books but products that have nothing to do with literature.

By 1974, in the wake of the motion picture version of *The Great Gatsby* featuring Robert Redford, the commercialization of F. Scott Fitzgerald and his works began in earnest. Bars and restaurants called Gatsby's sprang up everywhere. Host Favorite sugar packets of the late 1970s, available in coffee shops, featured various symbols of the Roaring Twenties, including Babe Ruth, Al Capone, raccoon coats, flagpole sitting, and in tribute to his role as historian "F. Scott Fitzgerald— *This Side of Paradise*, *The Great Gatsby*, *Tender Is the Night*. The spirit of the Jazz Age comes alive in the novels of this great writer. Nowhere else does one find a more vivid picture of the 1920's."

By the late 1990s, both Hemingway and Fitzgerald were being marketed as brand names in far more sophisticated ways. According to Marla A. Metzner, president of Fashion Licensing of America, thirteen separate manufacturers have opted to use Hemingway's name and image in connection with their products. Most notable among these is the "Ernest Hemingway Collection" from Thomasville Furniture Industries: "96 pieces of living, dining, and bedroom furniture and accessories" in four themes—Kenya, Key West, Havana, and Ketchum. Among the other items scheduled for marketing, as of May 1999, were Hemingway pillows, picture frames, desk sets, and African masks. A similar campaign was just getting under way for Fitzgerald, with two companies strongly interested, Metzner added. "We're going back to the great icons of the century, as heroic brands." To borrow a phrase from Hemingway, he and Fitzgerald were as dead as they would ever be. What harm could come from conjuring up his name and slapping it on a dining room suite?

In the halls of academe, Hemingway's work has customarily generated much more criticism than that of Fitzgerald. According to Susan Beegel's research, the amount of critical attention to Hemingway has been steadily growing since his death, with the number of books and articles published each year doubling between 1961 and 1991. The annual chapter on the two authors in *American Literary Scholarship* normally runs at least twice as long for Hemingway as for Fitzgerald. One reason for this disparity, as Andrew Hook has pointed out, is that most of Fitzgerald's writing "has been victimized critically by the success of *The Great Gatsby*." In the 1998 Modern Library poll of the best books of fiction in English of the twentieth century, *Gatsby* finished second, behind only James Joyce's *Ulysses* and far in advance of anything of Hemingway's. The great preponderance of Fitzgerald criticism has focused on that one book, to the relative neglect of his three and a half other novels and nearly two hundred stories. "Because his other novels are not *Gatsby*," Hook sums up the situation, "they are failures."

The very word "failure" summons up another reason for the relative inattention to Fitzgerald's fiction. His characters repeatedly fail, and he seemed to covet his own failure, as in his declaration that unlike Hemingway he could speak with "the authority of failure." Many have been inclined to take him at his word, but as Hook demonstrates there is a paradox here. At the same time that critics recognize Fitzgerald as a major American writer, they tend to ignore or denigrate much of his work as having somehow failed. The cause, in good part, has been the lingering sense of Fitzgerald as a popular magazine writer of lightweight stories, and as an immature artist: the fool with a jewel of Edmund Wilson's 1922 formulation. Hook poses a rhetorical question to illustrate the point. "Has there ever been an author more patronized, more put down, more condescended to, by an established critical orthodoxy than Scott Fitzgerald?" The answer, patently, is no.

"It is characteristic of operations on the literary exchange that critics usually praise an author by disparaging others. They know, but keep forgetting, that true authors can seldom he compared in any real sense, each being unique," observed Malcolm Cowley, in his 1957 book *The Literary Situation*. Given impetus by the competitive drive in the culture, the process of invidious comparisons has continued, though as Cowley commented, no single measuring stick could accurately judge the achievement of any two writers accomplished enough to have found their own individual voice. Certainly that apple vs. orange distinction is true of Fitzgerald and Hemingway. As Matthew J. Bruccoli concluded in *Scott and Ernest*, "their work was utterly dissimilar in style, themes, material, and technique." Style, most of all.

When she was twelve or thirteen, Didion fell in love with the first paragraph of *A Farewell to Arms*.

> In the late summer of that year we lived in a house in a village that looked across the river and the plain to the mountains. In the bed for the river there were pebbles and boulders, dry and white in the sun, and the water was swiftly moving and blue in the channels. Troops went by the house and down the road and the dust they raised powdered the leaves of the trees. The trunks of the trees too were dusty and the leaves fell early that year and we saw the troops marching along the road and the dust rising and leaves, stirred by the breeze, falling and the soldiers marching and afterward the road bare and white except for the leaves.

She fancied that if she studied hard enough she might one day be able to arrange 126 words herself that captured the premonitory power of that paragraph written in a vocabulary stripped of modifiers and of much specific detail. The tension in the writing, she later decided, came from the information that was deliberately withheld. The speaker, who is Hemingway's protagonist Frederic Henry, does not use many words. He holds things back, and he has reasons.

It's a prose poem, that beginning, and in its simplicity of language at an opposite pole from the poetic incandescence Fitzgerald was capable of creating. In college, he had fallen in love with Keats, from whom he borrowed the title of *Tender Is the Night* and the technique of the unexpected verb conveying emotion. Gatsby and Daisy are together after five years apart, and Gatsby is showing her his mansion.

> In the music room Gatsby turned on a solitary lamp beside the piano.
> He lit Daisy's cigarette from a trembling match and sat down with
> her on a couch far across the room where there was no light save what
> the gleaming floor bounced in from the hall.

This is description too, like the first paragraph of *Farewell*, but what a difference! Gatsby's excitement comes alive in the match (not the hand) that is trembling and in the light (not his heart) that bounced on the gleaming floor. Fitzgerald was proud of this passage, as he should have been, and in one of his letters to his daughter directed her to compare it with the lines in "Ode to a Nightingale" that provided its inspiration.

Joseph Epstein offered another example of Fitzgerald's magically evocative gift in description, this one from *Tender*. "They drank the bottle of wine while a faint wind rocked the pine-needles and the sensuous heat of early afternoon made blinding freckles on the checkered luncheon cloth." In a single short sentence, he called up the French Riviera.

Hemingway and Fitzgerald were different, not better. Each was great in his own way. In that league, no one had to lose for both of them to be winners.

CHAPTER II

THE MASTER AND THE ACTOR

> People like Ernest and me were very sensitive once and saw
> so much that it agonized us to give pain. People like Ernest
> and me love to make people very happy, caring desperately
> about their happiness. And then people like Ernest and me had
> reactions and punished people for being stupid, etc., etc.
> People like Ernest and me...
> —F. Scott Fitzgerald, *Notebooks*

It is hard to take the note above any way but ironically. The first sentence makes some sense, for only two writers of great sensitivity could have produced the wonderful fiction of the 1920s and 1930s. But it was Scott who cared desperately about making other people happy, including Hemingway, and Ernest who punished others, including Fitzgerald, for their stupidity. "People like Ernest and me" presupposes a likeness between the two men that simply did not exist. They could hardly have been more different.

It was the difference that made the quirky and difficult relationship possible, and that converted it finally into an exercise in sadomasochism. Hemingway felt a compulsion to dominate, to lord it over others, and Fitzgerald had a complementary need to be dominated. If Ernest liked to kick, Scott wore a sign on his backside saying "Kick Me." In a piece of light verse, Theodore Roethke captured something of this intermixture of psychological shortcomings:

> It wasn't Ernest; it wasn't Scott —
> The boys I knew when I went to pot;
> They didn't boast; they didn't snivel,
> But stepped right up and swung at the Devil...

Roethke knew his readers would understand who did the boasting, who the sniveling.

In an important article, Ruth Prigozy examined the psychodynamics of the Fitzgerald-Hemingway relationship. Leaving aside the issue of rivalry, she suggested that they responded to each other on the basis of "mutual personal need." Fitzgerald, in his boyish romanticism, found an embodiment "for his dreams of personal heroism and physical superiority" in Hemingway. As he wrote in his notes, when he liked men he wanted to *be* like them, to absorb into himself those qualities that made them attractive. In the attempt to achieve this impossible goal, he was willing—more than willing—to abase himself before the objects of his hero worship, courting "humiliation as others did success" and in the process gratifying "his own self-destructive impulse, his perverse need for punishment."

Hemingway was put off by the fulsome admiration Fitzgerald lavished upon his work at their first meeting. Praise to the face, he felt, was open disgrace. Later, he repudiated the role of being "Scott's bloody hero" as "embarrassing." In fact, Hemingway was embarrassed by all public displays of feeling, considering them demonstrations of weakness or effeminacy. In Fitzgerald, Prigozy proposed, he located an alter ego, a repository for his own "very real insecurities and sexual worries." Consciously or not—and Prigozy thinks Fitzgerald intuitively understood the situation—Scott became "outwardly the walking model of Hemingway's fears, the symbol of his despair." By attacking Scott, Ernest tried to dispose of those fears.

This view of the Fitzgerald-Hemingway connection does not, of course, address the *sources* of the feeling between them, nor does it minimize the genuineness and depth of that feeling. Even in his ill-spirited assaults after Fitzgerald's death, Hemingway repeatedly proclaimed that he spoke out of love. The usual formulation followed the "I loved Scott, but..." pattern. "We both loved him," he wrote to Perkins, "I cared for Scott so much" to Wilson. Readers might be inclined to take such statements with a grain of salt, inasmuch as they were customarily followed by derogatory comments. On the other hand, it was extremely difficult for Hemingway to confess his love for anyone. I know of no other man that he said he loved. Certainly there is no one he said he loved as often and as openly as he did of Fitzgerald. And Fitzgerald said the same thing about Hemingway, even after the abuses Ernest visited upon him in "The Snows of Kilimanjaro" and elsewhere. No matter what he did, "[s]omehow I love that man," he wrote Perkins. He confessed that love in his notebooks, as well. As Wilson summed up the situation, Scott "began by adoring" Ernest and "remained more of less obsessed by him" all his life.

That Hemingway and Fitzgerald loved each other does not provide a warrant for the assertion that they were lovers. Only Zelda Fitzgerald, among those who knew them, ever proposed that possibility, and Zelda made her accusation at a time when she felt a strong sexual attraction to another woman and may have wanted to ameliorate her own feelings of guilt.

In his public persona as in his (mostly posed) photographs, Fitzgerald appears as an elegant young man—fine-featured, well-dressed, well-mannered, charming, clever, and romantic, if unfortunately afflicted by alcohol and victimized by fate. For the Triangle Club show "The Evil Eye," his photograph was taken in drag and circulated as a picture of Princeton's "most beautiful showgirl." (At the time, there were no female undergraduates, and their roles were played by men.) With "a touch of the feminine" in his nature, Fitzgerald possessed an unusual capacity to put himself in the shoes of his fictional women.

Hemingway's public image, on the other hand, bears an unmistakably masculine cast. He is ruggedly handsome, decked out in outdoor gear, and wearing a signature beard. The precise details of Fitzgerald's appearance are somewhat hazy in the public imagination, but everyone knows what Hemingway looks like: so much so that there is an annual contest in Key West for Hemingway look-alikes. His reputation as sportsman and warrior—as an outdoorsman who managed to do some writing—appealed to the anti-intellectual strain in the American imagination. At the same time, however, it stigmatized him as egregiously macho.

Octavio Paz construed the typical *macho* figure as a stoical man capable of bravery and endurance in the face of adversity, much like such Hispanic heroes in Hemingway's fiction as the bullfighter Manuel Garcia in "The Undefeated" and the fisherman Santiago in *The Old Man and the Sea*. Hemingway aspired to such behavior himself, and at times succeeded, as under fire during World War II. But he also resembled the prototypical macho in another and more important way. Such a man, Paz wrote, is "a hermetic being, closed up in himself," for to open himself to others would both demonstrate weakness and invite rejection. The stereotyping of Hemingway has concentrated on his aggressively masculine appearance and pursuits, and not taken his psychologically withdrawn side into account. He was macho all right, but in a different way than most observers think.

In the light of these public perceptions of the two men, and of their fiction, it is somewhat surprising to discover a fascination with unconventional sexual arrangements permeating the work of Hemingway. Living in Paris in the early 1920s, he met and befriended a number of independent and sexually liberated women, mostly lesbians. These included not only Stein and Toklas, but also Sylvia Beach, Natalie Barney, Margaret Anderson, Bryher (Winifred Ellerman), and Janet Flanner. Hemingway made fewer such friends among the gay male community of the Left Bank. To do so would have been to invite speculation about his own orientation. But he did of course observe, and depicted both gays and lesbians in some of his early fiction, as for example in "The Battler" (probably), "A Simple Enquiry," "The Mother of a Queen," and "The Sea Change."

In Paris, too, he encountered the New Woman, or her reasonable facsimile in the liberated person of Lady Duff Twysden, a woman who took on and disposed of lovers as casually as a male Lothario. In her fictional form as Lady Brett Ashley in *The Sun Also Rises*, this dangerous creature succeeded, Circe-like, in transforming the men around her into swine, without herself gaining the least glimmer of happiness. "Promiscuity no solution," Hemingway noted. But Lady Ashley remained a basically sympathetic character on the page, reflecting Ernest's own feelings about Duff. Throughout his early fiction, and particularly in the stories of love and marriage in disrepair, his sympathy seems to reside with the female characters—the neglected wife in "Cat in the Rain" and the woman reluctant to undergo an abortion in "Hills Like White Elephants," for example.

As many have noticed, there are few truly successful man-and-woman relationships in the fiction of Ernest Hemingway. In stories that look back to his own parents, women dominate and emasculate their husbands, like Mrs. Adams in "The Doctor and the Doctor's Wife" and "Now I Lay Me." In stories that deal with figures contemporaneous with himself, young men resent or resist the marital commitments that get in the way of their doing what they like to do—skiing, fishing, traveling around Europe without undue encumbrances. When Hemingway does invent an apparently idyllic love, as in *A Farewell to Arms* and *For Whom the Bell Tolls*, death soon intervenes to bring it to an end.

The very absence of successful lasting relationships, Rena Sanderson believes, suggests an implicit yearning for them. In effect, Hemingway posits an ideal prelapsarian world where a man and a woman are united against the rest of the world. Hemingway's stories are full of the problems that get in the way of such an idyllic state, among them "homoeroticism, divorce, abortion, venereal disease, infidelity." But as Sanderson points out, the greatest single problem is male passivity, as in the various self-abasements Jake Barnes undergoes for Brett and the humiliations Dr. Adams silently accepts from his wife.

The most vivid and compelling portrait of such a man comes in the 1936 story "The Short Happy Life of Francis Macomber," where the title figure—

a wealthy and weak character who is good at court games but little else—under-goes a series of mortifications during an African safari. After he runs from a charging lion in full view of his beautiful wife, Margot, she exacts a double vengeance upon him. She taunts him cruelly in the presence of white hunter Robert Wilson, and then cuckolds him with Wilson, despite having promised that "there wasn't going to be any of that" on safari. These events lead Wilson, who carries a double-sized cot to take advantage of any such "windfalls," to reflect on relations between American women and their husbands in an extremely misogy-nistic passage.

> They are, he thought, the hardest in the world; the hardest, the cruelest, the most predatory and the most attractive and their men have softened or gone to pieces nervously as they have hardened. Or is it that they pick men that they can handle?

However it may have begun, the marriage of the Macombers degenerated into the worst of accommodations. "They had a sound basis of union. Margot was too beautiful for Macomber to divorce her and Macomber had too much money for Margot ever to leave him." But the wife must maintain the upper hand. At the end of the story, when in his fury at her infidelity Francis bravely confronts a wounded buffalo, Margot shoots him dead. Whether accidentally or on purpose is left ambiguous, although Hemingway commented twenty years later that, in his experience, the percentage of husbands killed accidentally by bitchy wives was very low.

Hemingway's misogynistic tendencies peaked during the 1930s, following the suicide of his father and his own marriage to a woman who—like Helen in "The Snows of Kilimanjaro," a companion story to "Macomber" published in the same year—was rich enough to support him. Thereafter they receded in his fiction, if not entirely in his life. Among the papers Hemingway left behind in his Cuban home was a fragment generalizing about the fitness of women as wives for male writers. Women can be wonderful friends, the passage reads, but also make dreadful enemies. They break the rules: "Woman is the only two legged animal that stands upright and will always hit after the bell." They always have to be jealous, "and if you give them no cause for jealousy except your work they will be jealous of that." They are far more interested in your ability to fuck than your ability to write. They are greedy, and will "remember for a hundred years any cashable asset they did not get" from their husbands. You must never say anything against a woman's family, but also never agree with anything bad she may say about it. Still, real bitchery was abnormal. "Most lovely women bat over .750 at not being bitches."

Such reflections conform to the public perception of Papa Hemingway as a man's man more comfortable on the Gulf Stream than in the bedroom. But that image was severely challenged in the posthumously published *The Garden of Eden* (1986). A novel of 250 pages cobbled together from a manuscript several times that length, *Garden* tells the story of David Bourne and his erotically adventurous wife, Catherine, who draws him into cross-sexual roles. In bed, for example, she mounts him, calling herself "Peter" and him "my girl Catherine." Subsequently, both David and the devilish Catherine make love to the bisexual Marita, forming an uneasy ménage à trois. At the end, after the mentally disturbed Catherine has burned her husband's manuscripts, David is living contentedly with Marita, his capacity to write having survived the destructive yet oddly invigorating effects of the sexual experimentation.

More than any other book put together from Hemingway's voluminous manuscripts, *The Garden of Eden* stimulated a critical re-examination of his work. Several of the themes it explored—male androgyny, female madness, unconventional sexual behavior, and the relationship between sex and creativity—were at least implicitly present in his previous writing. Consider, for example, the erotic role that haircuts play in Hemingway's fiction, most notably in *A Farewell to Arms*. Catherine Barkley proposes to Frederic that she cut her hair and he grow his so they will look alike. It will give them something to do while they await her baby, she suggests, and he happily assents. A similar scene is enacted in the first chapter of *Garden*, though it was omitted from the published version by editor Tom Jenks of Scribner's. Catherine Bourne goes to the barbershop in order to bring back to David a "dangerous" surprise: hair cut to precisely his length. He then dyes his hair blond to look like hers and the two of them take the sun for identical tans, in order to become "the same one" (as Catherine Barkley remarked) and/or to eradicate gender distinctions in lovemaking.

As J. Gerald Kennedy has discovered, Hemingway wrote a very similar haircut scene in a chapter cut from *A Moveable Feast*, which he was composing more or less simultaneously with *The Garden of Eden* in the late 1950s. This nineteen-page sketch focused on Ernest and Hadley after their return to Paris in 1924. They had their own private customs at the time, Hemingway wrote, their own standards and taboos and delights. One such delight came when they agreed on an androgynous project of identical hairstyles. He would grow his out, and she'd get hers evened and wait for him to catch up. It would probably take four months, Hadley estimated.

"Four months more?"

"I think so."

We sat and she said something secret and I said something secret back.

"Other people would think we are crazy."

"Poor unfortunate other people," she said. "We'll have such fun Tatie."

"And you'll really like it?"

"I'll love it," she said. "But we'll have to be very patient. The way people are patient with a garden."

When she returned from the hairdresser's to show him her newly cut hair, Hadley said, "Feel it in back," the exact words Catherine utters to David in the opening chapter of *Garden*. And when he did so, his fingers shaking, she commanded him to "[s]troke it down hard." Again he said "something secret" as he held his hand against the silky weight of her hair. "Afterwards," she said.

Ernest played similar sexual games, involving hair and role-changing, with his fourth wife Mary. She was "Pete," he was "Catharine." Mary had no lesbian leanings, but always wanted to be a boy, he wrote in December 1953. Though he disliked all tactile contact with other men, embracing Mary introduced him to "something quite new and outside all tribal law."

In *Feast* as in *Garden*, then, Hemingway revealed the excitement he felt about crossing the conventional boundaries between men and women. Yet there was every good reason for him to excise the passage about unisex hairstyles from *A Moveable Feast*, a memoir in which he consistently portrayed the protagonist—a young writer named Ernest Hemingway—as a figure of strictly conventional sexual orientation who regarded gay men with derision and lesbians with disgust. In *The Garden of Eden*, which he had no plans to publish, he could more freely explore what Kennedy calls "the unstable terrain of sexual ambivalence." After the appearance of *Garden* in 1986, it became clear that Hemingway's feelings about sex, like everything else about him, were too complicated to conform to a simple macho image. Scholars began to write books about Hemingway's battle with or immersion in androgyny. "The Hemingway you were taught about in high school," Nancy Comley and Robert Scholes announced, "is dead."

Fitzgerald could never have written about, or even conceived of, an arrangement like that of the Bournes and their mutual lover Marita in *Garden*. His attitudes toward sex were rigorously traditional, the product of his midwestern Catholic upbringing, and he felt a visceral abhorrence toward homoerotic relationships. The story that fascinated him, because it was so nearly his own, was that of the young man rejected by a beautiful and desirable young woman of higher social status. He saw such encounters as part of a game—later, a war—that the poor young man could not hope to win.

This is precisely the situation of Amory Blaine and Rosalind Connage in *This Side of Paradise*. Rosalind, a New York debutante, plays off one beau against another as she moves toward a decision about who to marry. She is in control of these relationships, throughout. "Given a decent start," she asserts, "any girl can beat a man nowadays"—and with her beauty and wealth she has been given far more than that. Following the advice of her mother, Rosalind decides to turn down Amory in favor of a rival who can promise her a future to compare with her privileged past. Her love for Amory cannot make up for what she stands to lose should they marry. As she tells him, "I like sunshine and pretty things and cheerfulness—and I dread responsibility. I don't want to think about pots and kitchens and brooms. I want to worry whether my legs will get slick and brown when I swim in the summer."

Fitzgerald does not condemn Rosalind for her hard-hearted if sensible choice, any more than he could condemn Ginevra King for making the same choice. At a time when prospects of a career were minimal and divorce carried a definite stigma, young women were hardly to be faulted for following a course of economic and social security. Instead of blaming Ginevra for rejecting him, or Rosalind for rejecting Amory, Fitzgerald continued to put these golden girls on a pedestal because of their unavailability. If the male protagonists of his fiction lost the game, at least they could keep their illusions. This placed the women in his fiction, and in his life, in an untenable position. They could only preserve their status as idealized creatures by repudiating the love of their suitors, as Daisy turned down Gatsby. The issue of social class is central in that novel as in many of the stories. The two characters who dare to fall in love above their station—Gatsby and Myrtle Wilson—end up dead, while Tom and Daisy Buchanan safely retreat into their money and their "vast carelessness."

On the other hand, should such a desirable woman elect to marry one of Fitzgerald's male protagonists, the marriage was usually compromised by the "fine, full-hearted selfishness" characteristic of a Rosalind or of a Judy Jones (in "Winter Dreams") or, as Scott maintained, of his wife Zelda. In "The Adjuster," a story published like *Gatsby* in 1925, Fitzgerald dramatized the difficulties confronting Charles Hemple, who cracked under the strain of supporting all the responsibilities of the household while his wife Luella pursued various avenues of excitement. Otherwise Charles was strong and capable: his attitude toward his wife was his weak point. "[H]e was aware of her intense selfishness, but," the author intrudes to comment, "it is one of the many flaws in the scheme of human relationships that selfishness in women has an irresistible appeal to many men," particularly when accompanied as in the case of Luella Hemple by "a childish beauty."

The irresponsible and narcissistic (if still somehow enchanting) belle of Fitzgerald's early fiction grew into the more dominant and independent woman of his later work. In good part, the changing situation in his fiction was a response to the cultural revolution in morals and manners. In a 1930 essay, Fitzgerald announced the arrival of the independent woman. The flapper had been replaced by "the contemporary girl," who possessed courage as well as beauty and radiated poise and self-confidence. In a rather frightening development, she had also become sexually liberated and no longer identified virtue with chastity. Fitzgerald expected wonders from this newly independent woman. It was "the poor young man" he worried about.

In *Tender Is the Night*, this confident new woman engaged the young man he worried about in a dramatic struggle, and emerged victorious. In portraying Nicole Diver's progress from dependent mental patient to a woman sure of her ground and hard as Georgia pine, ready to discard her husband Dick to take on a lover—Why not? she thinks, other women do—Fitzgerald was developing on the page some of his own fears about the battle of the sexes.

Here he was influenced by his reading, in 1930, of D.H. Lawrence's *Fantasia of the Unconscious*. In Lawrence's view, contemporary man was losing sight of his principal objective in life—a "disinterested craving...to make something wonderful" of himself—as a consequence of his sexual desire. Trying to please the female led to weakness in males, Lawrence believed, and the modern woman filled the vacuum, becoming "a queen of the earth, and inwardly a fearsome tyrant." These ideas fitted into Fitzgerald's own concept of a deadly competition between the sexes, and his apprehension that the women were winning.

His private life was very much on his mind in this connection. In *Tender,* Nicole Diver recovers her strength while Dick suffers a moral, physical, and professional decline. It was as if she drew health and energy from her husband, leaving him depleted. By 1932 or 1933, Fitzgerald became convinced that he and Zelda were engaged in a marital war from which only one of them would emerge whole. In a document among his notes, he even envisioned a diabolical plot to *"attack on all grounds,"* driving Zelda further into madness by suppressing her creative work, disorienting her schedule, and detaching her from Scottie.

Tender Is the Night contained Fitzgerald's frankest and most antagonistic portrayals of homoerotic characters, both gays and lesbians. He became closely acquainted with this subculture during the late 1920s in Paris, some years after Hemingway, and responded to it with abhorrence. A section excised from *Tender* makes a stronger statement of repulsion than anything in the published novel. Francis Melarkey, the hero of the novel (in its first draft), is attracted to Wanda Breasted. He meets her at a bar where three tall, slender women make slurring remarks about Seth and Dinah Piper (the original names of the Divers). Annoyed by these insults to friends of his but with expectations of a tryst with Wanda to follow, Francis joins her on a drinking spree. His hopes are dashed when he finds her in the embrace of another woman, but he extricates Wanda, takes her home, and stays with her after she threatens suicide. It is morning before he can escape. "Good God, this is getting to be a hell of a world," he thought. "God damn these women!"

Love does not work out for Hemingway's characters because the fates are against them. There are no lasting marriages in his fiction. Death intervenes when they threaten to develop, as for Catherine Barkley or Robert Jordan. You cannot go back to a prelapsarian Garden. Love doesn't lead to happy endings for Fitzgerald's characters, either, though for different reasons. In his universe, love can only endure if the lover is rejected by the object of his love, who thus preserves her status as an idealized object. Let the two marry, and the illusions that make the love possible will inevitably vanish, leading at best to the disillusionment or—in Fitzgerald's later fiction—to the destruction of the lover.

The relationships that failed in the stories and novels of Hemingway and Fitzgerald were paralleled in their lives. Hemingway, who was married four times, broke off the first three marriages himself and tried to break off the fourth. Fitzgerald was married only once, but his union with Zelda was far from happy. If love could not last for either of them, neither could friendship.

PSYCHOLOGICAL SPECULATIONS

> In the end is my beginning...The end is where we start from.
> —T.S. ELIOT, "Four Quartets"

In *The Psychopathic God: Adolf Hitler*, Robert G.L.Waite attempted to combine the techniques of psychological investigation with the rigorous findings of history.

He was aware of the danger that such an approach might reduce "complex personalities" to a mere diagnosis, while historical scholarship argued for multiple causation. But Waite also pointed out what the psychologist Erik Erikson had to say on the subject: that those very biographers who categorically repudiated systematic psychological interpretation nonetheless permitted themselves "extensive psychologizing" justified in the name of "common sense." Whenever the question "Why" intruded itself, some sort of psychological explanation was sure to follow.

Well, then, *why*? What was there about Ernest Hemingway and Scott Fitzgerald that led their intimate friendship to degenerate into a painfully cruel exercise in sadomasochism? Rivalry played its part in the deterioration of the friendship, particularly as it found expression in Hemingway's comments after Fitzgerald's death and subsequent critical resurrection. But there must have been other powerful forces at work, also. Almost all literary relationships are contaminated to some degree by rivalrous feelings. Few of them end as bitterly as did that of Fitzgerald and Hemingway. Why?

Hemingway had a dark side to his nature, blacker than Zimbabwe granite. When visited by the demon of depression, he could be tremendously cruel and critical of others, much as in the end he visited the final judgment upon himself. From boyhood on Hemingway was fascinated by death, and especially by suicide. His first printed story, in the Oak Park high school literary magazine, ended with a suicide. The subject came up often in his correspondence. He could imagine how a man could be so weighed down by obligations as to take his own life, he wrote Gertrude Stein in 1923. Three years later, when he and Pauline agreed to spend one hundred days apart, he wrote Fitzgerald that he had struggled through "the general bumping-off phase."

His feelings about suicide changed when his father killed himself in December 1928. Ernest blamed his mother for this tragedy. She had bullied his father into it, he decided. But he could not condone what his father had done. His suicide was an act of weakness, even of cowardice. He addressed the topic directly in the ending of *For Whom the Bell Tolls* when Robert Jordan, wounded and in pain, rejects the option of taking his own life. Jordan's mind, running in triple time, reminds him of the experience of his father and grandfather, who closely resemble Hemingway's own. His grandfather, like Anson T. Hemingway, distinguished himself in combat during the Civil War. His father, like Clarence Edmunds Hemingway, shot himself with a Smith and Wesson revolver because he could not stand up to his wife. Jordan forgave his father that weakness, but he was also "ashamed of him." He did not "want to do that business his father did."

So Ernest resisted for a long time the pull of oblivion, even in the extremity of pain. On shipboard following his terrible injuries of the two 1954 plane crashes, he gazed with longing at the restful water flowing by—and did not jump. Finally, he could resist no longer.

The sole attempt at a psychological interpretation of Hemingway was published by psychiatrist Irvin D. Yalom and his wife Marilyn, a literary scholar, in 1971. Admitting the difficulty of arriving at a "dynamic formulation" of a man they never met, the Yaloms used as resources Hemingway's published fiction and letters and the biographical information available at the time, abetted by consultation with General Buck Lanham.

They began, logically enough, with the "powerful imposing figure" Hemingway presented to the world.

> Whatever else we can see, always there is virility, strength, courage: he is the soldier searching out the eye of the battle storm; the intrepid hunter and fisherman compelled to pursue the greatest fish and stalk the most dangerous animal from the Gulf Stream to Central Africa; the athlete, swimmer, brawler, boxer; the hard drinker and hard lover who boasted that he had bedded every girl he wanted and some that he had not wanted; the lover of danger, of the bullfight, of flying, of the wartime front lines; the friend of brave men, heroes, fighters, hunters, and matadors.

This was not only Hemingway's public image, the Yaloms concluded—it was the *idealized image* he tried to live up to.

The idea of the idealized image they borrowed from Karen Horney, who in her *Neurosis and Human Growth* (1950) argued that a child deprived of acceptance by his parents or finding in them no realistic model to emulate would instead construct "an idealized image—a way he must become in order to survive and to avoid basic anxiety." Hemingway's idealized image, according to the Yaloms, "crystallized around a search for mastery." He became the man who would be master, a goal beyond the reach of any human being. And because his idealized image was unattainable, he was afflicted by recurrent self-doubt and self-contempt and became highly sensitive to any adverse criticism from others.

Living the dangerous existence he demanded of himself, Hemingway was often hurt. He proceeded on the assumption that he could withstand pressures that would fell an ordinary mortal. "[H]e boasted that he had an unusually indestructible body, an extra thickness of skull, and was not subject to the typical biological limitations...being able, for example, to exist on an average of two hours and 32 minutes sleep for 42 straight days." Similarly, he believed — or made himself believe — that he could work harder and better than others, learn more, drink more, make love more, and so on. Throughout his life, the Yaloms asserted, Hemingway attempted to abolish the necessary discrepancy between his real self and this superhuman idealized self. When he could not do so, he was overcome by anxiety and depression and, in the last years of his life, by paranoia — projecting onto others his hatred for his own real and sometimes unmasterful self.

Where relations with others were concerned, Hemingway carefully kept his distance. In love, he brooked no disapproval and ceded little of himself to his partners. Giving of oneself he saw as a sign of emasculation, and he was determined not to "do that business" of his father, either. Nor would he put himself in a position to be hurt, after his youthful repudiations by Agnes von Kurowsky and his mother. His wives may have loved him — three of them undoubtedly did — but they were not loved back.

In friendship, too, Hemingway withheld commitment. In his edition of Hemingway's selected letters, Carlos Baker called attention to Ernest's highly gregarious nature: a longing "to gather his closest male friends around him for hunting, fishing, drinking, or conversational exploits." Ernest had a rare capacity for the kind of male camaraderie — the whiskey around the campfire — that could ward off loneliness but required no strong emotional investment. His closest companions, in the last decades of his life, were men he fished or hunted or boxed with. In such company, as Baker put it, he "could relax, boast, show off, gossip and listen to gossip, tell tall tales, make rough jokes, shoot, fish, drink — often competitively — and share what he had and what he knew with those who were close to him in size, strength, or adventurous disposition." But they were emphatically not close to him in intellectual attainments, and none of them were writers.

Systematically and often with excessive cruelty, he broke off all his literary relationships. Donald Ogden Stewart, who knew Ernest well during the 1920s and was the model for the sympathetic Bill Gorton in *The Sun Also Rises*, was one of those spurned by Hemingway. In an interview, Stewart tried to puzzle out the reason why. "The minute he began to love you, or the minute he began to have some sort of obligation to you of love or friendship or something, then is when he had to kill you. Then you were too close to something he was protecting. He, one-by-one, knocked off the best friendships he ever had. He did it with Scott; he did it with Dos Passos — with everybody."

What he was protecting, in the Yaloms' formulation, was his idealized image as a master, a self-created artist beholden to no one and unwilling to be contaminated by any trace of weakness. Fitzgerald was guilty on both counts. He laid Hemingway under obligation during the first years of their friendship, providing Ernest with precisely the sort of professional and personal debt he felt compelled to cast aside. And in many ways—as artist and husband and drinking companion—Fitzgerald demonstrated a vulnerability that Hemingway regarded as contemptible. It may well be that he detected aspects of his own weakness in Fitzgerald's characterological shortcomings and hence responded to them with seemingly undue vitriol. The extremity of Ernest's viciousness toward Scott in *A Moveable Feast*, Jacqueline Tavernier-Courbin commented, "suggests a projection of [his] own fears of personal and professional failure."

In the glow of his early success, Fitzgerald wrote in "The Crack-Up," he held the serene belief that "[l]ife was something you dominated if you were any good." Then he cracked up and discarded that illusion. Sara Murphy, reading the essay, scolded Fitzgerald for the arrogance of his youthful confidence, but it was Ernest and not Scott who clung to the idea that life could be dominated if you were masterful enough. His son Jack observed that he could not conceive of his father receding into an amiable old age. Given his idealized image of himself, such an accommodation to reality was unthinkable. As Hemingway's health deteriorated and his artistic powers flagged, the man who could not master life chose not to live at all.

If Hemingway needed to think well of himself to survive, Fitzgerald seemed to covet his imperfections. In a document composed when he was fifteen years old, for example, he simultaneously celebrated his superficial attractiveness and condemned his deeper moral failings. Among his positive qualities Fitzgerald listed "superior mentality," good looks, charm, "a sort of aristocratic egotism," and an ability to exert a "subtle fascination over women." On the negative side, he considered himself "rather worse than most boys, due to a latent unscrupulousness." He was cold, cruel, and "mordantly selfish." He had a "streak of weakness" in his character, and lacked "the essentials"—a sense of honor, courage, perseverance, and self-respect. His inordinate vanity, he added, "was liable to be toppled over at one blow by an unpleasant remark or a missed tackle."

Such a harsh self-assessment, unusual from anyone, was astounding from a boy of fifteen. The most interesting things about it were 1) that young Scott Fitzgerald seemed to enjoy chastising himself for his moral shortcomings fully as much as he enjoyed listing his mental and physical virtues, and 2) that his sense of self-worth depended so much upon the opinion of those who *watched* him avoid the tackle and could devastate him with "an unpleasant remark." The inner-directed Hemingway drew his strength—and used it up—by trying to conform to the image of himself he carried around inside his head. With so little self-respect, the other-directed Fitzgerald was forever seeking the approval of others, and regarded himself as despicable for making the effort. His compulsion to alienate the very people he wanted to please offered tacit evidence of his failure to value himself. By outrageously demonstating his unworthiness in alcoholic misbehavior, he forestalled others from arriving at a sober reasoned judgment of his inferiority.

Fitzgerald's family background was essential in the formation of his flimsy self-image. No more than Hemingway did he have a father who gave him a paternal image to pattern himself upon. The well-mannered but ineffectual Edward Fitzgerald bequeathed him little beyond fine features, a few courteous gestures, and a fondness for lost causes. But instead of building an unrealizable ideal like Ernest, young Scott took his cue from his mother's ambitions for him. Mollie Fitzgerald spoiled her only son, and pushed him into social worlds beyond his depth. Taking pride in his good looks and charm and "superior mentality," she encouraged him to show off for the entertainment of others. Scott inherited from her a lasting sense of social insecurity and a demeaning eagerness for the applause of other people. Above all, Fitzgerald wanted to please. In his notebooks he jotted down an Egyptian proverb about the worst things in life:

> To be in bed and sleep not,
> To want for one who comes not.
> To try to please and please not.

Inevitably, he sometimes failed in his efforts to please. "I must be loved," he told Laura Guthrie in 1935. "I have so many faults that I must be approved of in other ways." His need to be loved may have been the most serious fault of all.

The continual exercise of his charm, Fitzgerald fully understood, involved him in artifice, and he excoriated himself for this indulgence. In a note written during his Hollywood years, he resolved not to go around "saying I'm fond of people when I mean I'm so damned used to their reactions to my personal charm that I can't do without it. Getting emptier and emptier." In his fiction, both early and late, he considered the destructive consequences of pleasing others through charm. Amory Blaine, in *This Side of Paradise*, aspires to become a personage instead of a personality. The difference is that a personage makes his mark through accomplishment and "is never thought of apart from what he's done," while a personality depends on the approval of others for his self-image. Dick Diver, in *Tender Is the Night*, represents an almost clinical study of a man emptied of vitality by the exercise of an increasingly insincere charm. There is something unwholesome as well as destructive in Diver's overweening need to be loved.

In his campaigns to please, Fitzgerald was far more successful with women than with men. "He liked women," Zelda said after Scott's death, and they usually "lionized" him. He "kept all the rites," knew how to flatter and entertain, and was sensitive to shades of meaning in converation. With men, on the other hand, Fitzgerald felt ill at ease and unconfident. He tried too hard, asked too many questions, and often ended by abasing himself.

Unfairly or not, he tended to associate his mother with this failure. In 1931, Fitzgerald became the intimate friend of Margaret Egloff, a psychiatrist then "working with the Jung group" in Switzerland. At her suggestion he wrote out the details of what Egloff called "a Big Dream."

> I am in an upstairs apartment where I live with my mother, old, white haired, clumsy and in mourning, as she is today. On another floor are a group of handsome & rich, young men, whom I seem to have known slightly as a child and now want to know better, but they look at me suspiciously. I talk to one who is agreeable and not at all snobbish, but obviously he does not encourage my acquaintance— whether because he considers me poor, unimportant, ill bred, of of ill renown I don't know, or rather don't think about—only I scent the polite indifference and even understand it. During this time I discover that there is a dance downstairs to which I am not invited. I feel that if they knew better how important I was, I should be invited...I go downstairs again, wander into the doorway of a sort of ballroom, see caterers at work, and then am suddenly shamed by realizing this is the party to which I am not invited. Meeting one of the young men in the hall, I lose all poise and stammer something absurd. I leave the house, but as I leave Mother calls something to me in a too audible voice from an upper story. I don't know whether I am angry with her for clinging to me, or because I am ashamed of her for not being young and chic, or for disgracing my conventional sense by calling out, or because she might guess I'd been hurt and pity me, which would have been unendurable, or all those things. Anyway I call back at her some terse and furious reproach....

The dream patently revealed Fitzgerald's feelings of social inferiority. *I scent the polite indifference and even understand it.* According to Egloff, who knew Fitzgerald well, he felt that the rich, powerful, and chic were the people to identify with. "The fact that he was not born into that society galled him, and he hated himself for his own and everyone else's snobbery. He hated his mother for her upward aspirations, and he despised his father for not setting his goal and his career in that direction. But with all his ambivalence his underlying value system was very similar to his mother's."

One way of winning approval, Fitzgerald discovered in boyhood, was through performing in public. Presented proudly to company by his mother, he recited poems and sang songs. In prep school he cultivated his theatrical bent by writing and acting in plays. At Princeton he wrote for both the *Lit* and the *Tiger* humor magazine, but expended most of his efforts on the book and lyrics for Triangle Club shows. Had he not been sent home in junior year, he would almost certainly have become Triangle president in senior year. He had extremely high hopes for the success of *The Vegetable*, his 1923 comedy—hopes that were encouraged by Edmund Wilson, who had been his collaborator on "The Evil Eye" at Princeton. When his daughter Scottie got involved in the theater at Vassar, he suggested that she might consider starting a career "following the footsteps of Cole Porter and Rodgers and Hart." He might have "gone along with that gang" himself, he added, had he not been too much a moralist at heart with a desire "to preach at people in some acceptable form rather than to entertain them." There was a detectable twinge of regret in that November 1939 letter, as if Fitzgerald felt he might have been better off writing musical comedy rather than some of the best stories and novels of the century.

Such a career would have satisfied his lifelong propensity for showing off, often under the influence of alcohol. In marrying Zelda, he found a mate who enjoyed putting on performances as much as he did. During the first years of their marriage, both in an around New York City and in France, the two of them seemed determined to command the attention of their friends through their ostentatious and often shocking misbehavior. They didn't just *go* to parties or *give* parties. They *were* the party.

Biographer James Mellow characterized the Fitzgeralds as "masters of invention...acting out their stories in real life." The way they acted out was strikingly different. Zelda liked to skirt the edge of the precipice, drawing all eyes to her recklessness, and dragged her husband after her into dangerous pursuits. Scott, on the other hand, was content to attract an audience through demeaning himself in public. This was his pattern, particularly, when dealing with the very talented and successful. In 1920, upon hearing that Edith Wharton was in Charles Scribner's office, he burst into the room and knelt at her feet in literary homage. In 1928, he threatened to throw himself from the window of a Paris apartment in tribute to the genius of dinner companion James Joyce. When Hemingway was on the scene, Fitzgerald's self-abasement became especially embarrassing. At least twice—at the Murphys' party for Ernest at Juan-les-Pins and at the dinner with Wilson and Hemingway in New York—he actually crawled around on the floor.

In 1931, Fitzgerald took one drink too many at a Sunday party given by Irving Thalberg and Norma Shearer in Hollywood and decided to entertain the assembled actors and directors with his humorous song "Dog." He was roundly booed for his trouble. Fitzgerald used the incident—somewhat transformed to put his fictional counterpart in a better light—in his excellent story "Crazy Sunday," just as he wrote other humiliations into *Tender Is the Night*. These fictional confessions must have been difficult to put down on paper. They are painful even to read about.

According to Arnold Gingrich, Fitzgerald possessed a "strange, almost mystic Celtic tendency to enjoy ill luck as some people enjoy ill health." Scott, he thought, was as much fascinated by failure as Ernest was enamored of success. "If anything was wrong in his life, and something always seemed to be...then everything was all wrong, and he seemed rather to enjoy saying so." It was this trait, Max Perkins believed, that drove Scott to write the "Crack-Up" essays and so put his career in jeopardy. He was, in Samuel Johnson's wonderful word, a "seeksorrow" who took pleasure in dramatizing his defeats.

This would seem to qualify Fitzgerald as a thoroughgoing masochist—that is, as someone who "enjoyed" or "took pleasure" in or was made "happy" by his failures and humiliations. But these terms often require redefinition, Shirley Panken asserted in *The Joy of Suffering*. "What might be meant is need for drama, crisis, sensation, stimulation, or a high tension level, thereby emphasizing one's identity or acquiring a spurious feeling of aliveness." The need for drama seems to fit Fitzgerald's situation. In a moment of deep intimacy, Rosemary Hoyt says to Dick Diver, "Oh, we're such *actors*—you and I," and clearly that is true of the series of performances Diver puts on throughout the novel.

Fitzgerald's personality like Hemingway's was far too complex to be reduced to a simple formulation. Much of his behavior, however, corresponded closely to what Avodah K. Offit classified as the "histrionic personality." Usually but not always women, such people must be the stars in the series of performances that make up their lives. They seek the approval of others through a show of pleasingness, and should that fail, through dramatic presentation of their "black vapors." Often they seduce and discard serial lovers. Though demanding and self-obsessed, histrionics are nonetheless appealing because of their intuitive insights and their "uncanny ability to make sensitive and perceptive observations about others."

For such people, as often seemed to be true of Fitzgerald, infamy was better than no notice at all. When he did something almost unforgivable—broke the wineglasses, insulted the guests, picked a fight—he followed up with extravagant exhibitions of regret. His first letter to Hemingway took the form of an apology for drunken misbehavior, and throughout their relationship he seemed to find himself invariably in the wrong. With others, too, most notably the Murphys, Scott tried to correct his nighttime indiscretions with morning-after notes and visits. "My God, did I say that? Did I do that?" he would ask. Couldn't they possibly forgive him, considering how bad he felt about what had happened?

When drinking Fitzgerald was apt to become belligerent, as he did on first meeting young Robert Penn (Red) Warren in 1929. After a dinner party in Paris that Zelda skipped, the two writers stopped by the Fitzgeralds' apartment long enough for Warren to overhear a "frightful hissing quarrel" between husband and wife. He and Scott then proceeded to a café where Warren made a flattering remark about *Gatsby*. "Say that again," Fitzgerald responded, "and I'll knock your block off." The next morning Red got a *pneumatique* from Scott "full of apology, saying he had been under great strain and drunk besides, and asking me to dinner." Fitzgerald was constantly testing the tolerance of others, as if to see if he could still command their forgiveness. Not everyone reacted as he must have wished. "Between being dangerous when drunk and eating humble pie when sober, I preferred Scott dangerous," writer Anita Loos commented. And in London, one lady of title simply refused to accept his contrition. He was terribly, despairingly sorry, Fitzgerald wrote her in abject next-day remorse. Oh, was he? she replied.

In a note written around 1931, Scott set down a list of those who responded to his misconduct by snubbing him.

Snubs—Gen. Mannsul, Telulah phone, Hotel O'Connor, Ada Farewell, Toulman party, Barrymore, Talmadge and M. Davies. Emily Davies, Tommy H. meeting and bottle, Frank Ritz and Derby, Univ. Chicago, Vallambrosa and yacht, Condon, Gerald in Paris, Ernest apartment.

Some of the people have disappeared in the mist. But it is possible to reconstruct snubbings by Tallulah Bankhead, Bijou O'Connor, and Ada MacLeish, by Hollywood's John Barrymore, Constance Talmadge, and Marian Davies, by socialites Emily Davies Vanderbilt, Tommy Hitchcock, and Ruth Vallombrosa, and of course by Gerald Murphy and Ernest Hemingway. Fitzgerald would have been particularly sensitive to any slight from three of the men: the war hero and polo player Hitchcock, the elegant and socially impeccable Murphy, and the writer as man of action Hemingway. They were the very three Ernest placed on the roster of those Scott made heroes of. In choosing Hitchcock, Murphy, and himself, Hemingway added, Fitzgerald had certainly "played the field."

Fitzgerald at his best was a man of great charm and absolute loyalty, generous and supportive. Fitzgerald at his worst was an almost impossible friend, as annoying in his torrents of apology as in the episodes that inspired them. Hemingway found him disturbing in both manifestations, and was as much troubled by the generosity as the groveling.

As a friend, Hemingway treated Fitzgerald with extraordinary cruelty. He used Scott's support and later repudiated it. He insulted Scott in his letters and in his fiction, and after his death conducted a campaign against his reputation. And yet, the feeling between them ran deep.

What Scott loved about Ernest was the idealized version of the sort of man—courageous, stoic, masterful—he could never be. What Ernest loved about Scott was the vulnerability and charm that his invented persona required him to despise. It made for a poignant story, really: one great writer humiliating himself in pursuit of a companionship that another's adamantine hardness of heart would not permit.

SOURCES

The notes below track the text of the book, and are keyed to the bibliography that follows.

ABBREVIATIONS:
SD   Scott Donaldson
FSF   F. Scott Fitzgerald
ZF   Zelda Fitzgerald
EH   Ernest Hemingway
MP   Maxwell Perkins
EW   Edmund Wilson

JFK   Hemingway Collection, John Fitzgerald Kennedy Library, Boston
Neville   Collection of Maurice and Marcia Neville
PUL   Firestone Library, Princeton University
Yale   Beinecke Library, Yale University

Fitzgerald's letters have been printed in several different volumes.

As Ever   *As Ever, Scott Fitz —*
Correspondence   *Correspondence of F. Scott Fitzgerald*
Letters   *The Letters of F. Scott Fitzgerald*
Life in Letters *F. Scott Fitzgerald: A Life in Letters*
Scott/Max   *Dear Scott/Dear Max*

To date there are two significant collections of Hemingway correspondence.

Only Thing   *The Only Thing That Counts*
SL   *Selected Letters of Ernest Hemingway*

Loveshocks: At Home

St. Paul and FSF's Parents:

FSF, "My Generation," *Esquire* 70 (October 1968), 121. FSF, "The Death of My Father," *Apprentice Fiction*, 1-6. Bruccoli, *Grandeur*, 19. SD, *Fool*, 10-11, 189, 16. SD, "Scott Fitzgerald's Romance with the South," 15-17. FSF to O'Hara, July 18, 1933, *Letters*, 503. FSF, "Author's House," *Afternoon*, 184. FSF, "Imagination—and a Few Mothers,"

Ladies' Home Journal 40 (June 1923): 21, 80-81. FSF to MP, February 20, 1926, *Life in Letters*, 138. FSF, *Ledger*. FSF, "Scott Fitzgerald's 'Thoughtbook,'" *Princeton University Library Chronicle* 26 (Winter 1965): 102-108 and unpaginated facsimile. FSF to Annabel Fitzgerald, ca. 1915, *Life in Letters*, 7-10. Spencer, "Where Has All the Glamour Gone?" unpaginated.

Oak Park and EH's Parents:

Lynn, *Hemingway*, 34-37. Sanford, *At the Hemingways*, 26-27, 31-33, 39. EH, "Fathers and Sons," *Short Stories*, 491. Baker, *Life Story*, 160. Lynn, *Hemingway*, 28-33, 38-43. Sanford, *At the Hemingways*, 49, 55-62. SD, *By Force of Will*, 188-190. Baker, *Life Story*, 5. Reynolds, *Young Hemingway*, 82-87, 69-70, 78-81, 129-133, 134-138. Comley and Scholes, *Hemingway's Genders*, 24-27. EH to Carol Hemingway, ca. 1945, in Fuentes, *Hemingway in Cuba*, 387.

Loveshocks: Jiltings

FSF and Ginevra King:

FSF, *Ledger*, 165, 167, 169-173. FSF, *Notebooks*, 205. SD, *Fool*, 48-52. FSF, *Paradise*, 58-71. Lehan, *Craft of Fiction*, 92-93, 189. FSF, *Crack-Up*, 77. Friskey, "Visiting the Golden Girl," 10-11. Martha Blair, "These Charming People," FSF Scrapbook, PUL. FSF to Scottie Fitzgerald, October 8, 1937, *Life in Letters*, 338. FSF, "One Hundred False Starts," *Afternoon*, 132. Lehan, *Craft of Fiction*, 95. FSF to Annabel Fitzgerald, ca. 1915, *Life in Letters*, 8.

EH and Agnes von Kurowsky:

Baker, *Life Story*, 43, 46-56. SD, "The Jilting of Ernest Hemingway," 661-673. Villard and Nagel, editors, *Hemingway in Love and War*, 48, 118-119, 135. EH to Smith, December 13, 1918, *SL*, 20. EH to Gamble, March 3, 1919, *SL*, 21-23. EH to Jenkins, 16 June 1919, *SL*, 25. SD, "'A Very Short Story' as Therapy," 99-105. Gullo and Church, "Love Survival: How to Mend a Broken Heart," 51-53, 77.

A Friendship Abroad

EH, *Feast*, 149-152 and "Preface." Bruccoli, *Scott and Ernest*, 3. EH, Item 486, JFK. Diliberto, *Hadley*, 82. Reynolds, *Young Hemingway*, 241. FSF to MP, ca. October 10, 1924, *Scott/Max*, 78. FSF to MP, ca. December 20, 1924, *Scott/Max*, 91. MP to FSF, February 24, 1925, *Scott/Max*, 95. FSF to MP, May 1, 1925, *Scott/Max*, 104. FSF, *Notebooks*, #1002. FSF, *Crack-Up*, 66-67, 70. EH to FSF, December 15, 1925, *SL*, 176. Gingrich, "Coming to Terms with Scott and Ernest," 60.

The City of Light

Kennedy, *Imagining Paris*, 10-13, 84-87, 100-103. EH, "The Snows of Kilimanjaro," *Short Stories*, 69-70. FSF to EW, May 1921, *Letters*, 326. EW to FSF, July 5, 1921, *Letters on Literature and Politics*, 63-64. Mellow, *Invented*, 136-139. LeVot quoted in Kennedy, *Imagining Paris*, 192-193. EH, *Feast*, 168. FSF, "How to Live on Practically

Nothing a Year," *Afternoon*, 113. Bruccoli, *Grandeur*, 221. FSF to ZF, Summer (?) 1930, *Correspondence*, 239. Meyers, *Scott Fitzgerald*, 138. EH, *Feast*, 154-155, 165-166, 174-176. Mellow, *Hemingway*, 290. EH to MP, June 9, 1925, *SL* 162-163. EH to FSF, April 12, 1931, *SL*, 339. Mellow, *Invented*, 241. George Wickes, "The Right Place at the Right Time," *French Connections*, ed. Kennedy and Bryer, 5-7. Baker, *Life Story*, 82-87. EH to EW, November 25, 1925, *SL*, 105. Simon, *Biography of Alice B.Toklas*, 143-147. Mellow, *Hemingway*, 291. Stein to FSF, May 22, 1925, *Correspondence*, 164. FSF to Stein, June 1925, *Letters*, 484-485.

Two Weaknesses

FSF, *Notebooks*, #1996. EH, *Torrents*, 76. EH to Poore, May 21, 1953, JFK. Reynolds, *Paris Years*, 339. Dos Passos quoted in Braudy, *Frenzy of Renown*, 550. EH, Item 593a, JFK. EH to FSF, May 4, 1926, *SL*, 203. EH, Item 185a, JFK. EH, Item 486, JFK.

Special Delivery to Scribner's

EH to FSF, July 1, 1925, *SL*, 165-166. FSF to EH, November 30, 1925, *Letters*, 295. Reynolds, *Paris Years*, 314-315. FSF to T.R. Smith, late May 1925, *Life in Letters*, 114. FSF to MP, ca. June 1, 1925, *Life in Letters*, 115-116. MP to EH, February 21, 1925, *Only Thing*, 33. FSF to MP, ca. October 6, 1925, *Letters*, 192. Stephens, *Critical Reception*, 7, 13. Mellow, *Hemingway*, 314-315. John J. Fenstermaker, "The Search for an American Audience: Marketing Ernest Hemingway, 1925-1930," *Oak Park Legacy*, ed. Nagel, 179-181. EH to Loeb, ca. November 25, 1925, JFK. EH to Pound, 30 November 1925, Yale. EH to Liveright, December 7, 1925, *SL*, 172-174. FSF to Liveright and Smith, before December 30, 1925, *Correspondence*, 183. EH to MacLeish, ca. December 11, 1925, *SL*, 140. EH to Cowley, 8 November 1951, Neville. FSF to MP, ca. December 27, 1925, *Letters*, 193. Liveright to EH, December 30, 1925, University of Virginia library. EH to FSF, December 31, 1925-January 1, 1926, *SL*, 183-185. Mellow, *Hemingway*, 320. FSF to MP and MP to FSF, telegrams, January 8, 1926, *Correspondence*, 187. MP to FSF, January 13, 1926, *Scott/Max*, 129. Liveright to FSF, December 30, 1925, *Correspondence*, 184-185. FSF to MP, ca. December 30, 1925, *Scott/Max*, 127-128. EH to Liveright, January 19, 1926, *SL*, 190-191. MP to FSF, March 4, 1926, and FSF to MP, ca. March 1, 1926, *Scott/Max*, 135-136.

"Fifty Grand" and Money

FSF to MP, 1 December 1925, *Correspondence*, 182. FSF to MP, ca. January 19, 1926, *Scott/Max*, 130-131. MP to EH, February 1, 1926, *Only Thing*, 34-35. MP to FSF, February 3, 1926, *Scott/Max*, 132. EH, "The Art of the Short Story," 88, 91. SD, "Wooing," 694-695. EH to MP, March 10, 1926, *SL*, 197. MP to EH, March 15, 1926 and March 24, 1926, PUL. EH to MP, April 1, 1926, *SL*, 198. Beegel, "'Mutilated by Scott Fitzgerald?': The Revision of Hemingway's 'Fifty Grand,'" *Craft of Omission*, 13-15, 24-26. FSF to Mencken, March 1926, *Correspondence*, 190. FSF, "How to Waste Material," *Afternoon*, 117-122. FSF to MP, ca. June 1, 1925, *Life in Letters*, 117, 119. EH to FSF, December 15, 1925, *SL*, 176. FSF to MP, before May 10, 1926 and ca. June 25, 1926, *Letters*, 203, 206. EH to FSF, ca. April 20, 1926 and ca. May 20, 1926, *SL*, 199-200, 204. Wescott, "The Moral of Scott Fitzgerald," *Crack-Up*, 324-325. Kathleen

Cannell to Carlos Baker, October 13, 1965, PUL. EH to FSF, ca. April 20, 1926, *SL*, 199-200. Mellow, *Invented*, 266-267. Hadley Hemingway to EH, May, 1926, in James Nagel, "Kitten to Waxin: Hadley's Letters to Ernest Hemingway, May 1926," *Journal of Modern Literature* 15 (Summer 1988), 156-157. EH, *Feast*, 209-210. Reynolds, *Paris Years*, 349-351.

A "Golden Couple": Gerald and Sara Murphy

Stewart quoted in Miller, *Lost Generation*, xv. Vaill, *So Young*, on Murphys: 6, 36, 46, 64-65. Miller, *Lost Generation*, xvi. Vaill, *So Young*, on Fitzgeralds: 138-139, 146-147,154-155; on Hemingways: 167-168, 170, 172; on party at Juan-les-Pins: 2-5, 176-177. Sara Murphy to FSF, ca. summer 1926, in Miller, *Lost Generation*, 17-18. Meyers, *Fitzgerald*, 115.

Making the Sun Rise

EH, *Feast*, 184-185. Reynolds, *Paris Years*, 308. Svoboda, *Hemingway and Sun*, 106-107. EH to FSF, ca. April 20, 1926, *SL*, 199-201. FSF, *Gatsby*, 99. EH to FSF, ca. May 20, 1926, *SL*, 204-205. MP to EH, May 18, 1926, *Only Thing*, 38. Berg, *Perkins*, 95-98. Svoboda, *Hemingway and Sun*, beginning cut: 131-137; FSF to EH thereon: 137-140. Delmore Schwartz, "The Fiction of Ernest Hemingway," *Perspectives U.S.A.*, No. 13 (Autumn 1955), 71. Reynolds, *Paris Years*, 40-42. EH to MP, June 5, 1926, *SL*, 208-209. MP to FSF, May 29, 1926, *Only Thing*, 41-43.. FSF to MP, ca. June 25, 1926, and ca. August 10, 1926, *Scott/Max*, 144, 145. MP to FSF, August 17, 1926, PUL. MP to EH, July 20, 1926, PUL. SD, "Wooing," 702-710. EH to FSF, ca. September 7, 1926, *SL*, 216-217. MP to EH, October 30, 1926, *Only Thing*, 47. EH to MP, November 16, 1926, *SL*, 223-224. FSF to EH, December 23, 1926, *Letters*, 298-299. FSF to O'Hara, July 25, 1936, *Letters*, 538.

The End of Something

FSF to MP, ca. August 10, 1926, *Letters*, 230. EH to FSF, ca. December 24, 1925, *SL*, 182. Mellow, *Invented*, 271-273. Bruccoli, *Composition*, 33, 39. FSF to Ober, July 1926, *As Ever*, 92. Ober to FSF, August 12, 1926, PUL. EH to FSF, ca. September 7, 1926, *SL*, 216-217. FSF to EH, fall 1926, *Letters*, 296-297. Sara Murphy to EH, ca. fall 1926, and Gerald Murphy to EH, September 6, 1926, Miller, *Lost Generation*, 24, 23. EH to Hadley Hemingway, November 18, 1926, *SL*, 228. Stephens, *Critical Reception*, 31-35. Reynolds, *Homecoming*, 81-82. EH to FSF, ca. November 24, 1926, *SL*, 231-233. FSF to EH, December 1926 and December 23, 1926, *Letters*, 298.

The Case of Harold Stearns

FSF to EH, December 28, 1928, *Letters*, 207. EH to Stein, ca. May 15, 1924 and January 20, 1925, *SL*, 118, 121. FSF to Woollcott, fall 1925, *Letters*, 486-487. EH to FSF, December 15, 1925 and ca. December 24, 1925, *SL*, 177, 180-181. EH to FSF, May 4, 1926 and ca. May 20, 1926, *SL*, 203, 204. EH, *Sun*, 42-51, 73. FSF to EH, December 28, 1928, and FSF to MP, October/November 1928, *Life in Letters*, 161, 159. EH to Mizener, April 22, 1950, *SL*, 243.

Oceans Apart

Bruccoli, *Grandeur*, 257-260. FSF to EH, March 14, 1927, PUL. Bruccoli, *Scott and Ernest*, 56-58. FSF to EH, March 1927, *Letters*, 299. EH to FSF, March 31, 1927, *SL*, 248-250.. FSF to EH, telegram, March 27, 1927, PUL. FSF to EH, April 18, 1927, *Life in Letters*, 149. MP to FSF, May 10, 1927, and FSF to MP, ca. May 12, 1927, *Scott/Max*, 146-147. MP to EH, April 13, 1927 and October 14, 1927, *Only Thing*, 61, 66-67. MacLeish to EH, ca. November 1927, *Letters of Archibald MacLeish*, ed. R.H. Winnick (Boston: Houghton Mifflin, 1983), 199. FSF to EH, November 1927, *Letters*, 300-301. FSF to Mencken, inscribed in *Men Without Women*, ca. October 1927, *Life in Letters*, 210. Woolf, "An Essay in Criticism," *New York Herald Tribune Books*, October 9, 1927), 1, 8.. SD, "Woolf vs. Hemingway," 340-342. F.P.A., "The Importance of Being Ernest," "The Conning Tower," JFK. EH to FSF, ca. November 1927, PUL. MP to EH, June 8, 1927, *Only Thing*, 62. FSF to MP, September 1927, *Life in Letters*, 207. EH to MP, September 15, 1927, *Only Thing*, 64. EH to FSF, September 15, 1927, *SL*, 260-262. FSF to EH, December 1927, *Letters*, 302-303. FSF, "Babylon Revisited," *Short Stories*, 618-619. EH to FSF, ca. December 15, 1927, *SL*, 267-268. EH to FSF, ca. December 25, 1927, PUL. Baker, *Life Story*, 189-190. "The Bruiser and the Poet," *Times Literary Supplement*, July 9, 1964, 613, and September 3, 1964, 803. Alan Margolies, "'Particular Rhythms' and Other Influences: Hemingway and *Tender Is the Night*," *Hemingway in Italy*, ed. Lewis, 69. FSF to MP, after January 24, 1928, *Correspondence*, 213. EH to MP, March 17, 1928, *SL*, 273-274. MP to EH, April 10, 1928, *Only Thing*, 70. Mellow, *Invented*, 315-316.EH to MP, April 21, 1928, *SL*, 276-277. MP to EH, April 27, 1928, *Only Thing*, 73. FSF to MP, ca. July 21, 1928, *Scott/Max*, 152. ZF to FSF, late summer/early fall 1930, *Correspondence*, 248. FSF to ZF, late summer (?) 1930, *Correspondence*, 240-241. FSF to EH, ca. July 1928, *Correspondence*, 220-221. EH to FSF, ca. October 9, 1928, *SL*, 287-289. MP to EH, September 17, 1928, *Only Thing*, 77. EH to MP, September 28, 1928, *SL*, 285. MP to EH, October 2, 1928, *Only Thing*, 81. EH to MP, October 11, 1928, *SL*, 289-290.

"Une Soirée Chez Monsieur Fitz . . ."

EH, Item 720b, JFK. Meyers, *Fitzgerald*, 181. EH, Item 183, JFK. Mellow, *Hemingway*, 365-366. Reynolds, *Homecoming*, 204, 208-209. Mellow, *Invented*, 328. EH to FSF, ca. December 9, 1928, *SL*, 291. EH to MP, December 16, 1928, *Only Thing*, 83-84. EH to MP, January 8, 1929, *SL*, 292. MP to FSF, January 23, 1929, *Correspondence*, 223.

1929: Breaking the Bonds

Reynolds, *1930s*, 3. FSF to MP, November 1928 and ca. March 1, 1929, *Life in Letters*, 159-160, 161. Mellow, *Invented*, 330, 333. EH to MP, April 3, 1929, *Only Thing*, 97. FSF to EH, May 17, 1929, *Letters*, 304. FSF to ZF, late summer (?) 1930, *Correspondence*, 240.
A Farewell to Criticism

FSF to MP, ca. April 1, 1929, *Letters*, 214. FSF to EH, June 1929, *Correspondence*, 225-228. Mann, "Fitzgerald's Critique," 141-153. Oldsey, *Hidden Craft*, 72-73. EH, "Valentine," *Little Review* 12 (May 1929), 42. FSF to EH, June 1, 1934, *Life in Letters*,

262-264. EH to MP, December 28, 1934, *Only Thing,* 219. FSF to O'Hara, July 25, 1936, *Letters,* 538. EH to Speiser, 1942, Yale. EH to Mizener, January 11, 1951, *SL,* 719. EH to Poore, January 23, 1953, *SL,* 800. SD, "Censorship," 85-93. EH to MP, June 7, 1929, *SL,* 297. EH to FSF, July 1929, PUL. MP to EH, August 14, 1929, *Only Thing,* 115. FSF to MP, ca. June 1929, *Letters,* 215. EH to MP, July 26, 1929, *Only Thing,* 110. FSF to EH, August 23, 1929, *Letters,* 331. FSF to EH, August 23, 1929, *Letters,* 305. Mellow, *Invented,* 342-345, 348. EH to FSF, September 4, 1929, *SL,* 304-305. FSF to EH, September 9, 1929, *Letters,* 305-307. EH to FSF, September 13, 1929, *SL,* 306-307.

The Bout with Morley Callaghan

FSF to MP, after January 24, 1928, *Correspondence,* 213. Callaghan, *That Summer,* 30, 68, 99-101, 124-126, 149-155, 156-159, 167, 189, 195-196, 209-216, 241-250, 254-255. Callaghan to FSF, June (?) 1929, *Correspondence,* 228-229. EH to MP, August 28, 1929, *Only Thing,* 116. EH to Mizener, January 4, 1951, *SL,* 716. Meyers, *Fitzgerald,* 184. EH to FSF, December 12, 1929, *SL,* 312-314. MP to FSF, December 17, 1929, *Scott/Max,* 160. MP to EH, December 27, 1929, *Only Thing,* 137-138. EH to Callaghan, January 4, 1930, *SL,* 318-319. EH to MP, January 10, 1930, *Only Thing,* 143. FSF to MP, January 21, 1930, *Letters,* 217.

Roiling the Waters

Ober to FSF, February 9, 1929, *As Ever,* 125-126. Ober to FSF, telegram, September 21, 1929, *As Ever,* 146. Paul Revere Reynolds to FSF, September 23, 1929, *As Ever,* 147. Ober to FSF, October 8, 1929, *As Ever,* 148-149. FSF to EH, after October 8, 1929, *Correspondence,* 230-231. FSF to Ober, late October 1929, *As Ever,* 153. FSF to Ober, mid-November 1929, *As Ever,* 157-159. EH to MP, October 3, 1929, *Only Thing,* 118-119. FSF to MP, ca. June 1929, *Scott/Max,* 156. MP to FSF, October 30, 1929, *Scott/Max,* 157. MP to EH, November 12, 1929, *Only Thing,* 122-123. EH to MP, November 20, 1929, *Only Thing,* 128-129. MP to EH, December 10, 1929, and EH to MP, November 17, 1929 (unsent) and November 19, 1929, *Only Thing,* 134, 123-125, 126. EH to MP, December 15, 1929, *Only Thing,* 134-135.

Une Soirée Chez Mademoiselle Stein

EH, "My Own Life," *New Yorker* 2 (February 12, 1927), 23. Reynolds, *1930s,* 29-31. Kirk Curnutt, "In the Temps de Gertrude," *French Connections,* ed. Kennedy and Bryer, 128-131. Mellow, *Invented,* 350-352. Stein, *Autobiography,* 220. FSF, ca. December 5 or 12, 1929, *SL,* 309-311. FSF to MP, March 4, 1934, *Letters,* 247. Bruccoli, *Scott and Ernest,* 161. SD, *By Force of Will,* 208-209. Munson, "Our Post-War Novel," *Bookman* 74 (October 1931), 142. Margaret C.-L. (Egloff) Gildea to Andrew Turnbull, December 16, 1958, PUL. EH, *Feast,* 27, 20-21, 118-119, 110-111.

The Slanderers

Baker, *Life Story,* 106-107. EH to MP, October 3, 1929, *Only Thing,* 119. MP to FSF, October 30, 1929, *Scott/Max,* 157-158. FSF to MP, ca. November 1,5 1929, *Letters,* 216. EH to MP, December 10, 1929 and December 15, 1929, *Only Thing,* 132-133, 135.

MP to EH, December 26, 1929 and December 27, 1929, *Only Thing*, 137. Smith, *Reader's Guide*, 224. FSF, *Notebooks*, #62. SD, *By Force of Will*, 208. EH, *Feast*, 186, 180-181. SD, "Fitzgerald's Nonfiction," in press. FSF, "I have often thought" fragment, PUL. ZF to FSF, late summer/early fall 1930, *Correspondence*, 248-250. EH, *Feast*, 183. SD, *Fool*, 73, 75-77. FSF to ZF, summer (?) 1930, *Life in Letters*, 198. ZF to FSF, late 1930 (?), PUL. Mellow, *Invented*, 358-360, 356. EH, *Feast*, 189-191. Meyers, *Fitzgerald*, 149-150.

Long Distance

SD, *Fool*, 97. Bruccoli, *Fitzgerald and Hemingway*, 206. EH to FSF, April 12, 1931, *SL*, 340, 339. Bruccoli, *Grandeur*, 312, 322. FSF to MP, ca. January 15, 1932, *Scott/Max*, 173. SD, "A Short History," 177, 188. ZF to FSF, December 1931, *Correspondence*, 279. FSF to MP, ca. May 14, 1932, *Scott/Max*, 176. MP to EH, 19 April 1932, and EH to MP, 2 June 1932, *Only Thing*, 166-169. EH to MP, November 15, 1932, *SL*, 376-377. MP to EH, June 11, 1932, *Only Thing*, 170. EH to MP, April 4, 1932, *Only Thing*, 162. EH to John Dos Passos, ca. April 12, 1932, *SL*, 356. EH to MP, July 27, 1932, *Only Thing*, 175. Hobson, *Mencken*, 346-348. EW, *Thirties*, 473-474. EW to Mizener, 1949, *Letters on Literature and Politics*, 233.

Dinner at the Aurora

Mellow, *Hemingway*, 416-419. FSF to MP, January 19, 1933, and FSF to EW, ca. February 1933, *Life in Letters*, 226-227. FSF, *Crack-Up*, 200. EH to MP, early February 1933 and February 23, 1933, *Only Thing*, 181, 184. EH, "Homage to Switzerland," *Short Stories*, 426. EW to FSF, October 21, 1933 and 4 November 1933, 230-231. FSF to MP, September 25 ,1933, *Scott/Max*, 182-183.

Missed Connections

FSF, "A Preface," ca. 1934, PUL. SD, "A Short History," 195. FSF to MP, March 4, 1934, *Scott/Max*, 194. FSF to Bishop, April 23, 1934, *Life in Letters*, 255. FSF to EW, ca. February 1933, *Life in Letters*, 277. EW, *Sixties*, 222. Eliot, blurbs on jacket of *Tender*. FSF to Eliot, May 21, 1934, *Correspondence*, 362-363. FSF to Samuel Marx, May 21, 1934, *Correspondence*, 364. Warren to FSF, October 12, 1934, PUL. FSF to MP, March 4, 1934 and August 24, 1934, *Letters*, 272, 277. FSF to MP, December 3, 1934, *Correspondence*, 394. ZF to FSF, after April 12, 1934, *Correspondence*, 354. SD, "A Short History," 196-197, 190-192. Reynolds, *1930s*, 168. MP to EH, February 7, 1934, and EH to MP, April 30, 1934, *Only Thing*, 207, 208-210. FSF to EH, May 10, 1934, *Letters*, 307. EH to FSF, May 28, 1934, *SL*, 407-409. FSF to EH, June 1, 1934, *Letters*, 308-310. ZF to FSF, after April 12, 1934, *Correspondence*, 355. EH to Gingrich, November 26, 1934, telegram, Neville. FSF to EH, December 3, 1934, in Bruccoli, *Scott & Ernest*, 125. EH to MP, December 28, 1934, *Only Thing*, 219. MP to FSF, February 18, 1935, *Scott/Max*, 216-217. MP to EH, February 27, 1935, *Only Thing*, 222. FSF to MP, April 15, 1935 and May 11, 1935, *Scott/Max*, 219-220, Bruccoli, *Scott and Ernest*, 127. EH to FSF, December 21, 1935, *SL*, 427-429. Stein, *Autobiography*, 216. Gauss quoted in Goldhurst, *Contemporaries*, 161. Kirk Curnutt, "In the Temps de Gertrude," *French Connections*, ed. Kennedy and Bryer, 131, 122. EH to Gingrich, November 16, 1934, *SL*, 410-411. EH to MP,

July 26, 1933, and MP to EH, September 22, 1933,*Only Thing*, 193, 201. Simon, *Biography*, 156, 209-210. FSF, *Notebooks*, #2068. Mellow, *Invented*, 431-432. FSF and ZF, "Auction — Model 1934," and FSF, "Sleeping and Waking," *Crack-Up*, 62, 63. SD, *By Force of Will*, 210-211. FSF. *Notebooks*, #1031, #1034. Bruccoli, *Grandeur*, 387-388. FSF to MP, April 23, 1938, and FSF to MP, December 24, 1938, *Life in Letters*, 360, 374. FSF to MP, November 20, 1934 and November 26, 1934, *Scott/Max*, 212, 214.

The Question of Influence

Emerson, "The American Scholar," *Selections from Ralph Waldo Emerson*, ed. Stephen Whicher (Boston; Houghton Mifflin Riverside, 1957), 68. Eliot, "Tradition and the Individual Talent," *Selected Essays* (New York: Harcourt, Brace, 1950), 4-6. Bruccoli, *Scott and Ernest*, 159. EH, *Death*, 2. FSF, *Gatsby*, 188-189. EH, *Farewell*, 331-332. FSF, "Ring," *Crack-Up*, 35. FSF to Bishop, January 30, 1935, and FSF to EH, June 1, 1934, *Letters*, 364-365, 309. Bruccoli, *Composition*, 121-122. Alan Margolies, "'Particular Rhythms' and Other Influences: Hemingway and *Tender Is the Night*," *Hemingway in Italy*, ed. Lewis, 69-74. Goldhurst, *Contemporaries*, 163-164. EH, *Sun*, 241-243, 245. Prigozy, "Measurement," 106. EH, *Across*, 34. FSF, "My Lost City," *Crack-Up*, 33.

Afternoon of an Author

Hobson, *Mencken*, 389. Laura Guthrie journal, PUL. FSF, note on bicycle racing, PUL. FSF, genius chart, PUL. SD, *Fool*, 133. MP to EH, August 30, 1935, and EH to MP, September 7, 1935, *Only Thing*, 224, 227. MP to FSF, September 28, 1935, *Scott/Max*, 225. Lounsberry, "Holograph," 38-39. EH, *Green Hills*, 23-24. MP to FSF, October 26, 1935, *Scott/Max*, 226. Lynn, *Hemingway*, 414. Mellow, *Hemingway*, 459. EH to FSF, December 16, 1935, *SL*, 424-425. EH to Dos Passos, December 17, 1935, *SL*, 427.

"The Crack-Up" and the Crack in "Snows"

SD, "Fitzgerald's Nonfiction," in press. FSF, "Ring," *Crack-Up*, 38-40. EH to John and Katharine Dos Passos, January 13, 1936, *SL*, 433. EH to MP, February 7, 1936, *SL*, 437-438. MP to EH, February 27, 1936, *Only Thing*, 238. EH to MP, April 9, 1936, *SL*, 444. FSF to Sara Murphy, March 30 ,1936, *Life in Letters*, 298. Gingrich, "Scott, Ernest and Whoever," 186. EH, "Snows," *Short Stories*, 72. FSF, "Rich Boy," *Short Stories*, 318. Lynn, *Hemingway*, 426. Bruccoli, *Scott and Ernest*, 131. FSF to EH, July 16, 1936, *Life in Letters*, 302. FSF to Beatrice Dance, September 15, 1936, *Letters*, 542-543. EH to MP, July 23, 1936, *Only Thing*, 245-246. Mellow, *Hemingway*, 470-471. FSF to MP, September 19, 1936, *Letters*, 267. FSF, *Crack-Up*, 77. EH, *Feast*, 208. Brenner, "Are We Going," 539-541. SD, *By Force of Will*, 55. Reynolds, *1930s*, 238. FSF to MP, before March 19, 1937, *Letters*, 272. MP to FSF, March 19, 1937, and FSF to MP, ca. May 10, 1937, *Scott/Max*, 236-237. FSF to MP, March 4, 1938, *Letters*, 276. MP to EH, August 23, 1938, *Only Thing*, 268-269. MP to FSF, September 1, 1938, *Scott/Max*, 248. FSF to MP, February 25, 1939, *Scott/Max*, 255. EH to Mizener, January 4, 1951, *SL*, 716. Eddy Dow, "The Rich Are Different," *New York Times Book Review* (November 13, 1998), 70.

Last Encounters

SD, *Fool*, 98. FSF, *Ledger*. FSF, "One Hundred False Starts," *Afternoon*, 131-132. FSF, *Notebooks*, #447. Bruccoli, *Grandeur*, 414. Mellow, *Invented*, 452-453. Mok, "The Other Side of Paradise," *F. Scott Fitzgerald in His Own Time*, ed. Bruccoli and Bryer, 294-299. Bruccoli, *Fitzgerald and Hemingway*, 194-195. EH to FSF, October 1936, telegram, JFK. MP to EH, October 1, 1936, *Only Thing*, 246-247. Meyers, *Fitzgerald*, 278-280. Mizener, *Far Side*, 266-267. Bishop, "Missing All," 106-121. FSF to MP, May 20, 1940, *Life in Letters*, 445. Lynn, *Hemingway*, 443. Reynolds, *1930s*, 270-271. Bruccoli, *Scott and Ernest*, 136. FSF to EH, June 5, 1937, *Life in Letters*, 324. Dardis, *Thirsty*, 151, FSF to EH, July 13, 1937, telegram, JFK. FSF to MP, ca. July 15, 1937, *Scott/Max*, 238.

Ambivalent to the End

MP to EH, August 5, 1937, *Only Thing*, 252. Baker, *Life Story*, 241-242, 317-318. FSF to MP, ca. August 20, 1937, MP to FSF, August 24, 1937, and FSF to MP, September 3, 1927, *Scott/Max*, 238, 239-240, 240-241. MP to EH, February 3, 1938, and EH to MP, mid-February 1938, *Only Thing*, 255, 256-257. SD, *By Force of Will*, 106-108. MP to FSF, April 8, 1938, and FSF to MP, April 23, 1938, *Scott/Max*, 243, 244. FSF, "Dame Rumor" playscript, PUL. Ring, *Current*, 66-67. FSF to Frances Turnbull, November 9, 1938, *Letters*, 578. FSF to Scottie Fitzgerald, November 15, 1938, November 25, 1938, and December 1938, *Letters*, 41, 45, 46. FSF to Morton Kroll, August 9, 1939, *Letters*, 593. FSF to Scottie Fitzgerald, November 29, 1940, *Life in Letters*, 472. FSF to MP, December 24, 1938, and MP to FSF, March 9, 1938, *Scott/Max*, 250, 243. Meyers, *Fitzgerald*, 269. FSF, *Notebooks*, #1915. FSF, "Early Success," *Crack-Up*, 87. FSF, *Notebooks*, #612, #1819, #1868, #1177. Bruccoli, *Grandeur*, 456-459. EH to MP, 25 March 1939, *Only Thing*, 275. MP to FSF, September 19, 1940, *Scott/Max*, 266. FSF to ZF, September 28, 1940 and October 26, 1940, *Letters*, 125, 128-129. EH to FSF, after October 24, 1940, inscription, *Correspondence*, 611. ZF to FSF, October 1940, PUL. FSF to EH, November 8, 1940, *Letters*, 312. FSF to ZF, October 19, 1940, October 23, 1940, and October 26, 1940, *Letters*, 127, 128, 129. FSF, *Notebooks*, #2066. Schulberg, conversation with Mizener, August 7, 1947, Mizener collection, Cornell. FSF to MP, October 14, 1940, PUL. Ring, *Current*, 96. Warren to FSF, December 21, 1940, PUL. MP to EH, December 28, 1940, *Only Thing*, 301.

Alcoholic Cases

FITZGERALD'S CASE

EH, *Feast*, 166. Goldhurst, *Contemporaries*, 174. Goodwin, *Alcohol*, 40-42. FSF, *Ledger*. Bruccoli, *Grandeur*, 57, 135-136, 143-144, 149, 185, 186-187, 221, 253-256. FSF to Robert D. Clark, February 9, 1920, *Life in Letters*, 45. Dardis, *Thirsty*, 103, 117-118. FSF to MP, August 24, 1921, *Life in Letters*, 48. Boyd quoted in Woodward, *Public Figure*, 84. FSF to EW, January 1922, *Life in Letters*, 50-51. FSF, "A Short Autobiography," *New Yorker* 5 (May 25, 1929), 22-23. FSF to MP, ca. April 10, 1924, *Life in Letters*, 67. EH, *Feast*, 166-167, 162-164, 171-174. Diliberto, *Hadley*, 193. EW, *Twenties*, 95. FSF to EH, September 9, 1929, *Letters*, 306. FSF to Dr. Oscar Forel, summer (?) 1930, FSF to Dr. Mildred Squires, March 1932 and spring 1932, FSF to Dr. Adolf Meyer, spring 1933, *Life in Letters*, 196-197, 211, 213, 231-233.

The Fictional Evidence

Gilmore, *Equivocal Spirits*, 98-100, 103, 104-105, 107-109, 111-118.. FSF, "A New Leaf," *Short Stories*, 636-638. FSF, *Ledger*. FSF to MP, November 8, 1934, *Scott/Max*, 210. FSF to Ober, December 8, 1934, *Life in Letters*, 273-274. SD, *Fool*, 158-161, 168-173, 198-203. Meyers, *Fitzgerald*, 146. Boyd quoted in Woodward, *Public Figure*, 85. FSF to MP, March 11, 1935, *Life in Letters*, 277-278. Ring to Turnbull, April 12, 1961, PUL. FSF to Dr. Robert S. Carroll and Dr. R. Burke Suitt, April 7, 1938, *Life in Letters*, 356. Dardis, *Thirsty*, 152. FSF to Hayward, January 16, 1940, *Life in Letters*, 429. SD, "A Death in Hollywood," 106. Goodwin, *Alcohol*, 36.

HEMINGWAY'S CASE

EH to his family, July 21, 1918, *SL*, 12. EH, *Farewell*, 143-145. Dardis, *Thirsty*, 158-159, 180, 175, 163, 157, 190, 188-189, 199-200, 201. EH to Smith, December 13, 1918, and EH to Jenkins, June 16, 1919,*SL*, 20, 25. EH to Dos Passos, April 22, 1925, *SL*, 158. SD, "Writers and Drinking," 313. Diliberto, *Hadley*, 99. EH to MP, August 28, 1929, *Only Thing*, 116. EH, *Green Hills*, 28. EH to Kashkin, August 19, 1935, *SL*, 420. EH to MP, ca. 4 or February 11, 1940, *SL*, 500. Meyers, *Fitzgerald*, 366. EH to FSF, December 16, 1935, *SL*, 425. Goodwin, *Alcohol*, 63, 58, 65-71. EH to Mizener, April 22, 1950, *SL*, 690. Ross, "Portrait." Fuentes, *Cuba*, 63-66. Gingrich, "Coming to Terms with Scott and Ernest," 64. Reynolds, *Final Years*, 300-301.

A Writer's Disease

Dardis, *Thirsty*, 14-15. SD, "Writers and Drinking," 315-324. SD, *Fool*, 160, 169. Goodwin, *Alcohol*, 47-48. Cowley, *Situation*, 206-207. Percy, "Orbiting Self," 250, 252, 254. Hamill, *Drinking Life*, 17, 256, 261, 264.

That Prone Body

MP to EH, December 31, 1940, *Only Thing*, 301-302. MP to Lemmon, January 3, 1941, PUL. FSF, *Tycoon*, introd. Bruccoli, lxvii-lxxiii, lxxv-lxxvi. MP to EH, April 4, 1941, *Only Thing*, 307. EH to MP, April 29, 1941, *SL*, 523. EH to MP, November 15, 1941, *Only Thing*, 313-314. EH to Scribner, August 13, 1948, PUL. EH to Scribner, October 4, 1949, *SL*, 678-679. MP to EW, June 18, 1941, Yale. SD, "Remaking of Reputation," 2. SD, *Fool*, 149. MP to EW, February 16, 1941 and 24 February 1941, Yale. Laughlin to EW, August 3 and August 17, 1943, and EW to Biggs, August 10, 1943, Yale. EH to Speiser, 1943, PUL. EH to MP, February 25, 1944, *Only Thing*, 329-330. EH to MP, July 23, 1945, *SL*, 594-595. EH to Scribner, ca. October 1948, PUL. EH to Scribner, August 16, 1949, PUL. EH to Scribner, May 18-19, 1951, *SL*, 726. EH, "The Art of the Short Story," 100. EH to Cowley, September 5, 1948 and February 10, 1949, Neville. Cowley to EH, August 11, 1951, Neville. EH to Cowley, July 24, 1951, September 16, 1951, and November 8, 1951, Neville. EH to Mizener, July 6, 1949, *SL*, 657-658. EH to Mizener, April 22, 1950 and May 12, 1950, 689-690, 694-695. EH to Breit, January 17, 1951, and EH to Mizener, January 18, 1951, JFK. Bruccoli, *Fitzgerald and Hemingway*, 222. Dardis, *Thirsty*, 208. EH to Cowley, May 13, 1951, June 1, 1951, and June 2, 1951, Neville. EH to Fenton, June 12, 1952, Neville. EH to Poore, April 3, 1953, JFK. Baker, *Life Story*, 491. O'Hara, review of *Across*, *New York Times Book Review* (September 10, 1950), 1. EH to Poore, March 16, 1953, JFK. EH to Breit, August 18, 1954, *SL*, 834-836.

Poor Butterfly

Flaubert quoted in "Along Publishers Row," *Authors Guild Bulletin* (Summer 1998), 28. Worcester, *Satire*, 26-27. EH, *Dateline*, 114, 255. SD, "Hemingway's Attack," in press. EH to Mizener, May 12, 1950, *SL*, 694. EH, *Feast*, 207-208. EH to Scribner, September 14, 1949, PUL. EH to Mizener, July 6, 1949, *SL*, 657. EH to Breit, May 12, 1953, JFK. SD, *By Force of Will*, 68-69. EH to MP, November 15, 1941, *SL*, 528. EH to Wallace Meyer, March 4 and 7, 1952, *SL*, 758. EH, Item 486, JFK. EH, *Feast*, 147. Tavernier-Courbin, *Hemingway's Feast*, 11-12, 99. Egan, "Lies," 68-69, 79-80. Nabokov, "Invitation to a Transformation," *New York Times Book Review* (April 25, 1999), 35. Kronenberger, *Cutting Edge*, viii, xii.

The Spoils of Posterity

Lynn, *Dream*, 248. Lingeman, "Mencken and Dreiser," 1. EH to Breit, July 8, 1950, *SL*, 701. Hall, *Glittering*, 9. Baker, *Life Story*, 461, 495, 503, 526, 532. SD, *By Force of Will*, 252-253. EH, "The Art of the Short Story," 96-97.

Bejeweled by Bunny Wilson

SD, "Death," 106. Woodward, *Public Figure*, 77, 51, 295. Epstein, "Third Act," 52-54. EW to FSF, November 21, 1919, *Letters on Literature and Politics*, 45-47. Meyers, "Fitzgerald and Wilson," 375, 377-378, 382. Cohen, "Regret," 64-75. Elias, "Composition and Revision," 253-256. EW, "F. Scott Fitzgerald," *Shores of Light*, 27-33. FSF to EW, January 1922, *Letters*, 330. Rascoe quoted in Woodward, *Public Figure*, 102. EW and FSF, "Dog," Bruccoli, *Grandeur*, 136. EW to Mencken, May 12, 1922, *Letters on Literature and Politics*, 82. EW, "The Delegate from Great Neck," *Shores of Light*, 141-142, 151-155. FSF, *Crack-Up*, 79. FSF to EW, May 16, 1939, *Letters*, 348. SD, "Remaking of Reputation," 5-6. FSF to MP, before December 12, 1921, *Letters*, 151. EW to Basso, May 9, 1929, and EW to MP, October 18, 1938, quoted in Cohen, "Regret," 71. Dolan, *Modern Lives*, 148, 126-127, 119-120. Eliot to FSF, December 31, 1925, *Crack-Up*, 310. Rosenfeld, "F. Scott Fitzgerald," *Crack-Up*, 317-318. Wescott, "The Moral of Scott Fitzgerald," *Crack-Up*, 327-329, 334-337. Dos Passos, "A Note on Fitzgerald," *Crack-Up*, 338-339. Bishop, "The Hours," *Crack-Up*, 344-345. EW, "Dedication," *Crack-Up*, 7-9. Goldhurst, *Contemporaries*, 62-63. MP to EH, June 21, 1941 and January 7, 1929, *Only Thing*, 326, 84. Way, *Social Fiction*, 146-148. Hook, "Cases for Reconsideration," *Promises of Life*, ed. Lee, 20. FSF, *Gatsby* (New York: Modern Library, 1934), vii. Clark, "The Love Song of F. Scott Fitzgerald," *Commonweal* 56 (25 April 1952), 72. Baker, "Curses! Robbed Again!" *New York Times* (30 December 1971), 25.

The Writer as Celebrity

SD, "Hemingway and Fame," *Companion*, 1, 4, 6-7, 9, 10-11. SD, *By Force of Will*, 2. Reynolds, *1930s*, 14-15, 105. Baker, *Life Story*, 518-522. EW, "Emergence of Ernest Hemingway," *Shores of Light*, 115-124. EW to EH, January 7, 1927, May 4, 1927, and May 18, 1927, *Letters on Literature and Politics*, 140-141. EW, "The Sportsman's Tragedy," *Shores of Light*, 339-344. EH, "Valentine," *Little Review* 12 (May 1929), 42.

EH to MP, August 12, 1930, December 1, 1930, and December 8, 1930 (telegram), *Only Thing*, 145, 150-151, 152. EW to FSF, March 26, 1933, *Letters on Literature and Politics*, 229. EW, "Letter to the Russians about Hemingway," *Shores of Light*, 618-622. Stephens, *Nonfiction*, 22. EW to Cowley, October 20, 1938, *Letters on Literature and Politics*, 310. EW, "Hemingway and the Wars," *Nation* 147 (December 10, 1938), 630. EH to EW, ca. December 10, 1938, JFK. Raeburn, *Fame*, 55. EW, "Return of Ernest Hemingway," *New Republic* 103 (October 28, 1940), 591-592. EW, "Hemingway: Gauge of Morale," *Atlantic* 164 (July 1939), 36-46. EW to Florine Katz, March 7, 1941, and EW to MP, June 9, 1941 and July 3, 1941, *Letters on Literature and Politics*, 387-388. EH to Mizener, May 12, 1950, *SL*, 694-695. EW to Stein, April 17, 1942, and EW to Alfred Kazin, July 8, 1961, *Letters on Literature and Politics*, 346, 602. EW, *Sixties*, 47. EW, "That Summer in Paris," *Bit*, 525. Mary Hemingway, "Department of Amplification," *New Yorker* 39 (March 16, 1963), 160, 162-163. SD, interview of Mary Hemingway, September 1975.

Commercializing the Product

Didion, "Last Words," 79-80, 77, 74. EH to MP, April 29, 1941, *SL*, 523. SD, interview of Marla A. Metzner, May 5, 1999. Beegel, "The Critical Reception," *Companion*, ed. SD, 278. "Modern Library's Classics," *F. Scott Fitzgerald Society Newsletter* 8 (December 1998), 17. Hook, "Cases for Reconsideration," *Promises of Life*, ed. Lee, 18-20. Cowley, *Literary Situation*, 127. Bruccoli, *Scott and Ernest*, 159. FSF to Scottie Fitzgerald, spring 1938, *Letters*, 29. Epstein, "Third Act," 56.

The Master and the Actor

FSF, *Notebooks*, #1918. Roethke, "Song for the Squeeze Box," *Collected*, 111. Prigozy, "Measurement," 108-109. Mellow, *Invented*, 244. EH to MP, July 23, 1945, *SL*, 594. EW, *Twenties*, 94. Bruccoli, *Grandeur*, 62. Hobson, *Mencken*, 389. SD, *By Force of Will*, 188-189. Sanderson, "Hemingway and Gender History," *Companion*, ed. SD, 175-179. Fuentes, *Cuba*, 415-416. Kennedy, "Gender Trouble," 196-199. Reynolds, *Final Years*, 156, 271. Comley and Scholes, *Genders*, 146. FSF, "Girls Believe in Girls," *Liberty* 7 (February 8, 1930), 22-24. SD, "Short History," 186-167. SD, *Fool*, 86. FSF, "Wanda Breasted," *Tender Is the Night*, ed. Cowley (New York: Scribner's, 1951), 338-345.

Psychological Speculations

Eliot, "Four Quartets," *Complete*, 129, 144. Waite, *Psychopathic*, xii-xiv. SD, "Hemingway and Suicide," 287-295. Yaloms, "Psychiatric View," 487-494. EH, *SL*, introd. Baker, xvii-xix. Stewart, "An Interview," *Fitzgerald/Hemingway Annual 1973* (Washington, D.C.: NCR Microcard Editions, 1974), 85. Tavernier-Courbin, *Hemingway's Feast*, 119. FSF, *Crack-Up*, 69. Sara Murphy to FSF, April 3, 1936, in Miller, *Lost Generation*, 161. Reynolds, *1930s*, 195. Mizener, *Far Side*, 20-21. FSF, *Notebooks*, #23. SD, *Fool*, 191, 192, 59, 13-15, 164-165. FSF to Scottie Fitzgerald, November 4, 1939, 63. Mellow, *Invented*, xx. Bruccoli, *Grandeur*, 135, 267, 322. Gingrich, "Coming to Terms," 58. Panken, *Joy in Suffering*, 139. Offit, *Sexual Self*, 57-58, 62-64. Mellow, *Invented*, 353. FSF, *Notebooks*, #728. EH to Mizener, April 22, 1950, *SL*, 690.

BIBLIOGRAPHY

Astro, Richard, and Jackson J. Benson. *Hemingway in Our Time*. Corvallis: Oregon State University Press, 1974.

Baker, Carlos. *Ernest Hemingway: A Life Story*. New York: Charles Scribner's Sons, 1969.

Banta, Martha. *Failure & Success in America: A Literary Debate*. Princeton, NJ: Princeton University Press, 1978.

Beegel, Susan F. *Hemingway's Craft of Omission*. Ann Arbor: UMI Research Press, 1987.

Beegel, Susan F., editor. *Hemingway's Neglected Short Fiction: New Perspectives*. Tuscaloosa: University of Alabama Press, 1989.

Berg, A. Scott. *Max Perkins: Editor of Genius*. New York: Dutton, 1978.

Berman, Ronald. *The Great Gatsby and Modern Times*. Urbana: University of Illinois Press, 1994.

Bishop, John Peale. "The Missing All." *Virginia Quarterly Review* 13 (Winter 1937): 106-121.

Braudy, Leo. *The Frenzy of Renown: Fame and Its History*. New York: Oxford University Press, 1986.

Brenner, Gerry. "Are We Going to Hemingway's Feast?" *American Literature* 54 (November 1982): 528-544.

Bruccoli, Matthew J. *The Composition of "Tender Is the Night": A Study of the Manuscripts*. Pittsburgh: University of Pittsburgh Press, 1953.

———. *F. Scott Fitzgerald: A Descriptive Bibliography*. Pittsburgh: University of Pittsburgh Press, 1972.

———. *Supplement to F. Scott Fitzgerald: A Descriptive Bibliography*. Pittsburgh: University of Pittsburgh Press, 1980.

———. *Fitzgerald and Hemingway: A Dangerous Friendship*. New York: Carroll and Graf, 1994.

———. *Scott and Ernest: The Authority of Failure and the Authority of Success*. New York: Random House, 1978.

———. *Some Sort of Epic Grandeur: The Life of F. Scott Fitzgerald*. New York: Harcourt Brace Jovanovich, 1981.

Bryer, Jackson R., editor. *F. Scott Fitzgerald: The Critical Reception*. New York: Burt Franklin, 1978.

Burwell, Rose Marie. *Hemingway: The Postwar Years and the Posthumous Novels*. New York: Cambridge University Press, 1996.

Callaghan, Morley. *That Summer in Paris*. New York: Coward-McCann, 1963.

Cohen, Milton A. "Fitzgerald's Third Regret: Intellectual Pretense and the Ghost of Edmund Wilson." *Texas Studies in Literature and Language* 33 (Spring 1991): 64-88.

Comley, Nancy R., and Robert Scholes. *Hemingway's Genders: Rereading the Hemingway Text*. New Haven, CT: Yale University Press, 1994.

Cowley, Malcolm. *The Literary Situation*. New York: Viking, 1954.

Crowley, John W. *The White Logic: Alcoholism and Gender in American Modernist Fiction*. Amherst: University of Massachusetts Press, 1994.

Dardis, Tom. *The Thirsty Muse: Alcohol and the American Writer*. New York: Ticknor and Fields, 1989.

Didion, Joan. "Last Words." *New Yorker* 74 (November 9, 1998): 74-80.

Diliberto, Gioia. *Hadley*. New York: Ticknor and Fields, 1992.

Dolan, Marc. "The Good Writer's Tale: The Fictional Method of Hemingway's 'Scott Fitzgerald.'" *Hemingway Review* 12 (Spring 1993): 62-71.

———. *Modern Lives: A Cultural Re-reading of "The Lost Generation"*. West Lafayette, IN: Purdue University Press, 1996.

Donaldson, Scott. *By Force of Will: The Life and Art of Ernest Hemingway*. New York: Viking, 1977.

———. editor. *Cambridge Companion to Hemingway*. New York: Cambridge University Press, 1996.

———. "Censorship and *A Farewell to Arms*." *Studies in American Fiction* 19 (Spring 1991): 85-93.

———. "A Death in Hollywood: F. Scott Fitzgerald Remembered." *Iowa Review* 26 (Spring 1996): 105-112.

———. "Fitzgerald's Nonfiction." *Cambridge Companion to Fitzgerald*. Edited by Ruth Prigozy. New York: Cambridge University Press, in press.

———. "F. Scott Fitzgerald: The Remaking of a Reputation." *William and Mary Alumni Gazette* (Winter 1983): 2-8.

———. *Fool for Love: F. Scott Fitzgerald*. New York: Congdon & Weed, 1983.

———. "Hemingway and Suicide." *Sewanee Review* 103 (Spring 1995): 287-295.

———. "Hemingway's Attack on Fitzgerald's Reputation," in press.

———. "The Jilting of Ernest Hemingway." *Virginia Quarterly Review* 65 (Autumn 1989): 661-673.

———. "The Political Development of F. Scott Fitzgerald." *Prospects* 6, 313-355. Edited by Jack Salzman. New York: Burt Franklin, 1981.

———. "Scott Fitzgerald's Romance with the South." *Southern Literary Journal* 5 (Spring 1973): 3-17.

———. "'A Very Short Story' as Therapy." *Hemingway's Neglected Fiction: New Perspectives*, 99-105. Edited by Susan Beegel. Ann Arbor: UMI Press, 1989.

———. "Woolf vs. Hemingway." *Journal of Modern Literature* 10 (June 1983): 338-342.

———. "Writers and Drinking in America." *Sewanee Review* 98 (Spring 1990): 312-324.

Egan, Susanna. "Lies, Damned Lies, and Autobiography: Hemingway's Treatment of Fitzgerald in *A Moveable Feast*." *Auto/Biography Studies* 9 (1994): 64-82.

Elias, Amy J. "The Composition and Revision of Fitzgerald's *The Beautiful and Damned*." *Princeton University Library Chronicle* 51 (Spring 1990): 245-266.

Eliot, T.S. *The Complete Poems and Plays, 1909-1950*. New York: Harcourt, Brace and World, 1952.

Epstein, Joseph. "F. Scott Fitzgerald's Third Act." *Commentary* 98 (November 1994): 52-57.

Fetterley, Judith. *The Resisting Reader: A Feminist Approach to American Fiction*. Bloomington: Indiana University Press, 1978.

Fitzgerald, F. Scott. *The Apprentice Fiction of F. Scott Fitzgerald, 1908-1917*. Edited by John Kuehl. New Brunswick, NJ: Rutgers University Press, 1965.

————. *Afternoon of an Author*. Introduced and annotated by Arther Mizener. Princeton, N.J.: Princeton University Press, 1957.

————. *As Ever, Scott Fitz —: Letters between F. Scott Fitzgerald and His Literary Agent Harold Ober, 1919-1940*. Edited by Matthew J. Bruccoli. Philadelphia: J.B. Lippincott, 1972.

————. *The Beautiful and Damned*. New York: Charles Scribner's Sons, 1922.

————. *Correspondence of F. Scott Fitzgerald*. Edited by Matthew J. Bruccoli and Margaret M. Duggan. New York: Random House, 1980.

————. *The Crack-Up*. Edited by Edmund Wilson. New York: New Directions, 1945.

————. *Dear Scott/Dear Max: The Fitzgerald-Perkins Correspondence*. Edited by John Kuehl and Jackson R. Bryer. New York: Charles Scribner's Sons, 1971.

————. *F. Scott Fitzgerald: A Life in Letters*. Edited by Matthew J. Bruccoli. New York: Simon and Schuster, 1994.

————. *F. Scott Fitzgerald in His Own Time: A Miscellany*. Edited by Matthew J. Bruccoli and Jackson R. Bryer. Kent, OH: Kent State University Press, 1978.

————. *F. Scott Fitzgerald on Authorship*. Edited by Matthew J. Bruccoli. Columbia: University of South Carolina Press, 1996.

————. *F. Scott Fitzgerald's Ledger: A Facsimile*. Introduced by Matthew J. Bruccoli. Washington, D.C.: NCR/Microcard Editions, 1973.

————. *The Great Gatsby*. New York: Charles Scribner's Sons, 1925.

————. *The Last Tycoon*. Edited by Edmund Wilson. New York: Charles Scribner's Sons, 1941.

————. *The Letters of F. Scott Fitzgerald*. Edited by Andrew Turnbull. New York: Charles Scribner's Sons, 1963.

————. *The Love of the Last Tycoon: A Western*. Edited by Matthew J. Bruccoli, New York: Cambridge University Press, 1993.

————. "My Generation." *Esquire* 70 (October 1968): 119, 121.

————. "Scott Fitzgerald's 'Thoughtbook.'" Introduced by John Kuehl. *Princeton University Library Chronicle* 26 (Winter 1965): 102-108 and unpaginated plates.

————. *The Short Stories of F. Scott Fitzgerald*. Edited by Matthew J. Bruccoli. New York: Charles Scribner's Sons, 1989.

————. *Tender Is the Night: A Romance*. New York: Charles Scribner's Sons, 1934.

————. *Tender Is the Night: A Romance*. Edited by Malcolm Cowley. New York: Charles Scribner's Sons, 1951.

————. *This Side of Paradise*. Edited by James L.W. West III. New York: Cambridge University Press, 1995 [1920].

Friskey, Elizabeth. "Visiting the Golden Girl." *Princeton Alumni Weekly* (October 8, 1974): 10-11.

Fuentes, Norberto. *Hemingway in Cuba*. Secaucus, NJ: Lyle Stuart, 1984.

Gilmore, Thomas B. *Equivocal Spirits: Alcoholism and Drinking in Twentieth-Century Literature*. Chapel Hill: University of North Carolina Press, 1987.

Gingrich, Arnold. "Scott, Ernest and Whoever." *Esquire* 66 (December 1966): 186-189, 322-325.

———. "Coming to Terms with Scott and Ernest." *Esquire* 99 (June 1983): 54-56, 58, 60, 62, 64.

Goldhurst, William. *F. Scott Fitzgerald and His Contemporaries*. Cleveland, OH: World, 1963.

Goodwin, Donald W. *Alcohol and the Writer*. Kansas City, MO: Andrews and McMeel, 1988.

Graham, Sheilah, and Gerold Frank. *Beloved Infidel*. New York: Holt, 1958.

Gullo, Stephen, and Connie Church. "Love Survival: How to Mend a Broken Heart." *Health* 20 (August 1988): 50-53, 77.

Hall, Donald. *Those Ancient Glittering Eyes*. New York: Ticknor & Fields, 1992.

Hamill, Pete. *A Drinking Life*. Boston: Little, Brown, 1994.

Hanneman, Audre. *Ernest Hemingway: A Comprehensive Bibliography*. Princeton, NJ: Princeton University Press, 1967.

Hemingway, Ernest. *Across the River and into the Trees*. New York: Charles Scribner's Sons, 1950.

———. "The Art of the Short Story." *Paris Review* 79 (Spring 1981): 85-105.

———. *Complete Poems*. Edited by Nicholas Gerogiannis. Lincoln: University of Nebraska Press, 1992.

———. *Dateline: Toronto*. Edited by William White. New York: Charles Scribner's Sons, 1985.

———. *Death in the Afternoon*. New York: Charles Scribner's Sons, 1932.

———. *A Farewell to Arms*. New York: Charles Scribner's Sons, 1929.

———. *The Fifth Column and the First Forty-Nine Stories*. New York: Charles Scribner's Sons, 1938.

———. *For Whom the Bell Tolls*. New York: Charles Scribner's Sons, 1940.

———. *The Garden of Eden*. New York: Charles Scribner's Sons, 1986.

———. *Green Hills of Africa*. New York: Charles Scribner's Sons, 1935.

———. *The Hemingway Reader*. Selected by Charles Poore. New York: Charles Scribner's Sons, 1953.

———. *A Moveable Feast*. New York: Charles Scribner's Sons, 1964.

———. *The Old Man and the Sea*. New York: Charles Scribner's Sons, 1952.

———. *The Only Thing That Counts: The Ernest Hemingway/Maxwell Perkins Correspondence, 1925-1947*. Edited by Matthew J. Bruccoli. New York: Scribner, 1996.

———. *Selected Letters, 1917-1961*. Edited by Carlos Baker. New York: Charles Scribner's Sons, 1981.

———. *The Short Stories of Ernest Hemingway*. New York: Charles Scribner's Sons, 1954.

———. *The Sun Also Rises*. New York: Charles Scribner's Sons, 1926.

———. *The Torrents of Spring*. New York: Charles Scribner's Sons, 1926.

———. *To Have and Have Not*. New York: Charles Scribner's Sons, 1937.

Hemingway, Jack. *Misadventures of a Fly Fisherman: My Life with and without Papa*. Dallas: Taylor, 1986.

Hobson, Fred. *Mencken: A Biography*. New York: Random House, 1994.

Kennedy, J. Gerald. *Imagining Paris: Exile, Writing, and American Identity*. New Haven, CT: Yale University Press, 1993.

———. "Hemingway's Gender Trouble." *American Literature* 63 (June 1991): 187-207.

———, and Jackson R. Bryer. *French Connections: Hemingway and Fitzgerald Abroad*. New York: St. Martin's, 1998.

Kronenberger, Louis. *The Cutting Edge*. Garden City, N.Y.: Doubleday, 1970.

Lee, A. Robert, editor. *Scott Fitzgerald: The Promises of Life*. New York: St. Martin's, 1989.

Leenaars, Antoon A. "Psychological Perspectives on Suicide." *Current Concepts of Suicide*, 159-167. Edited by David Lester. Philadelphia: Charles Press, 1990.

Lehan, Richard D. *F. Scott Fitzgerald and the Craft of Fiction*. Carbondale: Southern Illinois University Press, 1966.

Le Vot, Andre. *Scott Fitzgerald: A Biography*. Garden City, NY: Doubleday, 1983.

Lewis, Robert W., editor. *Hemingway in Italy and Other Essays*. New York: Praeger, 1990.

Lingeman, Richard. "Mencken and Dreiser: Friends, When Speaking." *New York Times Book Review* (March 8, 1992): 1, 25.

Lounsberry, Barbara. "The Holograph Manuscript of *Green Hills of Africa*." *Hemingway Review* 12 (Spring 1993): 36-45.

Lynn, Kenneth S. *The Dream of Success: A Study of the Modern American Imagination*. Westport, CT: Greenwood, 1955.

———. *Hemingway*. New York: Simon and Schuster, 1987.

Mann, Charles. "F. Scott Fitzgerald's Critique of *A Farewell to Arms*." *Fitzgerald/Hemingway Annual 1976*, 141-153. Edited by Matthew J. Bruccoli. Englewood, CO: Information Handling Systems, 1978.

Mellow, James R. *Hemingway: A Life without Consequences*. Boston: Houghton Mifflin, 1992.

———. *Invented Lives: F. Scott and Zelda Fitzgerald*. Boston: Houghton Mifflin, 1984.

Mencken, H.L. *My Life as Author and Editor*. New York: Knopf, 1993.

Meyers, Jeffrey. *Edmund Wilson: A Biography*. Boston: Houghton Mifflin, 1995.

———. *Hemingway: A Biography*. New York: Harper and Row, 1985.

———. *Scott Fitzgerald: A Biography*. New York: HarperCollins, 1994.

———. "Scott Fitzgerald and Edmund Wilson." *American Scholar* 61 (Summer 1992): 375-388.

Miller, Linda Patterson, editor. *Letters from the Lost Generation: Gerald and Sara Murphy and Friends*. New Brunswick, NJ: Rutgers University Press, 1991.

Nagel, James, editor. *Ernest Hemingway: The Oak Park Legacy*. Tuscaloosa: University of Alabama Press, 1996.

Offit, Avodah. *The Sexual Self*. Philadelphia: J.B. Lippincott, 1977.

Oldsey, Bernard. *Hemingway's Hidden Craft: The Writing of* A Farewell to Arms. University Park: Pennsylvania State University Press, 1979.

Panken, Shirley. *The Joy of Suffering: Psychoanalytic Theory and Therapy of Masochism*. New York: Jason Aronson, 1973.

Percy, Walker. "The Orbiting Self." *Lost in the Cosmos*. New York: Farrar, Straus and Giroux, 1983.

Pizer, Donald. *American Expatriate Writing and the Paris Moment*. Baton Rouge: Louisiana State University Press, 1996.

Prigozy, Ruth. "A Matter of Measurement." *Commonweal* 72 (October 29, 1971): 103-109.

Raeburn, John. *Fame Became of Him: Hemingway as Public Writer.* Bloomington: Indiana University Press, 1984.

Reynolds, Michael. *Hemingway: The American Homecoming.* Cambridge, MA: Basil Blackwell, 1992.

———. *Hemingway: The Final Years.* New York: W.W. Norton, 1999

———. *Hemingway: The 1930s.* New York: W.W. Norton, 1997.

———. *Hemingway: The Paris Years.* Cambridge, MA: Basil Blackwell, 1989.

———. *The Young Hemingway.* Cambridge, MA: Basil Blackwell, 1986.

Ring, Francis Kroll. *Against the Current: As I Remember F. Scott Fitzgerald.* Berkeley, CA: Creative Arts, 1985.

Roethke, Theodore. *The Collected Poems of Theodore Roethke.* Seattle: University of Washington Press, 1982.

Ross, Lillian. "Portrait of Hemingway." *Reporting.* New York: Simon and Schuster, 1964.

Sanford, Marcelline Hemingway. *At the Hemingways: With Fifty Years of Correspondence between Ernest and Marcelline Hemingway.* Moscow: University of Idaho Press, 1999.

Siegel, Ronald K. *Whispers: The Voices of Paranoia.* New York: Crown, 1994.

Simon, Linda. *The Biography of Alice B. Toklas.* New York: Avon, 1978.

Smith, Paul. *A Reader's Guide to the Short Stories of Ernest Hemingway.* Boston: G.K. Hall, 1989.

Spencer, Elizabeth. "Where Has All the Glamour Gone?" *F. Scott Fitzgerald at 100.* Rockville, MD: Quill and Brush, 1996.

Spilka, Mark. *Hemingway's Quarrel with Androgyny.* Lincoln: University of Nebraska Press, 1984.

Stein, Gertrude. *The Autobiography of Alice B. Toklas.* New York: Harcourt, Brace, 1933.

Stephens, Robert O. *Ernest Hemingway: The Critical Reception.* New York: Burt Franklin, 1977.

Svoboda, Frederic Joseph. *Hemingway &* The Sun Also Rises: *The Crafting of a Style.* Lawrence: University Press of Kansas, 1983.

Tavernier-Courbin, Jacqueline. *Ernest Hemingway's* A Moveable Feast. Boston: Northeastern University Press, 1991.

Vaill, Amanda. *Everybody Was So Young—Gerald and Sara Murphy: A Lost Generation Love Story.* Boston: Houghton Mifflin, 1998.

Villard, Henry Serrano, and James Nagel. *Hemingway in Love and War: The Lost Diary of Agnes von Kurowsky, Her Letters, and Correspondence of Ernest Hemingway.* Boston: Northeastern University Press, 1989.

Wagner-Martin, Linda. *"Favored Strangers": Gertrude Stein and Her Family.* New Brunswick, NJ: Rutgers University Press, 1995.

Waite, Robert G.L. *The Psychopathic God: Adolf Hitler.* New York: Basic Books, 1977.

Way, Brian. *F. Scott Fitzgerald and the Art of Social Fiction.* New York: St. Martin's, 1980.

Wilson, Edmund. *The Bit Between My Teeth: A Literary Chronicle of 1950-1965.* New York: Farrar, Straus and Giroux, 1965.

———. *Classics and Commercials: A Literary Chronicle of the Forties.* New York: Farrar, Straus and Giroux, 1950.

———. *The Fifties.* Edited by Leon Edel. New York: Farrar, Straus and Giroux, 1986.

————. *The Forties*. Edited by Leon Edel. New York: Farrar, Straus and Giroux, 1983.

————. *Letters on Literature and Politics, 1912-1972*. Edited by Elena Wilson. New York: Farrar, Straus and Giroux, 1977.

————. *A Prelude*. New York: Farrar, Straus and Giroux, 1967.

————. *The Shores of Light: A Literary Chronicle of the Twenties and Thirties*. New York: Farrar, Straus and Young, 1952.

————. *The Sixties*. Edited by Lewis M. Dabney. New York: Farrar Straus Giroux, 1993.

————. *The Thirties*. Edited by Leon Edel. New York: Farrar, Straus and Giroux, 1980.

————. *The Twenties*. Edited by Leon Edel: New York: Farrar, Straus and Giroux, 1975.

Woodward, Jeffrey Harris. *F. Scott Fitzgerald: The Artist as Public Figure. 1920-1940*. Ph.D. dissertation, University of Pennsylvania, 1972. Ann Arbor, MI: University Microfilms, 1974.

Worcester, David. *The Art of Satire*. Cambridge, MA: Harvard University Press, 1940.

Yalom, Irvin D. and Marilyn Yalom. "Ernest Hemingway—A Psychiatric View." *Archives of General Psychiatry* 24 (June 1971): 485-494.

Young, Philip. *Ernest Hemingway: A Reconsideration*. New York: Harcourt, Brace and World, 1966.

INDEX